Public Finance and the Price System

PUBLIC FINANCE and the PRICE SYSTEM

Edgar K. Browning
University of Virginia

Jacquelene M. Browning
Sweet Briar College

MACMILLAN PUBLISHING CO., INC.
New York
COLLIER MACMILLAN PUBLISHERS
London

TO OUR FAMILIES

Macmillan Publishing Co., Inc.
866 Third Avenue, New York, New York 10022

Collier Macmillan Canada, Ltd.

Library of Congress Cataloging in Publication Data

Browning, Edgar K
  Public finance and the price system.

  Includes bibliographies and index.
  1. Expenditures, Public.   2. Public goods.
3. Finance, Public—United States.   I. Browning,
Jacquelene M., joint author.   II. Title.
HJ7461.B75   336.73   78-21583
ISBN 0-02-315650-3

Printing: 2 3 4 5 6 7 8   Year: 9 0 1 2 3 4 5

PREFACE

Public Finance and the Price System is a textbook in public finance with an emphasis on policy analysis. Its broad purpose is to develop an understanding of the economic principles needed to examine the government's role in the economy, particularly those principles useful in a microeconomic analysis of tax and expenditure policies. A distinguishing feature of the book is the attention given to the analysis of a number of important expenditure programs, such as social security, unemployment insurance, food stamps, Medicare, and Medicaid. These programs are analyzed in Chapters 3–8 along with a number of reform proposals such as national health insurance and negative income taxation. By showing how the relevant theoretical principles can be applied to a variety of actual and proposed policies, we hope to instill an ability to use economics to identify and evaluate the major consequences of tax and expenditure programs.

It will be noticed that our applications of expenditure policy analysis are taken from the general category known as "social welfare expenditures," or those programs that provide cash or services (such as medical care or housing) directly to individuals. (See Chapter 7 for a breakdown of social welfare expenditures.) In part, this reflects our own research interests as well as where we think economic analysis can contribute the most toward understanding the relevant issues. It should also be emphasized that this category of expenditures currently accounts for more than 60 percent of total government expenditures, up from a third only twenty years ago. Not only is this type of expenditure policy quantitatively the most important but it is also the most rapidly growing. Consequently, we feel it is appropriate for a public finance text to stress the analysis of this type of policy.

Apart from the analysis of expenditure programs, the remainder of the text is more conventional in its content. Public good and externality theory (Chapter 2) and public choice theory (Chapter 9) are shown to have important implications for policy analysis. Federalism is considered in Chapter 14, and taxation is the subject of Chapters 10 through 13. The discussion of the federal income tax (Chapters 11 and 12) is comprehensive; however, other forms of taxation receive relatively less attention. This selective treatment was necessary to keep the text to a practical length. Readers who want additional analysis of taxes will find numerous suggested readings at the end of the relevant chapters.

Overall, the text reflects our view that it is better to analyze carefully and systematically selected topics that illustrate principal concepts and techniques than to cover a wide variety of topics superficially. The emphasis is theoretical, with factual and institutional material introduced when necessary to advance the analysis. We feel this approach is best suited to the development of true analytical ability, which is the major goal of *Public Finance and the Price System.*

Most readers of this text will probably be economics majors who have completed a course in intermediate microeconomic theory. Because of the increasing interest in the subject matter, however, we have made the text accessible for those who have only had a principles of economics course by including an appendix on indifference curve analysis. Indifference curve analysis is used throughout the text, and those unfamiliar with it (or needing a quick review) should read this section first. With that preparation, readers with a limited background in economic theory should have no difficulty with the material.

We would like to extend our appreciation to a number of people who have helped in the preparation of this text. Colleagues at the University of Virginia, William Breit and Roland N. McKean, provided encouragement and numerous suggestions throughout our work on the manuscript. Colin D. Campbell of Dartmouth College and C. M. Lindsay of the University of California, Los Angeles, provided helpful comments on large segments of the manuscript. Our especial thanks go to Wallace Oates of Princeton University, who reviewed the entire manuscript and provided detailed comments and suggestions. In addition, we are grateful to June Morris and Barbara Lowe for their prompt and competent assistance with typing.

E.K.B.
J.M.B.

CONTENTS

INTRODUCTION

Public finance is the study of how government policy, especially tax and expenditure policy, affects the economy and thereby the welfare of its citizens. No one can doubt that the influence of government on the operation of the economy is immense. The average U.S. household in 1977 contributed about $7000 of its income to governments (federal, state, and local) through a variety of taxes. In return, it received services in varying degrees from literally thousands of different expenditure programs that were financed by these taxes.

Government expenditures and taxes are now clearly an important part of our everyday lives. In recent years they have become increasingly important, as Table 1–1 suggests. In 1929 total government spending was $10.3 billion, or only 11 percent of net national product (NNP). At that time combined state and local government expenditures were nearly three times as large as federal expenditures. By 1977 all this had changed dramatically. Government expenditures were then $621.2 billion, or 36.7 percent of NNP, with the federal government spending 60 percent more than state and local governments.

Our subject is the investigation of these expenditures and the taxes that finance them. Some of the most pressing social issues of the day fall squarely in this domain. Public finance provides the framework for the study of such diverse policies and issues as income tax reform, national health insurance, social security, welfare reform, and revenue sharing. All of these issues, and many others, will be considered in later chapters. In this chapter the analytical framework that will be used in the analysis will be discussed.

Table 1-1. Government Expenditures, Selected Years ($ in Billions)

Year	Federal Government Expenditures	State and Local Government Expenditures	Total Government Expenditures	Expenditures as Percent of NNP
1929	$ 2.6	$ 7.8	$ 10.3	11.0%
1950	40.8	22.5	61.0	23.3
1960	93.1	49.8	136.4	29.8
1970	204.2	132.2	311.9	35.0
1977	423.5	265.3	621.2	36.7

Note: Federal grants-in-aid to state and local governments are included in both federal and state and local expenditure figures. Total expenditures are adjusted to avoid this duplication.
Source: Economic Report of the President, 1978, Tables B-73 and B-17.

The Nature of the Economic Effects of Policies

It will be helpful to begin by explaining three quite different types of effects tax and expenditure (or other) policies may have.[1]

Allocation

Almost all government policies have an effect on the allocation of resources. In other words, the mix of goods and services produced by the economy is altered as a result of the policy. If the government spends money to build missiles, it bids resources—manpower and capital—away from the production of other goods and services. The result is that economic resources are reallocated so that *more* missiles are produced and *fewer* other goods and services. Economic resources are scarce, and their use to produce one type of good necessarily implies sacrificed production of other goods.

One of the most important issues in public finance is the determination of exactly how each of the vast array of government tax and expenditure policies affects the allocation of resources. What goods and services do we get more of, and at what cost in terms of smaller quantities of other goods and services? In some cases, the impact on resource allocation is fairly obvious, but in others it is not. As will be seen, some government subsidies have little or no effect on resource allocation: If the government provides free food to people, they may simply curtail their private purchases of food. Other policies have seemingly counterintuitive effects, as when public housing leads to lower consumption of housing for some recipients.

---

[1] Richard A. Musgrave developed the following useful classification in his *The Theory of Public Finance* (New York: McGraw-Hill, 1959), Chapter 1.

To understand the allocative effects of government policies, it is necessary to know both how the policy operates and how the economic behavior of people is influenced by the policy. Does a welfare program undermine incentives to work? If so, the earnings of the poor will fall when they are provided assistance. Does the provision of social security pensions lead people to save less privately for retirement? If so, the economy's rate of growth will be affected. Economic analysis does not provide unambiguous answers to all such questions concerning the allocative effects of policies, but it provides some, and it represents a general framework that is helpful in evaluating such effects.

Distribution

Over any period of time, the economic system produces a certain mix of goods and services that is consumed by its citizens. Not only is the total output of goods and services of interest, but also the manner in which they are distributed among the public. Government policies often affect not only resource allocation—the mix of goods and services—but also the distribution of these goods, that is, the distribution of real income. Knowing that a particular medical policy increases the amount of medical care and reduces the total amount of other things consumed does not imply that each person, or income class, ends up with more medical care and less of other goods. Some may have more of both and others less of both than before. If this is so, the policy also alters the distribution of real income by benefiting the former group at the expense of the latter group.

When trying to determine the distributional impact of any policy, we are basically trying to answer the question: Who is benefited and who is harmed by the policy? Popular discussion often obscures this issue. Advocates of any policy generally stress that the "nation" will be benefited, whereas opponents argue that "we" would be better off without it. As far as we know, there has never been any policy that literally benefits everyone, or one that harms everyone. Most policies benefit certain persons and groups at the expense of others. In some cases, this may be intentional (e.g., redistributional welfare programs), and in other cases it may be unintended (a defense program harming "doves"). In any event, the extent to which income is redistributed, and the direction of that redistribution (whether in favor of the poor, the elderly, homeowners, etc.), is an important effect of government policies.

Economic analysis is often essential in determining how government policies affect the distribution of real incomes. In some cases the effects are more obvious than in others. It is fairly clear, for example, that several of the welfare programs comprising our welfare system redistribute income in favor of certain low income groups. But who is benefited and **3** who is harmed by social security or unemployment insurance? Who bears the true burden of the corporation income tax? What is the overall effect of all taxes and expenditures on the distribution of income? Questions such as these pertaining to the distributional effects of policies are not easy to answer, but they are clearly important issues and will be considered in later chapters.

Stabilization

The overall level of expenditures and taxes, in conjunction with monetary policy, can have important effects on the aggregate level of employment, output, and prices. Indeed, most people first study taxes and expenditures in terms of their impact on aggregate demand. Stabilizing the economy at high (and perhaps growing) levels of output and employment is today considered a major responsibility of the federal government.

In this textbook, these macroeconomic effects of the fiscal operations of government will be ignored. Our neglect of this set of important issues stems from the fact that most students will take a separate course in macroeconomic analysis, and any treatment given in a chapter or two would necessarily be repetitive and probably inferior to the more detailed discussions in other courses. There is, however, a more substantive reason for giving little attention to macroeconomic effects: Macroeconomic effects are of little importance in the analysis and evaluation of individual tax and expenditure programs. Only when all taxes and expenditures are considered in the aggregate do these effects become significant. This point will be elaborated further when the effects of expenditure policies are studied in more detail in later chapters.

Positive Analysis and Value Judgments

Most people study economics, we suspect, with the intention of learning what types of economic policies are desirable and what types are undesirable. Because most of public finance deals with public policies, it is important to understand what economic analysis can contribute to determining what is a good policy.

Logically, an argument that a policy is good depends on two steps: positive analysis and a value judgment. First, it is necessary to determine what the consequences of the policy—its effects on resource allocation and income distribution—will be. This is the realm of positive economic analysis, dealing with the measurable or observable outcomes of policy. We might consider, for example, how minimum wage law affects unemployment, or whether a particular tax loophole works to the

4

advantage of the wealthy, or how national health insurance would affect the prices of medical services. Positive analysis of policies therefore consists of propositions about the effects of policies. The distinguishing feature of positive analysis is that it deals with propositions that can be tested, with respect to both their underlying logic and empirical evidence.

Economic analysis can assist in determining what is desirable government policy by providing a framework for positive analysis that generally yields correct propositions about the consequences of policy. Knowing the consequences of a policy, however, is not sufficient to determine that it is desirable. A second step is necessary: It must be held that the consequences themselves are desirable. To make this evaluation, it is necessary for each person to make a subjective judgment, a value judgment, to determine if he believes the consequences are desirable. By its nature, this judgment is nonscientific: It cannot be proven to be right or wrong by facts or evidence. For example, a belief that a more equal distribution of income is desirable is of this type. People may agree that a particular government policy produces greater equality, but some may hold that this outcome is desirable and others that it is undesirable. Their value judgments are different.

Although the distinction between positive analysis and value judgments, and the role each plays in the evaluation of policies, may seem abstruse, it is nonetheless essential to clear thinking. Economic analysis cannot demonstrate that any policy is desirable (and neither, for that matter, can any other scientific branch of knowledge). Holding that something is desirable requires a nonscientific judgment of what constitutes "desirability" that cannot be supplied by a technique of analysis; only individuals can make this type of judgment. Nonetheless, economics can assist in making that judgment by helping us to determine the likely consequences of policies, which is an important contribution. Many people disagree about the desirability of policies not because of differences in their values but because they have different conceptions about their effects.

Criteria for Policy Evaluation

In a general sense, we have seen that the evaluation of a public policy must be based on a value judgment about the consequences of the policy. Some types of value judgments are widely shared and frequently used in evaluations of public policies, and further discussion of these may be helpful. Although the following criteria for the evaluation of policy do embody explicit value judgments and therefore cannot be demonstrated to be "desirable," they are so widely (and often unthinkingly) **5** used that it is important to understand the strengths and weaknesses of each.

Equity

Perhaps the most widely used criterion in discussions of policy is that of equity, or fairness; government policies should be equitable in their effects on people. This criterion has the advantage of being accepted by virtually everyone; no one thinks unfairness in a policy is desirable. Yet the superficial consensus in favor of equitable treatment obscures a real difficulty in defining exactly what is meant by "equity." Although everyone approves of equity, very few people interpret the term in the same way.

A few examples will illustrate the difficulty of making a judgment about equity. Is minimum wage law equitable? It results in higher wage rates for some people, unemployment for others, and higher costs for the consuming public. Are its effects on all groups fair? How about public schools? Is it equitable for families without children to pay taxes to finance public schools? Is it equitable for persons to be required to provide for their retirement through social security rather than in other ways they might prefer? If questions like these are considered seriously, as they should be, some of the difficulties in making an equity judgment will become apparent.

Consider the following statement: "The tax exempt status of state and local government bonds enables the wealthy to avoid their fair share of the tax burden by receiving tax free interest income." Is the tax exemption granted these bonds fair? Judging from the frequency of statements like the preceding, it is generally considered unfair. Yet the statement misconstrues the effects of this tax exemption: People who hold tax-free bonds are not the major beneficiaries of this policy. Instead, state and local governments can sell bonds bearing a lower interest rate than other borrowers and are the major beneficiaries (as evidenced by the fact that state and local governments, not wealthy taxpayers, have lobbied extensively in the past to defeat tax reform efforts to end the tax exempt status of state and local bonds). For example, a tax-free bond might require an interest rate of, say, 5 percent to compete with a 9 percent (taxable) corporate bond. Elimination of this tax exemption would mean that state and local governments would have to pay 9 percent to compete with the other bonds. Wealthy taxpayers would then pay taxes on the higher interest income, but it is not clear that their net after-tax incomes would be any lower.

The case of the tax exemption granted these bonds is a good example of the importance of positive analysis in making equity judgments. Most people are prone to make judgments without a careful consideration of the actual effects of economic policies. Yet the equity issue is concerned with the actual consequences of policies, and positive analysis is necessary to determine these consequences.

It is obvious that few people have a clearly defined idea of what equity really means, and even if they did, individual interpretations would differ. Consequently, equity is a difficult criterion to use in practice, but this does not imply that it is unimportant. The concept of equity may be difficult to pin down precisely, but there may still be wide agreement at a fairly general level. For example, few people would argue that a policy that taxes poor people to subsidize the yachting activities of the wealthy is equitable. Unfortunately, most real-world issues are not so clear-cut.

Among economists, the question of equity often takes on a very narrow meaning, referring to the distributional effects of a policy. If a policy results in any redistribution, the major emphasis is on whether the people benefited are poorer (or more deserving in some sense) than the people harmed. Economics is well designed to explore how policies affect the distribution of income, but that is probably only one dimension of the equity issue. Although economics can help in identifying the consequences of policies—notably the distributional effects—each person must ultimately decide whether these consequences are equitable.

Economic Efficiency

Economic efficiency, or as it is sometimes called, Pareto optimality, is a criterion widely used by economists in policy evaluation. It is not so widely used by noneconomists and is, in fact, often disparaged as dealing with materialistic issues, cost minimizing, profit maximizing, and so on. In part this rejection of efficiency as a criterion reflects a misunderstanding of its meaning as used by economists. Far from being materialistically oriented, efficiency is defined in terms of the well-being of people. Roughly speaking, an efficient economic system is one that makes people as well off as possible, taking into account all the ways the economy influences their well-being. Interpreted in this way, economic efficiency is a criterion that would probably command wide acceptance.

A more careful definition of efficiency can be stated. An efficient allocation of resources is one in which it is impossible, through any change in resource allocation, to make some person or persons better off without making someone else worse off. In short, when the economy is operating efficiently, there is no scope for further improvements in anyone's welfare unless some people are benefited at the expense of others. A corollary to this definition is that an inefficient allocation of resources is one in which it is possible, through a change in resource allocation, to make some person or persons better off without making anyone else

7

worse off. Inefficiency implies waste in the sense that the economy is not catering to the wants of people as well as it could.

These definitions can be made clearer with the aid of a diagram. To make matters simple, assume that society consists of only two people, Sam and Oscar, although the discussion can be generalized for any number of people. In Figure 1–1, the level of well-being, or welfare, of Sam is measured horizontally and the welfare of Oscar is measured vertically. The farther to the right we are in the diagram, the better off Sam is (the higher indifference curve attained), whereas the farther up in the diagram we go, the better off Oscar is.[2] Any allocation of resources corresponds to a certain level of welfare for each person and can thus be plotted in the diagram.

Because of limitations in the amount of resources available to produce goods and services, there are limits to how well off Sam and Oscar can be. These limits are shown by the welfare frontier (or "utility frontier") $Z_1 Z_2$. Any point that lies outside this frontier is unattainable. The society, for example, cannot produce a mix of goods and services that would make Sam and Oscar as well off as indicated by point K. By contrast, any point lying on or inside the frontier is attainable. It is physically possible to allocate existing resources in a way to achieve any combination of welfare for Sam and Oscar that lies inside or on $Z_1 Z_2$.[3]

Using this construction, it can be seen that any allocation of resources that implies a point lying on the $Z_1 Z_2$ frontier is efficient. For example, point A represents an efficient allocation of resources because it is not possible to make Sam better off without making Oscar worse off— because it is impossible to move outside the frontier. It will be immediately noticed, however, that this is also true of point B; any possible move from point B makes at least one of the two worse off. Indeed, every point *on* the frontier satisfies the definition of efficiency, so there are really innumerable efficient allocations. The efficiency criterion does not allow us to claim that there is only one best state of affairs.

The different efficient points on the welfare frontier represent different distributions of welfare, or real income, between Sam and Oscar. Efficiency does not resolve the question of how real income should be distributed among people. Suppose there is only one good produced, food, and an efficient use of resources yields 100 units of food. Point A could represent the situation when Oscar has 60 units and Sam 40 units,

---

[2] In effect, the diagram tells us only how each person ranks alternative resource allocations. It does not tell us by how much better or worse Sam or Oscar believe one allocation to be in comparison to another.

[3] For a discussion that demonstrates how this utility frontier can be derived, see Francis Bator, "The Simple Analytics of Welfare Maximization," reprinted in William Breit and Harold Hochman (eds.), *Readings in Microeconomics* (New York: Holt, Rinehart and Winston, 1968), and Peter Kenen, "On the Geometry of Welfare Economics," *Quarterly Journal of Economics,* 71:426 (Mar. 1957).

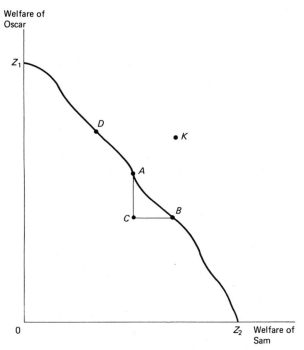

Figure 1-1. Welfare frontier.

whereas at point B, Oscar has 40 units and Sam 60 units. Both ways of dividing the food are efficient because there is no way to make one person better off except by giving him more food, and that requires taking food from the other person. The efficiency criterion provides no way of comparing points like A and B because they are both efficient. Instead, an explicit value judgment is required to compare different distributions of real income.

Consider now point C. This is an inefficient point, perhaps where the economy is producing only 80 units of food. (Even in our simple one good world, this need not imply unemployment of resources—resources may simply be used unwisely and then produce less output than is possible.) Point C is inefficient because it is possible to change things so as to benefit one person without harming the other. By moving from C to A, Oscar is made better off without harming Sam; alternatively, moving from C to B would benefit Sam without harming Oscar. Indeed, moves within the CAB area benefit both. Thus, inefficiency implies that there are changes in resource allocation possible that will be of mutual benefit to people. Most people would make the value judgment that changes making everyone better off are desirable; thus, economists tend to think that efficiency is a good thing.

It should not be inferred that *all* efficient points are better than *all* inefficient points. Consider a move from point D, an efficient point, to point C, an inefficient point. Admittedly, this is a change from an efficient to an inefficient allocation of resources, but the change benefits Sam at Oscar's expense. Only, however, if we are unconcerned about the distribution of real income would we unequivocally say that D is better than C. Perhaps Sam is poor and Oscar wealthy, so the move from D to C is a redistribution in favor of the poor person. A person who makes the value judgment that greater equality is highly desirable might prefer point C to D despite the fact that it is inefficient. Economists, however, would generally argue that if we are going to redistribute from Oscar to Sam (starting at point D), it would be better to do so in a way that ended up on Z_1Z_2 in the AB range rather than at point C. A redistribution from D to A, for example, would benefit Sam as much as a move from D to C, and it would leave Oscar better off. In this way efficiency considerations are relevant in situations involving redistribution. There are efficient and inefficient ways to redistribute income.

The efficiency criterion clearly does not resolve all questions of economic policy. In particular, it is neutral with respect to distributional questions; these still require nonobjective value judgments. Furthermore, there are some practical questions about applying the criterion. For example, in the complex real world, it is not an easy matter to determine exactly what policies will be most efficient, because a great deal of information (that we often don't have) is required to make that judgment. In addition, we may sometimes object to a criterion based on the assumption that the welfare of all individuals *as they themselves evaluate their well-being* is what counts. Do we want to cater to the wants of children, the mentally retarded, or criminals?

Despite these obvious drawbacks, it is a widely used criterion. If, in your view, a good policy is one that promotes the welfare of people as they themselves judge their welfare, then you will be led to give some weight to efficiency in evaluating policies.

Paternalism

Government policy may, in some cases, be intentionally designed to provide services that would not be chosen by people if they had a choice. Instead of catering to the wants of people, the government overrides, or disregards, their wants. A policy of this type could be described as paternalistic and is ultimately based on the premise that some individuals are not competent to make wise choices.

A few examples may help to illustrate this criterion. A justification sometimes given for social security is that people would not independently save enough for their old age. If we assert, however, that the level of savings someone would choose to make is "too small," then we are ignoring his expressed wants and substituting someone else's conception of the proper level of saving. Similarly, many welfare programs do not permit the poor to spend the government assistance as they wish, but require that it be spent on housing, medical care, and so on. Children are required to attend schools until a specified age regardless of their (or their parents') desires. The fact that 10 percent of the public has no form of health insurance is sometimes cited as an argument for mandatory health insurance (national health insurance) for everyone despite the fact that the uninsured 10 percent have decided they were better off purchasing something other than health insurance. (We don't mean to imply that these policies can be supported only by paternalistic arguments, but merely to suggest how paternalistic considerations can play a role in the evaluation of policies.)

Many people support some government policies, we believe, not because they think these policies give the public what it wants but because they think the government knows better what is good for the public than the public itself. This does not imply that paternalism is in any sense bad (a value judgment); we all approve of paternalistic policies in some cases. For example, most people agree that small children should not be permitted to purchase liquor or drugs or guns even if (and perhaps especially if) they want to. The government may be in a better position to evaluate highly specialized knowledge and in some cases make "better" (in some sense) choices than people could on their own.

Paternalism does not, however, supply any clear basis for the evaluation of policies. Because there is no absolute standard by which people's choices can be judged, there is no limit to what could be justified on this basis. Moreover, paternalism as a criterion contains a definite antidemocratic element. If individuals are not thought competent to make decisions that mainly affect themselves (like saving for retirement), then, taking this a step farther, they must be even less competent to make decisions that affect everyone in society through the voting process.

Individual Freedom

Many people place a high value on individual freedom and wish to see government restrict that freedom as little as possible. Actually, the concept of freedom is difficult to pin down precisely. It is generally taken to mean, at least in the economic sphere, that economic arrangements are voluntary. The many exchanges that characterize economic organization take place through a series of mutual agreements between buyers and sellers, with the terms of trade (prices) agreeable to both parties.

Although a case can clearly be made for individual freedom, it is not clear that this criterion provides much guidance for policy issues dealt with in the field of public finance.[4] Whenever the government taxes people to finance public expenditures, it deprives them of the freedom to spend part of their incomes as they would have individually chosen. With subtle interpretation, in some cases it may be possible to argue that some taxes or expenditures are more consistent with freedom than others. On the expenditure side, for example, it might be argued that a welfare program of cash transfers that permits recipients to spend cash assistance as they wish is more consistent with the notion of individual freedom than a program where the assistance is restricted to food or housing. Even so, in the bulk of cases, it is difficult to hold that one tax is a greater infringement on freedom than another. This is not to say that individual freedom is unimportant, but only that it may not offer much specific guidance for choices among alternative tax and expenditure policies.

Tradeoffs Among the Criteria

The four criteria discussed so far do not exhaust all the ways in which economic policies may be evaluated, but they do provide some idea of the range of effects that may be considered. Forming an overall evaluation of a policy is clearly a difficult task. Not only is it necessary to determine how well the policy satisfies each of the criteria deemed relevant, but a decision of how much weight to give each separate criterion is also necessary. It will generally be impossible to satisfy all criteria simultaneously. For example, a policy that is considered equitable may be quite inefficient, or a policy to achieve greater efficiency may necessitate a loss of equity. Some of the criteria, in fact, are inherently contradictory. This is true of paternalism and efficiency, because efficiency involves catering to the wants of people as they themselves define those wants, whereas paternalism substitutes another judgment of what people should have. In short, a policy evaluation must reflect not only how it performs according to the separate criteria but also how the relative importance of each criterion is judged.

Economists typically emphasize two of these criteria, efficiency and equity, more than any others. In part, this simply reflects the fact that economic analysis is better suited to identifying how efficient policies are likely to be and how they affect the distribution of real income (generally felt to be relevant to making equity judgments). This emphasis also reflects the value judgment that these two broad criteria emphasize worthwhile goals. In the final analysis, however, each person must de-

[4] For contemporary arguments emphasizing the importance of individual freedom, see Friedrich Hayek, *The Constitution of Liberty* (Chicago: University of Chicago Press, 1960), and Milton Friedman, *Capitalism and Freedom* (Chicago: University of Chicago Press, 1962).

cide what criteria are important. As pointed out earlier, economic analysis cannot demonstrate that policies are good or bad, but we hope to show in the remainder of this book that it can help in making that judgment by clarifying many of the consequences of tax and expenditure policies.

The Price System

Much economic activity is organized through private markets in which competitive forces determine prices. These market-determined prices are signals that guide resource allocation, and a system that relies on prices determined in open markets to coordinate economic activities is generally referred to as a price system. In studying public finance, an understanding of how the price system functions is important for two somewhat different reasons. First, relying on the price system is the major alternative to the use of government tax or expenditure policies as a means of resolving economic problems. For example, the price system provides methods by which individuals can insure against medical risks and provide for their retirement; these methods are alternatives to using government policies such as national health insurance and social security to perform these functions. Thus, in evaluating how well social security operates, it should be compared to the way the price system works in this area.

Second, the way in which tax and expenditure policies interact with and influence the price system has important implications for the effects of these policies. Often government policies create incentives that change the functioning of private markets. When state and local government bonds are made tax exempt, for example, the price system responds by generating a lower interest rate on these securities, which will induce heavier borrowing by state and local governments. Similarly, the provision of social security benefits may lead to less private saving for retirement, and national health insurance may result in higher prices for medical care. Therefore, to understand the full effects of tax or expenditure policies, it is important to analyze how the price system will respond to them.

This is not the place, of course, to explain in detail how a price system functions; it is assumed that the reader already has a basic understanding of microeconomic, or price, theory. It may be helpful, however, to consider briefly the performance of a price system in terms of the criteria just discussed.

Economic Efficiency

One of the major conclusions of modern economics is that a competitive price system tends, under certain conditions, to produce an efficient allocation of resources. Business firms in competition with one another for the patronage of consumers have incentives to provide goods in the quantities and qualities that are most preferred by consumers. The incentives provided by prices encourage resource owners to employ their resources in ways that are valued most highly by consumers. If the output of one good, say, beer, is too high, and the output of clothing is too low, the price of beer will be too low to cover costs and beer producers will suffer losses. Clothing producers will be making profits, and the lure of higher profits in clothing production will encourage resources to move from the overexpanded beer industry to the clothing industry. In the end, the mix of clothing and beer output will reflect consumer preferences as indicated in market demands for the goods.

The nature of the attainment of efficient levels of output in competitive markets can be explained in greater detail by examining a specific market. In Figure 1–2, the competitive demand and supply curves for beer are shown. For well-known reasons, the competitive equilibrium rate of output is 1500 units at a price of $7 per unit. Our question is whether this equilibrium level of output is the most efficient level. To explore this question, suppose that for some reason output is only 1000 units. Now we wish to know if the additional, or marginal, benefits of a larger output are greater than the marginal costs of producing it. If so, the net benefits—the excess of benefits over costs—of the public can be increased by producing more beer.

At an output of 1000 units, the marginal benefit, or marginal value, of output is equal to $9 per unit. Nine dollars is a measure of how much consumers are willing to pay to get an additional unit (the 1001st unit) of beer. This is simply the price that will prevail if 1000 units are placed on the market, given by the height to the market demand curve at that rate of output. Note that each consumer will be willing to pay $9 (more precisely, infinitesimally less than $9) for another unit of beer; that is why we can say *the* marginal value of beer is $9 because it is the same for all beer consumers. This can be seen by noting that each consumer will consume beer up to the point where the marginal unit is worth $9. (Individual A, for example, with demand curve d_A, will be consuming five units, at which point his marginal valuation of beer is $9.) Equivalently, recall that each consumer is in equilibrium where his marginal rate of substitution between money spent on other goods and beer is $9. The marginal rate of substitution between money and beer is, of course, a measure of the marginal benefit of more beer, that is, how much the consumer will pay for another unit.

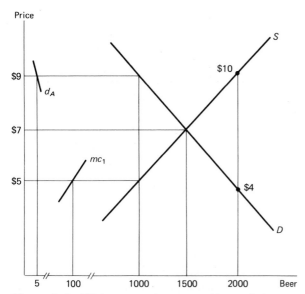

Figure 1-2. Efficient output in a competitive market.

The market demand curve is thus a measure of the marginal importance of the good to consumers. Although this marginal benefit is commonly measured in dollars, it should be recalled that this is just a means of registering the importance of beer in comparison to other goods. Saying that the marginal benefit is $9 means that consumers are willing to give up $9 worth of other goods to get another unit of beer.

Now let's consider the cost of producing more beer. The height to the competitive supply curve measures the marginal cost of beer production. At an output level of 1000 units, the marginal cost is $5. (It is also $5 for each firm producing beer, just as firm 1 would be operating on its marginal cost curve, mc_1, at an output rate where marginal cost is $5.) This $5 measures the cost of the resources needed to produce one more unit of beer. To produce more beer, $5 worth of resources must be withdrawn from the production of other goods. If other markets are competitive, when $5 worth of resources is diverted to beer production, output of other goods will fall by exactly $5. In other words, when the marginal cost of beer production is $5, this is a measure of the value of other goods that must be sacrificed to produce one more unit of beer.

Interpreting the competitive demand and supply curves as measures of marginal benefits and costs makes it easy to determine the efficient rate of output. At 1000 units of ouput, consumers are willing to give up $9 in other goods to get one more unit of beer, but it is only necessary to sacrifice $5 worth to produce one more unit. Additional beer production

15

is worth more than it costs; thus, 1000 is an inefficient (too low) rate of output because more beer and less of other things are preferred by consumers.

The efficient rate of output is where marginal benefit and marginal cost are equal. This occurs where output has expanded to 1500 units, at which point marginal benefit and cost are equal at $7. By reasoning analogously to the preceding, it can be seen that any output in excess of 1500 units will be too great. At an output of 2000, for example, the marginal cost of beer production is greater than its marginal benefit, and consumers will be better off with less beer and more of other things. Thus, because 1500 units is the competitive equilibrium output, the competitive output with its careful balancing of benefits and costs is also the most efficient rate of output. (It should be noted that 1500 is the efficient output even if the beer market is not competitive; the important thing is the real schedule of marginal benefits and costs, and these remain unchanged regardless of the market structure.)

Recalling our earlier discussion of efficiency using a welfare frontier (Figure 1–1), this analysis implies that a competitive price system yields a resource allocation that places us at one point on the welfare frontier. There is then no way to change a competitively determined resource allocation without harming someone. Although our discussion has emphasized only one aspect of the efficiency issue—the rate of output of a good—the results hold generally when the framework is broadened.[5]

A competitive price system generally gets high marks with respect to the criterion of economic efficiency. Nonetheless, the price system may not always function as smoothly as the preceding analysis suggests. In particular, there are certain conditions under which a private market, even a competitive one, will not function efficiently. These conditions have to do with the presence of public goods and externalities, and will be considered in some detail in the next chapter.

Equity

As was suggested by our earlier general discussion of equity, this criterion must reflect nonobjective and individual standards of fairness. As such, it is not possible to prove that the price system is equitable or inequitable in the way that efficiency can be appraised. Nonetheless, there are a few observations that perhaps should be made.

One frequent objection to the contention that a price system is efficient runs like this: How can we say that markets cater effectively to genuine needs when the children of the poor go without toys or milk, and yet the pets of the wealthy wear diamond collars? This raises a valid

[5] See Bator, op. cit.

objection to total reliance on the price system, but it is important to see that the issue is really one of equity, not efficiency. Those with larger incomes influence resource allocation to a greater degree than those with smaller incomes. This is not perverse; the market is merely responding to people's desires and other relevant circumstances, including the distribution of income. *Given* the distribution of income, a competitive price system efficiently caters to needs as backed up by money. One may object to the fact that some people end up with more goods and services than others, but this is not inefficient, because it simply reflects the fact that some have more income than others. (Put somewhat differently, in terms of Figure 1–1, this objection is that we are at one efficient point, *D,* but another one, *B,* would be better.)

Inequality in the distribution of income can be, and frequently is, objected to on equity grounds. In general, a person's income in a competitive price system depends on how well he can meet the demands of consumers by supplying labor and other productive resources. Because incomes typically reflect productivities, those who are, for whatever reason, less productive will have lower incomes, and their needs will be less fully catered to by the market. Our view of what income a person ethically deserves may differ from what he receives when paid according to his productivity; the distribution of income generated by the price system may not necessarily conform to one's notion of equity.

Despite the evident importance of income distribution from an equity standpoint, it would probably be a mistake to view equity solely in terms of how the system distributes incomes. The process by which incomes are determined (as distinct from the end result) is also important. Is the price system a "fair game" in which people have reasonably fair opportunities to influence the size of their income? It is sometimes pointed out that a person's income is, after all, voluntarily given to him by the purchasers of his productive services, and everyone is free to compete in trying to offer more valuable services. To a large extent, the price system rewards traits such as ambition, foresight, and hard work, and that seems equitable to many people. Nonetheless, some persons are not fortunate enough to own productive resources that are highly valued by markets and will end up with low incomes in a price system. For them, the fact that the process is believed by many to be fair will be little consolation for their lack of income. Both the nature of the process and the results are relevant in making an equity judgment.

Paternalism and Individual Freedom

Paternalism and individual freedom can be dealt with briefly. From a paternalistic perspective, a price system will not function well. It gives people what they want and not what someone else thinks they should want. Some people may deplore the fact that the "system" allocates resources to the production of professional wrestling matches, motorcycles, cigarettes, carnival side shows, fattening foods, and comic books, but these goods are produced only because some people are willing to pay for them. A person who dislikes the preferences of other people has only one avenue of influence: to try to persuade others that there are better ways to spend their money. The slow and gradual process of persuasion is a frustrating one for those who think they know (and perhaps some do) what is good for the rest of us. A paternalist will probably not consider a price system to be the best way of allocating resources in all cases.

On the other hand, a price system receives high marks in preserving individual freedom. People can choose what jobs to perform and how to dispose of their incomes, subject only to the constraint that they cannot force other people into involuntary exchanges.

What Role for Government?

If a price system is efficient, what role is there for government policy? As the preceding remarks suggest, efficiency is not the only criterion by which an economic system may be judged. A case can clearly be made for government to redistribute incomes in the interest of equity. In some instances paternalistic government policies may be warranted. In addition, a price system requires certain government actions if it is to attain an efficient allocation of resources; property rights must be defined, contracts must be enforced, and perhaps antitrust measures are needed to insure that markets are competitive. A still further role can be rationalized because of the existence of public goods and externalities. That is the subject of the next chapter.

Supplementary Readings

Bator, Francis M. "The Simple Analytics of Welfare Maximization," reprinted in William Breit and Harold Hochman (eds.), *Readings in Microeconomics.* New York: Holt, Rinehart and Winston, 1968.

Baumol, William J. *Welfare Economics and the Theory of the State.* Cambridge, Mass.: Harvard University Press, 1965.

Friedman, Milton. *Capitalism and Freedom.* Chicago: University of Chicago Press, 1962.

Hayek, Friedrich A. *The Constitution of Liberty.* Chicago: University of Chicago Press, 1960.

Head, John G. *Public Goods and Public Welfare.* Durham, N.C.: Duke University Press, 1974, Chapter 10.

Kenen, Peter. "On the Geometry of Welfare Economics," *Quarterly Journal of Economics,* 71:426–447 (Mar. 1957).

Musgrave, Richard. *The Theory of Public Finance.* New York: McGraw-Hill Book Company, 1959, Chapter 1.

Scherer, Frederic. "General Equilibrium and Economic Efficiency," *The American Economist,* 10(1):54–70 (Spring 1966).

MARKET FAILURE: PUBLIC GOODS AND EXTERNALITIES

CHAPTER 2

In Chapter 1 we explained how a competitive price system tends to produce an efficient allocation of resources. The demonstration of efficiency was incomplete, however, because it depended on the implicit assumption that there were no public goods or externalities. Public goods, as we shall see, have peculiar characteristics that make it unlikely that private markets will provide the efficient quantity. When this happens, *market failure* is said to occur. The modern economic rationale for many types of government intervention is based on the inability of the price system to function efficiently in such situations. To appreciate how government intervention may improve on the workings of the price system, it is necessary to understand what public goods and externalities are and how they affect the allocation of resources.

The Nature of Public Goods

The term *public good* does not necessarily refer to a good that is provided by the government. Instead, it refers to a good (or service) that has two characteristics, regardless of whether or not the government provides it. These two characteristics are *nonrival consumption* and *nonexclusion*.

Nonrival Consumption

A good is nonrival in consumption when, with a given level of production, consumption by one person need not diminish the quantity consumed by anyone else. In other words, a number of people may simultaneously consume the same good.[1] Some examples will clarify this concept. Consider an antimissile system that reduces the likelihood of

---

[1] Nonrival consumption is sometimes referred to as collective consumption or indivisibility of benefits.

foreign attack. Note that the protection of your property and person does not reduce the protection received by others; even if you did not exist, the level of protection available to others would be unaffected. Thus an antimissile system simultaneously protects a large number of people.

National defense—of which an antimissile system is a component—is generally considered to be one of the most clear-cut examples of a good that is nonrival in consumption. Note, however, that this characteristic does not mean that people are necessarily benefited to the same degree. A given defense effort could afford greater protection to some geographic areas than to others. Possibly, if you lived near a missile base, you might actually feel that your life and property are in greater danger because a foreign attack might concentrate on wiping out our missile systems. Similarly, if you are a pacifist, you might secure negative benefits from the defense effort. Nonetheless, an antimissile system is still a good that is nonrival in consumption because it simultaneously affects (to different degrees) a large number of people.

Once the nature of nonrival consumption is understood, it is an easy matter to find many examples. A flood control project, for instance, is nonrival in consumption for those living in the region where the probability of flooding is reduced. (Of course, the project would not benefit those living in other regions, but it is still nonrival for people in the protected area. As we shall see later, the geographic extent of the nonrivalry is important in considering what level of government is best equipped to deal with the good.) Weather forecasting, pollution abatement, and some public health measures that reduce the spread of disease are other examples.

By contrast, most goods and services that we deal with in economics are rival in consumption. For a given level of production of hamburgers (or watches, shoes, houses, or cars), the more you consume, the less will be available for others. In these cases, consumption is rival because there is a problem in deciding how to ration output among the competing (rival) consumers. The price system resolves this problem by allocating a larger quantity to those who place a higher value on the good (i.e., those who are willing to pay more for it). With a good that is nonrival in consumption, there is no rationing problem: Once the good is produced, it can be made available to all consumers without affecting any individual's level of consumption.

Nonexclusion

The second characteristic of a public good is nonexclusion. This means that it is impossible, or prohibitively costly, to confine the benefits of the good (once produced) to selected persons. A person will then benefit from production of the good regardless of whether or not he pays for it. Although nonrivalry and nonexclusion often occur simultaneously, there is a distinction between the two concepts. Recall that our definition of nonrivalry said that consumption by one person *need not* (not *does not*) interfere with consumption by others; this means that, although all *could* consume simultaneously, it is still possible for one person to consume the good while others do not. There are cases where we have potential nonrival consumption but where it is possible to prohibit consumption by some people at moderate cost; in this case the good in question does not fit the definition of a public good.

Television broadcasting can make the distinction between nonrivalry and nonexclusion clear. When a television program is broadcast, any number of people (in the relevant area) can watch and not interfere with the reception of others. Thus, a broadcast has the nonrival characteristic of a public good. Note, however, that it is possible to exclude some people from viewing the program. Those without television sets, for example, will be unable to watch. Or metering devices could be installed on all TV sets so that only on payment of a price could a person view the programs; nonpayers would be excluded. Therefore, a television broadcast is nonrival in consumption, with exclusion possible at moderate cost; such a good then does not have both necessary characteristics of a public good.

In many situations nonrivalry and nonexclusion go together; then we have a public good. National defense is a case in point. How could we protect you and not your neighbor? Your neighbor could, of course, be deported and thereby excluded from securing any benefits from the defense effort. Similarly, the same means could be used to exclude potential beneficiaries of the flood control project. In both cases exclusion is possible, but it involves high costs. Whether a good is nonexclusive is ultimately a matter of degree, because in some cases the cost of exclusion is higher than in others. The relevant question is whether the cost is low enough to make exclusion feasible. In the case of national defense, most people would agree that exclusion is too costly; thus, national defense fits our definition of a public good. In contrast, most people would probably agree that exclusion is feasible with television broadcasting, so it is not a public good.

The existence of public goods creates problems for a price system. Once a public good is produced, a number of people will automatically benefit, regardless of whether or not they pay for it (because they cannot be excluded), so it is difficult for private producers to provide the good: Unless they can collect money for producing the good, they will be unable to cover their costs. On the other hand, with private goods—where consumption is rival and nonpayers can be excluded—private producers have incentive to provide the goods because they can extract payment from consumers. With private goods the price system can function effectively, but with public goods voluntary cooperation encounters a serious hindrance: the free rider problem.

Public Goods and the Free Rider Problem

A crucial question is whether voluntary cooperation through the price system will provide the appropriate quantity of a public good. To understand why voluntary cooperation often will not work, consider a community of ten people thinking of financing the construction of a dam to lessen the probability of flooding; the dam is, of course, a public good. Assume that the dam provides protection valued at $1000 to each person and that the total cost of the dam is $5000. If the dam is built, the benefit to each of the ten people is $1000; thus, the total benefit is $10,000. Because the benefit exceeds the cost, it is in the community's interest to build the dam. Note in particular that the dam could be built if each person contributed $500, and then everyone would be better off (i.e., each would receive a benefit of $1000 at a cost of $500).

Will voluntary agreement among the ten persons lead to the dam being built? Actually it is not possible to give an unequivocal answer, but we can see the problem that could arise. Suppose one of the ten people believes that the other nine will finance the good whether or not he contributes anything. Because of the high cost of exclusion, if the dam is built, he will receive protection regardless of whether he participates in its funding. Because he will be far better off if he can enjoy the benefit of the dam at no cost, he has incentive not to make any voluntary contribution. He is behaving as a free rider, attempting to avoid bearing any cost in the financing of a public good.

In this particular example it is possible that the dam would be financed despite the free rider problem, with the remaining members of the community bearing somewhat higher costs. Whether this occurs depends on how prevalent free rider behavior is within the group. If, however, enough people in the community behaved as free riders, the dam would not be built. Although the outcome of this example is indeterminate, we can explain under what conditions the free rider problem would be most likely to create a serious misallocation of resources. Basically, it is a matter of the size of the group over which benefits are nonrival.

The larger the group, the more severe the potential free rider problem, and hence the more likely that a public good could not be financed by voluntary contributions. Consider a small group of two neighbors where the public good is the removal of a dead tree lying precisely on the property line separating their properties. Only two people need agree on financing the tree removal, and each will recognize that without his participation the tree may not be removed. It is probable that both will contribute, and the tree will be removed. (There is an element of indeterminacy concerning exactly how the cost will be shared, but as long as the combined benefit of the neighbors exceeds the cost, it is likely they will bargain until agreement on financing is reached.)

Note that the dam and tree examples differ in a significant way. With the dam, each person will realize that his own contribution will have only a small effect on whether or not the dam gets built. Even if he contributes nothing toward the project, other people may finance the dam, and he will receive the benefit at no cost. Of course, the problem is that if enough people reasoned this way and withheld their contributions, the project would not be undertaken. On the other hand, in the tree case each neighbor will realize that his own contribution has a significant impact on the outcome. Unless both contribute, the tree will probably not be removed, so it is more likely that both will contribute.

As the group size increases, it is more likely that everyone will behave as a free rider, and the public good will not be provided. If we change the dam example slightly and assume the dam benefits 1000 people, each by $10 (so the total benefit is the same as before), it is less likely the good will be financed than in the previous examples. In this case, each person's contribution will have virtually no effect on the ultimate result. Put differently, the outcome depends mainly on what the other 999 people do, and whether any one person contributes will not affect what others do. Choosing not to contribute is the most rational behavior.[2] Because this is true for every person, no one will contribute, and the good will not be provided.

Therefore, when the benefits of the public good are nonrival over a large group, it is unlikely that the good will be provided (or, if provided through the contributions of a few, it will not be provided in sufficient quantity). This is true even though it is in the interest of people to have the good provided, that is, even though the benefits exceed the costs. The failure of the price system—based as it is on voluntary cooperation—to function efficiently in providing public goods is a major economic justification for government intervention. In the last example, the government could levy a tax of $5 on each person and use the $5000 in tax revenue to finance the dam. Each person would be better off: He would receive services from the dam worth $10 at a cost of $5 in taxes. The government expenditure of $5000 on the dam would lead to a more efficient allocation of resources than would the price system.

Exactly how large the group must be before the free rider problem

[2] A formal analysis of the relationship between group size and the free rider problem can be found in James M. Buchanan, *The Demand and Supply of Public Goods* (Skokie, Ill.: Rand McNally, 1968), Chapter 5.

becomes serious is unclear because it depends on the bargaining and negotiating costs, the strategies adopted by people in these negotiations, and so on. There is little doubt that, generally, a group of 1000 people would encounter great difficulties in reaching voluntary agreement on the financing of a public good. (Consider, however, that many small communities—but not large ones—manage to provide fire protection through *volunteer* fire companies.) It is in the large group setting, such as national defense, that the strongest case for government action can be found.

There are many real-world examples that provide empirical support of the importance of free rider behavior. A particularly good example occurred in 1970, when General Motors tried to market pollution control devices for automobiles at $20 (installed) that could reduce the pollution emitted by 30 to 50 percent. Pollution abatement is, of course, a public good, at least over certain geographic areas. We may suppose that the benefits of a 30 to 50 percent reduction in pollution far outweighed a cost of $20 per car. (If this assumption is not valid, the government has made a sizable mistake, because it now requires pollution control devices on all new cars that reduce pollution by about 95 percent at a cost of several hundred dollars per car.) Yet GM withdrew the device from the market because of low sales. This was simply the large group free rider problem at work: Everyone might have been better off if all drivers used the device, but it was not in the interest of any single individual to purchase it because the overall level of air quality would not be noticeably improved as a result of his action.

It should not be thought that the free rider phenomenon is necessarily bad. In some cases it serves a useful function. For example, the free rider problem may inhibit the formation of collusive agreements among businesses to restrict output and raise prices. It also makes it more difficult to finance lobbies that try to persuade Congress to adopt (or reject) certain policies.[3]

Our examples of free rider behavior have dealt primarily with public goods—goods with nonrival consumption and infeasible exclusion. When a good has both characteristics in a large group setting, the market will fail to provide the good or to provide it in sufficient quantity. If, however, a good is nonrival in consumption, but exclusion is feasible, markets can provide the good, and there are many examples of this type of good. Movie theaters, for instance, provide a good with nonrival benefits, at least up to a group size equal to the capacity of the theater. However, exclusion is possible because only those who pay the

---

[3] A reader who wonders how some groups containing hundreds of thousands of people have been able to partially overcome the free rider problem and finance lobbies (such as union members, doctors, and farmers) should consult Mancur Olson, Jr., *The Logic of Collective Action* (New York: Schocken Books, 1968).

admission cost are permitted to see the movie. Thus, theaters can collect money from consumers, and this provides an inducement to incur the costs necessary to produce the good. Concerts, circuses, and sporting events, as well as schooling, are quite similar to movies in this regard. Pay television, where viewers must pay for each program they view, is also possible because the necessary metering devices are not overly costly.[4]

We have seen that the price system will not provide public goods efficiently in the large group case. In the following section we will see how, in principle, the efficient level of output can be determined, as well as the difficulties encountered in attempting to put this theory into practice.

The Efficient Output of a Public Good

As with most other economic decisions, determination of the efficient output of a public good involves a comparison between the marginal benefits and marginal costs associated with different levels of output. The marginal cost of a public good simply reflects the cost of resources used to produce the good, just as in the case of a private good. However, the marginal benefit of a public good differs from that of a private good because of the nonrival nature of the former. With a private good like hamburgers, the marginal benefit of producing an additional unit is simply the value of the hamburger to the single person who consumes it. With a public good like defense, the marginal benefit of producing an additional unit is not the value that you alone place on it, because a large number of other people also benefit simultaneously from the same unit. Instead we must add the marginal benefit of every person who values the additional unit of defense, and the resulting sum indicates the combined willingness of the public to pay for more defense, that is, its marginal benefit.

The way in which we derive the social marginal benefit of a public good—in this example, a dam designed to control flooding—is illustrated in Figure 2–1, where units of the public good are in terms of the

[4] Although private markets can clearly provide goods where exclusion is possible at low cost, even if the benefits are nonrival, there is some disagreement over whether the private markets will operate with perfect efficiency. For some interesting discussion of this question, see Harold Demsetz, "The Private Production of Public Goods," *Journal of Law and Economics,* 13:293 (Oct. 1970), and comments on this paper by Robert B. Ekelund, Jr., Joe R. Hulett, and Earl A. Thompson in *Journal of Law and Economics,* 16:407 (Oct. 1973). See also William H. Oakland, "Public Goods, Perfect Competition, and Underproduction," *Journal of Political Economy,* 82:927 (Sept./Oct. 1974). With special reference to television, see Roger G. Noll, Merton J. Peck, and John J. McGowan, *Economic Aspects of Television Regulation* (Washington, D.C.: Brookings, 1973).

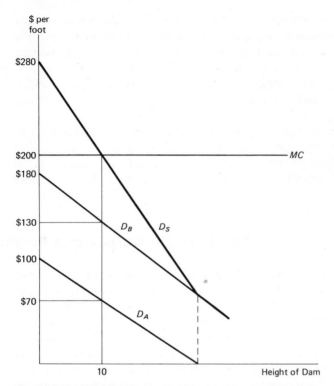

Figure 2–1. Efficient output of a public good.

height of the dam. For simplicity assume that only two people, *A* and *B,* benefit from the dam, although the analysis can be generalized for any number of people. The demand curves of the two consumers are shown as D_A and D_B. Recall that the demand price on a consumer's demand curve at any rate of output (i.e., the height to the demand curve) measures the marginal benefit for that consumer. In moving from the marginal benefit of each consumer to the marginal benefit for society, we must add the demand prices of all consumers. Geometrically, this involves a vertical summation of the consumers' demand curves. For example, in Figure 2–1 we add the marginal benefit to *A* for the first unit ($100) to the marginal benefit of *B* for the first unit ($180) and arrive at the social marginal benefit of $280 for the first unit. Proceeding in this way we can derive the social demand or marginal benefit curve, D_S, from the sum of D_A and D_B.

It is now easy to see that at any output where D_S lies above the marginal cost curve, *MC*—drawn here as horizontal at $200 for simplicity—people are willing to pay more for additional units of output than their marginal cost; thus efficiency requires an expansion of output. In

Figure 2–1 at any level of output below 10, A and B together are willing to pay more for another unit of output than the marginal cost of $200 (because D_S lies above MC). Thus, an increase in output can be financed by A and B in a way that will benefit both (with each paying somewhat less than the maximum amount he is willing to pay). At any output greater than 10, on the other hand, too much of the public good is being produced; because the cost of the additional output is less than the combined benefit to A and B, a reduction in output can benefit both A and B. Therefore, the most efficient rate of output is 10, where A's marginal benefit of $70 plus B's marginal benefit of $130 just equals the marginal cost.

In general, the efficient output of a public good is that level of output where D_S, obtained by vertically summing the demand curves of all consumers, equals the marginal cost of production. Note that our discussion has been in terms of finding the efficient level of output, a 10-foot dam. There is no presumption that this output will be the actual, or equilibrium, output. We have already noted that voluntary cooperation in the large group case would *not* lead to production of the efficient output. Whether the government would actually finance the efficient output depends on how political forces determine public policies, a matter to be examined in a later chapter. Here we have simply identified the efficient level of output.

Nothing has yet been said about who is to pay the $2000 cost of producing the 10-foot dam. There is a good reason for this omission because there are many different ways to divide this cost between A and B, and all of them may be equally efficient. The distribution of taxes is, in part, a matter of equity. One way to finance the output would be to charge each taxpayer a price per unit of the public good equal to the taxpayer's marginal benefit at the efficient output level. Because A's marginal benefit is $70 per unit, his tax liability will be $700 ($70 times 10 units, or $700), and B's tax liability will be $1300. Financing the public good in this way covers the toal cost of provision and has the advantage of ensuring that everyone on balance benefits from the government tax-expenditure package. In addition, if taxes were apportioned in this way, taxpayers would unanimously agree that ten was the most appropriate output. The argument that taxes should be determined in this way is called the *benefit theory of taxation*. It holds that it is just (a value judgment) to make beneficiaries of government expenditures pay for their benefits in this way.[5]

Alternatively, a different distribution of the tax burden could be used. Individual A could pay $800 and individual B could pay $1200 for the same quantity of the public good. The total cost of providing the

---

[5] Chapters 10 and 12 contain a further discussion of the benefit theory of taxation.

good would still be covered, but, compared to the tax distribution above, this would represent a redistribution of $100 from A to B because A would be paying more than his marginal benefit and B would be paying less. Note that ten is still the efficient output, at least as a first approximation. If, however, the redistribution shifts D_S by changing A's and B's relative demands for the good, the efficient level of output will be affected by the way the taxes are distributed.[6] Thus, our analysis shows how to determine the efficient output for a given distribution of income; it does not, however, indicate that any particular allocation of the tax burden is preferred. This is not to say that the tax distribution is solely a question of distributional equity; there are relevant efficiency aspects to this question, but they are simply not incorporated in this analysis. For example, if A is heavily taxed, he might emigrate from the taxing jurisdiction. Furthermore, taxation unrelated to benefits would lead those who pay little (or no) tax to favor a larger output and those who pay heavy taxes to favor a smaller output, thereby creating conflicting pressures within the political process. These matters too will be discussed in later chapters.

Government financing of a public good with taxes overcomes one aspect of the free rider problem, the tendency of people to withhold payment. It circumvents this problem by forcibly collecting the money. There is, however, another aspect of free rider behavior that government financing does not overcome: People have no incentive to reveal their demand accurately for the public good. In order to determine the efficient output, we must know every person's demand curve (so we can vertically add them to obtain D_S). How can we find out how much a public good, like defense, is worth to millions of people? This is probably the most difficult practical problem in implementing the analysis.

The (marginal) value of consumers for private goods is revealed in their purchasing decisions so that market-determined prices reflect the relative values of private goods. If the government is financing a public good, however, the political process does not reveal the value of that good to the taxpayer-voter with any degree of accuracy. When a person votes for candidate A rather than for candidate B, his vote reveals very little about how much incremental amounts of defense, education, or welfare are worth to him. Nevertheless, it is conceivable that, despite this problem, there is an "invisible hand" in the political process that works to promote efficiency. We will examine this question in a later chapter.

One other matter deserves some attention. The use of vertically added demand curves to determine efficient output is a consequence of the

[6] The efficient output is unchanged if the income effects on A's and B's demand are negligible, *or* if B's increase in demand (because he has $100 more income) is exactly offset by A's decrease in demand.

nonrival characteristic of a public good and is not related to whether exclusion is feasible. Where exclusion is feasible, private producers face demand curves that reflect some form of vertically added individual demand curves. For example, the marginal cost of showing movies in theaters is covered by the sum of the admission prices paid by the viewers. (In contrast, the marginal cost of a Big Mac is covered by the price that the individual consumer pays.) It is clear that with exclusion possible, the price system can provide goods with nonrival benefits. However, is the result of private provision an efficient allocation, that is, should potential customers be excluded where it is possible?

A case can be made that consumers should not be excluded from a good with nonrival benefits even if it is possible. Once a good with nonrival benefits has been produced, an additional person can consume the good and not interfere with the consumption of others. Excluding a person from consuming the good will then harm that person without benefiting anyone else, so it is often argued that it is inefficient to exclude him. This has led some economists to maintain that the nonrival characteristic of certain goods alone will lead to market failure because the use of prices by private firms will exclude some consumers.

On the other hand, it should be pointed out that the charging of prices by, say, movie theaters does not necessarily exclude anyone: People who are willing to pay the price do consume the good. Only those who are willing to pay less than the price of admission will be excluded, and even this problem is often mitigated by using lower prices for some groups, such as children and senior citizens. There may be some inefficiency, but it must be weighed against the advantage of having production linked closely (if not perfectly) to consumer demands and having market-determined prices as a guide (possibly incomplete) to the value of the good. In any event, it is clear that the degree of inefficiency in market provision will be far less for a nonrival good when exclusion is possible than when it is not. Hence, the more serious problems occur for goods with both characteristics, that is, public goods.[7]

Externalities

Sometimes in the production, distribution, or consumption of certain goods, there are harmful or beneficial side effects that are borne by people who are not directly involved in the market exchanges. These side effects of ordinary economic activities are called externalities—external benefits when the effects are beneficial and external costs when they are harmful. The term *externality* stems from the fact that these effects are

[7] See the references in footnote 4 for interesting analyses of these issues.

outside, or external to, the price system; their impact is not determined through mutual agreement among all those affected. A few examples will make the nature of these effects clear.

Immunization against a contagious disease is an example of a consumption activity involving external benefits. When a person is inoculated, he benefits directly, because his chance of contracting the disease is reduced (this benefit is not the external benefit). The decision to be inoculated also confers benefits indirectly on others, because they are less likely to catch the disease, and this is the external benefit. The fact that other people benefit from his actions will not influence the person's decision as to whether he is willing to pay to be immunized. What the person is concerned with is the effect on his own health. Thus, the benefit his inoculation generates for others is external to his decision.

Maintenance of a person's lawn or home may also produce external benefits for neighbors. If the neighbors' well-being is improved by living in a more attractive neighborhood, then there is an external benefit associated with home lawn maintenance. On a somewhat grander scale, education is often alleged to involve external benefits such as a reduction in juvenile delinquency, an improvement in the functioning of the political process, or greater social stability.

External costs are also quite common, and the best examples can be found in the area of pollution. Driving an automobile or operating a factory with a smoking chimney pollutes the atmosphere that other people breathe; thus the operation of a car or factory imposes costs on people not directly involved in the activity. Similarly, operating a motorcycle produces a level of noise that is often irritating to those nearby, just as the noise level of a supersonic (or subsonic) airplane may be annoying to many people. Congestion is also an external cost: When a person drives during rush hour, the road becomes more congested not only for him, but for other drivers as well.

At a formal level, externalities and public goods are very similar. If a person is inoculated for a contagious disease, there are nonrival benefits; both he and others benefit from his inoculation. In addition, it would be very difficult to exclude other people from benefiting from his inoculation. The same is true of pollution, but here there are nonrival costs. A large number of people are simultaneously harmed if the atmosphere is polluted, and it would obviously be difficult to have the atmosphere (in a particular area) polluted for some and not for others.

If there is any difference between externalities and public goods, it may be the fact that external effects are unintended side effects of activities undertaken for other purposes. For example, no one pollutes because he enjoys breathing a polluted atmosphere—he simply wants to transport himself in a car from one place to another. In addition, the distribution of the benefit (say) from consuming a good with external benefits is usually very skewed. We may receive some benefit from your becoming better educated, but clearly the benefit you receive is many, many times greater; public goods tend to benefit people more evenly. These distinctions, however, are matters of degree, and there remains a basic similarity between the concepts.[8]

Recognizing the similarity between externalities and public goods greatly facilitates appreciation of the significance of externalities. Externalities lead to an inefficient allocation of resources, or market failure, just as public goods do. Market demands and supplies will reflect only the benefits and costs of the participants in the market; the benefits and costs that fall on others will not be taken into account in determining production. For example, a person may decide against being immunized because the improvement in his health is not worth the cost involved. If, however, the benefits of improved health for others are added to his benefit, the combined benefit could exceed the cost. In this case, his decision not to be immunized would represent an inefficient use of resources.

External Benefits

To examine the implications of externalities more fully, assume that consumption of some product generates external benefits. The competitive supply and demand curves are shown in Figure 2–2 as S (drawn horizontally, implying a constant cost competitive industry) and D_P; D_P reflects only the private demand of individual for the product. Given these relationships, the market equilibrium occurs with an output of Q_1 and a price of \$5. External benefits can be represented by the curve D_O, which reflects the marginal benefit to people other than the direct consumer. D_O is simply the vertically summed demands of people other than the immediate consumer of the product, vertically summed because of the nonrival nature of the benefits.

The competitive output, Q_1, is inefficient. At Q_1 the benefit to consumers of another unit is \$5 (the height to D_P). If another unit is consumed, however, people other than the direct consumer of the product receive a benefit valued at \$2 (the height to D_O). Thus, the combined marginal benefit of another unit of output is \$7, and this exceeds the \$5 cost of producing the good. The combined, or social, marginal benefits are shown by D_S, which is derived by vertically adding (again because the benefits are nonrival) D_O and D_P. The competitive output is too low because the marginal benefits of the greater output exceed the marginal

[8] For attempts at making a rigorous analytical distinction between externalities and public goods, see S. E. Holtermann, "Externalities and Public Goods," *Economica,* 39:78 (Feb. 1972), and Ezra J. Mishan, "The Relationship Between Joint Products, Collective Goods, and External Effects," *Journal of Political Economy,* 72:329 (May 1969).

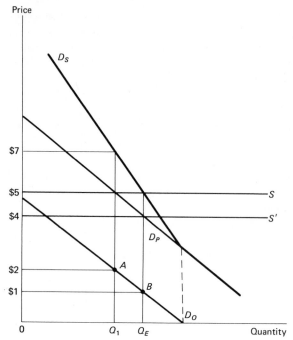

Figure 2-2. External benefits in a competitive industry.

costs. Yet there is no tendency for competitive pressures to produce a larger output because the additional benefits to the direct consumers are less than the $5 price per unit they must pay.

Figure 2–2 illustrates the general tendency of an activity to be underproduced when external benefits are involved and when production is determined in competitive markets. The competitive output is Q_1, whereas the efficient output is Q_E—where D_S intersects S. Government could step in with a policy designed to increase output to the efficient level. The policy most often recommended is an excise subsidy. If the government pays firms $1 for every unit of output they sell, the supply curve confronting consumers shifts to S'. Although the marginal cost of production is still $5, the government is in effect bearing $1 of this cost through the subsidy, so consumers need only pay $4. At the lower price of $4, consumers would be led to purchase Q_E units, and this is the efficient output. By using appropriate subsidies, the government can expand output in situations where external benefits lead competitive markets to produce too little.[9]

---

[9] It might be mentioned that this analysis is based on the assumption that external benefits are related to total consumption of the good, irrespective of who consumes the output. In some cases, external benefits will depend on the level of individual consump-

Note that the price to consumers has been lowered by $1, exactly the amount of the marginal external benefit at the efficient level of output, Q_E. (At Q_E the marginal external benefit is given by the height of D_0 or $1.) The subsidy is not equal to the marginal external benefit of $2 at the competitive equilibrium. A $2 per unit subsidy would confront consumers with a price of $3, and the resulting level of consumption would be in excess of the efficient quantity.[10]

External Costs

The analysis of external costs is symmetrical to that of external benefits. Suppose that firms in a constant cost competitive industry produce wastes as a by-product of their production and dispose of the effluents by dumping them into a nearby river. For a variety of reasons, these wastes irritate (i.e., harm) people living downstream, so the production of the industry's product involves external costs. In this case, the competitive output will be too large, because the external costs are not taken into account in the production decisions of the firms.

Consider Figure 2–3. The competitive demand and supply curves are shown as D and S_P, and the equilibrium output is Q_1, with a price of $5 per unit. The marginal damage suffered by people downstream is shown by the marginal external cost, or MEC, curve. It is drawn sloping upward to reflect the assumption that additional amounts of pollution inflict increasing costs on people living downstream as the water becomes more polluted. (Nothing important would be changed if the marginal external costs were constant, however.) At Q_1, the marginal external cost is $2, implying that people downstream would be $2 better off if one unit less of the product (and the waste) were produced.

With external costs the competitive output is too large. Firms expand output as long as consumers will pay a price that covers their costs, but the resulting price will not cover all costs of production—it ignores the damage done by pollutants to people living downstream. At Q_1, firms incur costs of $5 per unit, which is just covered by the price paid by consumers, but there is still a cost of $2 borne by people downstream. At the competitive level of output, Q_1, the product is not worth what it costs to produce: The social marginal cost of production is $7, whereas

tion, and it may be desirable to subsidize only those who would consume very little on their own rather than subsidize all consumers as in Figure 2–2.

[10] Although the subsidy depicted in Figure 2–2 attains an efficient output, it does not benefit everyone relative to the competitive equilibrium. Assuming that those who receive the external benefit bear the cost of the subsidy, the cost is $1 times Q_E, or $1BQ_E0$. The benefits they receive come from the expansion in output from Q_1 to Q_E and are equal to ABQ_EQ_1, clearly below the costs. In principle, a subsidy could be designed that would benefit both consumers and externally affected parties. Check to see if you understand how a subsidy of $1 per unit for consumption only in excess of Q_1 might achieve this.

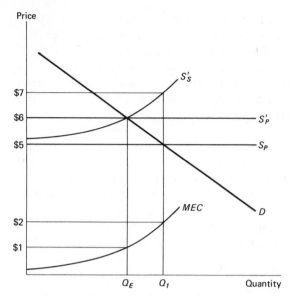

Figure 2–3. External costs in a competitive industry.

the marginal benefit to consumers is only $5. The social marginal costs of production are shown by the curve S_S, obtained by vertically adding *MEC* to the private supply curve, S_P. An efficient output occurs where S_S, which includes all production costs, intersects D, or at output Q_E. Competitive pressures, however, lead to an output of Q_1, larger than the efficient output.

As a corrective action, an excise tax could be used to induce firms to produce at the efficient level. A tax of $1 per unit of output would shift the supply curve up by $1 to S'_P, and firms would curtail production until the consumers were willing to pay a price of $6. The result, at Q_E, is where the marginal benefit to consumers equals the social marginal cost of production. Note that pollution is not eliminated; it is simply reduced to the point where a further reduction in production and pollution would cost more than it is worth.[11]

To summarize: Activities involving external benefits will be underproduced and those involving external costs will be overproduced by a competitive price system. We have seen how policies can be designed to achieve efficient outcomes, but to implement these policies it is necessary to know the size of the externalities. Unfortunately, this determina-

[11] The analysis depicted in Figure 2–3 is fully correct only if the waste bears a fixed relationship to output, and it must be disposed of in the river. In more realistic cases, it would be desirable to use a policy that induced firms to employ production processes that generate less waste per unit of output.

tion involves the same difficulties as in determining the demand for a public good.

Applying Externality and Public Good Analysis

Understanding how public goods and externalities lead to market failure provides important insight into the possible use of government intervention to produce greater efficiency. In such cases, there are potential mutual benefits from government action, so it is understandable that economists attach much significance to these phenomena in their discussions of public policy. Our brief introduction to public goods and externalities, however, has ignored some relevant issues, so we will now consider some common objections, misunderstandings, and problems in applying the analysis.

Voluntary Bargaining in the Small Group

In an important theoretical paper, Ronald Coase has shown that voluntary bargaining can lead to efficient outcomes even when externalities exist.[12] Coase developed his analysis by considering a rancher and a farmer with adjoining properties. The rancher's cattle would occasionally stray onto the farmer's property and destroy some of his crops: an external cost associated with cattle raising. Our earlier analysis would suggest that there would be too much crop damage, but Coase argued that this might not be correct. If the rancher is legally liable for damage caused by his cattle, he will bear a cost as a result of straying cattle. The damage caused by his cattle will not then be an external cost, but a direct cost borne by the rancher (and therefore taken into consideration in his decision making), because the rancher will have to compensate the farmer for crop damage.

Coase went further and argued that, even if the rancher were not liable, an efficient solution could emerge without government action. This would happen because the farmer has incentive to offer to pay the rancher to reduce the number of cattle that stray because a reduction in crop damage will increase the farmer's profits. An agreement could therefore be struck that would reduce cattle straying to the efficient level.

Coase's ingenious analysis shows that voluntary bargaining can lead to efficient outcomes, and at the same time illustrates the intimate connec-

[12] Ronald H. Coase, "The Problem of Social Cost," *Journal of Law and Economics,* 3:1 (Oct. 1960).

tion between external effects and property rights. As long as property rights are clearly defined and enforced, bargaining resolves the problem. Interestingly, it does not matter exactly how property rights are assigned. Whether the rancher is or is not liable for damage, cattle straying will be reduced. It is true that the *distributional* effects depend on the exact definition of property rights. When the rancher is liable, he will compensate the farmer; alternatively, when the rancher is not liable, the farmer will pay the rancher to reduce cattle straying. In both cases, cattle straying and crop damage are reduced to the efficient level, but different people bear the cost.

There are many examples of situations when the price system operates efficiently despite what may *appear* to be externalities. Consider noise in an apartment complex; noise from your neighbor's apartment interferes with your cramming for an exam. Is there an inefficiency? Probably not. It is likely that the market has already adjusted and that the noise level is efficient. If renters value quiet enough, then they will pay more for quiet apartments. Apartment owners, therefore, have incentive to soundproof apartments, require television sets to be operated at moderate levels, prohibit parties after midnight, and so on. As long as the additional quiet is worth the extra cost, apartment owners have incentive to provide it. Note that not all noise will be eliminated (so your studying may still be disturbed), but it will be reduced to efficient levels by the bargaining between renters and apartment owners. In this case, noise is not an externality, because it has been taken into account by the market mechanism.

Is there then ever a need to rely on government in these situations? We have already provided the answer in our discussion of the free rider problem. Private bargaining can work efficiently when there are small numbers involved, as in the Coase example where only one farmer is harmed by the straying cattle. When a factory pollutes the atmosphere breathed by thousands of people, however, private bargaining cannot be expected to lead to an efficient outcome. Our earlier conclusion of market failure is correct, therefore, in the large group case. Many issues of great importance, such as defense, pollution, and police protection, are large group externalities or public goods, and the price system cannot be expected to function effectively in these areas. Coase's analysis should caution us, however, against concluding that every phenomenon that appears to be an externality requires government intervention.

Choice of a Policy to Deal with Market Failure

External effects and public goods, at least in the large group setting, imply that voluntary behavior within a competitive price system will not result in an efficient allocation of resources. The identification of this distortion, however, does not tell us what type of government policy is preferred. Analysis of pollution, for example, shows that an unhampered price system will produce too much pollution, that is, that the benefits of reducing pollution exceed the costs. There are many different policies that could be used to reduce pollution, and it is unlikely that one policy will dominate others in terms of its efficiency.

Refer back to the analysis of Figure 2–2. There we saw that external benefits lead to underproduction of the good and that an excise subsidy, as a corrective measure, could be used to stimulate output to the efficient level Q_E. Other policies, however, could lead to this efficient output. For instance, the government might simply require people to consume larger quantities (to total Q_E), much as there are now requirements concerning school attendance and vaccinations. This is also an efficient policy, but the distribution of benefits and costs differs from that of the excise subsidy. With the excise subsidy, taxpayers bear the cost of expanding consumption through taxes to finance the subsidy; consumers of the product do not. With a consumption requirement, the consumers alone pay the additional cost. In each case, an efficient allocation results, but with a different distributional impact.

Choosing among alternative policy prescriptions to deal with externalities is a problem not fully answered by externality theory, but theory does help by suggesting the nature of the corrective action required. The use of taxes (for external costs) and subsidies (for external benefits) is quite popular among economists. These policies have numerous advantages: They are very flexible, because the rate of subsidy or tax can be easily adjusted depending on whether an increase or reduction in the external effect is desired; often fewer administrative problems are encountered; markets can still adjust in a decentralized way to changes in supply or demand; and information concerning the private benefits and costs is still provided by market prices and costs. Yet no unequivocal preference for taxes and subsidies should be inferred. Each alternative policy must be examined on its own merits. Externality theory can assist by pointing in the proper direction, but it is not a detailed blueprint for action.

One further problem in designing a corrective policy lies in determining how far to pursue the corrective policy, that is, how large a tax or subsidy should be used. If we knew the exact size of the benefits and costs involved, it would be a simple matter to determine the appropriate tax or subsidy as we did in Figures 2–2 and 2–3. But the magnitude of the external effects cannot be easily (if at all) determined. The danger here is that we will go too far: In the case of external benefits, expanding the output too far can be worse than doing nothing at all, as is true with reducing external costs too far below the efficient level.

Figure 2–4 can illustrate this, as well as several other points. It is

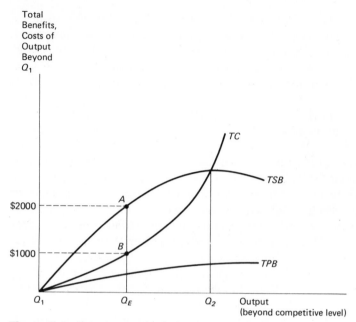

Figure 2–4. Output expansion in the presence of external benefits.

based on the external benefit example in Figure 2–2. In Figure 2–4, however, the horizontal axis measures output in excess of the competitive output, Q_1. On the vertical axis we are measuring the total benefits and costs associated with expansion in output beyond Q_1. The TC and TPB curves show the total private costs and benefits, respectively, of additional output; they are derived from the private demand and supply curves in Figure 2–2. (The curves in Figure 2–2 show the marginal costs and benefits; these are simply the *slopes* of the respective total curves.) The total social benefit curve, TSB, is the sum of the benefit to consumers (TPB) plus the external benefits associated with greater levels of outputs.

If there were no external benefits, the TC and TPB curves would reflect all the benefits and costs of output levels beyond the competitive level. In that event, an expansion of output would be inefficient because the costs exceed the benefits. When external benefits are involved, the relevant total benefit curve, TSB, lies above the total cost curve over a region of output. This means that the competitive output is too low, because an expansion of output will confer benefits greater than costs. The most efficient output occurs where there is the largest excess of total benefits over total costs, that is, where there is the largest *net* gain. This occurs at Q_E, where the slopes of TSB and TC (marginal social benefit and marginal cost) are equal, because there is then the greatest distance between the curves. At Q_E, the total benefit of the additional output, AQ_E, exceeds the total cost, BQ_E, by \$1000—the net gain. As we saw, an appropriate excise subsidy could be used to induce this expansion of output to Q_E.

If a mistake is made and the subsidy (or other policy) increases output beyond Q_2, we would be better off with no subsidy at all. Beyond Q_2 the total cost of the additional output exceeds its total benefit, even including the external benefits. This illustrates the danger of having too much of a good thing. Yet without knowing the magnitude of the external benefits, it is impossible to ascertain when we have gone too far. This is a serious problem, given the difficulty of estimating the magnitude of the external benefit, which is, of course, based on a precise knowledge of the value individuals place on the external effect.

It must be recognized that, given this problem, it is unlikely the government will use a subsidy of exactly the proper size. Nevertheless, we should not necessarily conclude from this that the government should do nothing. Note that a subsidy that achieves an output between Q_1 and Q_2 in Figure 2–4 is better than no subsidy at all. Although Q_E is the most efficient output, all the outputs in the Q_1–Q_2 range do involve some excess of benefits over costs in comparison to the competitive level of output, so some potential gain is possible. Just because the optimal level of output, Q_E, may not be achieved is no reason to oppose or reject a policy. As long as a program represents an improvement over the status quo, it should be considered, and perhaps eventually a more efficient policy will be found. However, the possibility that some policy might be worse than none should also be kept in mind.

Identifying the Externality or Public Good

A first step in correctly applying externality (or public good) theory is to identify exactly what constitutes the external effect. With air pollutants emitted by automobiles, it is not the production or use of automobiles that is an externality, it is the emission itself. Externality theory predicts that there will be too much pollution, not necessarily that there will be too many cars. An efficient policy must be designed to reduce pollution directly, not indirectly, for example, by reducing the stock of automobiles or by making it harder to get a driver's license. A tax on automobiles would be inappropriate because it would do nothing to induce auto manufacturers to produce cars that pollute less. An automobile tax would reduce the output of all cars by increasing their cost to drivers—irrespective of whether, or how much, they pollute. Instead an efficient tax should be levied on pollution itself. (The rate of tax should vary with the amount of damage done by pollution; for example, the pollution damage in large metropolitan areas—because there are more people to pollute and to be polluted—would be greater than the damage done in rural areas. As a consequence, the pollution tax would be higher in the larger, more densely populated areas.) This would give producers and consumers the proper incentive to reduce pollution in any way that costs less than the taxes levied.

The importance of determining exactly what constitutes the externality is frequently overlooked in policy analysis. Consider the frequent assertion that education produces external benefits—possibly in the form of a more stable society. Exactly what type of education produces these effects? Is instruction in dance, music, home economics, and physical education beneficial to anyone other than those who receive it? Yet if only certain types of education generate external benefits, then only these types should be subsidized. A policy that induces students to acquire skills they are unwilling to pay for—if these skills fail to generate external benefits—is simply inefficient.

Or consider the claim that education generates external benefits because it enables students to earn higher incomes and hence makes it less likely they will become criminals. Note that it is criminal activity that is the harmful effect. A subsidy to education would be inefficient because it would encourage overconsumption of education by pupils who would never become criminals. An efficient policy would be one that penalized, and thus deterred, criminal activity per se. To see the problem intuitively with this argument, note that it really claims that raising the incomes of potential criminals will reduce crime. This may be true, but the fact that there is some relationship between income and crime does not mean that raising the incomes of criminals is the least costly way of reducing crime. Generally, it will not be.

As a final example, consider the various proposals to stop economic growth. The reasons given usually involve external costs: economic growth is accompanied by more pollution and congestion. But the growth in pollution and congestion, or even their absolute levels, may be reduced without directly reducing the growth in other goods and services. A corrective policy would be more effective if designed to deal with pollution and congestion explicitly and not with economic growth.[13]

---

[13] There can be exceptions to the argument developed in this section, and the reader may wish to pursue the matter further. Generally, the exceptions involve cases where it is infeasible, or administratively too costly, to deal with the externality itself, and some indirect means may be the only possibility. Such cases are probably fairly rare, and as a general rule, it appears that attempting to deal with the externality directly will be more efficient.

Inframarginal Externalities

Inframarginal externalities are externalities with a marginal value of zero at the privately chosen equilibrium. An example of an inframarginal external benefit is shown in Figure 2–5. Individual A's demand curve is shown as $d_A d_A'$, and it is assumed that his consumption of the good generates marginal external benefits according to the schedule D_0. The marginal external benefit becomes zero at q_1; note that the point where D_0 becomes zero is less than q_A, the level that A would choose to purchase independently. This means that the marginal value of the external benefit at the private equilibrium is zero. This type of externality is called an inframarginal ("inside the margin") externality, and the importance of inframarginal external benefits is that they do *not* result in any inefficiency. The social demand curve reflecting all marginal benefits is $D_S d_A'$, and at q_1 it coincides with individual A's demand curve. In other words, only A receives any benefit if his consumption is extended beyond q_1, and, because his benefit (shown by $d_A d_A'$) is not worth the cost, it is inefficient to increase consumption beyond the level A chooses independently.

Because our primary concern is with externalities that result in inefficiencies in resource allocation, we should make sure that the externalities we are considering have nonzero values at the private equilibrium. In other words, would a little more (or less) of the activity in question confer *more* benefits (or costs) on the externally affected parties?

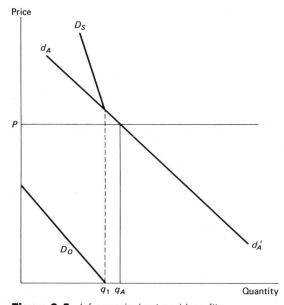

Figure 2–5. Inframarginal external benefits.

Frequently this distinction is obscured. Consider the statement, "We all benefit from living in an educated society." This statement is correct even if the external benefits are entirely inframarginal at the private equilibrium, because it can be interpreted to refer to total external benefits rather than marginal ones. Therefore, it does not necessarily imply a misallocation of resources by the price system. The fact that we benefit from living in an educated society is no reason for using government to encourage more education than people would choose on their own unless we would be even better off in a more educated society, that is, unless the externalities are marginally relevant.

Pecuniary Externalities

Suppose that the demand for housing by college students increases and drives up the price of housing for nonstudents in a college community. Although the demand for housing by nonstudents has not increased, they will be paying a higher price, and consequently are made worse off. The increase in demand by students harms nonstudents. Is this an external cost we need to worry about? The answer is no. This damage to nonstudents is transmitted through the price system (in the form of higher prices), not outside it. It is not external to the price system. Unfortunately, this type of effect has been given the name "pecuniary externality," meaning that it is monetary rather than real. All the externalities we have discussed so far are real, or as they are sometimes called, "technological externalities."

Pecuniary externalities are intrinsic to the workings of a price system. Every time a price, wage rate, or interest rate changes, as thousands do every day, some people are harmed and others are benefited. There is no inefficiency produced by these effects; the markets are simply adjusting efficiently to changes in the underlying demand or supply conditions. The reason there is no inefficiency involved is that the harm done to, say, nonstudents when housing prices rise is not a *net* cost to society. Instead it is simply a *transfer* of purchasing power from renters to owners of rental housing. A higher price harms the buyer but benefits the seller to the same degree, and there is no net loss. The situation is quite different with pollution, where the harm done to the pollutee is not offset by a gain to the polluter. Technological externalities, or just "externalities," as we refer to them, reflect net costs or benefits not taken into account by the market system. Because of this, they are a source of inefficiency, whereas pecuniary externalities are not.

Pecuniary externalities can easily be confused with the real thing. It is sometimes argued, for example, that vocational education of welfare recipients is a (technological) external benefit for taxpayers: vocational education may increase the earning capacity of welfare recipients, thus permitting a reduction in welfare payments (and a reduction in tax liabilities for taxpayers). This effect on taxpayers is a pecuniary externality, not a technological one, although in this case it is transmitted through a government policy rather than through the price system. The reduction in welfare payments and tax liabilities is simply a transfer from welfare recipients to taxpayers, with the loss to transfer recipients equal to the gain to taxpayers. Vocational education for recipients does not, of itself, lower taxes. Instead, it is the decision to reduce welfare payments that lowers taxes, and this has a purely redistributive effect.

From now on when we refer to "externalities," we will mean the technological variety that can cause resource misallocation, not the pecuniary variety that only indicates transfers of income.

Multiple Distortions

The efficiency implications we have drawn from our analysis so far are correct only when the economy is perfectly efficient except for the distortion produced by the public good or externality being examined. In other words, our conclusion that the output of a competitive industry will be too small if there are external benefits depends on the assumption that the remainder of the economy is without distortions, that is, the external benefit is the only distortion in an otherwise efficient economy. When this assumption is not correct, as is often the case, it is no longer possible to infer from the existence of externalities that there is necessarily any inefficiency. With many distortions in the economy, some may operate to offset others, and the end result is not clear.

To see this, suppose consumption of some industry's product yields external benefits *and* production of that product imposes external costs. If the external benefit is the only distortion, we can conclude that output is too low; on the other hand, the external cost by itself tends to produce too large an output. The two distortions operate in opposite directions and can cancel out, resulting in an efficient output. Similarly, a monopoly whose production involves external costs can be efficient, but a monopoly whose production involves external benefits will be more inefficient than a competitive industry with external benefits. (Can you see why?) In addition, more remote distortions in other industries can also have an effect, because all markets are interrelated.

Because there are many distortions in an economy, it is a difficult if not impossible task to take all into account, as a completely rigorous analysis should. In many cases, the quantitative significance of this problem is trivial: Because there is a monopoly in the safety pin industry, our conclusion that cars will pollute the atmosphere too much in the absence of government action is not likely to be altered. For that reason, in addition to the fact that we must first understand the complications of

45

single distortions before we can hope to comprehend the more involved cases of interacting distortions, we will largely ignore this problem. There are, however, a few important cases that we will evaluate later.

The Individual Demand for Public Goods

How much would you be willing to pay for a 50 percent reduction in the level of nitrogen oxide in the atmosphere? How much is a base of ICBMs outside Atlanta worth to you? If you have difficulty giving fairly precise answers to these questions, then you do not have a well-defined demand for the public good or externality in question. Our analysis, however, was based on the assumption that people do have well-defined demands for such goods: Recall that the marginal external benefit and cost curves simply reflect the sum of everyone's answers to questions like the preceding. If people cannot place a precise value on these goods, then the notion of efficiency becomes fuzzy and inexact. That is, how can we determine the efficient quantity of the good, the type of policy to pursue, or the size of the corrective action if people don't know how much the good is worth? Because of this, it will be difficult to evaluate resource allocation with regard to its efficiency.

This is a troublesome problem. People can also be uncertain about the value of some goods purchased in private markets (such as, perhaps, some type of medical care), but this problem is clearly more prevalent with public goods and externalities. Although economic analysis can still be used to determine some of the consequences of public policies, efficiency judgments must be made subject to a range of indeterminancy.

Public Goods and Externalities: A Summary

Understanding how public goods and externalities affect resource allocation provides significant insight into cases where competitive markets will not function with peak efficiency. Analysis of these phenomena is also of assistance in determining what types of policies are most likely to improve resource allocation. It is not surprising then that economists examine the price system for these (and other) sources of inefficiency in their evaluation of public policy. Where externalities and public goods are quantitatively significant, a case can be made that certain types of government intervention will generally be mutually beneficial.

Unfortunately, very little empirical evidence on the size, or even the existence, of external effects is available. (Information yielded by the burgeoning studies of pollution represent a partial exception to this and hold out promise that research in other areas will dispel some of our ignorance.) Some externalities, such as the effect of your attire on the well-being of others, are probably not important enough to bother with, particularly when we understand the difficulty of designing efficient policies. Others, such as pollution, are clearly more important. In the vast intermediate range between these extremes, there is considerable room for honest disagreement about the quantitative significance of public goods and externalities.

Appendix to Chapter 2 [14]

The greatest drawback to the partial equilibrium analysis used in Chapter 2 is that it fails to make precisely clear the implications of alternative distributions of the cost involved in altering the resource allocation. In this appendix we will develop a model that overcomes this shortcoming. [15]

Our example will be an external benefit. Assume individual B's consumption of good X is an external benefit for individual A. In Figure 2–6 MN is B's budget constraint, with his consumption of X measured horizontally and his consumption of other goods (money spent on goods other than X) measured vertically. We know how to show B's preferences with indifference curves and to determine his equilibrium in such a diagram. What we want to see is how A's preferences can be represented in this diagram. Any consumption pattern of B indirectly implies a certain level of welfare for A, and a change in B's consumption pattern will influence A's welfare in one or both of two ways. First, if B consumes more X, this tends to benefit A, because B's consumption of X is an external benefit. Second, if a subsidy to B is used to increase B's consumption above his private budget constraint, A (it is assumed) must finance the subsidy, and this tends to make A worse off. By combining these two factors, we can show A's preferences with adjusted indifference curves.

Assume that the price of X is \$1, so the slope of the budget constraint, P_X/P_M, equals 1. Select a point, C, where B is consuming 10 units of X and is paying their full cost (he is on his budget constraint). Point C represents a level of welfare for A that places him on the adjusted indifference curve, AIC_2^A. To understand the shape of this curve,

---

[14] The appendix contains advanced material that can be omitted without great loss.

[15] Paul Samuelson first developed the geometry employed here in "Diagrammatic Exposition of a Theory of Public Expenditure," *Review of Economics and Statistics*, 37:350 (Nov. 1955). The approach was reinvented by F. Trenery Dolbear, Jr., and later by Hirofumi Shibata in "On the Theory of Optimum Externality," *American Economic Review*, 57:90 (Mar. 1967), and "A Bargaining Model of the Pure Theory of Public Expenditures," *Journal of Political Economy*, 79:1 (Jan./Feb. 1971), respectively.

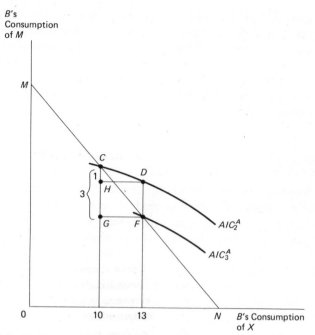

Figure 2–6. Adjusted indifference curves for externally affected party.

suppose B consumes three more units of X. If B were to pay for this additional consumption, he would be at point F, and A would then be better off because he would be receiving a larger external benefit without having to pay for it. We want to show, however, how B can consume more X and leave A as well off as at point C. For A to be equally well off, he must pay an amount equal to the additional external benefit received when B consumes the additional three units; assume this benefit is valued by A at $2. Then at point D, individual A is as well off as at point C, because in moving from C to D individual A has given up $2 (equal to DF), and B's consumption increases from 10 to 13. We know that A must have given up $2 to reach point D, because B's consumption at point D costs $2 more than his budget, and this additional cost must be borne by A.

Points C and D are two points on the same indifference curve for A. The slope of AIC_2^A tells us the size of the marginal external benefit for A caused by B's consumption of X. At point C, A is willing to pay $2 to have B consume three more units of X, so the marginal external benefit averages $2/3 over this range. Note that this is not the slope of AIC_2^A; the slope between C and D is $1/3$. In fact, the slope of an adjusted indifference curve is equal to the difference between the price of X and the marginal external benefit. More precisely, it is $P_X/P_M - MRS^A_{M X_B}$, or the difference between the market price ratio, P_X/P_M (the slope of the budget constraint), and A's marginal rate of substitution between other goods and B's consumption of X (i.e., the marginal external benefit). This means that the slope of an adjusted indifference curve is flatter than the budget constraint whenever there are positive marginal external benefits. This is intuitively plausible: When AIC^A_2 is flatter than MN, it means that A is willing to pay some of the cost of increasing B's consumption of X, and this will be true when there are positive marginal external benefits.

As we move down AIC^A_2, B is consuming larger quantities of X. As B consumes more X, A will be willing to pay less for still further increases (the marginal external benefit falls as B consumes more X). This means that the slope of AIC^A_2 will become steeper as we move to the southeast. At the point where the marginal external benefit becomes zero, AIC^A would have a slope equal to B's budget constraint. This explains the slope of a given adjusted indifference curve. Adjusted indifference curves representing higher levels of welfare for A are located closer to the X axis. One of these is shown as AIC^A_3, although, of course, an adjusted indifference curve passes through every point in Figure 2–6.

To complete the picture, we can now incorporate the more familiar indifference curves of individual B. These are shown in Figure 2–7. If B must operate along his own budget constraint, he would choose to consume at point C. Point C represents B's private equilibrium. Now that we understand the adjusted indifference curves, we can see why the private equilibrium is inefficient. When B's consumption of X is an external benefit, the AIC curves are flatter than B's budget constraint, so one passes through point C, as does AIC^A_2. The intersection of IC^B_1 and AIC^A_2 encloses the shaded area in Figure 2–7. *Any allocation within this region makes both A and B better off;* this shows the private equilibrium to be inefficient. At point D, individual B is better off (on IC^B_2), and individual A is equally well off as at C. At point K, individual A is better off (on AIC^A_3), and B is equally well off as at C. Note that all of the allocations within the lens-shaped area involve a greater consumption of X by B than at his private equilibrium. External benefits lead to underconsumption.

An efficient allocation occurs where it is not possible to benefit one person without harming another. This is true where A's adjusted indifference curves are tangent to B's indifference curves. There are, therefore, many efficient allocations, and they are shown by the contract curve JJ, which connects all points of tangencies between the indifference curves. Different efficient allocations correspond to different distributions of welfare between A and B.

The contract curve, which shows the efficient allocations, may be ei-

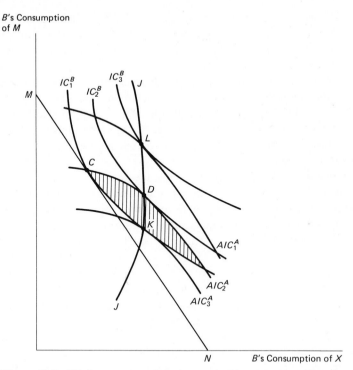

Figure 2–7. Efficient consumption of a good with external benefits.

ther upward sloping (over the region JK), vertical (over the region KD), or backward bending (over the region DJ); the contract curve can also have different slopes at different points as in Figure 2–7. This means that there is not any one unique efficient quantity of consumption of X by B. Instead, the efficient level may depend on the distribution of welfare. (This is true, of course, whether or not there are externalities.) It is possible for the efficient level of X to be independent of this distribution, as over the KD region of the contract curve, but we could not easily show that the efficient level could depend on the distribution in our earlier models (as in Figure 2–2). With a change in income distribution, the demand curves in Figure 2–2 shift in opposite directions. The important point, however, is that, with any distribution, a privately attained equilibrium will involve too little consumption of a good yielding external benefits.

An efficient allocation is shown in Figure 2–7 by a tangency of indifference curves, or where $MRS^B_{MX} = P_X/P_M - MRS^A_{MX_B}$. Rearranging this expression, it becomes $MRS^B_{MX} + MRS^A_{MX_B} = P_X/P_M$. In words, efficiency occurs where B's marginal benefit from X (MRS^B_{MX}) plus A's marginal external benefit from B's consumption of X ($MRS^A_{MX_B}$) equals the marginal cost of X (P_X/P_M—where it is assumed that market prices reflect marginal costs). This condition corresponds to equating the vertical sum of the demand curves (in Figure 2–2) to marginal cost. They are simply two different ways of expressing the same thing.

Figure 2–7 also shows clearly why voluntary bargaining can lead to an efficient outcome: By moving into the lens-shaped area, both parties benefit. When bargaining does not work—as it would not if A were a large group of people rather than a single individual—government policy may be capable of improving efficiency.

Several types of government policies are illustrated in Figure 2–8. An excise subsidy that lowers the price of X to B (the policy emphasized in the text) can lead to an efficient outcome. Originally, the private equilibrium is at point C, with B on IC_2^B and A on AIC_2^A. The excise subsidy shifts B's constraint to MN', and B's equilibrium occurs at point L—consuming more, of course, at the lower price. Point L is on the contract curve, JJ, and represents an efficient allocation. Note, however,

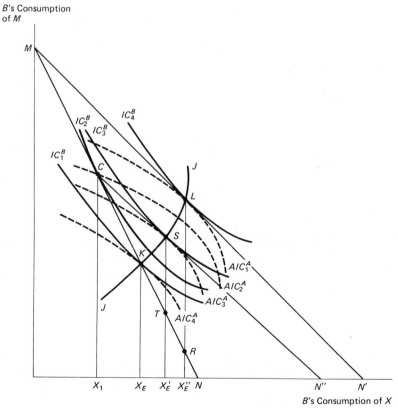

Figure 2–8. Policies to deal with a consumption externality.

that A was better off before B was subsidized. That is because the subsidy, the total cost of which is LR, applies to all units of X that B consumes, but only the additional X consumed, $X_E'' - X_1$, represents a benefit to A because B was consuming X_1 without the subsidy.

In principle, it is possible to design a subsidy that benefits both A and B. One example is a marginal excise subsidy that shifts B's budget constraint to MCN''. This subsidy lowers the price only of units consumed in excess of X_1, B's presubsidy consumption, and leads to an equilibrium at point S (in the lens-shaped area identified in Figure 2–7). Both A and B are better off than they were without the subsidy. Individual A is better off despite paying the cost of the subsidy, ST, because the additional external benefit received from the increase in consumption from X_1 to X_E^1 exceeds this cost.

A third policy that achieves efficiency is to simply require B to consume X_E units and pay for them himself. This forces B to consume at point K and makes him worse off than at C, but point K is an efficient allocation.

All three of these policies, and numerous others, are capable of achieving an efficient allocation. Externality theory does not imply that any of these policies is superior to any other. A major difference between the efficient outcomes of these policies lies in their distributional implications. To judge one to be superior, it is necessary to make a value judgment concerning what distribution is best.

Note that designing policies to achieve efficient outcomes requires knowledge of the adjusted indifference curves that represent the size of the marginal externalities. (Some policies, such as the law requiring consumption of X, would require knowledge of both sets of indifference curves. The excise subsidies have the advantage of generating information about B's preferences from B's response to the subsidy.) As stressed earlier, this type of knowledge is very difficult to obtain.

Supplementary Readings

Buchanan, James M. *The Demand and Supply of Public Goods.* Skokie, Ill.: Rand McNally & Company, 1968.

Burkhead, Jesse and Jerry Miner. *Public Expenditure.* Chicago: Aldine Publishing Company, 1971, Chapter 4.

Coase, Ronald. "The Problem of Social Cost," *Journal of Law and Economics,* 3: 1–44 (Oct. 1960).

Demsetz, Harold. "The Private Production of Public Goods," *Journal of Law Economics,* 13 (2): 30–43 (Oct. 1970).

Head, John G. *Public Goods and Public Welfare.* Durham, N.C.: Duke University Press, 1974.

McKean, Roland N. *Public Spending.* New York: McGraw-Hill Book Company, 1968, Chapter 5.

Mishan, E. J. "The Postwar Literature on Externalities: An Interpretive Essay," *Journal of Economic Literature,* 9:1–28 (Mar. 1971).

Tullock, Gordon. *Private Wants, Public Means.* New York: Basic Books, Inc., Publishers, 1970.

CHAPTER 3

PRINCIPLES OF EXPENDITURE ANALYSIS

Expenditure analysis involves using economic theory to determine the consequences of government expenditure programs. Unfortunately, there is no general analysis that is applicable to all expenditure programs, because these programs take many different forms. The consequences vary greatly, depending on exactly how the government spends the funds. Consequently, it is necessary to proceed case by case, although some types of programs are clearly more important than others. In this chapter we will examine some of the more significant economic effects of fairly common types of expenditure programs. Later chapters will consider specific programs in more detail.

The economic effects of expenditure programs fall primarily into two categories: allocative and distributive. Allocative effects refer to the way an expenditure program affects the pattern of goods and services produced by the economy. For example, does a particular subsidy lead to an increase in the output and consumption of the subsidized good? Although common folklore assumes that a subsidy increases output, there are important real-world subsidies that have had the opposite effect, at least for some of the people being subsidized. As we will see, subsidies to housing and education are of this type.

The distributive effects of government expenditures refer to their impact on the distribution of real income, or welfare. Put most briefly, who benefits and who loses from the programs? Many government expenditures benefit some groups at the expense of others and consequently redistribute income. Such effects are obviously important, but frequently are not self-evident. For example, there is reason to believe that urban renewal programs have actually operated to the detriment of low income families. Similarly, unemployment insurance, subsidies to higher education, and agricultural subsidies have benefited middle and upper income families far more than low income groups.

In this chapter we will analyze some of the important effects of various types of expenditure programs: expenditures on nonmarketed goods, fixed quantity subsidies, and variable quantity subsidies. In each case, we will be concerned with the allocative and distributive effects of these expenditures.

Expenditures on Nonmarketed Goods

Governments spend substantial sums of money to stimulate the production of goods and services that would not be provided by the price system (or, if provided, would be provided in negligible amounts). We call such goods, nonmarketed goods. Examples include defense programs, foreign aid, and space exploration. Economic analysis of these expenditure programs is somewhat limited, in part because the goods often have the characteristics of a public good so consequently there is no readily available measure of the value of the good to the public. Nonetheless, a few basic points can be made.

Allocative Effects

There are two basic ways the government can spend to stimulate output of some good that is not provided by private markets. One approach is to pay private firms to produce the good. In this case the government expenditure simply represents a market demand for the good that gives private firms the incentive to produce it. Another way is for the government to hire the resources (labor, capital goods, etc.) itself and oversee the production directly. There are numerous examples of both types of programs. For instance, the government purchases airplanes and rifles from private firms for use in defense activities; in providing postal services, however, it employs resources and oversees production directly.

Whichever method is used, the allocative effect is to increase output of the desired good. Moreover, in both cases, resources that would have been used to produce other goods in the private sector are used instead to produce goods in the public sector. Thus, we get more of one good and less of others. This is illustrated in Figure 3-1, where output in the government sector is measured horizontally and output in the private sector is measured vertically. ZZ is the production frontier that shows all combinations of these goods that can be produced. Initially, suppose we are at point C, with the economy producing $0G_1$ in the public sector and $0P_1$ in the private sector. Then the government increases its production so that government sector output increases to $0G_2$, or by G_1G_2. The result is a move to point B. Note that as a consequence private sector output is reduced from $0P_1$ to $0P_2$, or by P_1P_2. The opportunity cost as-

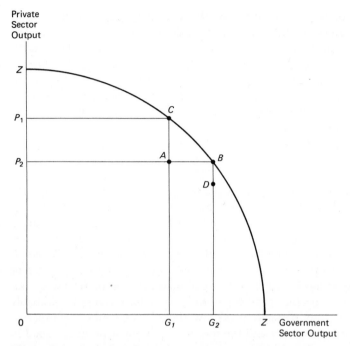

Figure 3–1. Allocative effects of government provision of goods and services.

sociated with the increase in government output, G_1G_2, is a loss of other goods and services equal to P_1P_2. This simply reflects the fact that the resources used in the government project must be drawn from the private sector, where they would have been used to produce other goods and services.

Government expenditures that stimulate the output of some non-marketed good therefore have an opportunity cost that takes the form of a reduction in other goods and services in the private sector. This is an extremely simple point but one that is frequently overlooked. Government-provided goods and services, even though they are not sold directly to the public, are not free. Yet this obviously does not mean that they are not worthwhile. It may be that the benefits accruing from the G_1G_2 increase in government sector output are greater than the costs associated with the P_1P_2 sacrifice of other goods. In Chapter 2 we saw that there are cases where the price system would not provide some goods even though benefits exceeded the costs. Here we are only pointing out the nature of the cost involved when the government undertakes to provide some good.

Although private sector output in the aggregate falls with an expan-

57

sion of output in the public sector, this does not mean that the output of each and every good produced in the private sector will decrease. The output of some goods—those complementary to the government-provided good—could increase. If the government provides recreational areas such as national parks, then motel bookings, camper and gasoline sales might increase because people would utilize these services while consuming the government's product. In the aggregate, however, private sector output must fall.

Distributive Effects

When the government stimulates production of nonmarketed goods, the distribution of benefits to different individuals or groups is generally difficult to determine, just as the overall benefit to the public is difficult to ascertain. This is because there are no market prices to register values that people either individually or collectively place on this type of good. It is clear, however, that different people may benefit to very different degrees, just as hawks may benefit more than doves from defense spending. Similarly, people who enjoy and can afford camping probably benefit more from national parks. Without considerable information about people's preferences and the specific government-produced good in question, very little can be ascertained about the distributional impact of the good.

Production Inefficiency

Recall that the opportunity cost of increasing government output by G_1G_2 is shown as P_1P_2 in Figure 3–1. Actually, this is the *minimum* possible opportunity cost associated with the production of the government good. Only if the government output is produced in the least costly way will P_1P_2 reflect the actual cost. There are many ways to combine resources to produce the additional G_1G_2 units of product, and some of them will involve a larger sacrifice than P_1P_2. In other words, if government production is inefficient, we could end up at point D in Figure 3–1 when $0G_2$ is produced. This involves a cost (sacrifice of other goods) of DB greater than is necessary to produce $0G_2$. Although D is inside the production frontier, this does not necessarily mean that resources are unemployed. If, for example, resources are misallocated so labor resources that would be relatively more productive in producing private goods are used in the government sector, then the economy will be operating inside the frontier.

Sometimes government sector output is produced inefficiently, with results like those depicted in Figure 3–1. For instance, it has been estimated that public housing projects actually cost about 20 percent more to produce than comparable housing built privately.[1] Likewise, it was argued that the Defense Department used too much labor relative to capital when it could draft soldiers and pay below market wages.[2] Similar concerns have been expressed about services produced by the post office and public schools.[3]

Why does it sometimes cost more to produce government goods than is necessary? In competitive resource markets, any given output is produced using the least costly combination of inputs, that is, at the least opportunity cost. Firms operating in private markets for a profit are normally led to produce efficiently because their profits are greater when they do so. With a government-produced output, however, the profit motive is absent. Sometimes it may even be in the interests of government agencies to pad their costs, because neither the agency nor its employees bear the cost of the resulting inefficiency. Even if the agency tries to operate efficiently, it is sometimes misled by prices that do not accurately reflect resource costs. This was the case with public housing where the federal government subsidized construction costs but not operating expenses of local housing projects. As a result, local housing authorities produced housing units that were highly capital intensive but very poorly maintained—an inefficient way to provide housing services. (The program was so unsatisfactory, in fact, that it has been phased out.)

Designing government expenditure programs to avoid inefficient production is a difficult problem. In some cases, it may be feasible to have the government purchase the good from private firms. Because firms are profit oriented, they have incentive to produce in the least costly way. Even here, though, some forms of government procurement, such as sealed bid contracting and cost-plus contracts, have led to inefficiency.

It is not known exactly how important such inefficiency generally is, and further research in this area is needed. However, the fundamental point is that expanding government sector output involves opportunity costs in sacrificed private sector output, and sometimes this sacrifice is larger than necessary.

The Role of Taxes

Considering the opportunity cost of government expenditure programs naturally brings taxes to mind. Because we have discussed the opportunity cost without any reference to taxation, one might wonder what role

[1] Richard F. Muth, *Public Housing: An Economic Evaluation* (Washington, D.C.: American Enterprise Institute, 1973).

[2] James C. Miller III (ed.), *Why the Draft?* (Baltimore: Penguin Books, 1968).

[3] Admittedly, these examples are not all of nonmarketed goods. Schooling, housing, and postal services could be provided by private markets, and in some cases are.

taxes play in the analysis of government expenditures. Actually, expenditures involving the use of resources have an opportunity cost irrespective of how they are financed. In terms of Figure 3–1, private sector output must fall by at least P_1P_2 when the government project is undertaken. This is true regardless of whether the government taxes, borrows, or simply prints money to finance the spending. Nonetheless, taxes are most often the tangible embodiment of this cost, and it is convenient to think of the opportunity cost of government spending as reflected in the taxes needed to fund the program.

The exact role of taxes in financing government expenditures is twofold. First, the tax (or other method of finance) determines the composition of the sacrificed output in the private sector. As mentioned earlier, P_1P_2 measures the aggregate reduction in private sector output, but whether this reduction is composed mainly of fewer cars, less food, smaller homes, or less of some other goods depends on the exact method of funding. A tax on cars, for example, would obviously concentrate the reduction in output more on cars than a tax on food. However, the overall reduction in output, P_1P_2 (considered as an index of all private sector output), would be the same.[4]

Second, the tax would also determine exactly who will bear the opportunity cost, P_1P_2. Although the opportunity cost for the community is P_1P_2, different taxes will distribute this burden differently among the public. For example, a progressive income tax would place a larger share of the cost on high income families than would a tax on food.

It is clear, then, that the precise method of finance used has allocative effects (what goods are sacrificed) and distributive effects (who sacrifices these goods) of its own, in addition to the allocative and distributive effects of the government expenditure. In a complete analysis of government policies, both tax and expenditure policies must be considered simultaneously. As a practical matter, however, this is seldom feasible, because expenditure programs are not linked to specific taxes. Consequently, expenditure programs are usually analyzed separately, without regard to the precise method of finance. In doing this, however, it must be remembered that the expenditures do have opportunity costs and that these costs normally take the form of a tax that someone must pay.

A more detailed consideration of alternative taxes is postponed to later chapters.

---

[4]We are ignoring here the fact that some taxes may have a larger real burden than others raising the same revenue because of the welfare costs of taxes. This point will be developed when we consider tax analysis in Chapter 10.

Macroeconomic Effects

So far our emphasis has been on the opportunity cost associated with a government project. The conclusion that private sector output must fall is based on the assumption that the economy is initially operating on its production frontier. In cases of involuntary unemployment of resources, the economy will be operating inside its frontier, as at point A in Figure 3–1. Starting at point A, a government expenditure program could conceivably result in a move to point B, employing previously unemployed resources to produce the G_1G_2 increase in public sector output. Note that the incremental government output does not result in a reduction in output from the private sector.

At first glance, it appears that the opportunity cost of government spending might be zero when there is substantial unemployment. This is wrong, but because in one form or another it is a common error, let's consider it in some detail. The error lies in failing to understand that the notion of opportunity cost relates to alternative uses of resources. In Figure 3–1, the alternative to using the unemployed resources in the public sector is to employ them in the private sector. In other words, we could move from point A to point C. (This could perhaps be accomplished by a tax reduction, an increase in money supply, or an increase in cash transfers by government to stimulate employment in the private sector.) Point C is an alternative to point B, so the opportunity cost of using previously unemployed resources in the government sector is that they cannot be used in the private sector to increase output from $0P_2$ to $0P_1$. The opportunity cost of increasing government output from $0G_1$ to $0G_2$ is thus correctly viewed as P_1P_2 even if resources are initially unemployed.

A similar error occurs in the frequent discussions of government spending programs that allegedly "create jobs." Government employment of workers in public works or other programs does not "create jobs"; instead it simply induces people to work for the government rather than in the private sector. Government spending diverts workers (and other productive resources) to the government sector. Just as in the preceding case, in the relevant sense, this is true even when the workers are initially unemployed. The important question is whether the workers' services are more valuable in the government sector or elsewhere, and the concept of opportunity cost forces us to face that question.

Possible impacts of government expenditures on the over-all price level (inflation) are frequently cited by presidents as a reason to veto a particular expenditure bill. This is also a source of confusion. An expenditure program is not intrinsically inflationary if taxes are used to finance the program. If taxes are not used and the government prints money to finance the program, inflation can result, but even then it is not an obvious reason to oppose the program. Inflation can be thought of as a type of tax that reduces the value of cash balances. An objection that an expenditure program is inflationary can then be seen as an objection to the particular type of tax used to finance it. Although it may be true that inflation is more harmful than other taxes as a method of financing an expenditure program, it must be recognized that the possible inflationary impact of an expenditure program is not a valid objection to the program itself. The same program could be financed by other, non-inflationary, means.

Therefore, the potential impact of government expenditures on the overall level of employment, output, or prices is largely irrelevant in an analysis of specific expenditure programs. Where these effects are important is in an examination of the combined impact of monetary policy and all taxes and expenditures on macroeconomic variables. Of course, entire courses on these matters are taught, and our neglect of these issues does not imply that we think them unimportant. But as long as there are many policy combinations compatible with full employment, macroeconomic considerations provide no method of analyzing and comparing the allocative and distributive consequences of different points on the production frontier (i.e., of different positions of full employment). The assumption of full employment is simply a convenient way to stress the relevant alternatives.

Fixed Quantity Subsidy for Marketed Goods

Much of the recent growth in government subsidies has taken the form of subsidies for goods that are, or could be, provided through the market mechanism. Subsidies for education, food, child care, housing, job training, old age pensions, and medical care (among others) involve subsidizing goods and services that people would have purchased anyway (but perhaps not in the same quantity). To understand the consequences of such subsidies, it is necessary to determine how people—both consumers and producers—respond to the subsidy, and this depends in part on what type of subsidy is used.

A common form of subsidy is one through which the government makes a certain quantity of a good available to a consumer at no cost, or perhaps at a cost below the market price. This is a form of "in-kind" subsidy, so called because the subsidy is linked to a particular good. The essential characteristic of this particular type of in-kind subsidy is that the quantity of the good being subsidized is beyond the control of the consumer; the government determines what quantity of the good is made available at the zero or subsidized price. For example, the government may provide food stamps a consumer can use to purchase $1500 worth of food, but if more food is desired the consumer must pay for the additional amount himself at the full market price. Here the subsidy applies only to a given quantity, $1500 worth of food. Similarly, public schools make available a certain quantity or quality of schooling, and if more is desired it must be paid for by the consumer. That is, if parents are not satisfied with the education provided by public schools, they can send their children to private schools at their own expense, or if parents wish to supplement their children's education (with tutoring or special classes), they may, but again they must bear the full cost. In both these examples, as well as many others that could be mentioned, the subsidy applies to a fixed quantity of the good being subsidized, with any additional quantities being purchased by consumers at the full market price.

Reduced Private Purchase

One major impact of this common type of subsidy is that it caused a reduction in the private purchases of the subsidized good. Such a reaction on the part of consumers is intuitively obvious because the government is providing a good the consumer would have purchased on his own. If, however, the reduction in private purchases is less than the quantity provided by government, then total consumption of the good may still rise.

To illustrate the consequences of this type of subsidy more clearly, consider a consumer whose presubsidy budget constraint relating the subsidized good to other goods is shown by MN in Figure 3–2. The budget constraint reflects the consumer's income of $1000 (equal to $0M$) and the market price of food, $10 per unit (the slope of MN). Prior to receiving any subsidy, the consumer is in equilibrium at point E, consuming 40 units of food and $600 worth of other goods and services.

Now suppose the government provides 30 units of food to the individual at no direct cost.[5] This means that the consumer could consume at point M'—accepting the 30 units of food and still have $1000 in income remaining to spend on other goods and services. If he wants, however, the consumer may also use his own income to purchase additional units of food at a price of $10 per unit. His entire budget constraint is therefore $MM'N'$; the $M'N'$ segment has the same slope as the original budget constraint because the consumer must pay the unchanged market price for each unit beyond 30. Note that if the government had given the consumer a cash transfer equal to the cost of 30 units of food ($300 in cash), his budget line would have been $M''N'$. ($M''M$ is the dollar cost of the subsidy.) The effect of this fixed quantity subsidy on consumption

---

[5] It makes no difference to the analysis whether the government provides the consumer with funds that must be spent on food.

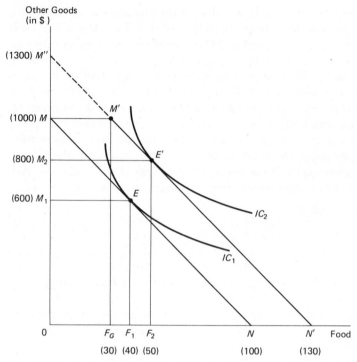

Figure 3–2. Fixed quantity subsidy: reduction in private purchases.

opportunities is the same as a cash transfer except that the dotted portion of the budget constraint, $M'M''$, is not available to the consumer. Actually, if the consumer is able to sell some of the food provided by the government at $10 per unit, he could move along the $M'M''$ part of the budget constraint. It is assumed, however, that resale is not allowed.

The exact response of the consumer depends on how the budget line is affected, which we have just determined, and on his preferences concerning food and other goods, which we will now consider. If we assume that food and other goods are normal goods, then we know that after receiving the subsidy the consumer will choose a point along $M'N'$ involving more consumption of both. This is illustrated by the postsubsidy equilibrium at E' on $M'N'$, with the consumer consuming 50 units of food and $800 worth of other goods. Recall that at the original equilibrium, E, the consumer purchased 40 units of food; after the subsidy, consumption of food has increased by only 10 units even though the government is providing 30 units of food. Private purchases of food by the consumer have fallen from 40 ($0F_1$) to 20 (F_GF_2) in response to the subsidy, but total consumption has risen to 50. Note also that the subsidy has allowed the consumption of other goods to increase. Before the subsidy, the consumer spent $400 on food and $600 on other things; after the subsidy the consumer spends $200 of his own income on food (and receives a $300 subsidy) and has $800 left for other goods and services.

A reduction in private purchases should be expected with a fixed quantity subsidy. As long as the quantity provided by government (30) is less than the consumer would purchase if given the subsidy in the form of cash (50 units would be consumed with an unrestricted cash transfer), this type of subsidy is equivalent in its effects to a cash transfer. Thus, consumption of the subsidized good increases only to the extent that the consumer would choose if given money instead of food.

Unchanged Total Consumption

Our analysis suggests that consumption of the subsidized good increases, but by less than the amount of the subsidy. However, we have been ignoring the impact of the taxes required to finance the subsidy. Taxes reduce disposable income, and this in turn tends to reduce consumption of food as well as other goods. To complete our analysis, we must consider the combined effects of a tax and subsidy together.

Assume that our consumer in Figure 3–2 pays a tax equal to the subsidy received ($300). Although this would not normally be true for all consumers, on average the tax paid must equal the subsidy (if the program is to be self-supporting), so this is a convenient starting point. Suppose, then, that the consumer's before-tax-and-subsidy budget constraint is $M''N'$, his income is $1300, and he is in equilibrium at point E'. A tax of $300 would shift his budget constraint to MN. When the government returns the tax to the consumer in the form of 30 units of food, his post-tax-and-subsidy budget constraint becomes $MM'N'$. Thus, the combined tax expenditure policy has no effect on his consumption expenditures apart from disallowing consumption along $M'M''$. The net effect is that the consumer ends up purchasing the same quantities of food and other goods after the tax-plus-subsidy as he did before.

Now let's consider how this subsidy affects the overall market for food. In Figure 3–3, the original equilibrium, with 100 consumers each consuming 50 units, is shown by the intersection of the demand and supply curves. When the government taxes the consumers and uses the proceeds to purchase food for them, two things happen. First, the consumers' private demand for food falls from D to D_P, resulting from the combined effect of the tax and subsidy. Second, the government's demand for food is shown as D_G. As we have seen, the government demand tends to be offset by a reduction in private demand. The post-subsidy-and-tax demand is the horizontal sum of the private demand, **65**

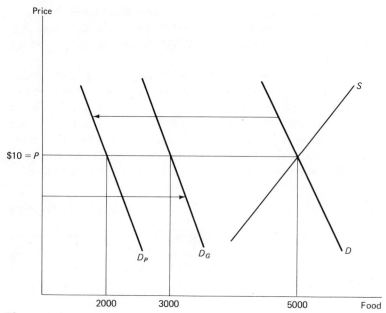

Figure 3-3. Fixed quantity subsidy: unchanged total consumption.

D_P, and the government demand, D_G. Thus, the aggregate demand, D, is unchanged and the price and output of food remain unaffected.

These conclusions suggest that many government expenditure programs have little or no effect on the allocation of resources. However, our analysis depended on a number of assumptions concerning the nature of the subsidy. In some cases these assumptions are not appropriate, and by modifying the analysis we can determine when and how this type of subsidy can affect resource allocation.

Overconsumption

There are times when a fixed quantity subsidy will increase consumption by more than a cash transfer. This happens when the quantity provided by the government is greater than the consumer would purchase if he had cash rather than the in-kind subsidy. Consider Figure 3-4. MN is the presubsidy budget constraint, with the consumer purchasing F_1 units of food. If the government provides F_G units of food at no cost, the budget line will shift to $MM'N'$. Given the consumer's preferences as shown by his indifference curves, his new equilibrium is at point M'. If the individual had been given cash equal to the cost of the subsidy (MM''), his budget constraint would have been $M''N'$, and he would have consumed less food, F_2, at E'. In this case, the fixed quantity sub-

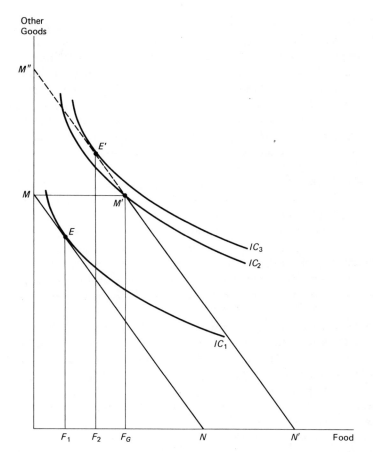

Figure 3–4. Fixed quantity subsidy: overconsumption.

sidy has increased consumption more than a cash transfer. Note, though, that the consumer would have been better off if given cash. That is, with a cash transfer equal to the cost of the subsidy, the consumer would be on indifference curve IC_3; with the in-kind subsidy the consumer is on IC_2, a lower indifference curve.

A fixed quantity subsidy can also increase consumption when the consumer pays taxes equal to the cost of the fixed quantity subsidy. In this event, $M''N'$ is the before-tax-and-subsidy budget constraint, MN the after-tax budget constraint, and $MM'N'$ the after-tax-and-subsidy budget constraint. In this situation, the consumer's equilibrium is altered from E' to M', involving a higher level of food consumption. Note, however, that when consumption of food is increased, the consumer is worse off; he was on a higher indifference curve at E' than now at M'. This is because a government subsidy does not increase consumption possibilities when the consumer must pay the tax; total expenditures on food and other goods are not changed. The only effect of the subsidy cum tax is to alter the position along the original $M''N'$ budget constraint from E' to M'. The consumer could have chosen to consume more food at M' in the absence of the government policy, but according to his preferences the additional F_2F_G units of food cost more than they were worth. When the government tax-expenditure policy is in effect, it leads the consumer to purchase the additional food and pay for it through taxes, and this understandably makes him worse off.

Thus, when the quantity of the subsidized good provided by the government exceeds the quantity the individual would choose if he could spend the subsidy as he wishes, the subsidy is successful in stimulating consumption. Only when the consumer's own preferences play no part in determining consumption, with the government policy, in effect, fully determining the consumer's food consumption, does this outcome occur. Such a policy also makes the consumer worse off than he would be with no subsidy or tax (in the case where the consumer pays taxes equal to the subsidy) or with an equal size cash subsidy (in the case where someone else pays the taxes).

Because the recipient is worse off with the fixed quantity subsidy than with a cash transfer, what is the justification for this type of subsidy? This is a good question. Although there are a number of possible reasons (such as the paternalistic one: "consumers don't know what's good for them"), one is of particular interest to economists. Recall that when consumption of a good involves external benefits the private equilibrium involves too little consumption. If food consumption generates external benefits, it is possible that M' in Figure 3–4 is a more efficient consumption pattern than E'.[6] Even though the immediate consumer would prefer to consume less food than at M', other people are better off when he consumes at M' rather than E'. Thus, there can be some justification on efficiency grounds for overriding the consumer's preferences. In the absence of such external benefits (or other sources of market failure), however, a fixed quantity subsidy that leads to overconsumption is unequivocally inefficient.

Underconsumption

It is often taken for granted that a fixed quantity subsidy will increase consumption, but we have seen that in some cases it may lead to no more consumption than a cash transfer. In addition, there are situations

[6] This can be demonstrated rigorously using the geometric device developed in the appendix to the previous chapter. Note that if the adjusted indifference curve of externally affected parties that passes through point M' is tangent to the recipient's indifference curve at that point, then the allocation at M' is Pareto optimal.

where this type of subsidy will actually reduce consumption! This paradoxical outcome can occur when it is very costly, or impossible, for the consumer to supplement the quantity of the good provided by government. Earlier we assumed that the consumer could purchase additional units of food at the market price and thereby supplement the subsidized quantity provided. For some types of goods and some types of subsidies, it is very costly to consume more than the quantity provided by the government.

An example will make this clear. Suppose the subsidized good is housing, and the government offers a consumer a two-bedroom apartment at no cost. The consumer may prefer a three-bedroom apartment and might be willing to pay the difference in cost between a two-bedroom and a three-bedroom apartment to obtain a larger apartment. The way the program is administered, however, this option is not open to him. The consumer cannot accept the government two-bedroom apartment and, by paying the cost of an extra bedroom, convert it into a three-bedroom apartment. Instead he must either accept the two-bedroom apartment or forego the subsidy altogether and pay the entire cost of housing himself. In this setting, it is quite possible that the consumer will choose the two-bedroom apartment when the government foots the bill rather than the three-bedroom apartment he would have chosen in the absence of the subsidy.

Note how the housing subsidy differs from the food subsidy considered earlier. With the food subsidy, the consumer could supplement the subsidized quantity by purchasing additional units of food at the market price. With the housing subsidy, the nature of the good provided by government makes supplementing it costly if not impossible. Housing is typical of a good that is not highly divisible into small units; it is "lumpy," and to increase the quantity consumed usually requires moving into a larger or better housing unit. A subsidy such as described earlier provides a housing unit of a given size and is therefore difficult to supplement.

Let's see how this looks in the framework we have been using. In Figure 3–5, the presubsidy budget constraint relating housing and other goods is MN. (Even though housing is "lumpy," the budget constraint is smooth, because the consumer can choose more or less housing by moving from one housing unit to another.) In the absence of any subsidy, H_1 units of housing are consumed. Now assume the government offers a smaller (or lower quality) housing unit of H_2 units at no cost. The budget constraint becomes $MM'RN$. Note the difference between this and the food subsidy. With the food subsidy the budget constraint is $MM'N'$, because the consumer could consume more of the subsidized good (to the right of M') by paying only the cost of additional units. But to consume more housing than H_2, the consumer must forego the

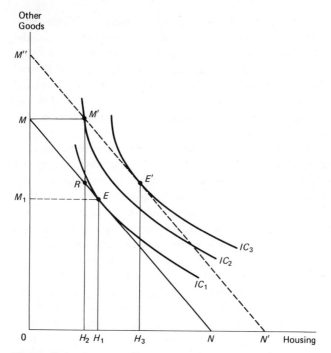

Figure 3–5. Fixed quantity subsidy: underconsumption.

subsidized housing unit and bear the entire cost of the housing units along the RN portion of the original budget constraint. Compare, for instance, the amount of income the recipient has available to spend on other goods and services when he consumes H_2 units of housing in contrast to H_1 units; if he opts for the government subsidy, he has $0M$ in income, his entire income, free to spend on other goods. If, instead, he were to consume H_1 units, he only has $0M_1$ in income remaining.

Confronted with the $MM'RN$ budget constraint, the consumer would choose to accept the subsidized housing and consume at M', even though this involves less housing than he consumed without the subsidy. Although the consumer sacrifices H_1H_2 units of housing, he gains M_1M units of other goods, and the net result is that he is better off at M' than at E.

Actually, the more relevant comparison is between the consumption pattern with the subsidy (at M') and with an equal-size cash subsidy that the consumer can spend as he wishes. Because MM'' is the cost of the housing subsidy, a cash transfer of this sum would yield the dotted $M''N'$ budget constraint, and the consumer would choose point E', with H_3 units of housing. The consumer would also be better off at E', on a higher indifference curve, because the extra H_2H_3 units of housing are worth more than their cost. H_2H_3 is a measure of the underconsumption produced by the housing subsidy.[7]

It is important to recognize that this type of subsidy can lead to underconsumption for some consumers, overconsumption for other consumers, and the appropriate level of consumption for still others. The exact outcome depends on the size of the subsidy in relation to the preferences and incomes of the recipients of the subsidy. (Verify this.) In general, it is most likely that the subsidy will restrict consumption when the quantity being subsidized is small, when the consumer's income is high, or when the unsubsidized quantity chosen by the consumer is large. The opposite combination of circumstances is likely to lead to overconsumption.

There are a number of real-world subsidies that can lead to underconsumption. Subsidies for public schools and institutions of higher education are probably the most important examples, because schooling is a "lumpy" good just as is housing. Similarly, public housing, medical services provided by public health clinics, and Medicaid are other obvious examples. It is theoretically possible for these subsidies to lead to underconsumption, but whether they actually do is, of course, an empirical question.

Two recent studies have investigated this question and concluded that some subsidies of this type have, in fact, operated to restrict consumption, at least for some recipients. Kraft and Olsen studied a sample of public housing tenants and estimated that 49 percent of the families were consuming less housing than if they had been given the subsidy as cash.[8] The remaining 51 percent were consuming the same amount of housing or more than they would with cash subsidies. However, the families in this sample had higher income levels and more children than the average of all public housing tenants, so Kraft and Olsen's estimate cannot be generalized to all recipients of public housing.

In another study, Sam Peltzman studied the effects of state-supported colleges and universities on the consumption of higher education.[9] He found that expenditures per student would be higher in the absence of subsidies to higher education, which supports our contention that some fixed quantity subsidies result in underconsumption. Peltzman also

---

[7] Note that the same diagram can be used to analyze the effects of a nonredistributive housing subsidy in which the consumer pays a tax equal to the subsidy he receives. In this case, $M''N'$ is the before-tax budget constraint, and the consumer is initially at point E'. The tax shifts the constraint to MN, and the subsidy then produces the $MM'RN$ budget constraint. The net effect of the tax-plus-subsidy reduces housing consumption and makes the consumer worse off.

[8] John Kraft and Edgar Olsen, "The Distribution of Benefits from Public Housing," paper presented at Conference on Research in Income and Wealth, May 1974.

[9] Sam Peltzman, "The Effect of Government Subsidies-in-Kind on Private Expenditures: The Case of Higher Education," *Journal of Political Economy*, 81:1 (Jan./Feb. 1973).

found that more students attended college as a result of the subsidies. Thus, some students are consuming less schooling and others (those who would not have attended college without the subsidy) are consuming more as a result of state support of institutions of higher education.[10] These studies, therefore, provide some empirical support for our analysis.

Other Relevant Factors

We have seen that the fixed quantity type of subsidy can increase, reduce, or have no effect on the consumption of the subsidized good. The exact outcome probably varies widely from one subsidy to another, and from one consumer to another. Although it is difficult to generalize, it appears likely that the quantitative impact of such subsidies on the allocation of resources is much smaller than widely believed. Before concluding, however, that they are unimportant, several factors should be mentioned that have been ignored so far.

One significant impact of subsidies like these is on the distribution of income. Frequently subsidies of the fixed quantity variety are used to redistribute income in favor of certain groups. For example, food stamps, housing subsidies, and Medicaid subsidies are concentrated exclusively on low income groups. Public schools and social security (subsidized old-age pensions) are more widely distributed, but it is important to consider the taxes used to finance the subsidies and who pays them, as well as the subsidies themselves, in determining their overall impact. In general, it is plausible to suppose that the way such subsidies operate to benefit some groups at the expense of others is more important than their impact on the level of consumption of the subsidized goods; that is, because these subsidies probably have little effect on consumption levels, their impact on the distribution of income may be of more significance.

Another interesting consequence of these subsidies is that they often cause us to lose information about the value of the subsidized goods to consumers. Earlier we noted that market prices reflect the marginal values of goods to consumers. With fixed quantity subsidies, this is sometimes not true. To see this, refer back to the equilibrium positions shown in Figure 3–4 and Figure 3–5. Note that the slope of the consumer's indifference curve at M' (which measures the marginal value to the consumer) is not equal to the slope of MN (indicating the market price ratio). In Figure 3–4 the marginal value of food is less than its market price, whereas the opposite is true in Figure 3–5. In short, with

[10] At the risk of pointing out the obvious, it should be noted that we are discussing estimates and not facts. Effects of this type cannot be directly observed, of course, so we must rely on empirical estimates.

such subsidies we are often unaware of the value of the subsidized good to consumers. This is a serious problem in designing and evaluating policies (although it provides employment for economists who try to estimate values to recipients!). It is also a problem that can be avoided through the use of other types of subsidies, as we shall see.

We have also ignored the administrative costs of the subsidies, as well as the administrative (and other[11]) costs of taxes. The significance of these costs is that the amount of subsidy returned to consumers is less than the taxes paid. The importance of this factor varies widely from one subsidy to another and from one tax to another. Administrative costs are sometimes as low as 1 percent, but occasionally may exceed 10 percent.

In view of these factors, and because of the importance of possible overconsumption and underconsumption, it would be premature to conclude that fixed quantity subsidies have unimportant consequences for the economic system. On the other hand, it is probably true that these subsidies are quite ineffective if their goal is to stimulate greater consumption of the subsidized goods.

Variable Quantity Subsidy: An Excise Subsidy

A fundamentally different form of subsidy is one where the government pays part of the per unit price of a good but allows the quantity of the good to be determined by consumer purchases. For example, suppose the government decided to pay the consumer $5 for each unit of housing consumed. The subsidized quantity, and hence the cost to the government, is variable. Such a subsidy is called an excise subsidy—just the opposite of the more familiar excise tax.

Examples of excise subsidies are less common than examples of fixed quantity subsidies. Unemployment insurance is a type of excise subsidy, but with some significant differences from the "pure" type considered here. Some welfare programs operate much like excise subsidies. (These programs will be discussed in greater detail in later chapters.) But perhaps the most common examples are found in special provisions of the tax laws. These "tax subsidies" or "tax loopholes" will also be examined in later chapters. Here we will simply consider how such subsidies affect output and consumption levels.

There are two types of excise subsidies, ad valorem excise subsidies and per unit excise subsidies. With an ad valorem excise subsidy the government pays a certain percentage of the consumers' total expenditures on a good (say, 40 percent of the consumers' medical care costs). In

[11] The principal hidden cost of taxation is a welfare cost produced by distorting resource allocation. This will be discussed in Chapter 10.

contrast, with a per unit excise subsidy the government pays a certain amount for each unit of the good consumed, as in the housing subsidy mentioned earlier. In this chapter, we will concentrate on per unit excise subsidies, although the allocative and distributive effects of both types of excise subsidies are identical. In Chapters 11 and 12, when we analyze tax loopholes, we will consider ad valorem excise subsidies in greater detail.

Allocative Effects

Suppose we have a competitive industry for food. The supply and demand curves are shown as S and D in Figure 3–6, and the competitive equilibrium price and quantity are $10 and Q_1. For simplicity assume the industry operates at constant costs in the long run; that is, the supply curve is perfectly elastic, or horizontal, at a per unit cost of $10. The effect of dropping this assumption will be considered later.

Now assume that the government decides to expand output in this industry through an excise subsidy. The government pays the firms $5 for every unit of food sold; this is shown by a downward shift in the supply curve to S', where S' is simply the result of subtracting the subsidy per unit, $R,$ from the original supply curve. The immediate or short-run effect (not shown in the diagram) would be to increase the firms' profits, giving them the incentive to expand output. As all firms increase production, the larger output can be sold only at a lower price, and a final equilibrium is established at the intersection of S' and D. The total outlay of the government is equal to $PADP'$, or the per unit subsidy times the quantity being subsidized.

The ultimate effect of this excise subsidy, even though it is paid to the firms, is to reduce the price to the consumers by $5, the amount of the per unit subsidy. As a result, consumers are confronted with a $5 per unit price, and, at the lower price, consumption increases to Q_2. With an excise subsidy, consumption and output unequivocally increase as long as consumers will purchase more at a lower price. In other words, as long as the law of demand is valid (as it always is), this subsidy stimulates greater consumption.

Some care is necessary in interpreting the results of this subsidy. Although we have analyzed the subsidy by shifting the supply curve, it is clear that the subsidy does not reduce the true cost of production. It will still cost $10 per unit to produce food; the S' curve simply reflects the fact that the consumers need only cover half the cost, when the government subsidy covers the rest. In other words, at the final equilibrium, firms are receiving $10 per unit—$5 from the government and $5 from consumers. The price received by firms including the subsidy is given by AQ_2, or $10, in this example. The price paid by consumers is DQ_2, or

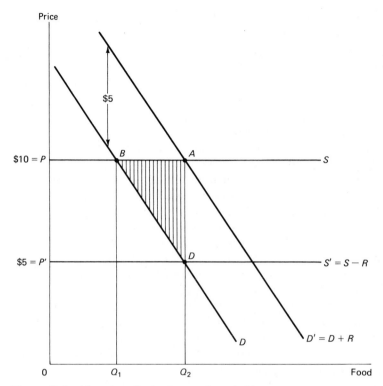

Figure 3–6. Allocative effects of an excise subsidy.

$5. Thus, the subsidy per unit enters as a wedge (AD) separating the price received by producers from the price paid by consumers.

As an alternative way of analyzing the effect of the subsidy, consider an excise subsidy of $5 per unit paid directly to the consumers. This subsidy increases the per unit price consumers will pay to firms. At Q_1, for instance, consumers are willing to pay a maximum of BQ_1 (the height of the demand curve) or $10 per unit out of their own pockets. However, because the government will give them $5 per unit, their demand price including the subsidy will be $15 (at Q_1). In other words, the subsidy per unit can be added to the original demand curve to yield D', the new demand curve confronting sellers of the product. With D' and the unchanged supply curve S, equilibrium occurs at A, with output Q_2. At Q_2, producers are receiving $10 per unit—just as they did when the subsidy was paid to them. Also, consumers are paying a net price of only $5, or DQ_2; the remaining $5, AD, reflects the government subsidy.

Thus, we reach the remarkable conclusion that an excise subsidy has the same effect regardless of whether it is paid to consumers of the product or to producers. In each case, the final equilibrium is at Q_2 with a price of $10 received by producers and a price of $5 paid by consumers. The price received by the producer and the price paid by the consumer are the same regardless of which side of the market is nominally subsidized. It is a matter of indifference, therefore, whether we analyze the subsidy as an upward shift in the demand curve or a downward shift in the supply curve.

The expansion of output from Q_1 to Q_2 results in overconsumption. The benefit of the additional Q_1Q_2 units to consumers is less than the cost of producing the additional output. In Figure 3–6, the benefit of increasing output from Q_1 to Q_2 is equal to BDQ_2Q_1, because the height of the demand curve gives the marginal value of each successive unit. The cost to the economy of producing this additional output is BAQ_2Q_1, or simply $10 per unit times the Q_1Q_2 increase in output. The cost of expanding output from Q_1 to Q_2 exceeds the benefit by the area BAD. This is a measure of the dollar value of the welfare cost, or inefficiency, associated with the subsidy-induced expansion of output.[12]

What this welfare cost means is that consumers would prefer that resources used to produce the Q_1Q_2 increase in output be used elsewhere to produce other goods and services. In other words, the subsidy artificially stimulates the output of food by drawing resources from other uses where they are more valuable to consumers. The subsidy results in an output level where the marginal benefit (DQ_2) to consumers is less than the marginal cost (AQ_2) of production.

Greater insight into the nature of the allocative effect of the excise subsidy can be gained by examining the choices of an individual consumer. In Figure 3–7, the presubsidy budget constraint is MN, and the consumer is in equilibrium at point E. The excise subsidy lowers the price of food, so the budget constraint pivots and becomes flatter, as shown by MN'. Faced with the lower price, the individual's new equilibrium is at E', with a larger consumption of food, q_2. The total cost of the subsidy is equal to $E'T$. This can best be seen by recognizing that, if the consumer purchased q_2 units without the subsidy, he would have had only Tq_2 dollars left to spend on other goods. With the subsidy, he consumes q_2 units and has $E'q_2$ dollars left to spend on other goods. Note, however, that the market cost of q_2 units is the same in both cases but that the $E'T$ reduction in cost to the consumer is borne by the government.

The postsubsidy equilibrium at E' represents overconsumption: The

---

[12] For those familiar with the concept of consumer's surplus, this conclusion can be reached by a different route. As a result of the lower price, there is a gain in consumer surplus equal to the area $PBDP'$. This is not a net gain, because the government must raise tax revenue equal to area $PADP'$ to finance the subsidy. The difference between the gain in consumer surplus and the cost to government is the net loss, or welfare cost, of area BAD.

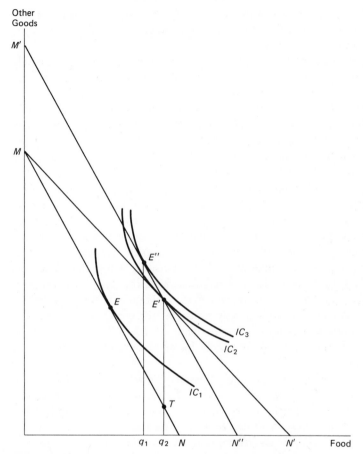

Figure 3–7. Allocative effects of an excise subsidy: individual consumer.

artificially low price encourages consumers to purchase more food and less of other goods, and this outcome is inefficient. This inefficiency can be demonstrated by assuming that the consumer is given the subsidy in cash rather than through a subsidy that lowers the price. Because the cost of the excise subsidy is $E'T$, the government can give, at no additional cost, cash equal to MM' (equal to $E'T$). This cash transfer produces a parallel movement of the budget constraint from MN to $M'N''$, with $M'N''$ passing through point E'. This means that the consumer could still choose the consumption mix at point E' if given the subsidy in the form of cash. Given his preferences, however, he would prefer point E'', purchasing less food and more of other goods. The consumer would therefore be better off with an unrestricted cash transfer. Compared to the cash transfer of equal cost, the excise subsidy produces a

77

welfare cost: The consumer is on IC_2 with the excise subsidy but can reach IC_3 by consuming a different combination of goods of the same total cost with a cash transfer.

We have assumed that people other than the recipient of the subsidy pay the taxes to finance the subsidy. The same analysis, however, applies when the consumers must pay the taxes themselves. In Figure 3–7, we can interpret $M'N''$ as the before-tax-and-subsidy budget constraint, MN as the after-tax budget constraint, and MN' as the budget constraint showing the combined effect of the tax and subsidy. In this case, the net result is to increase food consumption from q_1 to q_2 and to make the consumer worse off. Overconsumption of food and a loss in welfare are, once again, the outcome. Thus, the excise subsidy produces a welfare cost by artificially stimulating food consumption in both cases. The only difference is that the welfare cost associated with the subsidy when others pay the taxes reflects the fact that the consumers would be better off consuming less food with a cash transfer. (Recall that the recipient is on a higher indifference curve with a cash transfer.) When the consumers pay the taxes themselves, the welfare cost reflects the fact that consumers would be better off consuming less food without any tax or subsidy. (That is, before the tax-and-subsidy program, the consumer was on IC_3; after the program was implemented, he is on IC_2.) The nature of the welfare cost is the same; an artificially lower price stimulates too much consumption.

Figure 3–6 and Figure 3–7 both illustrate the welfare cost of an excise subsidy, but from different perspectives. In Figure 3–6, total overconsumption (or, equivalently, overproduction, because what is produced is consumed) equals Q_1Q_2, and area BAD is a measure of the total welfare cost. In Figure 3–7, overconsumption by an individual consumer is shown as q_1q_2, and the welfare cost is represented by the difference in welfare associated with consuming at E' rather than E''.[13]

Excise subsidies lead to a misallocation of resources. However, this conclusion is fully valid only if markets are competitive and if no externalities are present. When there are no externalities, competitive markets are efficient, and no form of subsidy can improve resource allocation. This underscores the importance economists attach to externalities. When external benefits exist, the market equilibrium is inefficient, and then some form of subsidy is capable of improving resource allocation by expanding output.

Regardless of whether externalities are present, it is clear that excise subsidies are more effective than fixed quantity subsidies in increasing

---

[13] In advanced courses in economic theory, the conditions under which these two approaches are exactly equivalent are discussed in detail.

consumption of the subsidized good. Fixed quantity subsidies are highly uncertain, cumbersome devices, so it is not surprising that most economists regard excise subsidies as a more effective means of stimulating the production and consumption of some desired good (for whatever reason). Another advantage of excise subsidies is that the marginal value of the subsidized good to consumers is readily ascertainable. Consumers adjust their consumption to the subsidized price so that the subsidized price is equal to the marginal value of the good. Thus, in Figure 3–6, DQ_2, or $5, is the marginal value of the good to all consumers. This valuable information is often difficult to obtain when fixed quantity subsidies are used.

Distributive Effects

Who benefits and who loses from a subsidy depend on the exact type and size of subsidy (as well as the distribution of the tax burden). Now let's consider another interesting dimension to the problem of determining the distributional impact: the relationship between the market structure and the incidence of the subsidy.

Economists use the term *incidence* to refer to the distributional effect of a tax, subsidy, or other policy. In the last section, the incidence of the excise subsidy fell on consumers because the price paid by consumers decreased by the full amount of the per unit subsidy. Thus, consumers benefited and sellers did not. Sometimes, however, the benefits do not accrue entirely to consumers.

Figure 3–8 illustrates the effect of an excise subsidy for a good produced by an increasing cost competitive industry. The only difference between Figure 3–8 and Figure 3–6 is that in Figure 3–8 the supply curve is assumed to be upward sloping, implying that per unit production costs rise as total industry output expands. The subsidy is $5 per unit, and this is shown by the upward shift in demand from D to D'. The final equilibrium occurs at K, where D' and S intersect. In this case, however, the net price to consumers is $7, only $3 below the unsubsidized price. Part of the subsidy is received by sellers who now are paid $12 per unit, $2 more than before. The incidence, or benefit, falls on both buyers and sellers.

The extent to which buyers and sellers benefit from an excise subsidy depends on the relative elasticities of the supply and demand curves. With a perfectly elastic supply curve (shown as S_1), the benefit accrues entirely to consumers. The more inelastic the supply curve, the smaller the price reduction for consumers and the larger the price increase for sellers. In fact, with a perfectly inelastic (vertical) supply curve the consumers receive no benefit, because the selling price rises by the full

79

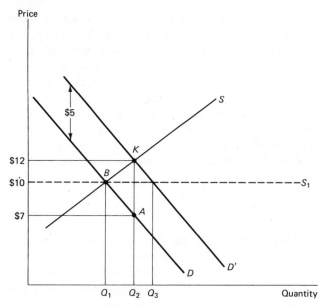

Figure 3–8. Incidence of an excise subsidy for an increasing cost industry.

amount of the subsidy. The reader should also be able to work out how the incidence varies with the elasticity of demand for any given supply curve.

We have been referring to "sellers" benefiting from the subsidy, and this requires some further explanation. Recall that in equilibrium competitive firms make zero economic profits (i.e., they earn a normal return on investment but no "abnormal" profits). Businesses per se probably do not benefit from an increase in the product price induced by the subsidy because their costs of production eventually rise. As industry output expands, its demand for productive factors—labor, raw materials, and so on—increases, bidding up wage rates, prices of raw materials, and so on. Higher wage rates represent higher production costs to firms and account for the upward slope in the supply curve. Those "sellers" who benefit from the higher selling price are typically owners of factors of production whose prices are bid up as total industry output expands. Thus, the benefit of the subsidy on the supply side will probably be dispersed among a number of economic groups, and it is unlikely that business profits will receive more than a temporary boost.

Where the benefits from a particular subsidy accrue depends on the structure and reaction of the market affected by the subsidy. Our discussion of incidence has been in the context of an excise subsidy, but the incidence of other subsidies (and taxes) can also be ascertained only by analyzing the reaction of the relevant market. For example, some of the benefits of fixed quantity subsidies can accrue to sellers of the subsidized product. If the fixed quantity subsidy does, on balance, increase consumption, this reflects an effective increase in demand. Coupled with an upward-sloping supply curve, a fixed quantity subsidy that increases demand will increase price, just like the excise subsidy in Figure 3–8. This may explain some of the support by educators (such as teachers' unions and colleges and universities) for subsidies to education, or by construction unions for housing subsidies.

With a constant cost industry, the incidence of an excise subsidy is entirely on consumers, and sellers derive no long-run benefit. Assuming a horizontal supply curve simplifies the analysis, because we need not worry about possible changes in wages and other input prices. Fortunately, research in industrial organization suggests that constant costs over the relevant range of output are quite common, so the assumption of a horizontal supply curve may be a reasonably close approximation in many cases.

Note that the welfare cost due to the excise subsidy in Figure 3–8 is shown by area BAK. The welfare cost due to overconsumption of Q_1Q_2 is measured by the difference in the cost associated with producing the additional output (given by the upward-sloping supply curve) and the benefits to consumers (given by the demand curve). If the supply curve were vertical, there would be no overconsumption and no welfare cost. (Verify this.)

Subsidies to Some Consumers and Not to Others

So far, our formal analysis has considered subsidies that apply to all consumers of some product. Actually, many subsidies are given to only some of the consumers of a particular product. This is true, for example, of food stamps, Medicaid, housing subsidies, Medicare, job training programs, and others. Our analysis can be modified to cover instances where a subset of all consumers is subsidized.

Suppose that only low income consumers of food are subsidized. In Figure 3–9 we can decompose the total market demand, D_T, into the separate demands of low income consumers, D_L, and high income consumers, D_H. Given the supply and demand relationships, the initial equilibrium price and quantity are P and Q_T. At a price of P, low income consumers purchase Q_L units and high income consumers purchase Q_H units. Of course, $Q_L + Q_H = Q_T$.

An excise subsidy given only to low income consumers increases their demand to D_L'. (A fixed quantity subsidy *could* increase demand in this way, also.) At the initial price, P, they would prefer to consume Q_L^*, or $Q_LQ_L^*$ more than before. Although the demand of unsubsidized con-

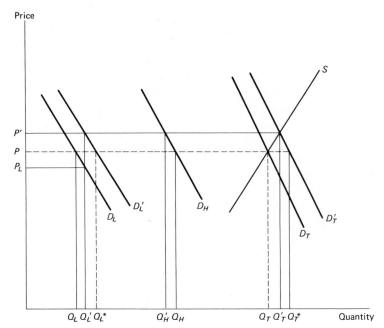

Figure 3–9. Excise subsidy for low income households.

sumers is not affected,[14] total demand has increased. The new total demand curve is D_T', obtained by summing D_L' and D_H (so $Q_L Q_L^* = Q_T Q_T^*$). It is the total market demand for the product in relation to supply that determines the market price and total output; hence, the market price rises to P' and quantity to Q_T'.

Higher income consumers are harmed by the subsidy because they must pay a higher price. Because their demand is unchanged, they curtail consumption to Q_H'. Unsubsidized consumers may also bear an additional cost if they pay some or all of the taxes needed to finance the subsidy. The benefits of the subsidy accrue to the subsidized consumers, who now pay a net price of P_L and consume Q_L'. In addition, sellers benefit because the price they receive has increased from P to P'. Note, however, that we have assumed an increasing cost industry. If the supply curve were horizontal, the product price would not rise, and the entire benefit of the subsidy would accrue to low income consumers.

This analysis suggests how the incidence of a subsidy may be spread widely and unevenly through society. And the analysis is of more than academic interest. It is precisely this combination of circumstances that,

---

[14] This assumes that the income effect of the tax on demand is small enough to be ignored.

in the opinion of many economists, contributed to the surge in medical care costs (prices) following the enactment of Medicaid and Medicare in the mid-1960s. Medicare and Medicaid are subsidies that apply to the elderly and poor, so an analysis that distinguishes subsidized from unsubsidized consumers is appropriate. Interestingly enough, one reaction to rising medical care costs has been the proposal that everyone be subsidized. As is now apparent, that would cause medical care costs to rise even more.

Appendix to Chapter 3: Benefit-Cost Analysis

Benefit-cost analysis is a technique that can be used to evaluate government projects. The basic concept is quite simple: Identify the benefits and costs of a project and then measure them in comparable units (such as dollars). If the benefits exceed the costs, the project will lead to a more efficient resource allocation. If the costs exceed the benefits, the project will lead to a poorer allocation of resources.

Because the benefit-cost technique is a logical method to use in appraising alternatives, it is not surprising that it is occasionally used to analyze government expenditure programs. Some government agencies, notably the Bureau of Reclamation and the Army Corps of Engineers, have employed benefit-cost analysis to evaluate alternative potential projects since the 1930s. In recent years the technique has been used by other agencies and practitioners outside government to analyze policies in such diverse areas as health, transportation, education, and social welfare programs. Such studies are sometimes available to Congress and provide information that is useful in its deliberations. Our main concern will not be, however, with how benefit-cost analysis has been employed within government but instead with the nature of the technique itself. A study of the nature and limitations of the benefit-cost approach provides further insight into the application of economics to government policy analysis.

Identifying and Measuring Benefits

Suppose we are trying to ascertain what benefits will result from a particular government project. Obviously, the first step is to determine the impact of the project: What goods or services will we have more of as a result of the project? Second, these effects must be expressed quantitatively; that is, the value of these effects to the public must be calculated. Usually this second step causes the greatest difficulty. An example will illustrate why.

Consider the construction of a dam to control flooding. One obvious

83

benefit is a reduction in the probability of flood damage. How do we measure this in dollars? The generally correct theoretical answer is that the dollar value of the benefit equals the maximum amount that people would be willing to pay to secure this service. Because of the free rider problem, however, we are unable to survey the potential beneficiaries to determine this figure. Instead an alternative means of estimating the benefit must be found, and that is the difficulty. Frequently there is no way to do this accurately.

Although it may be impossible to measure the benefit with perfect accuracy, analysts have shown considerable ingenuity in devising ways to approximate the magnitudes involved. Consider how this might be done in the present case. If flooding destroys farmers' crops, then we could estimate the average annual volume of crops destroyed and multiply this amount by their market price (the value to consumers). For a variety of reasons, this approach is unlikely to yield exactly the correct answer (i.e., how much farmers would be willing to pay), but it may be a fair approximation. In any event, it is likely to be better than relying on pure guesswork.

For some projects, the valuation of benefits is easier than for others. If, for example, the output is a good or service that is already produced and sold in private markets, we can use the market price to estimate the benefit. The production of electricity by nuclear power plants falls in this category. However, in many, perhaps most, cases the output of a government expenditure project is not sold and so is not valued directly in some market. In these situations, it is necessary to devise alternative methods to estimate benefits if benefit-cost analysis is to be used.

Benefit-cost studies usually distinguish between the direct and indirect benefits of a project. In the case of the flood control project, the direct benefit might be the reduced probability of flooding. An indirect benefit might be the recreational services of the lake behind the dam (e.g., swimming, fishing, camping, boating). The value of these services is as real a benefit as flood control and should also be counted as a benefit in a benefit-cost analysis.

In principle, there is no clear-cut distinction between direct and indirect benefits. All the effects of a project that are considered desirable by those affected are benefits and should be counted as such. Admittedly, some benefits are likely to be quantitatively less important than others; the recreational value of the lake may be very small in comparison to its flood control services. In addition, some benefits are likely to be much more difficult to estimate with any accuracy than others: How much is it worth to homeowners overlooking the lake to have a better view? What we call these indirect or intangible benefits is irrelevant as long as we generally recognize that all real benefits should, in principle, be counted. (In practice, however, many benefits may be too small or too costly to measure.)

One error frequently made in benefit-cost studies (especially in the past) was to count pecuniary externalities as benefits. Any government project is likely to affect the prices and quantities of other goods. It is important to distinguish between effects that provide clues to the net benefits and those that represent only transfers. For example, providing a recreational area may lead to higher prices for boats and fishing tackle, which benefit sellers of these items. At the same time, however, the higher prices are costs to people who purchase these items. Consequently, there are no net benefits. These effects may be treated in two ways. One is to recognize that a benefit accrues to the seller and include it along with other benefits. If this is done, the burden placed on the purchasers must also be entered as a cost. Alternatively, these effects can be disregarded altogether. In either case, the net effect is zero. The error arises when the benefit to sellers is included and not the cost to consumers, or vice versa.

Another common error is to double count benefits. An estimate of how much the view of the lake is worth to a nearby homeowner might be included as a benefit. But what about the higher property value of his home? The increased value of his home is not a separate benefit because the increase in the property value is a result of the house's commanding a better view. It might be possible to use the increment in property value as an estimate of the value of the view, but to include both is to count the same benefit twice.

It is clear that the identification and measurement of the benefits of a government project constitute a difficult task, one that is likely to be even more difficult when we consider such complex areas as national defense, education, health insurance, or welfare programs. Obviously, where externalities or public goods are involved, there is no accurate way to determine benefits. (This does not mean that the benefit-cost approach is faulty but only that its practical implementation is difficult.) Perhaps this explains why benefit-cost analysis has been widely used only in narrow areas where benefits are relatively easy to measure such as in irrigation, flood control, and transportation projects. Nonetheless, as our technical ability to estimate benefits improves, it is likely to find applications in other areas.

Identifying and Measuring Costs

The consequences of projects that involve burdens or sacrifices for people are its costs. In the case of a dam, manpower, concrete, equipment, energy, and other productive resources must be used for its construction and maintenance. Using these resources involves an opportunity cost because productive services in other sectors of the economy must be sacrificed. The task of placing a dollar figure on these costs is generally thought to be much simpler than valuing the benefits of the project. As a first approximation, the costs are what must be paid to attract the required resources into employment on the dam. Insofar as the economy is competitive, these payments will equal the value of sacrificed output elsewhere.

When the economy is not fully competitive, however, the payments necessary to attract resources into employment on the dam may either underestimate or overestimate the true costs. For example, the wage necessary to bid a worker away from a monopoly will underestimate the costs because the monopoly pays a wage below the marginal value product of workers. On the other hand, bidding workers away from subsidized industries requires wages above their marginal value products and so overstates the costs. It will seldom be possible to identify exactly where the resources employed by the government come from, so there may be little option but to use the actual payments as an estimate of their resource cost. Because there are biases in offsetting directions, this figure may in many cases be approximately correct.

Some analysts have suggested that if the project employs previously unemployed resources, the opportunity cost of using these resources is zero. As explained earlier in this chapter, this is generally incorrect. Not only are there practical problems (the value of leisure is not zero; a worker who is unemployed when hired may not remain unemployed very long even if the project were not undertaken), but also the basic point is that unemployed resources can be re-employed in a variety of uses. Using an unemployed worker to construct a dam means that he cannot be used elsewhere, and that involves an opportunity cost.

Although the costs of using resources to construct and maintain the dam will normally be the most important costs associated with the project, there may be additional costs. For example, damming a river might cause environmental damage. The lake could become a breeding ground for disease-carrying insects. In addition, the dam could break and cause a flood more severe than the floods it was built to prevent. Costs such as these should also be included, although clearly it would be difficult to measure them.

The funds to finance a project are normally raised through taxation. Note, however, that the burden on taxpayers is not (with a qualification noted later) a cost in addition to the payments to productive factors. Using taxes is simply a way of distributing the burden of diverting resources to the project; it is not a separate or additional cost. The owners of the resources that are used in constructing the dam do not necessarily bear any burden, because they are paid by the government.

As we said, the income they receive is a measure of the opportunity cost, but taxpayers are the ones who ultimately bear the burden.

There are, however, additional costs arising from the use of tax revenues to finance a project. To secure $100 in revenue to fund some government project, a burden greater than $100 must be placed on taxpayers. Part of this additional cost is the administrative cost of collecting taxes and the compliance costs borne by taxpayers. In addition, there is a more subtle cost that arises because taxes distort resource allocation in the economy. This cost, called an excess burden (or welfare cost) of taxation, will be considered in detail in later chapters. At this point, it is enough to recognize that these costs of taxation are costs associated with carrying out the project; they would not arise if the project were not funded. Consequently, if a project necessitated outlays of, say, $1 billion, the actual economic costs imposed on the economy might be $1.1 billion—with the extra $0.1 billion representing the administrative, compliance, and excess burden costs of the tax. Unfortunately, most benefit-cost studies have neglected these costs.

There is another cost that can be produced by the tax financing a project. If the taxpayers whose incomes are reduced by the tax spend part of their incomes in ways that generate external benefits, then there will be a reduction in such external benefits as a result of the tax. In this case, collecting the tax involves another cost. (The opposite case is also possible; expenditures that generate external costs may fall.) For example, the tax may lead some families to spend less on their children's education, and if education is an external benefit, others are harmed indirectly. This type of effect would generally be expected to be small, if not insignificant, in most practical situations. Benefit-cost analysts generally have little option but to ignore effects this remote and hard to measure.

This last point brings us to another one of the real difficulties in conducting a benefit-cost study. Benefits will generally be concentrated in a certain area or sector of the economy and will often be highly visible. The costs, on the other hand, are spread widely throughout the economy by taxation and may be hard to perceive. As an example, consider this list of alleged benefits from a low income housing project: reductions in crime, juvenile delinquency, and marital instability; reductions in fire and police protection costs; improved sanitation and reduced health-related costs; reduction in traffic congestion (dependent on location); more attractive neighborhoods and increased property values; improved access of tenants to jobs; improved competition in the housing market. It is easy for anyone familiar with housing projects to list these and other possible benefits—and some may conceivably be quantitatively important. However, a little thought concerning the impact on disposable incomes of the higher taxes needed to finance the project will also produce a similarly lengthy list of potentially harmful effects. The difference is that on a per taxpayer basis the costs are so small and uncertain that they will be neglected even though in the aggregate (because there are more taxpayers than beneficiaries) they may be significant.

In general, the more important costs are probably the use of resources by a project and the administrative, compliance, and excess burden costs of taxation. Other costs may be important in specific instances.

Comparing Costs and Benefits

Once all the costs and benefits have been identified and measured, our task is almost over. Now we must decide if it is efficient to undertake a project. Because benefits and costs are reckoned in dollars, the magnitudes can be compared. (In this section, we will assume that the benefits and costs occur in 1 year; the next section considers the issues involved when the effects occur over a period of several years.) The results are generally presented as a ratio. If benefits are estimated to be $1.5 million and the costs to be $1.0 million, the benefit-cost ratio is 1.5. This means that, on average, each dollar of cost in the project provides services worth $1.50 to the public.

Note that a benefit-cost study usually results in an estimate of the total benefit and total cost of a project of a specific scale. If the benefit-cost ratio exceeds 1, undertaking the project will lead to a more efficient allocation of resources than doing nothing. This does not mean, however, that such a project is the most efficient. To clarify this point further, consider Figure 3–10. The diagram plots the total benefits and costs for varying scales of a particular type of project. For example, the size of the dam used for flood control might be measured on the horizontal axis.

A benefit-cost study will generally estimate the costs and benefits of a specific project. For example, the project identified by the scale of V in the diagram has a benefit-cost ratio of AV/BV. Because total benefits exceed total costs, this project is more efficient than none at all. It is not, however, the most efficient scale. The most efficient dam size is where total benefits exceed total costs by the greatest amount, because this yields the largest possible net gain. The most efficient project is shown by point W in the diagram, where benefits exceed costs by CD, a larger amount than for any other scale of project. This occurs, of course, where the marginal benefits of changing the scale of the project equal the marginal costs. Although the results of a benefit-cost analysis are often summarized as a ratio of benefits to costs, the most efficient project is not the one with the largest ratio. The project of scale V, for example, has total benefits of, say, $4 million (equal to AV) and total costs of $1 million (equal to BV), for a ratio of 4/1. The project scale W, on the other hand, produces total benefits of $8 million ($CW$) and total costs of $4

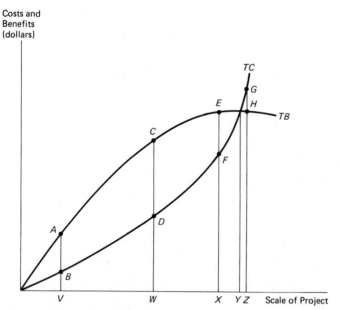

Figure 3–10. Benefit-cost ratios.

million (*DW*), a ratio of only 2/1. Nonetheless, the project of scale *W* is more efficient because its net benefit is $4 million compared with a net benefit of only $3 million for the project of scale *V*. Consequently, choosing the project with the highest benefit-cost ratio is not the appropriate strategy.

Clearly, if benefit-cost studies could be prepared costlessly, we would like to have one for each possible size of the project, for scales *V, W, X, Y, Z*, and all intermediate points, in Figure 3–10. With this information we could readily identify *W* as the most efficient project. Because of the cost and difficulty of preparing a benefit-cost study, however, we will generally have studies of only a limited range of options, frequently only one. Even in this case it can provide useful information—although there is no guarantee that a policy with benefits greater than costs is better than some alternative policies that were not analyzed.

Time and Discounting

With many, perhaps most, government expenditures, the benefits received by the public are experienced at approximately the same time that the costs are incurred. This, however, is not always true. In the case of our dam for flood control, for example, during the first few years (while the dam is being constructed) there are heavy costs and no benefits. During later years, there are benefits and much lower costs (only maintenance costs). For such projects, the time at which benefits and costs are experienced becomes an important consideration.

A benefit-cost study typically estimates the benefits and costs of a project over a number of years. We should realize, however, that a dollar in benefits received 10 years in the future is not worth as much as a dollar in benefits today. You would not be willing to pay a dollar today to receive a dollar 10 years from now because you could put the dollar in a savings account and it would grow to more than a dollar in 10 years. Thus, it is not correct to simply add the dollar value of benefits or costs that extend over a period of years in the future. Instead, all of the benefits and costs must be evaluated at their worth in today's dollars. To do this, benefits and costs to be experienced in the future are "discounted" using a discount (or interest) rate to arrive at a present value measure.

The very name "discounting" refers to the fact that future benefits and costs are worth less (must be discounted) today. If the discount rate is 5 percent, a dollar in benefits today is equivalent to $1.05 in benefits to be received 1 year later; that is, a person would be indifferent between receiving $1 today and $1.05 next year. Thus, the present or discounted value of $1.05 in benefits received is only $1 today. Putting this in a benefit-cost perspective, to consider an expenditure of $1 today, the project would have to produce a benefit of at least $1.05 a year from now (if next year's benefit were the only benefit). The present value of the benefit can be calculated from $B_1/(1+i)$, where B_1 is the benefit 1 year from now and i is the discount rate. Similarly, the present value of a dollar in benefits to be received 14 years from now is only 50 cents today: $B_{14}/(1+i)^{14}$, or $\$1/(1.05)^{14}$ equals $0.50.

When costs and benefits occur over a period of years, the total benefit of the project is the present value of the stream of benefits; similarly, costs must be evaluated at their present value. Having done this, we once more arrive at a single figure for the total benefit and for the total cost, and the project can be evaluated as in the previous section.

A major issue in discounting future costs and benefits concerns what discount rate to use. The results of a benefit-cost study can depend critically on the discount rate used to calculate the present value of benefits and costs. Consider a simplified example of a government project that has costs in the first year of $1 million and no benefits until 14 years later when there are $2 million in benefits; there are no other costs or benefits. If the discount rate is 3 percent, the present value of $2 million in benefits to be received 14 years in the future is $1.32 million, and the present value of $1 million in costs incurred in this year is, of course, $1 million. The benefit-cost ratio is 1.32, and the project appears worthy of consideration. Alternatively, suppose we use a discount rate of 6 percent; then the present value of the $2 million benefit is only $0.89 million today, and the benefit-cost ratio is 0.89. If the discount rate is instead 10 percent, the present value of benefits is $0.53 million, so the present value of costs is almost double the present value of benefits.

This example illustrates that the desirability of a project can depend heavily on what discount rate is used. The higher the discount rate, the smaller the present value of future benefits and costs. (We are discounting the future more heavily with a high discount rate.) Most government projects that yield benefits and costs over many years are similar to our example; there are high initial costs with benefits accruing later. This would be true, for example, of many irrigation, environmental, energy, and job training policies. In cases like these, the higher the discount rate used, the more unfavorable the project will appear.

What is the appropriate discount rate to use? This turns out to be a highly complex issue. Intuitively, it seems that the discount rate should be related to two different variables. One is the rate at which people are willing to sacrifice present consumption for future consumption. If the public is willing (at the margin) to give up $1 today in return for $1.05 a year from now, the 5 percent rate tells us how much the public discounts future benefits. This is sometimes called the time preference rate. On the other hand, public investment projects use resources that can alternatively be employed in private investment projects. If private investment projects yield (at the margin) 10 percent, then diverting resources from private investment to public projects entails an opportunity cost in the form of a sacrificed return of 10 percent. The return on private investments is sometimes called the opportunity cost rate. Which of these two rates should be used?

Frequently prices (in this case interest rates) determined in private markets can serve as a guide. If capital markets were perfectly competitive, and there were no risk associated with investments,[15] a single interest rate would be determined. This is illustrated in Figure 3–11, where the investment demand curve is shown as I and the saving supply curve is S. The equilibrium rate of return (interest rate) is 6 percent. At the equilibrium level of investment, I_1, the interest rate measures both the marginal return to private investments (the height of the I curve) and the return the public requires to sacrifice present consumption (the height of the S curve). The opportunity cost rate and the time preference rate are equal to one another at the competitive equilibrium. If this model were an accurate description of reality, most economists would agree that 6 percent would be the appropriate discount rate to use for discounting future benefits and costs.

[15] When investments differ in their degree of risk, there will be a wide range of interest rates in markets reflecting the varying risks of different projects. This is ignored in the text but is yet another reason why it is difficult to agree on a single interest rate to use in discounting.

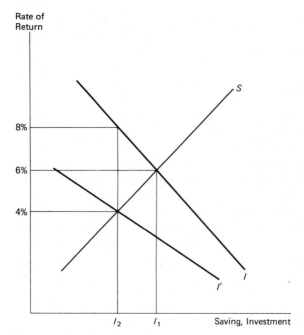

Figure 3–11. Taxation and discount rates.

For a variety of reasons, the real world differs from this model. Perhaps the most important difference is that the government taxes the return to private investments with the corporation income tax and property taxes. These taxes will be considered in detail in Chapter 13, but their relevance to the discount rate issue deserves mention here. Briefly, if a private investment yields a return of 10 percent, and the government taxes this yield, then less than 10 percent is left to be paid to investors (savers). The effect of a 50 percent tax is shown in Figure 3–11 by a pivoting downward of the I curve to I'. The I' curve shows the after-tax return that can be paid at each rate of investment; the I curve continues to show the before-tax return. The new equilibrium is at I_2. At this equilibrium, the net return to investors is 4 percent, in contrast to the before-tax return of 8 percent. Note that this means the time preference rate differs from the opportunity cost rate. The time preference rate is now 4 percent and the opportunity cost 8 percent. (These figures are intended only as illustrations; actually, empirical evidence suggests that the opportunity cost rate is around 10 percent.)

We now face a dilemma because we cannot choose one discount rate that simultaneously reflects the time preference of the public and the opportunity cost of private investments. Which rate, 4 percent or 8 percent, should be used? This question has been widely debated by economists, but no one answer seems to produce a consensus. Most economists seem in limited agreement that the 4 percent rate is too low, and that either the opportunity cost rate of 8 percent or some weighted average of the two rates should be used. In practice this means that many of the earlier benefit-cost studies have used discount rates that were far too low.

Whose Benefits and Whose Costs?

Generally, people receiving benefits from a project are not the same ones bearing the costs. The tax system usually distributes the costs widely among the public, and it would be only a coincidence if the benefits were distributed in a similar way. When this is true, exactly what meaning should be attached to the final benefit-cost ratio? To take an extreme case, suppose wealthy yacht owners receive $2 million in benefits from an irrigation project that imposes $1 million in costs on middle and low income families. Should this project, with a benefit-cost ratio of 2/1, be undertaken? Can we really compare the benefits and costs as evaluated by different people?

This issue has troubled many analysts. What is involved, of course, is that the project has both efficiency and distributional (equity) implications, and benefit-cost analysis has evaluated only the efficiency implications. Therefore, one must avoid thinking that any project with benefits greater than costs is necessarily desirable irrespective of its distributional implications. Value judgments must still be made concerning distributional effects of government policies.

An estimate that a project's benefits exceed its costs has a very definite meaning: It means that the beneficiaries *could* pay the entire cost and still be better off. If this were actually done, beneficiaries would be better off and no one else would be affected—a clear efficiency gain. When other people bear some of the costs, there is still an efficiency gain, but it is coupled with a redistribution of income. Thus, benefit-cost analysis, like any other economic analysis, cannot demonstrate desirability.

Some economists have suggested that the benefit-cost techniques be modified to permit an evaluation of distributional as well as efficiency effects. This could be done by using distributional weights that specify, for example, that a dollar of benefit to a wealthy person should be counted only as $.80, whereas a dollar of benefit to a poor person should be counted as $1.20. Such a procedure is an attempt to combine efficiency and distributional effects in one measure of "desirability." This would mean that an inefficient policy could be adjudged desirable if it redistributed income to low income persons. For example, if the government places a tax burden of $1 on a wealthy person and transfers $.80 to a poor person ($.20 being used up in administrative costs), the benefit-cost ratio is $0.96/$0.80, or 1.2 (using the weights above). **93**

There are several practical and conceptual problems with this procedure. For example, there is no objective way to choose a set of distributional weights. Obviously, people would disagree over what weights to use; to select one particular set of weights would require a value judgment. More importantly, there are many policies available that provide alternative means of redistributing income, and these should be explicitly compared if it is decided the government should redistribute income. Using distributional weights in benefit-cost analysis could easily lead to enactment of policies that help the poor, but do so less than would an alternative policy of the same cost to other people.

For these reasons, most benefit-cost analysts have not attempted to apply distributional weights. This does not imply a judgment that distributional effects are unimportant, but only that the benefit-cost analysis is more useful if it concentrates on efficiency considerations.

Benefit-Cost Analysis: A Summary

Benefit-cost analysis provides a technique that is helpful in weighing the advantages and disadvantages of government policies. Our discussion has only touched on the major problems in applying this technique, notably the identification and measurement of benefits and costs, and discounting to obtain present value measures. In particular, the difficulty of measuring benefits and costs has been emphasized, because this is the real problem in most attempts to grapple quantitatively with policy issues.

The remainder of this book will be dealing with many policy issues that are, in principle, amenable to benefit-cost analysis. Unfortunately, the problems of measuring benefits and costs are extremely difficult for many of the most important government policies. No attempt is made to construct a formal benefit-cost analysis of any of the policies discussed later, but the reader should find the benefit-cost approach a helpful guide in thinking about the economic effects that will be identified.

Supplementary Readings

Harberger, Arnold C. "On the Use of Distributional Weights in Social Cost-Benefit Analysis," *Journal of Political Economy,* **86** (2): S 87–120, Part 2 (Apr. 1978).

Haveman, Robert H., and Julius Margolis (eds.). *Public Expenditures and Policy Analysis.* Skokie, Ill.: Rand McNally & Company, 1977.

Layard, Richard (ed.). *Cost-Benefit Analysis.* Harmondsworth, Middlesex, England: Penguin Books, 1974.

McKean, Roland N. *Efficiency in Government Through Systems Analysis.* New York: John Wiley and Sons, Inc., 1958.

————. *Public Spending.* New York: McGraw-Hill Book Company, 1968.

McLure, Charles E., Jr., and Wayne R. Thirsk. "A Simplified Exposition of the Harberger Model, II: Expenditure Incidence," *National Tax Journal,* **28** (2): 195–208 (June 1975).

Mishan, E. J. *Cost-Benefit Analysis.* New York: Praeger Publishers, Inc., 1971.

CHAPTER 4

APPLICATIONS OF EXPENDITURE ANALYSIS: FOOD STAMPS AND UNEMPLOYMENT INSURANCE

In Chapter 3 we developed the analytical framework needed to study the allocative effects of different types of subsidies. Now we will examine an example of a fixed quantity subsidy, the food stamp program, and a variable quantity (excise) subsidy, unemployment insurance.

Food Stamp Program

President John Kennedy's first executive order in January 1961 directed the Secretary of Agriculture to establish pilot food stamp programs for needy families. After several years' experience with the pilot programs, Congress enacted the Food Stamp Act of 1964. Begun on a small scale with total expenditures of $30.4 million in 1964, the food stamp program has registered an impressive rate of growth, increasing to nearly $6 billion in 1978, as can be seen in Table 4–1.

Much of the expansion in the food stamp program reflects its growth throughout the country: In 1964 only forty-three counties and cities participated, but by 1976 approximately 3200 counties and cities (essentially, all regions of the country) were participating. In 1971 the program was amended to nationalize eligibility requirements and greatly expand benefits which accounts for much of the spurt in outlays between 1969 and 1972. Today, the program is one of the most important domestic economic programs assisting low income families.

From 1964 to 1977, the food stamp program was a type of subsidy program that economists refer to as a "priced voucher." Late in 1977 it was changed substantially. Our analysis will focus initially on the program prior to the 1977 reform. Much of the analysis of the earlier program is still relevant, but even those aspects not now directly applicable to the food stamp program are of more than historical interest. Not only

Table 4–1. Food Stamp Program: Total Expenditures and Participation, 1964–1978

Year	Total Federal Outlays* (millions)	Participation† (thousands)
1964	$ 30.4	367
1969	250.3	2,878
1972	1916.8	11,103
1974	2865.3	13,536
1976	3858.9‡	15,800
1978	5850.0‡	n.a.

*Kenneth Clarkson, *Food Stamps and Nutrition,* Table 5.
†Average per month.
‡Estimated.

is an understanding of the economic approach to the program important, but also a number of other programs, actual and proposed (part of the Medicare program, several housing subsidies, and proposed "energy vouchers," for example), have much in common with the food stamp program before its reform. At the end of the section on food stamps the 1977 reforms will be discussed.

To become eligible to receive the food stamp subsidy, households must satisfy both an income and an asset test. These tests specify that a family's net income and certain types of assets fall below specified amounts. For example, a family of four persons must have monthly net income less than $513 and assets below $3000 to qualify as of January 1975. In effect, these eligibility requirements operate to restrict benefits to families with low incomes and little wealth. For this reason the food stamp program is essentially a welfare program. (Prior to the 1977 reform, in fact, all welfare recipients were automatically eligible for food stamps.)

If eligibility requirements are met, households can receive food stamps. Food stamps can be thought of as checks signed by the government that can be used only to purchase food; some government pubications, in fact, refer to food stamps as "food money." The amount of food stamps that a family can receive is called the coupon allotment; the coupon allotment depends on family size and not on family income. The coupon allotment for a family of four people in 1975, for example, was $154 per month, but for a family of two it was $84, and for a family of seven it was $238.[1]

---

[1] There is a variable purchase option under which a family can purchase one fourth, one half, or three fourths of the basic coupon allotment. Because only about 6 percent of participants elect to take this option, it is ignored in the text.

The coupon allotment is the same for all families of a given size, but payment for food stamps varies with income. Thus, except for the very poorest families, recipients of food stamps must pay something to receive them. (This is why economists call them priced vouchers.) Table 4–2 shows how payments vary with income for four-person families. With income below $30 per month, the families receive $154 in food stamps free (a zero purchase price), so the net subsidy is $154. The purchase price for the same $154 worth of food stamps increases steadily with income until it reaches $130 at the $510–$539.99 level, so the subsidy in this range is only $24. Increasing the purchase price with income in this way has the effect of reducing the subsidy, so the larger subsidies are received by poorer families.

Equivalently, the relationship in Table 4–2 can be described as one where participants are required to purchase stamps in an amount equal to the purchase price and then they are given free food stamps in an amount equal to the subsidy. For instance, in the $150–$169.99 range participants must purchase $41 in food stamps and pay $41 for them, and then are given $113 in food stamps free, for a total of $154 in food coupons. The result is exactly the same, but looking at the relationships in this way accords more closely with the official terminology, which refers to the subsidy as "bonus food stamps." Bonus food stamps are "free" stamps received by the participant after making the mandatory purchase on his own.

The size of the coupon allotment itself is based on the cost of the "economy food plan" of the Department of Agriculture, a low cost plan for achieving a nutritionally adequate diet. Since 1974 the coupon allotment has been tied to a price escalator that changes the allotment semiannually to reflect changes in the prices of food items.

Table 4–2. Monthly Coupon Allotments and Purchase Requirements, January 1975 (Family of Four)

Monthly Net Income (selected intervals)	Monthly Coupon Allotment	Monthly Purchase Price	Subsidy per Month ("bonus" food stamps)
$ 0–29.99	$154	$ 0	$154
50–59.99	154	10	144
100–109.99	154	25	129
150–169.99	154	41	113
210–229.99	154	59	95
310–329.99	154	89	65
420–449.99	154	122	32
510–539.99	154	130	24

Source: Kenneth Clarkson, *Food Stamps and Nutrition,* Table 4.

Economic Effects of the Food Stamp Program

Welfare Cost. In effect, the food stamp program is a transfer program that places a floor under food consumption. Food stamps can be used only to purchase food, so selling (or giving) all four-person families $154 per month virtually guarantees that the families will purchase $154 worth of food. Families can consume more than the basic coupon allotment by purchasing additional food on their own. The food stamp program is an example of a fixed quantity subsidy because the $154 in food stamps is provided to all four-person families, but with the net subsidy for this fixed quantity varying with family income.

Before its reform in 1977, the food stamp program typically distorted the consumption pattern of participating families by inducing overconsumption of food. Available evidence indicates that most low income families would have preferred to consume somewhat less than $154 worth of food per month and have used the difference to spend on other needs considered more pressing. Because the program prohibited spending less than the coupon allotment on food, it forced an inferior consumption pattern on the recipients—a loss in welfare compared to what could be achieved at the same cost.

To see how a welfare cost is produced, assume that low income families would prefer to spend one third of their incomes on food if they could spend their incomes without restrictions. (This is, by the way, not an unrealistic assumption.) A four-person family with a monthly income of $210 would then spend $70 on food. Under the food stamp program (see Table 4–2), they would pay $59 for $154 worth of food stamps, which would be used to consume $154 worth of food. If this family had received the same subsidy of $95 as cash, bringing its total income up to $305, it would have spent $102 on food (one third of $305). Out of total expenditures of $305, the food stamp program leads recipients to consume $154 in food, or $52 more food ($154 − $102) than the family would prefer if it could spend the subsidy without any restrictions. The loss in welfare associated with the family consuming $52 more food than it wishes, and $52 less of other things, is the welfare cost of the program's effect on food consumption.

Figure 4–1 illustrates the point we are making. The presubsidy budget constraint is MN, and the initial equilibrium is at point E involving consumption of 70 units of food (a unit of food is defined so that it costs $1) and $140 of other goods and services. Our assumption that the family prefers to spend a third of its income on food is reflected by tangencies such as E, E'', and E', all of which imply one third of income being spent on food at different income levels.

With the food stamp program, the budget constraint shifts to $MARN'$. By giving up 59 (MM_1, equal to the purchase price), the

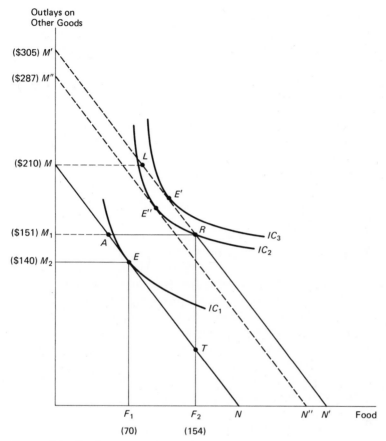

Figure 4–1. Food stamp subsidy: low income recipient.

family receives M_1R, or $154 worth of food stamps. The most preferred point on the $MARN'$ constraint is point R, where the family consumes exactly the coupon allotment in food. Note that not only more food but also more of other goods is consumed at R; in general, the program results in participants consuming more of other goods as well as more food. Point R is, however, an inferior consumption pattern involving too much food. To see this, suppose the family were given $95 to spend as it wished; the recipient's budget constraint would then be $M'N'$, because the subsidy equals RT. With that constraint, equilibrium occurs at E' on a higher indifference curve involving less food consumption ($102) and more consumption of other things ($203). Thus, the family would be better off at the same cost ($95) to the government if the subsidy were given in the form of cash. Note that the welfare cost does not mean that the recipient is worse off with the food stamps than with no

101

ANCE AND THE PRICE SYSTEM

subsidy, because he is clearly better off at point R than at point E. Instead, the welfare cost compares the welfare of the recipient under the food stamp program and an equal cost subsidy that does not distort consumption choices.

The welfare cost refers to how much worse off the family is at point R than at point E'. One way of measuring this cost is to determine how large an unrestricted cash transfer is required to make the family as well off as the food stamp program. In Figure 4–1, a cash transfer of $77 would produce the constraint $M''N''$, and equilibrium would occur at E'' on IC_2, the same indifference curve as attained with food stamps. To the recipient, a cash transfer of $77 is thus considered as desirable as the food stamp subsidy of $95. To put this differently, the $95 food stamp subsidy is worth only $77 to the recipient. The difference between the cost to the government and the benefit to the recipient, in this case $18 or $M'M''$, is the welfare cost, that is, the recipient considers himself to be $18 worse off consuming at point R rather than E'.

The size of the welfare cost will vary from family to family because it depends on the underlying preferences regarding food and nonfood items. Families with a relatively strong preference for food, who would spend a large proportion of their income on food anyway (more than one third), will find their consumption patterns less distorted than those who would prefer to spend less on food. In addition to preferences regarding desired levels of food consumption, the income of recipients is also likely to be related to the welfare cost. In general, the higher the income of the family receiving food stamps, the smaller the welfare cost. Higher income families normally spend more on food (in an absolute sense), so the $154 floor is less likely to represent too much food consumption for them.

How the food stamp program affects a higher income family in the program is illustrated in Figure 4–2. With a pretransfer income of $440, the family would receive a subsidy of $32 (see Table 4–2), and the constraint would become $MARN'$. With that constraint, equilibrium would occur at E', with more than $154 worth of food being consumed (assuming this family also chooses to spend one third of its income on food). For this family, the food stamp program has the same effect as an unrestricted cash transfer, and there is no welfare cost. That is, a cash transfer of $32 would yield the constraint $M'N'$, and equilibrium would still occur at E', because the family would prefer to spend $157 on food with an increase in income to $472. Paradoxically, the welfare cost is larger for poorer families than for higher income families in the program because $154 represents greater overconsumption at lower income levels.

In a study of the food stamp program, Kenneth Clarkson estimated

102 the welfare cost of the overconsumption of food induced by the pro-

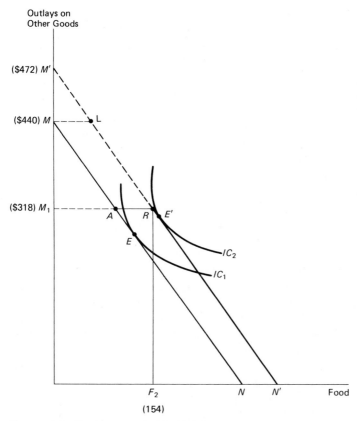

Figure 4–2. Food stamp subsidy: high income recipient.

gram.[2] Clarkson assumed, as we did, that low income families spend one third of their incomes on food; he also assumed unitary income and price elasticities. Using these assumptions, Clarkson found that a $1 subsidy under the food stamp program is worth, on average, $0.82 to recipients. This is an average figure for all participants in the program; at very low income levels the food stamp subsidy is worth only $0.50 per dollar of subsidy. Clarkson's estimates should probably be considered somewhat inexact but indicative primarily of the likely order of magnitude involved (as are most such estimates). They do, however, suggest substantial distortions in consumption patterns from the food stamp program.

[2] Kenneth W. Clarkson, *Food Stamps and Nutrition* (Washington, D.C.: American Enterprise Institute, 1975). See also his "Welfare Benefits of the Food Stamps Program," *Southern Economic Journal* 43(1):864 (July 1976).

Black Markets. Black markets refer to the illegal use of food stamps. There are a number of ways food stamps can be used illegally. For example, a recipient may sell some or all of his basic allotment of food stamps to other people who use them to purchase food. Or a recipient may purchase food first and then sell the food directly to other people. Alternatively, retailers may agree to accept food stamps in exchange for nonfood items.

All of these methods of circumventing the law have a common cause and a common effect. The common cause is the welfare cost of the program. The common effect is a reduction in food consumption below the basic coupon allotment.

To understand this better, recall that the food stamp program tends to impose an inferior consumption pattern on recipients. Recipients therefore have an incentive to try to substitute other goods for the food consumption mandated by the program. More formally, at the legally permitted equilibrium (R in Figure 4–1) the marginal value of a dollar's worth of food is less than a dollar. (The marginal value of the food is indicated by the slope of the indifference curve at point R.) Thus, food stamp recipients would be willing to sell food stamps at a price below the market value. To nonrecipients a dollar's worth of food is still worth a dollar, so nonparticipants are willing to pay up to a dollar for a dollar's worth of food stamps. There are, therefore, mutual gains possible when food stamp recipients sell food stamps at a price below their market value. The possibility of realizing mutual benefit by participants and nonparticipants is the reason black markets emerge, and this is possible only because the consumption pattern of recipients is distorted by the food stamp program.

In black markets, food stamps sell at a price below market value. This occurs because black market transactions are illegal, so buyers bear some risk when purchasing food stamps illegally and consequently are willing to pay less for them. The exact price at which black market transactions will occur cannot be determined without exact knowledge of the risk and penalties involved. We know, however, that the price will be below market value, and the general effects are illustrated in Figure 4–3. The legal equilibrium is shown as point R on the constraint $MARN'$. The alternatives open to the recipient by selling food stamps on the black market are shown by the line $M''R$. The slope of $M''R$ is the black market price. Confronted with these opportunities, the recipient will sell food stamps equal to F_1F_2 and move to point E. This makes the recipient better off because the increased consumption of other goods is worth more than the reduction of F_1F_2 in food consumption, as evidenced by the fact that the recipient is on a higher indifference curve after the black market sale. Note that the recipient may end up consum-

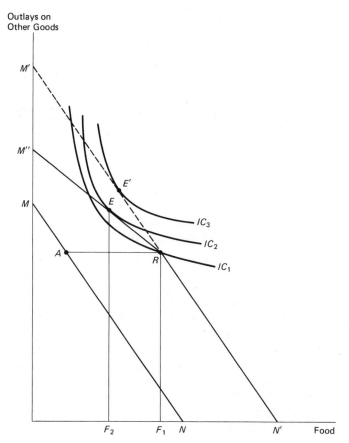

Figure 4–3. Food stamp resale in black markets.

ing less food than if he had received an unrestricted cash transfer equal to the cost of the food stamp subsidy.

Participation in black markets benefits both food stamp recipients and those who illegally purchase food stamps (otherwise, the black market would not exist). For this reason, food stamp black markets belong in the category of "crimes without a victim."[3] Some people, however, apparently do not agree with this assessment. Consider the statement made by Carl Williamson, Deputy U.S. Commissioner of Welfare:

> If a person gets $100 in food stamps that he wants to spend on rent or booze, he just sells them to a black marketeer, for, say, $80. This middle-

---

[3] There can be some harm to sellers of food, but when food purchases fall, purchases of other goods rise so sellers of these goods may benefit. There is thus no net loss to sellers, and this is just a pecuniary externality.

man than sells them for $90 to a crooked grocer who gets $100 from the Government. That way, everyone makes an easy profit, and the Government gets ripped off.[4]

Why it should be thought that the government is being ripped off is not clear, because its cost is the same whether the food stamps are used by the recipient or someone else. Presumably, the objection is that black markets lead food stamp recipients to consume less food than the basic coupon allotment.

Although there have been many reports of black market activity, it is not known how prevalent it really is. This is understandable, because black market transactions are illegal and hence tend to be covert. Black markets can also occur with other consumption subsidies, but these are often limited because of the nature of the subsidized good; for example, it is not easy to resell education or medical care once it has been received.

Other Effects. Although the impact on food consumption is the most widely emphasized effect of the food stamp program, there are other interesting aspects to the program. Some result from the deductions permitted. The monthly net income figure used to determine whether a family is eligible to receive food stamps is not a family's gross income, but instead is gross income minus certain deductions. Among the more important deductions permitted are local, state, and federal income taxes; social security taxes; medical costs (above $10 a month); child care expenses; educational expenses; and shelter costs (which include rent, insurance, and utilities in excess of 30 percent of income).

The most obvious effect of these deductions is that people with gross incomes well above the cutoff point can have net incomes low enough to make them eligible for food stamps. Thus, in 1973 approximately 20 percent of the four-person families participating in the program had gross incomes that exceeded the income cutoff point but were still eligible as a result of the deductions permitted.[5] A more subtle implication of the deductions is that it gives people incentive to spend more on deductibles to reduce their incomes in order to become eligible for the program, or, if they are already eligible, to increase their subsidy.

To illustrate, consider a family on food stamps spending 30 percent of its income on housing. If it increases its housing consumption by $50 per month, its "monthly net income" used to determine the food stamp

[4]Quoted in "Food Stamps, Out of Control?" *U.S. News and World Report* (Sept. 1, 1975), p. 13.

[5]Food and Nutrition Service, U.S. Department of Agriculture, *Food Stamp Program,* prepared for the Committee on Agriculture and Forestry, U.S. Senate, July 21, 1975 (Washington, D.C.: U.S. Government Printing Office, 1975), p. 65.

subsidy falls by $50. With a lower net income, the food stamp subsidy is larger (see Table 4–2), in this case by about $15. Consequently, the net cost of consuming more housing is only $35—because housing costs are deductible under the food stamp program, when the combined effects of housing expenditures and food stamps are considered, the cost of housing to recipients has been reduced. In effect, the deductibility provision has the same effect as an excise subsidy to housing.[6] Thus, the food stamp program also acts to subsidize the consumption of several goods (such as medical care and child care) other than food.

As mentioned earlier, households must meet an asset test as well as an income test to establish eligibility, and this serves to exclude those with considerable wealth but low incomes. Not all assets are counted, however. For instance, a family can own a home, car, life insurance policies, real estate, and personal property such as furniture or jewelry in any amount and still be eligible. By contrast, assets that are counted are essentially highly liquid assets such as cash, stocks, and bonds. The asset test gives people incentive to convert liquid assets into other forms to establish or retain eligibility.

Another peculiarity of the food stamp program stems from the fact that eligibility depends on *monthly* net income. Consequently, a family with a large *annual* income but a low income in certain months can receive food stamps. This is the provision that allows labor union members on strike to receive benefits; in this case the food stamp program acts to lower the costs of strikes to workers. In fact, although the average number of monthly recipients in 1974 was 17.3 million, it is estimated that 29.4 million individuals received food stamps for at least 1 month during the year.[7] Insofar as this is a problem, it could easily be avoided in part by having a year-end accounting, just as with the federal income tax, which is based on annual income but withheld on a monthly or weekly basis.

Administration of the Food Stamp Program

Food stamp subsidies are financed entirely by the federal government, but the administration of the program is the responsibility of state and local governments. State and local governments are reimbursed by the federal government for half their administrative costs. Estimates of these costs vary widely but appear to be about 11 percent of the cost of the

---

[6] More precisely, this is a marginal excise subsidy because it lowers the price of housing only in excess of 30 percent of net income. An example of how this affects the budget constraint is given in Figure 2–8, where MCN'' shows the effect of such a subsidy.

[7] *Food Stamp Program*, op. cit., pp. 1–2.

subsidy.[8] This means that governments must spend $1.11 to give a subsidy of $1.00 to food stamp recipients, which is worth only $0.82 to recipients (according to Clarkson's estimates). An administrative cost of 11 percent is relatively high in comparison to the cost of administering outright cash transfer programs. Social security, for example, involves an administrative cost of 3 percent. If food stamps were converted to a cash transfer, it should be possible to provide larger subsidies to recipients at no additional cost to taxpayers because of the savings in administrative costs.

Some of the financing arrangements of the food stamp program among federal, state, and local agencies also create problems that impair its effective administration. Robert Neilson, Director of the Office of Special Investigations of the state of Washington, pointed out one problem area concerning the identification and prosecution of ineligible food stamp recipients:

> Frankly, we felt we had higher priorities inasmuch as not a single dollar received by investigative and subsequent legal action resulting in restitution was retained by the State of Washington. All investigative and legal activities resulting in restitution meant money for the Federal Government, conversely, expenses for the State of Washington.[9]

In short, state and local administrators have little incentive to check eligibility carefully to avoid making overpayments to recipients; just the opposite occurs, in fact. If too many people receive benefits or the benefits are too large, the federal government bears the cost and local residents benefit. Conversely, to monitor recipients carefully or to investigate cases of potential fraud involves costs for local governments but no benefits.

This method of sharing responsibilities may account in part for the finding of a Department of Agriculture study in 1975 that the error rate in the food stamp program was 54 percent.[10] In other words, 54 percent of the participants in the food stamp program either were ineligible (17.3 percent), received too large a subsidy (26.0 percent), or received too small a subsidy (10.7) percent. The net overpayments made were 14.2 percent of total federal outlays.[11] These figures should not be in-

---

[8] Statement by Senator Patrick J. Leahy, Hearings before the Subcommittee on Agricultural Research and General Legislation of the Committee on Agriculture and Forestry, U.S. Senate, *Food Stamp Reform,* Part 2 (Washington, D.C.: U.S. Government Printing Office, 1975), p. 796. Henceforth referred to as *Food Stamp Hearings.* Clarkson, op. cit., estimates an administrative cost of 9 percent.

[9] Statement of Robert E. Neilson, ibid., p. 835.

[10] Food and Nutrition Service, Food Stamp Division, U.S. Department of Agriculture, *Quality Control in the Food Stamp Program, Non-public Assistance Households, July–December 1974,* reprinted in *Food Stamp Hearings,* op. cit., pp. 1314–1342.

[11] These estimates refer only to food stamp recipients who were not on public assistance.

terpreted as evidence that there is rampant fraud in the system. In the vast majority of cases, no doubt, they simply reflect honest mistakes by recipients and administrators as they attempt to comply with a complex, frequently changing set of rules and procedures.

Of course, there are some cases of deliberate fraud, and one case may be of interest to recount. Some residents of Pullman, Washington, site of Washington State University, had questioned the eligibility of many college students receiving food stamps, so a special investigator was sent to investigate. In October 1974, a year before the investigation, 1540 students applied for and received food stamps (36 applications were denied). A year later, following considerable advance publicity, an investigator was present at the application desk. Interestingly, when the investigator was there, applications from college students dropped drastically to 518, compared to 1576 the year before. Similar, but not so large, responses occurred when an investigator was present at two other colleges. As a consequence, the director of the investigation concluded: "There appears to be less reluctance on the part of college students to lie or deceive on his [sic] application as opposed to the noncollege population." [12] In defense of college students, however, it should be noted that no evidence was presented concerning the behavior of the noncollege population!

Although much publicity has been given to administrative problems in the food stamp program, one must avoid exaggerating their importance. The program is of relatively recent origin and has been expanded rapidly in recent years. With more experience, and possibly some reforms, administration should be expected to improve. With any program serving 20 million people, however, some errors and fraud are unavoidable, but this should be viewed in perspective.

Other Factors in an Evaluation of Food Stamps

Quite often, considerations that influence congressional decisions are quite different from those emphasized by economists. Food stamps are a case in point. Consider, for example, the testimony of the late Senator Hubert Humphrey in congressional hearings on food stamp reforms. Senator Humphrey summarized three arguments that were often heard in Congress:

The food stamp program plays a very critical role in enabling millions of low-income Americans to have a better diet.
It plays a very important role in the support of American agriculture.

[12] Statement of Neilson, op. cit., p. 837.

It also plays a very important role in keeping the economy from sliding into a deeper recession.[13]

Because these three arguments are frequently mentioned in discussions of food stamps, let's consider each in turn.

Nutrition. Improving the nutritional adequacy of the diets of poor families is frequently stated as the primary objective of the program. Clearly, the program is designed to increase food consumption, but a distinction must be made between the amount of food consumed and the nutritional adequacy of the diet. Somewhat surprisingly, available evidence does not indicate a significant improvement in the nutritional content of food consumed by recipients, and in some cases diets have apparently deteriorated. The evidence, however, is far from conclusive.[14]

The fact that nutrition is often not improved should come as no surprise. Food stamps can be used to purchase almost any kind of food including frozen TV dinners, candy, soft drinks, cakes, coffee, sugar, and other types of "junk" food. With a major expansion in food budgets, low income families often find it in their interest to obtain more palatable and easily prepared food, but not necessarily more nutritious food.

The effect on the overall level of food consumption and nutrition can be viewed from two different perspectives. First, relative to no subsidy at all, the program increases food and non-food consumption for recipients. However, the taxes that finance the program reduce disposable incomes of taxpayers and tend to reduce their food and nonfood consumption. Looking as the program in this way, we are explicitly recognizing its redistributive nature. Evaluating whether this redistribution is desirable raises issues that will be considered in more detail in Chapter 7.

The food stamp program redistributes income in a particular way that tends to increase food consumption more than would an alternative transfer of equal cost. Rather than consider the question of whether the redistribution itself is desirable, let's concentrate on the particular form of transfer. We know that food stamps increase food consumption more than a cash transfer, but even if this tends to lead to better nutrition than a cash transfer (which is not clear) the relevant question is whether this is desirable. Viewed in this context, any improvement in food consumption and nutrition comes at the expense of a reduction in consumption of other goods, which might include housing, medical care, education, clothing, drugs, or alcohol. In any event, the other goods sacrificed are considered more valuable to the recipient than the food or

---

[13] Statement of Senator Hubert H. Humphrey, *Food Stamp Hearings* op. cit., Part 1, p. 97.

[14] Clarkson, *Food Stamps and Nutrition,* op. cit.

nutrition gained. Why should an improvement in nutrition be considered desirable if the recipient is worse off than with a cash transfer? That is the basic question, irrespective of whether nutrition is improved or not.

To the extent that an improvement in the nutritional content of diets of low income families is considered a desirable goal, it is clear that the food stamp program is poorly designed to accomplish it because recipients are free to purchase foods that have little nutritional value. However, it would be a simple matter to redesign the program in a way that would improve nutrition: Simply restrict the use of food stamps to food items with a high nutritive content per dollar of cost. This would make recipients still worse off in their own view, but it would lead to better nutrition.

Effect on the Agricultural Sector. In recent years, food stamps have accounted for approximately 5 percent of total food expenditures. This, of course, does not mean that demand has been increased by 5 percent, for two reasons. First, food stamp recipients would have spent something on food in the absence of the program, and it is only the increased purchases of food that represent an increase in demand. (In Figure 4–1, the increase in demand is from F_1 to F_2, in contrast to total food stamp purchases, which equal F_2. And in Figure 4–2, the increase is even smaller for higher income recipients because the food stamps, in these cases, largely leave food purchases unchanged.) Second, taxes that finance the program reduce the demand for food by nonrecipients to some extent. On balance, the market demand for food is perhaps increased between 1 and 2 percent, probably closer to 1 percent.

No detailed study is required to see that the impact of a 1 percent increase in demand for food on the agricultural sector will be trivial. Less than half the retail food dollar reaches the agricultural sector; costs of retailing, transportation, and processing account for the remainder. Most, if not all, of what reaches agriculture will simply cover the costs of producing the small increment in output that results. Although the exact effects depend on the nature of the market (see Figure 3–9 in the last chapter for the relevant analysis), the quantitative impact is clearly very small.

If food stamp subsidies and eligibility were expanded, the program could, of course, have a sizable effect on the agricultural sector. The relevent question is whether such an impact is desirable. To the extent that the food stamp program increases the demand for food, it reduces the demand for other goods and services. Any increase in incomes, wages, or profits in agriculture is therefore accompanied by a reduction in income, wages, or profits in other parts of the economy. In short, any advantages derived by food producers reflect a redistribution of income away from other people; what farmers gain, others lose. So even if the agricultural sector does benefit, it is not clear why this should be considered desirable.

Employment and Business Expansion. Senator Humphrey buttressed his preceding remarks concerning the stimulative effect of food stamps by referring to a Department of Agriculture study on the impact of the program in Texas in 1972:

> The study found that $63.9 million in bonus food stamps provided in Texas that year generated $232 million in new business in Texas and appeared to generate at least $89 million in business elsewhere in the United States. In addition, the $63.9 million provided in bonus food stamps created 5031 jobs. Translated nationwide, this could mean that the food stamp program is now responsible for $27 billion in business in the United States each year and 425,000 jobs. . . . Furthermore, consider how much money we would have to spend to support those 425,000 workers and their dependents if they did not have the jobs that the food stamp program has apparently generated.[15]

Such arguments, frequently presented in Congress, represent a basic misunderstanding of the significance of the effects of the program on employment and output. The opportunity cost of the expansion of business and employment resulting from the expenditure on food stamp subsidies is a contraction of business and employment elsewhere. This expansion, if it occurs, is not a net effect because it involves drawing resources from other uses. This is easily seen when we recognize that the taxes that finance the program reduce taxpayers' demands for goods and services, reducing output and employment via multiplier effects through other markets.

At the end of his statement Senator Humphrey seemed to suggest that the workers were not bid away from other jobs, so the effects described represent a net increase in economic activity. This is highly unlikely; even if it were true, the implications drawn by Senator Humphrey would be wrong. As will be recalled from the last chapter, the opportunity cost of using these resources is that they could have been employed in other jobs producing different goods and services. Had the government spent the $63.9 million on a different subsidy, or had it cut taxes, these resources would have been drawn into the production of other goods. The food stamp subsidy simply leads to a different pattern of employment and output than alternative policies. Adding up the employment and output related to food stamp subsidies misses the point entirely that employment and output elsewhere could have been higher

[15] Statement of Humphrey, op. cit., p. 107.

with different policies. There is, therefore, no net gain in output and employment attributable to food stamps.

Of course, we have made this last point earlier: Impacts, if any, on the level of aggregate economic activity (macroeconomic effects) are irrelevant in the analysis of specific expenditure programs. The use of arguments like the one quoted, however, is so prevalent in discussions of many expenditure programs that we thought it useful to examine them in somewhat greater detail.

The 1977 Food Stamp Reform

In 1977 Congress passed a far-reaching reform of the food stamp program. The major change was elimination of the purchase requirement. Actually, this change had been proposed several times prior to 1977 but had never secured congressional approval. In 1977, however, the reform proposal had an easy trip through Congress, perhaps because it was incorporated in a general farm bill that increased crop price supports. This provides a good example of political logrolling, whereby a bill that could not secure majority approval on its own is combined with another bill and the two are voted on together. (Logrolling will be discussed in Chapter 9.)

Elimination of the purchase requirement means that participants will receive the "bonus" food stamps free. Referring back to Table 4–2, this would mean that families would receive free food stamps in the amounts shown in the last column. For example, a family with monthly net income of $50 would receive $144 free in food stamps, and a family with monthly net income of $310 would receive $65 free in food stamps. Note that this change does not directly affect the cost to the government, because the "bonus" food stamps already represent the previous cost of the subsidy. (There might be indirect effects on program costs, however, through changes in administrative costs and participation in the program.)

One issue that attracted a great deal of attention was whether this reform would reduce food consumption by participants. Proponents of eliminating the purchase requirement generally argued that food consumption would not fall. Senator Robert Dole stressed: "It [the proposed reform] will channel the same amount of government money into food and I assume the same or equal amount of private resources into food."[16] and Senator George McGovern elaborated:

> it [the argument that food consumption will fall] is based on the premise that people participating in the food stamp program, if given an option, would reduce what they are committing to food. I think given even the

---

[16] *Food Stamp Hearings,* op. cit., Part 1, p. 200.

present level of food prices in this country, it is very unlikely that at least the typical family is going to reduce that food budget, even though they don't have to shell out the entire amount in one lump sum.[17]

Senators Dole and McGovern notwithstanding, the elimination of the purchase price will lead to reduced food consumption, at least for many families, and we can employ some earlier analytics to make this clear. Consider Figure 4–1 again. The elimination of the purchase requirement shifts the budget constraint to MLN', and the consumer's equilibrium will then be point E' rather than point R. (For the higher income recipient shown in Figure 4–2, the constraint becomes MLN' and no change in food consumption results.) How do we know that many families are in a position like that shown in Figure 4–1? Budget studies indicate that lower income families would consume less food if they could spend their income without restrictions. Furthermore, the very existence of black markets is sufficient proof that many recipients would consume less food if allowed to.

The most obvious effect of eliminating the purchase price is to make most recipients better off. Note that the consumer in Figure 4–1 attains a higher indifference curve at point E' when no purchase price is charged. Overconsumption of food is reduced or eliminated for most recipients, so the related welfare cost is largely avoided. In effect, the minimum amount of food that can be purchased is reduced without decreasing the subsidy, thereby removing a restriction on the way recipients can spend their funds. In fact, eliminating the purchase price has the effect of converting the food stamp program into a program identical to an unrestricted cash transfer for most recipients (except for those with the lowest incomes, where, despite the reduction in required food purchases, some overconsumption may still occur). It is interesting that advocates of this reform did not stress this very real benefit to recipients. It is also noteworthy that this reform weakens three arguments that were popular in Congress (effects on nutrition, the agricultural sector, and aggregate economic activity), although these arguments are, as we pointed out, questionable in any event.

The major argument offered in support of this reform was that it would increase participation in the program. Only about half of all households thought to be eligible for the program were participating in it prior to the 1977 reform. It was argued that the necessity of coming up with a monthly purchase price in a lump sum was a deterrent to participation, especially for low income families. Low income families, it was held, did not have enough money at one time after paying other expenses (such as rent) to afford the purchase price.

This argument is of questionable importance. As it turns out, partici-

[17]*Food Stamp Hearings,* ibid.

pation rates are highest at the lowest income levels, understandable in view of the fact that the subsidy is largest among these groups. In addition, it has been estimated that the purchase price charged is less than the average family, at every income level, would have spent on food in the absence of the program, so the program did not require a family to devote more of its own money to food than it would normally. (This is true on average, but of course it need not be true for all families.) Moreover, Congress had already modified the program in 1971 in a way that greatly reduced this problem insofar as it existed. In 1971 Congress enacted a "variable purchase option" that enabled families to purchase a fraction of the full coupon allotment (either one fourth, one half, or three fourths) at the corresponding fraction of the normal purchase price. For example, a family with a monthly net income of $150 (see Table 4–2) could have purchased one fourth of the coupon allotment ($38.50) for one fourth of the purchase price ($10.25). With this option it is difficult to see how the purchase price could be a major deterrent to participation in the program.

Why, then, was participation so low? In large part it probably reflects the fact that, for some families, the costs of establishing eligibility (filling out forms, etc.) and traveling to purchase the stamps were greater than the benefits. This would be most likely for higher income families where the subsidy is small, and probably explains the low participation rates of families with incomes close to the ceiling amount. Why participation was not higher at lower income levels is not clear; it might have been that eligible families were not aware of the variable purchase option and were deterred by the full purchase price. (It might be mentioned that participation is not universal even under cash welfare programs; only 60 percent of those eligible for Supplemental Security Income, a cash program for the elderly poor, participate.)

Whatever the reason for the low participation rate, clearly it was unnecessary to eliminate the purchase price completely to avoid the deterrent effect of a lump sum payment. It would have been possible, for example, to allow participants to pay the purchase price gradually (such as one fourth each week) rather than all at once. Thus, to attain the major goal of the reform it was not necessary to eliminate the purchase price. It still seems true that the major issue involved in evaluating this reform is the reduction in food consumption and improvement in well-being of recipients.

Although we have emphasized what was considered to be the major issue, the elimination of the purchase price, the 1977 law involved several other significant changes in the food stamp program. The maximum net income that a family could have and be eligible for food stamps was reduced to the official poverty line. (Because the poverty lines are in terms of gross income, however, this still means that some families with incomes 50 percent above the poverty line would be eligible, because food stamp eligibility is determined by net income.) The system of deductions was simplified, and eligibility requirements for students were tightened. These and other changes were intended to simplify the administration of the program.

Unemployment Insurance

Government-provided unemployment insurance has been a part of American life since it was enacted into law as part of the Social Security Act of 1935. Systems providing unemployment compensation are operated by the states under federal guidelines. These guidelines assure that the state systems are quite similar, although some significant differences exist.

Workers who lose their jobs receive financial support from the unemployment insurance system while unemployed. In most states, the level of support provided is about 50 percent of previous wages up to some maximum amount. Some states replace as much as two thirds of previous wages, and several also use dependents' allowances, which provide an additional income supplement based on the number of family members. These benefits are normally payable up to a maximum of 26 weeks. As a result of legislation passed in 1970, however, benefits can be extended 13 additional weeks when the national (or state) unemployment rate is unusually high. (A temporary program enacted in 1974 extended benefits up to a total of 65 weeks.)

Total outlays under these programs are quite sensitive to the level of unemployment, as would be expected. Table 4–3 shows total outlays and related unemployment rates for recent years. Note the sharp increase to above $16 billion annually during the 1975–76 recession. The insured unemployment rate for jobless workers who receive benefits from the program is below the total unemployment rate because some unemployed persons had not worked long enough to establish eligibility, had just entered the labor force, or had quit (rather than been laid off from) their previous job.

Special (earmarked) taxes are used to finance unemployment insurance. To fund the system, employers pay taxes that are based on total taxable wages paid to workers. There is some variation in the tax base and rate among states. Typically, only the first $4200 of wages of each worker is taxable, and the tax rate is normally 3 or 4 percent. In other words, if the rate is 4 percent, an employer must pay $120 in taxes when employing a worker for $3000. For a worker who earns $4200 or more the tax is $168. Although this is paid by the employer, the incidence almost certainly is borne by workers in the form of lower wages.

Table 4–3. Total Expenditures on Unemployment Insurance, Related Unemployment Rates, and Insured Unemployment Rates, 1960–1976.

Year	Total Outlays (billions)	Unemployment Rate (percent)	Insured Unemployment Rate (percent)
1960	$ 3.0	5.5	4.8
1965	2.4	4.5	3.0
1969	2.3	3.5	2.1
1970	4.2	4.9	3.4
1971	6.2	5.9	4.1
1972	5.5	5.6	3.5
1973	4.5	4.9	2.7
1974	6.9	5.6	3.5
1975	16.8	8.5	6.0
1976	12.3	7.7	4.6

Source: Economic Report of the President, 1978, Table B-33.

Although the programs are nominally financed largely by the states, there is an indirect tax advantage granted by the federal government. A tax credit is used that has the effect of allowing states to tax employers at no additional cost to the employers—if the states did not collect the tax, the federal government would. This arrangement gives states a powerful incentive to implement an unemployment insurance program that qualifies for the tax credit, and all states have done so.

Distribution of Benefits

Because unemployment insurance (UI) benefits are paid to the unemployed, it is widely believed that the system disproportionately benefits those who would have low incomes without the program. This, however, turns out not to be true. In one of his several studies of unemployment insurance, Martin Feldstein has shown that in 1970 only 17 percent of the benefits went to the 28 percent of families with incomes below $5000.[18] In contrast, 15 percent of the benefits went to the 18 percent of families with incomes above $20,000. These income figures represent the incomes families had before receiving unemployment compensation.

Although benefits are not heavily concentrated on low income families, their overall impact may be modestly equalizing. The poorest 28 percent of families receive only 17 percent of total benefits, but they re-

[18] Martin Feldstein, "Unemployment Compensation: Adverse Incentives and Distributional Anomalies," *National Tax Journal,* 27(2):231 (June 1974).

ceive even less, approximately 7 percent, of total money income in the economy. The top 18 percent of the families receive 15 percent of UI benefits but almost 40 percent of total money income. Thus, UI benefits are more equally distributed than money income. As we will see, however, the distribution of money income tends to overstate the degree of inequality,[19] so whatever effect UI benefits have on the overall distribution of income is certain to be rather small. UI is not a strongly redistributive program (at least among income classes), in contrast to food stamps where virtually all the benefits accrue to families in the bottom third of the income distribution.

There are a number of reasons for this somewhat surprising conclusion. First and foremost, recall that UI benefits are related to previous earnings: Unemployed workers who had higher earnings receive higher UI benefits. Well-paid union members, for example, can receive sizable benefits while temporarily laid off. In addition, low income workers are more likely to have worked in one of the few occupations not covered by UI, or to have been employed too short a time period to be eligible for benefits. Finally, many low income individuals may have been unemployed long enough (more than 26 weeks) that benefit payments have ceased.

Replacement Rates

The replacement rate of UI for a family refers to the extent to which UI benefits replace lost earnings. It is frequently asserted that UI benefits provide only one third of the worker's usual pay. Consider, for example, the concern expressed on this point in a *New York Times* editorial (April 17, 1973): "The present national average benefit of roughly $55 a week is just a little over one-third of usual pay, a gap that causes unfair hardship to many." The size of the replacement rate is related not only to the financial protection against unemployment but also to the possible incentive unemployed workers may have to remain unemployed.

As Feldstein has shown, the relevant replacement ratios are generally well above one third. The *New York Times* comment is misleading for two reasons. First, it compares UI benefits, which are not taxable, to gross wages, which are taxable. Second, the average benefit refers to those actually unemployed, whereas the "usual pay" refers to the average wage of all covered workers whether unemployed or not. Because lower paid workers are somewhat more likely to become unemployed, $55 will represent a higher fraction of their lost earnings.

To see the importance of having UI benefits nontaxable, consider an example of a worker who earns $600 per month. If he is unemployed for

[19] See Chapter 7.

1 month, the worker's disposable, or take-home, earnings will fall by less than $600, because of the taxes he would have paid on his gross earnings. Suppose the worker's effective marginal tax rate is 25 percent; he might, for instance, be in a 15 percent federal income tax bracket and pay a 6 percent social security tax and a 4 percent state income tax. Then the worker's monthly disposable earnings are only $450. UI benefits will typically replace half his gross earnings of $600, or $300, and this payment is not taxable. Thus, in this case, UI replaces *two thirds* of lost disposable income.

The replacement rate varies widely from one worker to another. It depends on the state of residence, type of family, and number of dependents (several states have dependents' allowances that serve to increase the replacement rate), whether the spouse is working, and other factors. There are also usually minimum and maximum UI weekly benefits.[20] A minimum weekly benefit serves to increase the replacement rate of low paid workers and a maximum to reduce it for high paid workers. For example, if the minimum is $50 and a worker normally earns $80 a week, then the unemployed worker will receive over 60 percent of his regular gross earnings; in contrast, if the maximum is $100 per week, a worker with earnings of $300 a week will receive less than half his regular gross earnings.

Feldstein has studied the replacement rates for a variety of family structures in all 50 states. For workers earning less than 130 percent of the average wage in each state, he found that the replacement rate was quite high. For male earners, the replacement rates were typically above 60 percent, and for married women they were generally above 75 percent.[21] In fact, in several states the replacement rates for married women exceeded 100 percent, implying a higher net income for the family when the wife is unemployed than when she is working.

Actually, Feldstein's study is likely to have substantially underestimated the effective replacement rates for many families because it fails to include the effect of the food stamp program. Many unemployed workers may be eligible to receive food stamp subsidies, which also serve to replace lost earnings. Consider the example described earlier when the worker's regular pay is $600 a month. With a wife and two children, he would be ineligible for food stamps while employed (see Table 4–2).

---

[20] For a useful survey of the UI systems and their possible effects on incentives, see Raymond Munts and Irwin Garfinkel, *The Work Disincentive Effects of Unemployment Insurance* (Kalamazoo, Michigan: W. E. Upjohn Institute for Employment Research, 1974).

[21] Feldstein, op. cit.; Munts and Garfinkel find, however, replacement rates of 40 to 50 percent for Ohio, mainly by including fringe benefits in earnings. Feldstein has pointed out that Ohio has unusually low benefits and that it may be inappropriate to include all the fringe benefits. See Feldstein's remarks in *Brookings Papers on Economic Activity,* ed. by Arthur M. Okun and George L. Perry (Washington, D.C.: Brookings, 1975).

When unemployed, although his $300 in UI benefits counts as income under the food stamp program, his income is now low enough to entitle him to a food stamp subsidy of $71 per month. His net income, including the food stamp subsidy while unemployed, is thus $371, whereas his net (after-tax) pay if employed is $450. The effective replacement rate of UI and food stamps together is therefore 82 percent rather than the 67 percent calculated earlier when food stamps were ignored. If the family itemizes deductions, its monthly net income for food stamp purposes will be even lower, the food stamp subsidy will consequently be higher, and the effective replacement rate will be greater than 82 percent.

No study has been conducted yet to determine the importance of the food stamp program in augmenting the replacement rate of unemployed workers. A Department of Agriculture report, however, estimates that an increase in the unemployment rate of 1 percentage point increases participation in the food stamp program by 500,000 to 750,000 persons.[22] There seems little doubt that effective replacement rates are somewhat higher than Feldstein's estimates because of the interaction between UI and the food stamp program.

Duration of Unemployment

The most important potential effect of UI on the allocation of resources is its impact on the unemployment rate. UI does not, of course, very often cause people to lose jobs; instead, it creates an incentive for workers, once unemployed, to extend the duration of unemployment. The replacement rates of UI are the key to this effect. The greater the replacement rate (including food stamps), the lower the cost to the worker of extending the duration of unemployment.

When a worker is unemployed and does not receive UI benefits, the cost he bears is the sacrifice of net income earned if employed. UI substantially reduces this cost by replacing a large fraction of lost net earnings as long as the worker is unemployed. In the example previously discussed, a worker receives $371 in UI and food stamp benefits each month he is unemployed, or 82 percent of his previous net income. Such a worker has small financial incentive to search for a new job because his net income would rise by only $79 if he found a job paying the same salary as his previous one. Indeed, if he believes he cannot find a job that pays as much, or if there are expenses associated with his work (such as transportation), his gain from finding a job will be reduced even more. It is understandable then that a worker laid off from his previous job might simply wait to be recalled, or postpone searching for a new job in

[22] *Food Stamp Hearings,* op. cit., p. 5.

order to work some around the house. Such a reaction adds to the unemployment rate.

In understanding this effect, it may help to recognize that UI is really a type of excise subsidy, or variable quantity subsidy. UI reduces the price to the worker of a certain good—lengthening the spell of unemployment—and the law of demand reminds us that people generally consume more at a lower price. Not all people can be expected to react to this incentive in exactly the same way, but the general direction of the effect is clear.

It can now be seen that the replacement rate is significant for two very different reasons. First, a higher replacement rate means that workers are provided greater security against temporary loss of income due to unemployment. Second, a higher replacement rate lowers the cost to workers of remaining unemployed. The critical policy question involves how to strike a balance between providing security and undermining incentives.

Although the benefits paid by UI give workers incentive to extend spells of unemployment, there are several ways in which the UI system attempts to counter this effect. As mentioned earlier, UI benefits are normally payable for 26 weeks. Because benefits cease after that period, there is no incentive to remain unemployed indefinitely. (There is also no security provided for very long periods of unemployment.) In addition, UI benefits are generally (but not in all states) restricted to workers who have lost their jobs through no fault of their own. Workers who quit or who are discharged for misconduct are ineligible for benefits, although some states do permit such workers to collect benefits after a waiting period of 4 to 6 weeks.

In addition, unemployed workers are required to register for work at the State Employment Service and to accept a suitable job if offered one or lose their UI benefits. These provisions attempt to offset the financial incentives of workers to remain unemployed, but how effective they are is uncertain. Workers are required to accept "suitable work," but what constitutes suitable work is nowhere precisely defined and is largely left to administrative discretion. In practice, suitable work sometimes means a job paying the same wage rate as the one lost, with the same working conditions, and in the same location. This, of course, robs the provision of much of its force.

It is not clear how effective the Employment Service is at encouraging unemployed workers to seek new jobs actively. It sometimes requires workers to attend job interviews or lose their benefits, but an applicant can easily make sure he is not offered a job. As the president of a cab company testified at hearings on UI:

In 10 years I have not had more than one referral from your department [the Employment Service] and the man who came in made it certain that he would not be hired. I have had a standing order for cabdrivers here for 10 years, and I have not had one [sic] applicant.[23]

Moreover, although private placement agencies might have job listings suitable for unemployed workers, there is no attempt to coordinate their efforts with the State Employment Services. The chairman of the board of a private employment service complained that private employment services could place unemployed workers in jobs but that State Employment Services did not utilize these services. In fact, it is illegal for State Employment Services to refer an unemployed worker to a private service.[24]

It is probably true that these practices frequently fail to offset the financial incentive of workers to extend the duration of unemployment. No doubt, major abuses are avoided, and some workers lose UI benefits because of these practices, but it is not an easy matter to induce people to behave in a way they perceive as contrary to their best interests. Indeed, to make these provisions fully effective would probably lead to workers' having little freedom to choose among alternative jobs.

In judging the potential impact of UI on the unemployment rate, it is important to recognize some facts concerning the nature of unemployment. Many people believe unemployment consists of an unchanging pool of workers who will remain out of work unless the unemployment rate is reduced. Nothing could be farther from the truth. Actually, in most years nearly 50 percent of unemployed workers are out of work less than 5 weeks, and the average duration of unemployment seldom exceeds 12 weeks.

Table 4–4 provides some interesting facts concerning the duration of unemployment in recent years. As can be seen, most unemployment is of short duration. If the unemployment rate is 5 percent over 1 year, this means that many more than 5 percent of members of the labor force are out of work at some time during the year, but each person is unemployed for only a relatively short period of time. Reducing the unemployment rate is largely a problem of reducing the average duration of unemployment. What appears to be a small reduction in the duration of unemployment can have a significant effect on the unemployment rate. Suppose, for example, that in 1975, when average duration was 14.1 weeks, it would have been 10 weeks in the absence of UI. The unemployment rate would then have been 6.0 percent instead of 8.5 percent. (Obviously, we are not suggesting that this is the actual size of the impact of UI but are only trying to illustrate how a small reduction in

[23] Statement of James S. Metcaffe, Hearings before the Subcommittee on Unemployment Compensation of the Committee on Ways and Means, House of Representatives, *Phase III: Proposed Changes in the Permanent Federal-State Unemployment Compensation Programs* (Washington, D.C.: U.S. Government Printing Office, 1975).

[24] Statement of Robert O. Snelling, Sr., ibid., pp. 728–751.

Table 4-4. Unemployment Rates and Duration of Unemployment, 1960–1975.

Selected Years	Unemploy-ment Rate	Duration of Unemployment (percent)				Average Duration in Weeks
		Less Than 5 weeks	5–14	15–26	26 weeks or more	
1960	5.5	45	31	13	12	12.8
1965	4.5	48	29	12	10	11.8
1970	4.9	52	32	10	6	8.7
1971	5.9	45	32	13	10	11.3
1972	5.6	46	30	12	12	12.0
1973	4.9	51	30	11	8	10.0
1974	5.6	51	31	11	7	9.7
1975	8.5	37	31	16	15	14.1
1976	7.7	38	30	14	18	15.8
1977	7.0	42	30	13	15	14.3

Source: Economic Report of the President, 1978, Table B-31.

the average duration of unemployment would affect the unemployment rate.)

In our discussion of UI so far, its effect on unemployment as an "automatic stabilizer" has been conspicuously absent. At the risk of belaboring what is perhaps by now obvious, let's turn to Feldstein on this point:

> it is really irrelevant to argue that the program reduces unemployment because it automatically increases government spending when unemployment rises. We have come to accept the government's general responsibility for maintaining a high level of demand through variations in spending, taxation, and monetary policy. The fiscal stimulus now provided by unemployment compensation would alternatively be provided through other government expenditure increases or tax cuts.[25]

Actually, a tax cut rather than an expenditure increase (as with UI) would increase the incentive of unemployed workers to return to work because their potential take-home (after-tax) pay would be higher.

Encouraging Instability in Employment

The incentive provided by UI for workers to extend the duration of unemployment is clear, but there is another way UI operates to increase unemployment. UI encourages employment in industries where there are

[25] Martin S. Feldstein, "Unemployment Insurance: Time for Reform," *Harvard Business Review* (Mar./Apr. 1975).

high seasonal and cyclical variations in employment, that is, in short-lived jobs where there are frequent layoffs.

In the absence of UI a firm with a very unstable employment pattern would have to pay higher wages to attract workers. The higher wage would be necessary to compensate workers for the risk that their jobs would be short-lived. With UI benefits available, however, the government compensates workers who are employed in industries with frequent layoffs. This makes such unstable employment more attractive to workers and hence increases the supply of labor for such jobs. The result is a reduction in market wages and an increase in employment in industries where seasonal and cyclical unemployment is high. Unstable jobs are being subsidized by the UI program, and the lower market wage rates reduce the incentive for firms to organize production to reduce the instability in employment. Thus, sectors of the economy with unusually high unemployment rates are encouraged to expand at the expense of other sectors, and the result is a higher overall unemployment rate.

Empirical Evidence

Economic theory predicts that UI tends to increase unemployment, but empirical research is necessary to determine the size of the impact. In recent years much attention has been devoted to this question. Stephen Marston's study is one of the most careful attempts to determine the quantitative impact of UI. Marston compared the experience of insured and uninsured workers and found the duration of unemployment to be between 16 and 31 percent longer for the insured. If this difference is solely attributable to UI, the unemployment rate would be 0.2 to 0.6 percentage points higher as a result of UI. (This estimate ignores the effect of UI on the unemployment rate by encouraging unstable employment.) It is not clear, however, that the differences in unemployment between insured and uninsured workers measure the impact of UI, because these groups differ greatly. For instance, the uninsured unemployed are largely new entrants in the labor force or those who quit their last job, whereas the insured are primarily those temporarily or permanently laid off from a previous job. These groups would probably have different durations of unemployment even in the absence of UI.[26]

Kathleen Classen investigated the effect of raising weekly UI benefits (i.e., raising the replacement rate) by comparing similar, insured people in the same state (Pennsylvania) before and after an increase in benefits. She found that a $15 increase in weekly benefits increased the average

---

[26] Stephen T. Marston, "The Impact of Unemployment Insurance on Job Search," *Brookings Papers on Economic Activity,* op. cit. See also Feldstein's comments on Marston's paper on the same journal.

duration of unemployment by more than 1 week. (Note that this is not the total effect of UI on the total duration of unemployment but only the effect of a $15 increase.) As far as she could determine, there were no other changes in the economy that took place that would have led to this longer duration.[27]

Holen and Horwitz found that the rate at which people are denied benefits has an important impact. They estimated that simply doubling the denial rate would reduce the unemployment rate by 25 percent.[28]

Evidence from experience in other countries with UI suggests similar effects. Malkí and Spindler examined the British experience following the introduction of an extra "Earnings Related Supplement" into the UI system in Great Britain in 1966. Immediately following this increase in benefits the unemployment rate began a significant increase, rising from 1.6 percent (for males) the month before the change to 3.3 percent 5 months later. Not all of this increase is necessarily due to the Earnings Related Supplement, but Malkí and Spindler, after controlling for some other variables, estimate the overall unemployment rate to be 30 percent higher as a result of the increased benefit.[29] Similarly, Grubel, Malkí, and Sax, using time-series data for 1953–72, suggest that Canada's UI system has increased unemployment by more than one percentage point.[30]

None of these studies is definitive, but available evidence does point to a substantial impact on unemployment. Unfortunately, no existing study has examined the joint effects of UI and food stamps together, an important omission because the food stamp program tends to increase the effective replacement rate for many unemployed workers. Considerable research now in progress may help us understand more clearly the quantitative effects of UI.

Job Search

Contrary to popular opinion, many economists have emphasized that the longer duration of unemployment produced by UI is not unequivocally bad. An unemployed person may devote time to "job search," that is, to

[27] Kathleen Classen, "The Effects of Unemployment Insurance: Evidence from Pennsylvania," The Public Research Institute of the Center for Naval Analysis, PRI 166–75, April 1975.

[28] Arlene Holen and Stanley Horwitz, "The Effect of Unemployment Income and Eligibility Enforcement on Unemployment," *Journal of Law and Economics*, 17(2):403 (Oct. 1974).

[29] Dennis Malkí and Z. A. Spindler, "The Effect of Unemployment Compensation on the Rate of Unemployment in Great Britain," *Oxford Economic Papers*, 27(3):440 (Nov. 1975).

[30] Herbert G. Grubel, Dennis Malkí, and Shelley Sax, "Real and Insurance-Induced Unemployment in Canada," *Canadian Journal of Economics*, 8(2):174 (May 1975).

looking for a new job. The longer one looks for a job, the more likely it is that a good job will be found. UI reduces the pressure on an unemployed worker to take just "any job" that comes along and allows him to search more thoroughly for a job that could make better use of his skills. If greater duration of unemployment leads to a better matching of jobs and people, it may represent a productive investment.

It is important to determine whether longer spells of unemployment do lead to higher wages (implying, presumably, a better job) when workers ultimately return to work. Ehrenberg and Oaxaca found that longer periods of unemployment raise postunemployment wages. These effects, however, were statistically significant only in the cases of older males and females aged 30–44.[31] By contrast, Kathleen Classen found that longer durations of unemployment had no effect on post-unemployment wages.[32] Thus, it is not clear whether people find better jobs as a result of the longer duration of unemployment caused by UI.

Even if the longer spells of unemployment caused by UI do lead to higher postunemployment wages, it is not clear that this increase is efficient. There is an efficient level of job search that involves equating the marginal return from additional search to the marginal cost of continuing to look for a job. This does not generally involve waiting for the best possible job offer because there is a substantial cost—sacrificed earnings—to waiting. The problem with UI is that it greatly reduces the marginal cost of looking for a job, as perceived by workers, and encourages the unemployed to wait too long to take a job. The marginal cost of looking for a job is the earnings an unemployed worker sacrifices while searching, but as we have seen, UI makes the net sacrifice to the worker much lower by replacing a large fraction of his potential earnings. Workers receiving UI benefits have incentive to hold out for a better job as long as there is almost any hope, however small, because they are sacrificing very little income by not returning to work.

An example may clarify this point. Suppose a worker can return to work for $150 a week, but believes that if he searches or waits for 4 weeks he can find a job paying $160. The marginal cost of waiting for the $160 a week job is $600—his earnings at the $150 job for those 4 weeks. The marginal return is $10 extra per week for (we will assume) 50 weeks, or $500. In this case, the marginal cost is $600 and the marginal gain $500 so it is inefficient to wait for the higher paying job. If the worker receives $100 a week in UI benefits, however, his net cost

[31] Ronald G. Ehrenberg and Ronald L. Oaxaca, "Impact of Unemployment Insurance on the Duration of Unemployment and Post-Unemployment Wage," Paper presented at the Meetings of the Industrial Relations Research Association, Dallas, Texas, December 30, 1975.
[32] Classen, "The Effects of Unemployment Insurance: Evidence from Pennsylvania," op. cit.

of remaining unemployed for those 4 weeks is $200, because he could get only $50 more per week by returning to work. The costs and gains as he perceives them have changed; to wait for the higher paying job would cost him $200 in forgone earnings, compared to a gain of $500. Because the worker does not bear the entire cost of waiting with UI, he would then be led to wait for the better paying job even though this is inefficient.

Thus, UI could be expected to lead to excessive job search. Only if people would, in the absence of UI, tend to underestimate substantially the prospects of finding a better job by additional search and thus search too little would encouraging job search be an appropriate policy. Even if this were the case, UI is not well designed to deal with the situation because it reduces not only the cost of job search but also the cost of all other ways an unemployed person may use his time.

Proposals for Reform

Martin Feldstein has recommended a two-pronged reform that would greatly change the nature of the UI system.[33] First, he suggests that UI benefits be subject to the federal income tax. Second, he proposes that the current system of benefits be replaced by a combination of loans and nonrepayable benefits. Let's consider each of these proposals briefly.

UI benefits have been nontaxable since 1938. In 1938 only 4 percent of the population paid federal income tax, so the tax exempt status of UI benefits had very little effect on employment incentives. Today, with much broader income tax coverage and higher tax rates, the tax exempt status of UI benefits is quite significant. The effect of taxing UI benefits would be to reduce the net benefit to unemployed workers. Thus, a worker in a 20 percent federal tax bracket would pay $20 in taxes on a $100 UI benefit, leaving a net benefit of $80. In other words, taxing benefits would have the same effect as reducing benefits in proportion to the federal tax bracket of the worker. Because higher income workers are in higher tax brackets, benefits would be reduced most at high income levels. In fact, many low income families would not find their net benefits reduced at all because exemptions and deductions place many low income families in zero marginal tax brackets so they pay no federal income taxes. Therefore, taxing UI benefits would alter the distribution of UI benefits in favor of low income classes.

Taxation of UI benefits also would reduce the incentives of a worker to remain unemployed. Recall our earlier examples showing how nontax-

---

[33] Feldstein, "Unemployment Insurance: Time for Reform," op. cit. Actually, Feldstein's reform consists of three parts, the third to deal with what is known as "experience rating." We have ignored experience rating because it is very complex and does not materially affect the analysis in the text.

ation of benefits increases the replacement rates, especially for those in higher federal tax brackets. Many families would find replacement ratios reduced from in excess of 70 percent to 50 percent. This would tend to reduce but not eliminate the incentive to extend unemployment.

Feldstein's second proposal would have a far more drastic effect. He suggests that the government lend unemployed workers 60 percent of their previous wage rather than giving them benefits. These loans would be repaid after the worker returned to work. Only after a worker has been unemployed for a long period, 3 to 6 months, would he be eligible to receive nonrepayable benefits.

A loan program to provide support for the unemployed would virtually eliminate any incentives for a worker to extend inefficiently the duration of unemployment. Each week the worker borrowed money, he would increase his indebtedness to the government, and consequently he would bear the entire cost of remaining unemployed. This would give him a strong incentive to avoid extending unemployment unnecessarily and also make it more likely that the worker would use his time more actively to search for a job. On the other hand, those unemployed longer than 6 months would receive nonrepayable benefits and find unemployment subsidized thereafter.

In evaluating this proposal, it is important to recall that most unemployment is short-lived (see Table 4–4). Most unemployed workers would never become eligible for nonrepayable benefits. Only those with very long spells of unemployment would receive an outright subsidy, and this group would be more likely to be the most needy among the unemployed. (To avoid possible abuses in these few cases of extended unemployment, there would probably have to be some limitation on the duration of benefits.) Therefore, Feldstein's proposal would almost completely eliminate the adverse incentives inherent in the present system.

Would the repayment of loans be a great burden on workers after they return to work? Perhaps in some individual cases, but two points should be recalled. First, under the current distribution of benefits, most of the outlays are received by middle and upper income families. Second, using loans rather than nonrepayable benefits would allow the tax used to finance UI benefits to be reduced, and this would increase after-tax income and the ability of reemployed workers to repay the loan.

Actually, this proposal is a large step in the direction of eliminating UI altogether. Most unemployed persons would probably not borrow the money even if they could, but instead would finance their unemployment out of their own savings (at least unless the government lent at below-market interest rates). In that event, workers would be using savings to "self-insure" against unemployment. Indeed, people do not need a very large nest egg to provide the same degree of insurance currently provided by UI. Recall that the average duration of unemployment seldom exceeds 12 weeks. At a replacement rate of 50 percent, UI provides on average benefits equal to 6 weeks of wages. Thus, a worker requires savings of less than one eighth of his annual income to provide the same average protection as afforded by UI.

Having come this far, why not simply eliminate UI all together? The obvious reason is that some people would be too poor to have accumulated any savings. Yet if this is the reason, the real problem is a distribution of income with too many poor families, and that could be resolved by a welfare system that raised the incomes of low income families. Feldstein's proposal is a compromise that guarantees that those who cannot or simply do not provide for emergencies will be supported during periods of unemployment.

Supplementary Readings

Clarkson, Kenneth W. *Food Stamps and Nutrition.* Washington, D.C.: The American Enterprise Institute, 1975.
————. "Welfare Benefits of the Food Stamps Program," *Southern Economic Journal,* 43 (1):864–878 (July 1976).
Feldstein, Martin S. "Unemployment Compensation: Adverse Incentives and Distributional Anomalies," *National Tax Journal,* 27 (2):231–244 (June 1974).
————. "Unemployment Insurance: Time for Reform," *Harvard Business Review* (Mar./Apr. 1975).
Munts, Raymond, and Irwin Garfinkel. *The Work Disincentive Effects of Unemployment Insurance.* Kalamazoo, Michigan: W. E. Upjohn Institute for Employment Research, 1974.

FINANCING MEDICAL CARE

The role of government in the financing of medical care has expanded rapidly in recent years, and further expansion seems likely if some form of national health insurance is enacted. Health economics is a highly complicated field, and this chapter will focus selectively on issues related to the evaluation of publicly provided health insurance. Medicare and Medicaid will be considered because they are forms of health insurance for the elderly and the poor, and because the workings of these programs may provide some insight into the possible consequences of a system of national health insurance.

Public and Private Expenditures on Medical Care

Table 5–1 documents the rapid growth in medical care expenditures in recent years. Total expenditures were nearly 12 times as great in 1976 as in 1950; during the same period, GNP rose by a factor of only 6. Consequently, the share of GNP devoted to medical care nearly doubled, rising from 4.5 percent to 8.6 percent. By 1976 medical care expenditures in the United States were greater—in aggregate and on a per capita basis—than in any other country.

Both private and government expenditures on medical care have increased, but government spending has risen more rapidly. Note the particularly rapid growth in government spending since 1965, which marked the enactment of Medicare and Medicaid. By 1976 expenditures on Medicare and Medicaid alone totaled $33 billion, almost 60 percent of total government expenditures in the health care area. The remainder was devoted to a wide variety of purposes: public health, medical research, veterans' hospitals, child health programs, hospital construction, and others.

Table 5–1. Expenditures on Medical Care ($ in billions)

Fiscal Year	Total Spending	Total as a Percentage of GNP	Private Spending	Government Spending	Government as a Percentage of Total
1950	$ 12.0	4.5	9.0	3.0	25.5
1960	25.9	5.2	19.5	6.4	24.7
1965	38.9	5.9	29.4	9.5	24.5
1970	69.2	7.2	43.8	25.4	36.7
1976	139.3	8.6	80.5	58.8	42.2

Source: A. M. Skolnik and Sophie R. Dales, "Social Welfare Expenditures, Fiscal Year 1976," *Social Security Bulletin,* January 1977, Table 6.

Another significant recent development in the financing of health care has been the growth of private health insurance. Table 5–2 gives a percentage breakdown of personal health expenditures by sources of funds. In 1974 private insurance covered 25.6 percent of medical expenditures, three times as large as its share in 1950. Third party payments, that is, insurance plus government expenditures, covered almost two thirds of medical costs in 1974. (Third party payments are so called because they are expenses not directly incurred by either the provider or the consumer of the medical care; instead, the insurance company or the government bears the cost.) Although the public ultimately incurs the cost of third party payments in the form of insurance premiums or taxes, the fact that the patient does not bear the costs in proportion to his own use of medical care resources has important implications for the functioning of medical care markets, as we shall see later.

The figures in Table 5–2 give broad averages of total expenditures by people in the United States for all types of medical expenses. There is, however, a striking difference in the importance of third party payments for different types of medical care. For example, 90 percent of hospital care costs in 1974 were borne by third parties. By contrast, 60 percent of physician services were financed in this way, but less than one third of all other medical services (dental services, drugs, eyeglasses, nursing home care, etc.) were paid for by third parties. Private insurance covers only 5 percent of these latter services. The economic reasons for such variation in third party payments will be explained later.

Medical Care and Health

The "crisis in medical care" is a familiar topic thanks to the emphasis provided by the news media. In describing the "crisis", it is common to contrast the rapidly rising costs of health care with the health of the

Table 5-2. Percentage Distribution of Personal Health Care Expenditures*

Fiscal Year	Total	Private Direct Payments	Private Insurance Benefits	Government	Third Party Payments	Other
1950	100	68.3	8.5	20.2	28.7	3.0
1960	100	55.3	20.7	21.7	42.4	2.3
1965	100	52.5	24.7	20.8	45.5	2.0
1970	100	40.4	24.0	34.2	58.2	1.5
1974	100	35.4	25.6	37.6	63.2	1.4

Source: Compendium of National Health Expenditures Data, U.S. Department of Health, Education, and Welfare, Social Security Administration, Office of Research and Statistics Publ. No. 76-11927, January 1976, Table 2.
* Personal health care expenditures are about 10 percent smaller than the total expenditures shown in Table 5–1 because the former do not include medical research, public health activities, and so on.

American people. Although the United States spends more on health care than any other nation, its people are far from being the healthiest in the world. For example, in the late 1960s the United States ranked eighteenth in male life expectancy, eleventh in female life expectancy, and thirteenth in infant mortality.

Does this imply that our medical care system is generally inefficient? Not at all. A wealth of empirical evidence strongly suggests that differences in the quantity or quality of health care among developed countries are not significantly related to differences in health. Put another way, health levels in a country reflect a wide variety of factors; medical care is only one of these factors, and its independent contribution to the general level of health seems rather minor.[1] Thus, spending more on medical care or reorganizing the system is not likely to improve significantly the international standing of the United States.

With respect to mortality, it is easy to understand why medical care expenditures are unlikely to improve longevity significantly. The three leading causes of death in the United States are heart disease, cancer, and accidents (mainly automobile), accounting for seven of every ten deaths. More or better medical care is unlikely to prevent many of these deaths. In general, the health of a people depends heavily on other factors such as heredity, nutrition, smoking, drinking, exercise, education, environmental influences, and general "lifestyles." Provision of additional medical care will not alter these other influences and so cannot be expected to transform us into a healthy nation.

A striking example of the importance of nonmedical factors is provided by two adjacent states in the western United States, Utah and

[1] This theme is stressed in Victor R. Fuchs, *Who Shall Live?* (New York: Basic Books, Inc., 1974), Chapter 2. This section draws heavily on Fuchs's interesting work.

Nevada. These states enjoy similar levels of income and medical care, but the inhabitants of one state are apparently far healthier than those of the other. Death rates at all age levels, for males and females, are substantially higher in Nevada, typically 20 to 40 percent higher.

What explains these huge differences? Although we cannot know with certainty, it seems probable that the answer lies in the fact that Utah is predominantly Mormon. Devout Mormons lead temperate lives, neither smoking nor drinking.

No intent to disparage the contribution of medical care to health and well-being should be inferred, however. Here, as elsewhere, it is important to distinguish between *total* and *marginal* benefits of an economic use of resources. The total contribution of medical care to health in the United States is doubtless immense, at least at the present time. (It is now generally agreed that "it was not until well into the twentieth century that the average patient had better than a fifty-fifty chance of being helped by the average physician."[2]) One need only imagine what would happen if we had to do without *any* medical care to realize its importance. All or nothing, however, is not the relevant issue. Instead the issue is more correctly posed as a question of reorganizing the use of existing medical resources, or of devoting more or fewer resources to the provision of medical care. It should be understood that such *marginal* changes are not going to produce major differences in the average level of health.

If there is a medical care "crisis," it is not demonstrated by our international standing. Our ranking internationally probably tells us more about the lifestyles we have chosen (usually individually and voluntarily) than about our health care system. Nonetheless, there are important problems connected with medical care, as we will soon see.

Is Medical Care "Special"?

Just as with other goods and services, the provision of medical care requires the use of scarce resources that have alternative uses. To provide more medical care means that less of other desired goods and services can be produced. In this sense, there is an opportunity cost associated with the provision of medical care just as there is with other goods and services, and this raises the question of whether there are any special characteristics associated with medical care that require government intervention. Many economists believe that there are. Certain types of medical care have a public good or externality characteristic, implying that private provision would be inefficient. This is especially true of

[2] Ibid., p. 30.

medical research (where production of knowledge is a public good) and in the treatment of contagious disease (where there are external benefits for those not treated). A role for government in these areas can be rationalized. However, only a very small share—less than 5 percent—of medical expenditures fall in these two categories.

Another more subtle type of externality is suggested by statements such as "Medical care is a right" and "No one should have to go without needed medical attention because of inability to pay." These statements imply that the general public takes an interest in the consumption of medical care by those who are ill. Insofar as this is true, there may be external benefits from consumption of general types of medical care. It seems clear, however, that for the vast bulk of the population that is nonpoor these benefits are inframarginal, because adequate levels of care would be purchased privately without subsidization. This argument, then, may constitute a reason for subsidizing consumption of medical care by the poor. (This argument is considered in greater detail in a later chapter because it is often also made in connection with housing, food, and education.[3])

Apart from such fairly conventional externality considerations, there are two other peculiarities about medical care that are often stressed. First, medical expenses are irregular and unpredictable. In contrast to expenditures on goods like food and clothing, which tend to be steady and easily predicted, some types of medical expenses are incurred only in the uncertain event of illness. This particular characteristic of medical care accounts for the demand for insurance protection.

The second and probably most frequently noted characteristic of medical care is the difficulty the consumer has in evaluating the service received. In general, consumers don't know the consequences of different medical treatments, nor are they able to diagnose whether they require any treatment at all. This situation arises because knowledge is a scarce good, and it is not unique to medical care; education, legal services, and auto repairs share this characteristic. However, the lack of knowledge on the part of the consumer may be more pronounced and more important in the medical field. As a result, the consumer's demand for medical care depends in part on advice given by his doctor and raises the problem of whether individual demand reflects the true marginal value of the service. Although this "knowledge imperfection" is widely acknowledged, its implications for public policy are far from clear.

Finally, we should mention two characteristics of medical care markets. First, to practice medicine one must graduate from an accredited medical school. State governments have given the American Medical Association the task of accrediting medical schools. It is widely believed that the AMA has, by limiting entry into the profession through severe accrediting requirements, operated as a monopoly and restricted the number of doctors, thereby raising their incomes.[4] Second, most hospital care is provided by nonprofit organizations, either by state and local governments or by voluntary nonprofit hospitals. Because of these two characteristics of medical care markets, it is possible that the normal competitive model may not be an adequate framework for the analysis of health care.[5] Both noncompetitive features, however, are the result of deliberate government policy; there is nothing in the nature of the market that necessitates such a lack of competition.

For these reasons, both the positive analysis and normative evaluations of policies in the medical care field are difficult tasks.

Medical Expenses and Insurance

We live in a risky world, and one of the major risks is the probability of illness. The risk of illness carries with it the risk of incurring heavy medical expenses. Most people don't like to bear risk and are willing to pay to avoid it. Insurance provides this service. By pooling the risks of many people, insurance companies are able to provide insurance on favorable terms. A simple example can be used to show why insurance markets develop.

Suppose there is one chance in a hundred of contracting an illness that costs $20,000 to treat. An insurance company sells policies agreeing to cover this expense. If it sells a large number of policies, say 10,000, the statistical law of large numbers implies that the insurance company can be nearly certain of having to pay almost exactly 100 people (1/100 of 10,000). The number may be a few more or less than 100, but it is very unlikely to be far from 100. In effect, by pooling the risks of a large number of people, the risk borne by the insurance company is quite small. This makes it possible for the company to sell the insurance policy at a price (premium) slightly above $200 (1/100 times $20,000), which is the expected value, or average expense, incurred by the company for the people it insures. The price will have to be somewhat above $200 because the company must cover not only the expenses of those who become ill but also other costs (processing claims, selling costs, administrative costs, etc.).

[4] While this position is held by many economists, the evidence that the AMA has acted as a monopoly is not strong. See C. M. Lindsay and Keith B. Leffler, "The Market for Medical Care," in C. M. Lindsay (ed.), *New Directions in Public Health Care* (San Francisco: Institute for Contemporary Studies, 1976).

[5] An interesting attempt to analyze the behavior of hospitals is provided by M. Pauly and M. Redisch, "The Not-for-Profit Hospital as a Physicians Cooperative," *American Economic Review*, 63:87 (Mar. 1973).

Most people are what economists call *risk averse.* Technically, this means a person prefers to bear a given cost with certainty rather than an uncertain prospect of a greater cost with the same expected value. For example, most people would prefer to pay $200 for insurance than to remain uninsured and to take one chance in a hundred of losing $20,000. Depending on how strongly risk averse people are, they will be willing to pay more than $200 for an insurance policy that covers the $20,000 medical cost if they become ill. Because businesses are able to provide this service by pooling the risks of many people, markets for insurance will emerge.

It is not efficient to insure against all risks. To take an extreme case (where there is no risk), suppose you know with certainty that you will have a physical checkup costing $100 next year. An insurance company would be willing to sell you a policy to cover this expense, but only at a price of (say) $110, because it has to cover its own costs in addition to the cost of your physical. You would, of course, be better off paying the $100 bill directly and saving $10. In this case, there would be no insurance protection against risk because there is no risk, and the additional $10 payment to the insurance company would provide no service.

This simple example suggests some important principles. It is generally inefficient to insure against *predictable* expenses (where risk is small). In addition, it is generally inefficient to insure against small expenses because one can provide his own insurance more cheaply simply by saving a small sum. Thus, it is rational for people to bear many of the risks involved in living in an uncertain world. Insurance makes most sense (is most beneficial) in highly uncertain situations where the possible costs are quite large (consider life insurance, home insurance, and automobile liability insurance). This does not imply that there is one level of insurance coverage most suitable for everyone. People's abilities and willingness to bear risks vary greatly, so they prefer different types of insurance coverage.

In general, then, it would be expected that small and relatively predictable expenses would be left uninsured; large and unpredictable expenses, on the other hand, would be insured against. These expectations, however, are not fully borne out by the facts. Although over 90 percent of the nonpoor are covered by some form of private health insurance policy, the coverage is often "shallow." Shallow coverage refers to coverage of smaller and more predictable expenses but failure to provide much protection against very large expenses. (This might result from a policy that covers only the first 30 days of hospital costs, leaving the insuree to bear the risk of a lengthy hospital stay.) Only about half the population has insurance protection against major medical expenditures. To many observers this is an alarming statistic; from an outsider's point of view, it seems unwise to have extensive coverage of minor medical expenses while neglecting to insure against major medical calamities that could result in impoverishment.

Actually, there is a simple explanation for the prevalence of shallow coverage: The federal tax system subsidizes it. Through the use of special tax provisions (tax "loopholes"), the government has lowered the net price of shallow coverage to the extent that people benefit by purchasing it. Fringe benefits in the form of the employer contribution to group health insurance plans are not subject to income or payroll tax. Consider a worker in a 20 percent tax bracket. If he is paid $100 in cash by his employer, after taxes he will be able to purchase $80 worth of health insurance. At the same $100 cost to the employer, however, $100 in health insurance can be provided directly, and this fringe benefit is not taxable. Thus, it is substantially cheaper to the employee if his employer purchases health insurance for him.[6] The government loses tax revenue, of course, when the employer pays his employees with nontaxable fringe benefits rather than with taxable money.

This "tax subsidy" has actually made it financially expedient for many workers to cover small and predictable medical expenses through group health insurance. Recall that we explained why a person would normally never purchase insurance to cover a *certain* expense because he would have to pay a premium that was larger than the insurance benefit paid out. This is no longer true if health insurance is being subsidized. For group health insurance, policies can pay on average $100 in medical bills at a premium cost of $111—the $11 difference covers the cost to the insurance companies of providing the insurance. In insurance terminology, the "loading rate" is 11 percent. If the tax subsidy exceeds 11 percent, workers can cover their normal medical bills more cheaply by having their employers provide group health insurance plans covering expenses. As can be seen in Table 5–3, this is true for all income classes except the lowest.

Thus, the prevalence of inefficient shallow coverage is probably the result of the tax treatment of health insurance premiums. This does not explain, however, why people do not purchase greater insurance protection against catastrophic medical expenses. There are some government policies that produce a bias against the purchase of this type of insurance. For example, taxpayers can deduct large medical expenses (in excess of 3 percent of their income) under the federal income tax. Bankruptcy laws limit the liability that can be incurred. Moreover, some people of moderate incomes probably don't purchase major medical coverage because they believe that society will cover any large expense they can't

---

[6] There is another tax advantage granted health insurance: People can deduct up to $150 in premiums under the federal income tax. This tax advantage is also considered in the estimates in Table 5-3. For a fuller discussion of exactly how "tax loopholes" affect the economic decisions of taxpayers, see Chapters 11 and 12.

Table 5–3. Tax Subsidies and Group Health Insurance Policies, 1970

Income Class	Cost of (loading rate on) Group Premium (percent)	Tax subsidy as a Percentage of Premium
All classes	10.8	16.7
< $3,000	14.7	8.6
3,000–5,000	10.6	14.7
5,000–7,000	10.2	15.4
7,000–10,000	9.6	16.6
10,000–15,000	11.3	15.2
15,000–20,000	11.5	17.7
20,000–50,000	11.5	23.8
50,000–100,000	10.0	36.9

Source: Karen Davis, *National Health Insurance* (Washington, D.C.: The Brookings Institution, 1975), p. 16.

afford rather than letting them go without needed medical attention. Whatever the reason, some economists believe that many people have inadequate protection against major medical risk, and at the same time have too much protection against minor medical expenditures.

The Problem of Moral Hazard

Provision of insurance protection and payment by third parties creates a problem when the size of the loss a person suffers depends partly on his own behavior. Consider an insurance policy that covers all hospital expenses. When a person is hospitalized, he bears no financial cost if his stay is prolonged. In effect he pays a zero price for hospital care. This is likely to lead him to overconsume hospital services: Any medical care that has any benefit, no matter how slight, would seem worthwhile if the insurance company incurs the expense. His doctor is more likely to prescribe expensive tests and sophisticated treatments knowing that no financial responsibility falls on the patient. Although the value of the medical care to the patient is less than its actual cost, it seems worthwhile to the patient because he bears no cost.

In insurance terminology, this is called the "moral hazard" problem. It really has nothing to do with morality, and to an economist it simply represents the resource misallocations caused by a particular method of finance. Figure 5–1 can conveniently illustrate the moral hazard problem. The curve d_1 is a representative consumer's demand curve for a particular type of medical care if he becomes ill. (If he doesn't become ill,

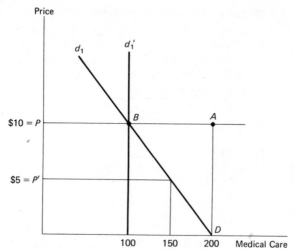

Figure 5-1. Moral hazard and insurance.

he has a zero demand.) At a price of $10 per unit, consumption would be 100 units at a total cost of $1000 in the absence of insurance. If the person is fully insured, the net price of care he bears at the time of his illness is zero and consumption will be 200 units. Consumption will be greater because of the law of demand; in fact, the moral hazard problem exists because the economic behavior of people is responsive to prices. Note that there is a welfare cost due to overconsumption of medical care; it is measured by the triangle *BAD*. In fact, insurance that covers all costs is identical to an excise subsidy that reduces the consumer's price to zero.

In this way, insurance induces increased consumption of medical care. Because out-of-pocket cost is so modest, there is little incentive for insured patients (or their doctors) to economize in the use of medical resources. This effect of insurance has several important consequences for an analysis of medical care financed by insurance. First, because effective demand of patients is increased, the price of medical care is likely to rise. Many economists, in fact, believe that the rapid growth in public and private insurance (third party payments) is directly responsible for the rapidly rising costs of health care in recent years.

Second, when the moral hazard problem exists, full insurance is no longer likely to be an efficient policy. Instead the welfare gain from having insurance protection must be weighed against the welfare cost of overutilization of medical resources. Note that the induced increase in consumption increases the total cost of medical care, and hence will increase the insurance premium needed to finance the policy. In Figure

5–1, if there is a 1 in 10 chance of being ill, the premium (ignoring the loading factor due to administrative costs) for full insurance coverage would be $200 (one tenth of the $2000 cost of 200 units of care). Because the cost is $1000 if uninsured, a person might prefer to remain uninsured and take a one tenth chance of bearing a $1000 cost rather than pay $200 for the insurance policy. Either may be efficient depending on his attitude toward risk.

There are several ways the moral hazard problem can be dealt with. Because it implies inefficiency associated with overconsumption, it is in the interest of insurance companies (as well as insured parties) to devise ways to avoid the problem. One way is to make a fixed payment to the insured party in the event of a specified illness. For example, the insured party might be given $1000 as a lump sum payment; this completely avoids the incentive to overconsume because the insurance benefit is fixed and does not depend on the quantity of medical care purchased. (This is, in fact, the way home fire insurance policies are written. The insurance benefit does not cover *all* costs incurred in purchasing a new house to replace a burned one, but is fixed in amount.) In the medical care field, this is sometimes difficult. For adequate protection, it would be necessary to specify a different payment for each illness, but because there are many possible complications and severities of illness within each category, this would be a complex and costly way of writing insurance. Nonetheless, some policies do place upper limits on the liability of the insurance companies, and that tends to place an upper limit on the moral hazard problem.

A second approach is to require the insured person to pay part of the costs. He might be required to pay, say, half the cost. In Figure 5–1, the price would then be P' or $5, and overconsumption would be reduced. The share of the cost borne by the insured person is called the *coinsurance rate,* a device that is widely used in insurance programs. It has the advantage of reducing the welfare cost of overconsumption but the disadvantage of requiring the insured party to bear some of the risk of illness. Focusing on where to set the coinsurance rate is a good way to understand the tradeoff between providing insurance protection and weakening the economic incentives necessary for efficient utilization of health care resources.

A third approach is the use of *deductibles.* This simply means that a patient must pay (say) the first $200 of hospital costs, and then the insurance company will cover all additional costs (full insurance), if any, or some fraction of these costs (using coinsurance rates). This gives insured patients incentive to be economical in the event of minor medical problems; it avoids, for example, the incentive for a person to enter a hospital for a brief treatment that could be just as easily provided at home or in a doctor's office. In addition, insurance itself is generally not efficient in the case of small expenses, and so deductibles are generally appropriate in any insurance policy.

Much of the discussion of how to structure a government policy of health insurance centers on the size of deductibles and the level of coinsurance rates. It is generally accepted that both features have a place in any program of health insurance, but their exact specification remains controversial. The basic issue should by now be clear: how to provide adequate insurance protection and preserve incentives at the same time.

One other factor is of considerable importance in determining the severity of the moral hazard problem, namely, the elasticity of demand for the type of medical care provided by insurance. In Figure 5–1, note that if the demand were perfectly inelastic—the vertical curve d_1'—consumption of medical care would not increase even at a zero price. If people's consumption of medical care is completely unresponsive to price, there is no moral hazard problem and full insurance coverage will not distort economic choices. In general, the more inelastic the demand, the less severe the problem of moral hazard. Although much popular discussion implicitly assumes vertical demand curves—"needs" that do not depend on price—a considerable body of evidence now exists showing that people, even sick people, consume more medical care at lower prices. For example, Rosett and Huang estimate that expenditures for physicians and hospital services would approximately double if the coinsurance rate were reduced from 35 percent to 10 percent.[7]

Demand elasticities may vary for different types of medical care. For example, it seems likely that the demand for hospital care is more inelastic than the demand for physician services. If so, this suggests that insurance is more efficient in the case of hospital care than in the case of physician services. In addition, because of the relative differences in demand elasticities, it would be efficient for coinsurance rates to be lower for hospital insurance than for physician services. This is, in fact, what we observe. As pointed out earlier in this chapter, third party payments are much more important in the area of hospital care than for physician services. Other medical services—eyeglasses, dental services, drugs, and so on—are likely to have high price elasticities of demand. This would explain why insurance is relatively unimportant in these areas.

[7] R. Rosett and L. Huang, "The Effects of Health Insurance on the Demand for Medical Care," *Journal of Political Economy*, 81(2):281 (Mar./Apr. 1973).

Medicare and Medicaid

Medicare and Medicaid were enacted as Title 18 and Title 19 of the 1965 amendments to the Social Security Act. Medicare is a program of medical assistance for the elderly, and Medicaid provides medical assistance to the poor. In fiscal 1976, government expenditures on Medicare were $18 billion and on Medicaid were $15 billion.

Medicare is a federally financed program with uniform benefit levels nationwide. It is actually composed of two separate programs. Part A is a program of mandatory hospitalization insurance that is provided to all the elderly (with minor exceptions) and is financed as a part of the social security system by a 1.8 percent payroll tax. Part B is called Supplemental Medical Insurance and covers physicians and other related services. Participation in Part B of Medicare is voluntary, but, because of the subsidy involved, 96 percent of the elderly participate. Part B is financed half by a monthly premium paid by participants ($6.70 a month in 1975) and half by contributions from general revenues. Thus, Part B is similar to the food stamp program before its 1977 reform in using a purchase price for a fixed benefit that is less than the cost of providing the benefit.

Medicare can best be thought of as government provision of a specified degree of insurance protection to the elderly. Part A uses a deductible ($92 in 1975) and then covers all hospital expenses up to 60 days. It uses a modest coinsurance payment for hospital stays from 61 to 90 days, but, because a very small percentage of patients stay in the hospital longer than 60 days, the incentive effects of this coinsurance payment are not significant. Part B uses a $60 a year deductible and then pays 80 percent of the cost of all other services (a 20 percent coinsurance rate).

Medicaid is a joint federal-state program, with the federal government paying from 50 percent (for high income states) to 83 percent (for low income states) of the costs. Medicaid is operated largely by states under federal guidelines. To receive federal subsidies, states must provide Medicaid services to all persons receiving public assistance; they may also choose to cover other low income people who are considered "medically indigent." In addition, the range of medical assistance provided to recipients varies from state to state. All states are required to cover hospital services, physician services, and nursing home services. Other types of medical care may be provided at the option of the states. With few exceptions, Medicaid covers all the costs of covered medical care services provided the eligible persons.

The Economic Effects of Medicare and Medicaid

Price and Output. Medicare and Medicaid represent heavy subsidies of medical care consumed by the elderly and poor. As such, the effective demand for medical care by these groups is increased, probably placing upward pressure on prices. Indeed, some observers believe that much of the recent acceleration in the rate of increase of medical care prices is due to these programs. Figure 5–2 will help us understand why this happens.

In the absence of Medicare and Medicaid, the demand for medical care by potential recipients is shown as D_P and the demand by all others is D_N. Total demand, D_T, is the horizontal sum of these curves, and the intersection of D_T and the supply curve determines price and output, P and M_T. Consumption levels of the two groups are M_P and M_N. As we have indicated, Medicare and Medicaid cover virtually all costs of medical care for recipients. In Figure 5–2 these policies have the effect of shifting the demand curve of recipients to the vertical curve D_P', indicating that subsidized groups would choose to consume M_P' whatever the market price, because the government pays it, and their net price is zero. Thus, there is a large increase in effective demand by subsidized parties, and this, coupled with an unchanged demand by the other group, causes the total demand curve to shift to D_T'. With an upward-sloping supply curve, price increases to P' and total quantity to M_T'. As a result, consumption by the unsubsidized group falls to M_N' and consumption by the subsidized group rises to M_P'.

This is a highly simplified exposition of a major cause of increasing health care costs. It explains, at least in part, why medical care prices rose by 29 percent between 1966 and 1970, whereas the overall consumer price index rose by only 20 percent. Nonetheless, this is an incomplete explanation because medical care costs were rising more rapidly than the average of all goods and services even before 1965. For example, for the period from 1950 to 1965 the overall price level rose by 31 percent; at the same time, medical care costs increased by 67 percent. The explanation for this longer term trend lies, it is widely believed, in the growth of government subsidies *plus* the increased use of insurance. Insurance tends to increase demand much as government subsidies do, especially when it emphasizes shallow coverage. Thus, it is probable that both the growth of insurance (fostered by the tax laws) and the introduction of Medicare and Medicaid have contributed to rising medical care costs.

More insight into the causes of medical care price increases is afforded by considering different types of medical care. Not all types of medical services have experienced similar increases. For example, since 1950 the cost of physician services has increased only slightly more than the

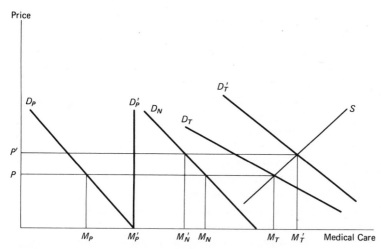

Figure 5-2. Economic effects of Medicare and Medicaid.

consumer price index, and no more rapidly than the price of other services generally. Drug prices have actually increased less than the average increase in all prices. In contrast, the average cost per patient day of hospital care increased from $16 in 1950 to $175 in 1976, a whopping 1000 percent increase! The problem (if it is a problem) of rising medical care costs is almost exclusively one of rising hospital costs. Recall that hospital services are the most extensively supported by third party payments, with patients bearing on average only 10 percent of hospital costs directly. It seems likely that the rapidly increasing role of third party payments for hospital care has been a major cause of hospital cost inflation.

Hospital administrators are quick to point out that these facts overstate the price increases for hospital care because they make no adjustment for quality changes. The quality of hospital care has improved markedly since 1950 so patients today are getting a better product for a higher price. To a large extent, this is true. Economists have contended, however, that hospitals are led to provide a more expensive product as a direct result of increased demand encouraged by public policy. In 1950 patients paid directly for over half of the cost of hospital care received; today patients pay only 10 percent of hospital costs. Because net out-of-pocket expenses are so low, doctors and patients choose more expensive and sophisticated hospital care. As long as the higher costs are paid by someone, hospitals will gladly provide higher quality care. (Their response in upgrading the quality of care may be even greater than in other markets because most hospitals are nonprofit.)

An example will show clearly why such a heavy subsidy is likely to

145

lead to better quality, more expensive products. Suppose the government pays 90 percent of the cost of the automobiles consumers purchase. It is possible that some consumers would respond by simply purchasing more of the Chevrolets, Fords, or Volkswagens they use now. But another plausible response would be to move up to a better quality car, to purchase a Cadillac or Lincoln Continental instead of a Chevy or Ford, or a Mercedes or BMW instead of a VW. We suspect that most people would purchase not only more cars but also more expensive cars. (We know we would!) Statistics would then show a sharp rise in automobile costs because the higher quality car costs much more.

It is likely that this has happened in the field of hospital costs. It is a source of concern because many experts believe that consumers would not want more expensive hospital care if they had to pay for it: To most people, the higher quality of Cadillac-care is not worth the extra cost. Patients and doctors choose this high quality care now only because its direct cost at the time of treatment is so low, even though the actual marginal benefit of the more expensive care is below the marginal cost of providing it. This, of course, is simply a statement of the welfare cost due to overconsumption—but here the emphasis is on the quality dimension rather than on the more familiar quantity dimension.

Our analysis of the impact of Medicare and Medicaid on resource allocation predicts that, at the lowered price, subsidized parties would increase consumption of medical care, and this is largely borne out by the facts. Indeed, in the early 1970s, the poor were consuming more medical care (according to some measures) than middle and upper income groups. For example, the poor have more doctor visits and hospital admissions than other income groups, and health expenditures (from all sources) per person are greater for low income groups.[8] The opposite was true before Medicaid and Medicare. (The change has not been great, however. Doctor visits per poor person increased from 4.3 per year in 1964 to 5.6 in 1973; for the nonpoor the increase was from 4.6 to 4.9.) These facts do not necessarily imply, however, excessive consumption by the poor. It should be noted that the poor, many of whom are elderly, typically have more health problems than other income groups.

Cost Controls. One important consequence of the Medicare and Medicaid programs for medical care prices is not made clear in Figure 5–2. In that diagram, it is implied that the price would settle at P'. However, with a subsidy that covers all (as distinguished from only part of) medical care costs, there is no economic pressure to keep the price of medical care for subsidized parties from rising even higher. If a doctor were to charge $500, or even $5000, for a physical checkup, a subsidized patient won't

---

[8] See *National Health Insurance Proposals,* Legislative Analysis No. 19 (Washington, D.C.: American Enterprise Institute for Public Policy Research, 1974).

care because he bears *no* cost. In this respect, a 100 percent subsidy is quite different from one that covers only part of the cost. When only part of the cost is covered, the patient still has some incentive to shop around for economical prices, and this behavior would keep the prices for subsidized patients from departing significantly from the market prices paid by unsubsidized patients. If the subsidy covers all of the costs, howvever, there is no market pressure to keep prices for subsidized patients from rising above market clearing levels.

This problem has necessitated the use of additional administrative devices to prevent uncontrolled price increases. Generally, these procedures involve the use of what amount to price controls. Under Medicare, for instance, physicians are reimbursed according to schedules of "reasonable and customary" fees; Medicaid will reimburse nursing homes for care they provide to poor patients but no more than a maximum fixed sum. Setting such price ceilings is a complex administrative task, but it is essential to contain prices when there are no incentives within the program to accomplish this task.

The setting of maximum upper limits that will be reimbursed by Medicare or Medicaid has several effects. In an open market for medical care, there will generally be a range of prices for similar services; for example, a physical checkup may range from $50 to $150, with the range reflecting differences in the thoroughness of the examination or the skill of the doctor—quality differences, in short. If Medicaid limits the "customary and usual" fee for a physical to, say, $75, this indirectly limits the quality of care that will be received by the poor. Highly skilled doctors whose services command $150 will be unwilling to provide the service to the poor for $75. Thus, those who are subsidized will receive poorer quality care; there will be a "shortage" of good quality care (a familiar result of price ceilings). At the same time, doctors who would otherwise have charged less than $75 will raise their fees to this level—indeed, to whatever level is permitted.

In August 1976 a U.S. Senate subcommittee held hearings in Miami, Florida, on fraud in the Medicaid program.[9] This hearing provided an interesting confrontation of views on nursing home practices under Medicaid. The state of Florida limited nursing home charges to $600 per month for Medicaid patients. Several nursing homes claimed the care they provided cost more than $600 per month. The homes would agree to accept a Medicaid patient only if the patient (or his relatives) agreed to "donate" an additional amount to the nursing homes. A number of instances of this practice were documented.

---

[9] U.S. Senate, *Fraudulent Payments in the Medicaid Program,* Hearings before the Subcommittee on Federal Spending Practices, Efficiency, and Open Government of the Committee on Government Operations, 94th Congress, Second Session, August 17, 1976, Miami, Fla. (Washington, D.C.: U.S. Government Printing Office, 1976).

The emphasis in this hearing was on the fraudulent behavior of nursing homes; it is illegal under Medicaid for the provider of care to charge anything to the patient or his relatives. Thus, the "donations" were illegal. Our only emphasis here will be to show why the structure of the program produced these donations and to note the consequences of stamping out such practices.

As already suggested, a limit of $600 per month reimbursement guarantees that Medicaid patients will not receive any care that costs more than $600 to provide if supplementary payments are not allowed. Many patients (or their relatives), however, were willing to pay $100 extra to get better care, and there were nursing homes willing to provide that care if they received $700 per month ($600 from the government and $100 from the patient). In such situations, it is in the mutual interest of both nursing homes and patients to agree to a supplementary payment or "donation" (the law could apparently be circumvented by calling the payments "donations") because both parties to the exchange would benefit. Hence, the illegal practice arose.

If "donations" were effectively eliminated, the quality of medical care received by some Medicaid patients would fall. In fact, by making it illegal to supplement the Medicaid subsidy, this policy in effect becomes a fixed quantity subsidy that can produce underconsumption of nursing home care. In addition, there is in this case another way that the program can lead to a reduction in the care received. Because the subsidy finances care only for patients in nursing homes, some people may be led to send their indigent relatives to nursing homes rather than take care of them at home. Medicaid does not reimburse relatives of Medicaid patients for caring for the patients at home, but it does provide a subsidy when the patients are in nursing homes.

These examples are intended only to illustrate some of the likely outcomes of types of "cost controls" now in use. The important point is to understand the reason why such controls become necessary in the first place, and to realize that, because of the controls, the subsidized parties will not receive as much care, or as good quality care, as they would like at the zero price they pay. The cost controls serve to ration the limited quantity of medical resources among competing patients, a function that is no longer being performed by the price system.

Other Effects of Medicare and Medicaid. One can view Medicare and Medicaid as the provision of health insurance coverage to eligible households. Viewed in this way, both policies are examples of fixed quantity subsidies that were considered earlier. The insurance protection provided is fixed in amount; the recipient does not have the choice of either less or more coverage than the government provides. (The amount of medical care that can be consumed by a person when ill is variable, but this variability is distinct from the fixed insurance coverage provided.) A relevant question is whether the amount and type of insurance protection provided are appropriate for the needs of the recipients.

Because the "optimal" amount of insurance depends on individual circumstances and preferences, there is no single answer to this question that would be correct for all recipients. Nonetheless, several studies have estimated that, on average, the insurance protection is greater than the recipients would prefer. Timothy Smeeding estimated a welfare cost of 32 percent for Medicare and Medicaid; Eugene Smolensky et al. estimated the welfare cost to be generally lower at 15 to 26 percent.[10] These figures mean that if recipients were given cash instead of insurance policies they would choose to purchase less insurance and more of other goods and services, and would be significantly better off with this different consumption pattern. The exact figures should perhaps not be taken too seriously, but these findings suggest that the poor and elderly are overinsured as a result of Medicare and Medicaid.

The administration of Medicaid provides a very interesting set of economic incentives for some low income families. Generally, eligibility is restricted to families with incomes below a certain level. For example, the income limit might be $5000, and all families below that level might receive insurance protection with an actuarial value of, say, $1000. Thus, a family with a cash income of $4900 would receive $1000 in insurance at no cost, but another family with an income of $5100 would receive no subsidy at all. There is an obvious inequity associated with the abrupt termination of all benefits at the $5000 level (in Chapter 8 we will see that this is called the "notch" problem that must be dealt with in the design of welfare programs), and it also strongly affects incentives. Families that would normally have earnings above the $5000 level have the incentive to reduce work effort to become eligible for the $1000 subsidy; they can actually increase their total real income by reducing their earnings. Similarly, families with income already below $5000 have incentive not to increase their incomes above that level because they would lose Medicaid benefits. Consequently, there are strong work disincentive effects built into the Medicaid program. This type of disincentive does not exist in Medicare because the subsidy is provided to the elderly regardless of income.

One other matter deserves mention because it has received so much

[10] Timothy Smeeding, *Measuring the Economic Welfare of Low-Income Households, and the Anti-poverty Effectiveness of Cash and Non-cash Transfer Programs,* unpublished Ph.D. dissertation, University of Wisconsin, Madison, 1975, and Eugene Smolensky, Leanna Stiefel, Maria Schmundt, and Robert Plotnik, *Adding In-Kind Transfers to the Personal Income and Outlay Account: Implications for the Size Distribution of Income,* Discussion Paper No. 199-74, University of Wisconsin (Madison: Institute for Research on Poverty, 1974).

public attention: the prevalence of fraud in Medicare and Medicaid. Allegations of widespread fraud have led to several congressional hearings devoted exclusively to the subject. Documented cases include laboratories billing for tests doctors do not request, doctors receiving illicit payments or kickbacks from laboratories in return for sending all Medicaid work to them, pharmacies billing for brand name drugs but providing the patient generic drugs, and laboratories billing for manual performance of a test (which is more expensive) when semiautomated tests are actually performed.

Why is there so much fraud in these programs? It should be clear that there will be some fraud in any program involving billions of dollars. Perhaps a better way to phrase the question is, Why is there more fraud in Medicare and Medicaid than in the social security retirement program, a program that involves twice as much government spending? It seems likely that the structure of Medicare and Medicaid is largely to blame, rather than simply poor administration. There are large monetary gains to be obtained when the government nominally covers all the costs of some economic activity. Patients do not monitor or police the activity when they have no financial stake involved. (In fact, patients frequently do not even see the bills submitted on their behalf to the government.) The laws are, of necessity, often vague; how is it possible to determine what bill, or what type of medical care, is "reasonable" or "customary"? As it turns out, very little fraud has been proven, because there is often no clear distinction between fraud and simple "abuse."

There has been remarkably little study of the relationships among program structure, the incentive for fraudulent behavior, and difficulties of detection and administration. Experience under Medicare and Medicaid suggests that some relationship probably does exist.

Comprehensive National Health Insurance

Much of the debate concerning the ills of the medical care system has centered around variations on a single policy option—national health insurance, or NHI. There are, in fact, a wide array of proposals that are popularly referred to as national health insurance, and there are vast differences among these proposals. Some would involve increases in the federal government's expenditures by as much as $100 billion, whereas others would involve negligible increases. It would take us far beyond the scope of this chapter to analyze or even describe all of these proposals, but we can consider briefly two general variants of NHI that typify the wide range of policies now being considered. One variant is a comprehensive approach to the financing of health care; the other limits the government role to that of assistance in the case of catastrophic medical expenses.

The comprehensive approach is embodied in the Kennedy-Corman bill (proposing the Health Security Act of 1977); indeed, it would be difficult to imagine a more comprehensive proposal. Kennedy-Corman would cover all U.S. residents, and the federal government would undertake to finance almost all kinds of medical services. This would include not only all hospital care and physician services but also dental services, eyeglasses, and prescription drugs. There would be no limit on benefits and no cost sharing by the patient. In effect, the federal government would become the primary and perhaps the sole purchaser of health care.

In 1975 the net budgetary cost (outlays in excess of those already undertaken for Medicaid, Medicare, etc.) has been estimated at nearly $73 billion, or more than $1000 per family in the United States. This cost is to be financed partly by a tax on wage and salary income and partly from general federal revenues. On balance, the proposal would redistribute income to those with lower than average incomes: Families with relatively low incomes would incur a smaller than average tax increase but receive the same insurance coverage as everyone else.

Probably the most obvious effect of this type of NHI would be a major increase in the demand for medical care, because the direct cost to patients would fall to zero. The impact would probably be greatest for those types of medical care that are not now so heavily subsidized: physician fees, dental services, and so on. (Recall that third party payments already account for 90 percent of outlays on hospital care, so effects in this market may not be as pronounced.) Prices would rise, as would the quantity and quality of care in these areas. The response would probably be similar to the effects produced by increasing subsidization of hospital care over the past several decades. Total cost—price times quantity—would, of course, rise, so the estimated budgetary costs would probably be conservative.

The analysis in the preceding paragraph, however, ignores one element found in most comprehensive NHI proposals: cost controls. As explained earlier, any subsidy paying the full costs of some activity must of necessity be accompanied by a regulatory mechanism to limit price and quantity. Kennedy-Corman, for example, envisions rather detailed supervision of the medical care system by regulatory agencies. Doctors would be reimbursed according to a schedule of fees, or they would elect to be reimbursed on a per capita basis according to the number of patients they treat. Hospitals would receive a fixed budget each year. The overall division of the total medical care budget among physicians, hospitals, dentists, and so on would also be determined by some agency.

151

How this regulatory mechanism would actually operate is the greatest uncertainty encountered in an attempt to analyze comprehensive NHI proposals. It is possible that the cost controls would be so strictly applied that price and quantity would not be permitted to rise in response to the increase in effective demand. Shortages would then result.

On the other hand, the controls might be completely ineffective and costs could rise without limit. Based on experience under Medicare and Medicaid, it seems likely that the actual result would fall between these extremes; costs would rise substantially but not by so much as they would if people could consume all the medical care they wished at a zero price.

There are still many unsettling questions concerning how this regulatory mechanism would function. For example:

1. Because there would certainly be major shortages (people would want more and better medical care at a zero price than would be supplied), how will the available quantities be rationed among the public? Will longer waiting times provide the rationing function now performed by prices?

2. In a similar vein, how will patients be allocated among hospitals, doctors, and dentists? There are good doctors, average doctors, and poor doctors; the same can be said of all other aspects of health care. At a zero price everyone would want the "best" care provided by the "best" practitioners, but it is physically impossible for all to have the "best." Will doctors be able to accept or reject patients, or will patients be assigned to doctors, as students are now assigned to public schools?

3. What criteria will be used to determine what fees and prices are permitted? Under Medicare and Medicaid, a large uncontrolled market in medical care provides some guidance as to what are "reasonable" fees and prices, but no private market would exist to generate this information under the Kennedy-Corman proposal. (This may not be exactly true: Some people might be so dissatisfied with the "free" medical care that they would forego the public subsidy and purchase care privately, just as some families send their children to private schools today.)

4. What incentives will doctors and hospitals have to provide good quality care? If doctors are reimbursed according to how many patients they treat, won't they have incentive to treat as many patients as they can, even if each receives only superficial treatment? (This seems to have happened in some cases under Medicaid.) What incentives would hospitals have not to devote their entire (government-funded) fixed budgets to research instead of providing medical care for patients?

These questions suggest a few of the problems that a regulatory mechanism would have to confront and resolve. Unfortunately, all of the proposals for NHI containing cost controls are very imprecise concerning exactly how they will operate. Yet clearly the answer to such "nuts and bolts" questions are of major importance in our analysis of comprehensive NHI. Direct controls may keep health costs down, but they also are likely to produce a major misallocation of medical resources.

The important point here is that the choice between comprehensive NHI and a system where the patient bears part of the cost is not really a choice between free and unfree care. Rather, the choice is between a bureaucratic mechanism to ration care and allocate scarce medical resources and a price system to perform these functions. In either case, the patients will ultimately bear the costs, either in the form of prices (or insurance premiums) or in the form of taxes.

Recognizing the difficulties created when the government finances all medical care costs, few economists favor a NHI plan of the Kennedy-Corman type. Instead those who support an expansion of the government's role in this area wish to have patients continue to bear part of the costs of the care they receive. (In other words, a coinsurance rate or rates would be used.) This avoids the most extreme of the problems suggested in the preceding discussion, but if the coinsurance rate is set relatively low, health costs would certainly rise.

The emphasis on the cost of health care (which depends on changes in price and quantity) is intentional. Limiting the rise in health care costs seems to be the only goal that advocates of NHI all share, probably because it is a cost that seems of paramount concern to the public. Increasing effective demand (which all comprehensive NHI proposals would do) is a strange way to hold costs down, but it is conceivable that the regulatory mechanisms could offset the policy-induced increase in demand.

Catastrophic National Health Insurance

"Catastrophic NHI" is the name applied to government-financed insurance protection against major medical expenses. In effect, a large deductible is employed and the government would finance medical expenses only in excess of the deductible. If the deductible is set at $3000 per year, then families with expenses below $3000 would bear the entire cost (either directly or through private health insurance). When expenses exceed $3000, the government would finance the excess. With expenses of $5000, for example, the government would pay $2000 of the total bill. The deductible thus places an upper limit on the out-of-pocket medical expenses incurred by any family.

Within the general framework of NHI restricted to catastrophic coverage, there is still a wide variety of specific approaches possible. In particular, it is possible to vary the deductible with family income. A $3000 medical expense is not a financial catastrophe for a family with an income of $50,000, but it is for a family with an income of $5000. Recognizing this, most proponents of catastrophic NHI specify the deductible as some percentage of total income. If the deductible were set at 10 percent of family income, a family with an income of $5000 would have to pay at most $500 for medical care, but for a family with $25,000 the sum would be $2500.

The appeal of catastrophic NHI stems from an understanding of the economic principles of insurance. As explained earlier, insurance is most advantageous when it covers large and unpredictable expenses. It is this type of medical expense that would be emphasized by a catastrophic NHI plan. Moreover, because there are certain biases against private purchase of catastrophic protection in the present system, a role for government may be justified.

Note that the provision of catastrophic NHI would not directly resolve the problem of too much shallow insurance protection. It is possible, of course, that once the risks of major expense are covered, people would not find it worthwhile to continue to insure against moderate and predictable expenses. But the present policies that subsidize shallow coverage would continue to exist. Most supporters of catastrophic NHI also favor an end to tax subsidies for private health insurance as well as the preferential treatment given Blue Cross. If these actions are taken, it is likely that the introduction of catastrophic NHI would lead to a reversal in the type of insurance protection most Americans have. In addition, it is frequently recommended that Medicaid and Medicare be terminated, because the poor and elderly would be covered by the catastrophic NHI plan.

The federal budgetary cost of catastrophic NHI is relatively modest. Although the exact figure depends on the specifics of the plan adopted, it seems probable that the gross budgetary cost of providing a plan with a 10 percent deductible for all those not now covered by Medicaid and Medicare would be in the neighborhood of $10 billion. This relatively low figure reflects the fact that only a small proportion of families have expenses exceeding 10 percent of income, and for these families only the expenditures in excess of 10 percent of income would be federally financed. If Medicare and Medicaid were abolished, the net budgetary cost would be less.

Three major advantages are claimed for catastrophic NHI. First, it ensures that everyone will have the most important type of insurance protection. Government aid will be concentrated on those who would be most heavily burdened by medical expenses; no one would be impoverished as a result of medical bills. Second, it will encourage more efficient use of medical resources. This advantage depends critically on the prediction that people will cease to insure against modest medical bills, an outcome that may depend on changes in other policies, as already noted. If that prediction is valid, then market incentives will be restored as doctors and patients take better account of the costs of alternative treatments. Medical care practices will be determined by comparing the expected benefits of more expensive care with the actual resource costs of providing that care, instead of largely ignoring costs as is frequently the case under present financing arrangements. Note, however, that this argument is valid only for families spending less than the deductible amount on medical care. For families who spend more than the deductible, the perceived marginal cost of more or better medical care will be zero, because the government pays the bill, and this creates disincentives in these situations—presumably, however, in the small minority of all cases.

The third major advantage claimed for catastrophic NHI is that it would moderate and possibly reverse the inflation in medical care prices. This follows directly from the preceding analysis; removal of the subsidies implicit in existing shallow health insurance (public and private) would reduce effective market demand. Hospital care would be the most strongly affected type of medical care because it is now the most heavily subsidized; other types of medical care would be affected to a much smaller degree.

Probably the major problem with catastrophic NHI concerns incentive effects for the families with expenditures above the deductible. Because the government would pay all the bills above this amount, it would be necessary to use a regulatory mechanism to control costs. Although the problems would be much less severe than with comprehensive NHI, it would still be necessary to provide some more or less arbitrary political controls as a substitute for market incentives. Supporters of catastrophic NHI have suggested a number of ways to ease this problem, but it cannot be avoided altogether. For example, raising the deductible amount to, say, 20 percent of annual income would greatly reduce the number of people affected by the plan, but it would also reduce the insurance protection provided and increase the risk people would have to bear. Alternatively, coinsurance rates could be used. The NHI plan could have the family pay the full cost of medical care equal to 5 percent of income, then have the government pay half the cost between 5 and 15 percent of income; thereafter, the government would pay all costs. This arrangement would still place an upper limit on medical expenses equal to 10 percent of income but would limit the extreme disincentive problem to an even smaller minority of families who spend more than 15 percent of their incomes on medical care. Whatever procedure is used, it is clear that there is a difficult tradeoff between preserving incentives and providing protection against medical risks.

Proponents of comprehensive NHI emphasize one major objection to catastrophic NHI: Because the bulk of medical care would still be privately financed, monetary considerations might still deter people from receiving needed medical care. Financial considerations, they argue, should not be a barrier to medical care. This objection raises the question of what is meant by "needed" medical care. The quantity and quality of care that is "needed" are not objectively fixed—the demand curve still slopes downward, implying that the quantity people want to consume depends on its relative cost. If market prices lead some people to consume less medical care than others think they should, then the actual problem may be a lack of income rather than an inappropriate barrier to care. This line of argument may suggest that the poor deserve special help (possibly through cash transfers so they can afford more medical care), but it does not seem to provide a case for comprehensive NHI for the nonpoor.

The more fundamental point is that the choice between comprehensive and catastrophic NHI plans is not a choice between a system without and a system with barriers to the consumption of medical care. Both plans incorporate "barriers" to ensure that people will get less care than they would like at a zero price. With comprehensive NHI, the barriers could take the form of bureaucratic rules, quantity and quality limits, and queues. With catastrophic NHI, the barrier to the use of medical resources (at least up to the deductible amount) is the price, the same barrier that exists for most other goods and services. Basically, the choice between the two approaches to NHI turns on whether one wishes to use a price system or a bureaucratic mechanism to allocate the bulk of medical resources and ration care among competing consumers.

Supplementary Readings

Andreano, Ralph L., and Burton A. Weisbrod. *American Health Policy*. Skokie, Ill.: Rand McNally & Company, 1974.

Arrow, Kenneth J. "Uncertainty and the Welfare Economics of Medical Care," *American Economic Review*, 53 (5):941–973 (Dec. 1963).

Cooper, Michael H., and Anthony J. Culyer (eds). *Health Economics*. Harmondsworth, Middlesex, England: Penguin Books, 1973.

Davis, Karen. *National Health Insurance: Benefits, Costs and Consequences*. Washington, D.C.: Brookings Institution, 1975.

Feldstein, Martin S. "A New Approach to National Health Insurance," *Public Interest*, 23:93–105 (Spring 1971).

Fuchs, Victor. *Who Shall Live?* New York: Basic Books, Inc., Publishers, 1974.

Lindsay, C. M. (ed.). *New Directions in Public Health Care*. San Francisco: Institute for Contemporary Studies, 1976.

Marmor, T. "Rethinking National Health Insurance," *Public Interest*, 46:73–95 (Winter 1977).

SOCIAL SECURITY

The set of programs popularly known as "social security" actually has a far more imposing official designation: Old Age, Survivors, Disability, and Health Insurance, or OASDHI for short. Enacted as part of the Social Security Act of 1935, social security was originally designed to provide only old age or retirement benefits; it was known as OAI then. Survivors benefits were added in 1939, and the system became OASI. In 1954 disability benefits were included, and the system was thus OASDI until 1965, when Medicare was enacted and it evolved to OASDHI. Today social security is perhaps the most important, and certainly the largest, domestic expenditure policy in the United States.

Table 6–1 summarizes information relating to the growth in social security since 1945. Total expenditures have risen from $0.2 billion in 1945 to $106.1 billion in 1977, representing an average annual growth of 17 percent per year—more than twice the rate of growth in net national product. Consequently, social security outlays have risen from 0.1 percent of NNP in 1945 to 6.3 percent in 1977. Part of the explanation for this rapid increase lies in the fact that only a small number of retired persons were receiving benefits in the early years. Only 8 percent of people over 65 received benefits in 1945, whereas more than 90 percent do today. Of the elderly not receiving benefits under social security, approximately one half receive benefits under other federal retirement programs.

Social security outlays are financed by an earmarked tax on earnings. (An earmarked tax is one whose revenues must be used to finance a specific program, in this case social security.) Workers in jobs covered by social security pay a flat rate tax on earnings up to a maximum amount. In 1977, for example, the tax was 11.7 percent of the first $16,500 in earnings.[1] Thus, the tax liability for a worker with $7000 in earnings

---

[1] The tax rate for self-employed persons is 7.9 percent on the same earnings base.

Table 6–1. OASDHI System, Selected Data

Year	Spending on OASDHI (in billions)*	Spending as Percentage of NNP†	Percentage of People 65 or over Receiving Social Security ‡	Covered Earnings	Tax Rate
1945	$ 0.2	0.1	8	$ 3,000	2.0
1950	0.9	0.3	17	3,000	3.0
1955	4.9	1.3	40	4,200	4.0
1960	11.0	2.4	62	4,800	6.0
1965	18.1	2.9	74	4,800	7.25
1970	38.7 (31.6)	4.3 (3.5)	84	7,800	10.2
1977	106.1 (84.3)	6.3 (5.0)	91	16,500	11.7

*Social Security Bulletin, April, 1978, Tables M-1, M-2, pp. 36–37. Figures include cash payments plus Medicare. Figures in parentheses exclude Medicare payments.
†Economic Report of the President 1977, Table B-17, p. 276.
‡Estimated from Future Direction of Social Security, statement of Robert Ball, Chart 22, p. 51.

was $819, whereas for another earning $16,500 it was $1930.50. Those earning above $16,500 also had tax liabilities of $1930.50 because only the first $16,500 is subject to tax. Actually, the social security tax is composed of two equal levies (of 5.85 percent in 1977) each on the employer and employee. There is little doubt, however, that the economic effects are the same as if a tax of 11.7 percent were paid entirely by the worker. (We will come back to the question of the incidence of the tax in Chapter 13.)

Social security is still primarily a system providing retired persons with benefits both in cash (in the form of pensions or annuities) and in kind (Medicare). To receive these benefits, a retired person must have worked in a covered job and paid social security taxes for a sufficient number of years to establish eligibility. The exact size of the benefits received depends on the taxes paid, in addition to other factors. As a result of legislation enacted in 1972, retirement benefits are automatically adjusted upward with increases in the consumer price index.[2] Benefits can be increased still further by congressional action, but no additional legislation is required to ensure that benefits keep pace with inflation.

Other details concerning the working of social security will become clear as we proceed with the analysis. Although our emphasis will be on

[2] Although Congress intended benefits to rise in proportion to prices, the 1972 legislation contained a mistake that resulted in double counting of price increases. This problem, referred to as "double-indexing inflation," means that benefits rose faster than prices. We have not discussed this problem because it was widely regarded as an unintended error and one that was corrected in legislation passed in 1977.

the provision of retirement benefits, it should not be forgotten that there are also disability and survivors benefits. The analysis can easily be extended to include these programs.

Pay-as-You-Go Financing

It is important to understand that social security does not operate like private insurance. When a person pays premiums to a private insurance company to purchase an annuity, the premiums are invested and build up a fund that will be adequate to finance the annuity, or pension. When a person pays social security taxes, however, the taxes are not invested on his behalf; no fund accrues. Instead, the taxes are immediately given to those currently retired. Today's social security taxes pay for today's social security benefits. This is called pay-as-you-go financing to distinguish it from the procedures employed by private companies.

The Social Security Administration does, however, have a trust fund. In 1977 this fund contained about $35 billion in government bonds. Note that less than half a year's benefits could be paid from this fund. Only if people continue paying taxes into the system can benefits to the retired continue to be paid out, at least beyond the 6 months that could be financed from the trust fund. The trust fund is therefore of negligible importance in the financing of the program. The fund does, however, serve a function, namely, to act as a contingency reserve that can be drawn on if for some reason current taxes fall temporarily below current benefit levels.

Recognition that the trust fund is inadequate to finance future benefits has led many people to conclude that the system is "bankrupt." It is true that social security would be considered insolvent if judged according to the same criteria applied to private insurance companies. A private insurance company must have a reserve fund sufficient to finance its obligations even if it never sells another insurance policy. If the social security system required a fund capable of meeting its already accumulated obligations, that fund would have to be more than *$3 trillion.* Judged by private insurance standards, the social security system is bankrupt because its fund is only $35 billion instead of $3000 billion.

Fortunately, it is incorrect to judge social security by private insurance standards. A *governmental* system of providing retirement benefits does not require a large fund to finance future benefits; these benefits can be financed out of future taxes. Pay-as-you-go financing is a viable method for the government to use to provide retirement benefits. Workers currently in the labor force can expect to receive pensions when retired because the government is able to tax the working generation at that time to finance these pensions. Social security is simply a different method of providing for retirement, and this does not imply that it is an inferior method.

Social security is different in a number of respects from private insurance, and we must now consider what the economic consequences of these differences are. To understand its consequences, it is necessary to understand how it functions over time. A simple arithmetic example will be helpful. Assume that the adult population consists of only three people, one young, one middle aged, and one retired. There is zero population growth, and each person has a 3-year life span: young in the first year, middle aged in the second, and retired in the third. The retired person dies at the end of each year and is replaced by a new young person the following year. Each year the young and middle-aged persons have equal earnings, and these earnings grow over time at the rate of 100 percent per year (in other words, the growth rate of the economy is 100 percent annually). These assumptions are obviously unrealistic, but are made to simplify the computations and to allow us to highlight some basic relationships in the simplest possible way.

Table 6–2 shows an economy growing over time according to our assumptions. Individuals are denoted by the letters A, B, C, and so on. In year 1, individuals C and B are young and middle aged, respectively, and have incomes of $250 each. In the same year, individual A is retired and has zero current income. In the following year, C becomes middle aged, B retires, and a new young person, D, has joined the labor force. C and D have incomes of $500 in year 2, double the per worker incomes of the previous year. Note that we can follow an individual through his lifetime by looking along a diagonal: C is young in year 1, middle aged in year 2, and retired in year 3. Now let's introduce a system of pay-as-you-go social security in year 2. A tax of 10 percent is levied on the incomes of the young and middle-aged workers each year, and the proceeds are transferred to the retired person. The tax payments and retirement benefits are shown by the figures in parentheses. Thus, C and D pay taxes of $50 in year 2, and B receives $100. By use of the same tax rate in subsequent years, the total tax revenue and retirement benefits grow along with the economy over time.

Table 6–2. Pay-as-You-Go Financing of Social Security

Year:	1	2	3	4	5
Tax Rate:	0	10%	10%	10%	10%
Young	C 250	D 500	E 1000	F 2000	G 4000
	(0)	(−50)	(−100)	(−200)	(−400)
Middle aged	B 250	C 500	D 1000	E 2000	F 4000
	(0)	(−50)	(−100)	(−200)	(−400)
Retired	A(0)	B(+100)	C(+200)	D(+400)	E(+800)

We are now in a position to consider how people fare under this system. Initially, consider individual D, because D is the first person to spend an entire lifetime under the system. D pays taxes of $50 and $100 in years 2 and 3, and receives retirement benefits of $400. D's retirement benefits are substantially larger than his taxes. This is also true for later generations: E, F, G, and so on also receive retirement benefits exceeding previous taxes paid. This would be true too if they saved privately, because they would earn interest on their savings. The relevant question is how large the rate of return is under social security. In other words, what rate of interest would produce a $400 sum if $50 were invested for 2 years and $100 for 1 year? The answer is 100 percent: $50 invested at 100 percent for 2 years will grow to $200, and $100 invested for 1 year will also grow to $200, for a total of $400. Thus, individual D is effectively receiving a rate of return of 100 percent under social security. This is also true of E, F, G, and later individuals, as long as income continues to grow at 100 percent per year and the tax rate remains 10 percent.

It is no accident that the rate of return on taxes paid is equal to the rate of growth in national income. An important implication of pay-as-you-go social security is that it can provide pensions that reflect a rate of return equal to the rate of growth of the tax base—in this case, national income. In a sense, social security allows people to "share in the growth of the economy." Of course, in reality income grows less than 100 percent per year. Taking a long-term perspective, the U.S. economy has grown at an average *real* (adjusted for inflation) rate of about 3 percent per year over the past 60 years. This growth has resulted from a growth in output per person of about 2 percent and a growth in population of about 1 percent per year. (In a more elaborate model, the rate of return under social security depends on the sum of the rates of growth of income per worker and the number of workers, a sum that gives the total rate of growth of national income.)

Present trends suggest a slowdown in economic growth due in part to slower (and perhaps nonexistent) population growth in the future. An annual real growth rate of 2 percent per year may be a reasonable prediction of the long-term prospect. Thus, persons retiring in future years may expect to receive social security benefits that represent a 2 percent rate of return on taxes paid. (Some qualifications are noted below.) Clearly, the most basic question is whether this is a good bargain. Is a mechanism that yields a real annual rate of return of 2 percent an attractive way to provide for retirement? Could we do better providing for retirement in other ways?

Actually, many individuals would have difficulty getting a real rate of return as high as 2 percent if they saved privately. Historically, the real rate of interest on savings accounts and government bonds has been below 2 percent. Corporate bonds and home ownership have yielded only slightly more than 2 percent. Corporate stocks have yielded well above 2 percent if we consider the last 30 to 40 years, but below 2 percent over the past decade. These comparisons suggest that a real return of 2 percent is not really too bad.

There is, however, an error in comparing these private investment yields with the implicit return under social security. Individuals receive a low return when saving privately largely because the government taxes the return to capital investment heavily. (See Chapter 13.) The after-tax returns to saving, such as those cited, are quite low, but the before-tax returns are the relevant measures to compare to social security. The before-tax return to capital investment is a measure of how much private saving that is channeled into capital investment contributes to future output—it is a measure of the real productivity of private saving. Even though the individual does not realize the before-tax return, society does. And the before-tax real return to capital investment is quite high, averaging about 10 percent in the postwar period. Thus, if we provide for retirement by accumulating real capital, we can receive a 10 percent return on our investment; under social security the yield is only 2 percent. Such a wide disparity in yields has led several economists to urge that we rely less on social security and more on real capital accumulation to provide retirement benefits.

There are two important qualifications to these comparisons between private investment yields and the rate of return on tax payments under social security. First, the real rate of economic growth can best be viewed as the long-run *potential* return that is available *on average* to participants in social security. There is no guarantee that any specific individual will achieve exactly this rate of return. The reason is simple: Under pay-as-you-go financing, the benefits received in retirement depend on the taxes enacted by Congress at that time. If the tax rate is raised after you are retired, your return could exceed 2 percent. Conversely, if the tax is reduced, your return could fall below 2 percent. Also, there are other reasons why each person cannot expect a return exactly equal to the rate of growth of the economy; these stem from the basic fact that the government can change the level of benefits or the schedule of benefits for different persons in the future.

Second, our calculations were based on people who spent their entire lifetimes under the social security system. Individuals B and C in Table 6–1 did not pay taxes throughout their working lives. Individual C received a pension in year 3 after paying taxes for only 1 year, and B received a pension without ever paying taxes. The rate of return these people received on their tax payments is far greater than the rate of growth of the economy. (Note that this does not keep subsequent generations from receiving a return equal to the rate of economic growth.)

This is a very important point to understand. People who retire shortly after the system is implemented will pay taxes for only part of their working lives and therefore will fare extremely well. This will also be the result for people working and paying taxes during years when the effective tax rate is low who then retire and receive benefits based on a higher tax rate enacted later on. Refer back to Table 6–1 and note how low the tax rate was until recent years. It is no surprise that calculations of the rates of return for persons retiring in the 1950s, 1960s, and even the early 1970s show extremely high returns. For example, persons retiring in 1970 received on average pensions that represented a real yield of 10.6 percent on their taxes. In earlier years the implicit returns were even higher. The reason for these high returns is, of course, that these persons spent most of their working lives when taxes were low, yet their pensions were based on the higher tax rates in effect after they retired. These persons, the early retirees, are clearly the major beneficiaries of social security because they receive a rate of return far higher than can be achieved by subsequent generations.

Social Security, Retirement, and Work Incentives[3]

Social security can have important effects on the labor supply decisions of the elderly. If the provision of retirement benefits creates work disincentives that lead older people to retire earlier or work less, the elderly will have lower earnings. Thus, granting them retirement benefits will not raise their money incomes by as much as it would in the absence of a work disincentive effect.

There are two distinct ways in which social security affects the labor supply of the elderly. One way is through the earnings test. Retirement benefits are not automatically received when a person reaches age 65. Under the earnings test, a person's pension is reduced if earnings exceed a certain amount ($2760 a year in 1976). For each dollar of earnings above $2760 the pension is reduced by 50 cents. If, for example, a person would receive a pension of $3000 if fully retired, this means that he would receive no pension if his earnings exceeded $8760 a year. In effect, the earnings test is like a 50 percent tax rate on earnings above $2760 up to the point where the pension is exhausted. In addition, social security taxes must be paid on earnings, and perhaps other taxes as well. As a result, workers over 65 have little incentive to earn above $2760—unless, of course, they are able to earn more than the cutoff

---

[3] This section draws heavily on the excellent article by Colin D. Campbell and Rosemary G. Campbell, "Conflicting Views on the Effect of Old-Age and Survivor Insurance On Retirement," *Economic Inquiry,* 14(3):369 (Sept. 1974).

point ($8760 in the preceding example). Unless part-time employment is readily available, some workers must stop working to receive their social security pension.

A second way social security can induce retirement is by providing a pension that is large relative to potential earnings. According to the formula used to calculate retirement benefits, low income workers typically are eligible to receive pensions that are quite large in relation to previous earnings. For example, a married couple retiring at age 65 in 1975 with earnings in 1974 of $3200 would receive a pension of $2934, or 92 percent of previous earnings. In addition, the social security pension is not taxable, whereas earnings are. This makes retirement an attractive alternative to working. For higher income workers, the pension is a smaller fraction of previous earnings, so this effect is not so important for them.

Taken together, these factors can be expected to lead some people to retire earlier and to contribute less to their own support by working less after age 65. These effects are likely to be greatest for low income workers, and for those unable to find part-time employment on attractive terms.

Evidence tends to support these hypotheses. Labor force participation among men over 65 fell from 46 percent in 1950 (when only 17 percent of the elderly received social security benefits) to 22 percent in 1974. It would be a mistake, however, to conclude that the entire decline is due to social security. There had been a trend toward earlir retirement for many years before social security, reflecting growth in real incomes and the ability to afford earlier retirement. In 1900, for example, over 60 percent of men over 65 were in the labor force, and the reduction to 46 percent by 1950 cannot be attributed in any significant degree to social security. Nonetheless, a number of careful studies have concluded that a significant part of the sharp drop since 1950 is due to social security.[4]

The earnings test, which restricts benefits to those who partially or completely withdraw from the labor force, has been one of the most unpopular features of the social security system. Its rationale is explicitly redistributive. With a given amount of revenue available for social security payments, a reduction in benefits for higher income wage earners makes it possible to settle larger benefits on those without earnings— many of whom are poor. If the earnings test were eliminated, about $5 billion in additional benefits would have to be paid to those over 65 still working. Such a change would necessitate an equivalent reduction of $5 billion for those not working, or for those working and earning under $2760.

---

[4] See the evidence discussed in Campbell and Campbell, ibid., and in Michael J. Boskin, "Social Security and Retirement Decisions," *Economic Inquiry* 17 (Jan. 1977).

Those who favor elimination of the earnings test argue that those who reach 65 and have paid sufficient taxes to be eligible should receive benefits whether or not they quit working. In addition, they point out that the earnings test is inefficient because it stifles incentives and leads to a smaller total money income for the elderly.

Social Security and Saving

In the absence of social security, people have strong incentives to save part of their incomes during their working lives to provide financial support for themselves during retirement. Social security, by promising pensions to retired workers, alleviates the need to save privately and may therefore lead to a reduction in saving. Consider a person who would normally set aside 10 percent of his income for retirement purposes. If the social security tax rate is 10 percent, and if he believes the pension promised by the system is comparable to what his private saving would produce, then he will stop saving altogether. Social security pensions would simply replace privately provided support for retirement.

Figure 6–1 can be used to show the impact of social security on private saving in a more rigorous fashion. Assume that an individual has a total income of $0M$ over his working life. If he consumes his entire in-

Figure 6–1. Effect of social security on saving: individual taxpayer.

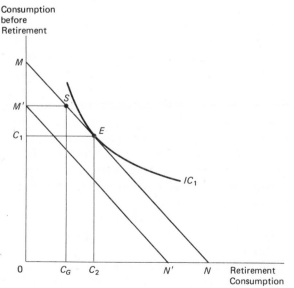

come, his consumption before retirement would be $0M$, and he would have no resources available to finance consumption during retirement. By consuming less than his total income before retirement, that is, by saving, he can accumulate resources for consumption after retirement. The budget constraint MN shows the combinations of before- and after-retirement consumption attainable; its slope reflects the interest return received on saving. With preferences shown by indifference curve IC_1, he would choose $0C_1$ consumption before retirement and $0C_2$ consumption after retirement. By saving MC_1 of his before-retirement income, he is able to finance consumption of $0C_2$ during retirement.

Now consider how social security will affect this individual. The social security tax of MM' will produce an after-tax budget constraint of $M'N'$. In return for paying the tax, however, the individual is promised a pension: We will assume the government pension is $0C_G$, or the same after-retirement consumption that the individual would receive if he saved MM' privately. As a result, his after-tax-and-pension budget constraint is $M'SN$. The individual remains in equilibrium at point E but has reduced private saving to $M'C_1$. In other words, his saving has fallen by the amount of the social security tax. (Note that it is not the tax alone that reduces his saving, but the tax combined with the promise of a future pension from the government.)

It might be thought that total saving is unchanged. After all, isn't the government now saving MM' for this individual? The answer to this question is unfortunately no. Recall that social security is financed on a pay-as-you-go basis, so current taxes are not invested but simply finance current benefits. Thus, the reduction in the individual's saving is not offset by any increase in saving by government, and the result is a *net reduction* in total saving. We will consider the consequences of a reduction in saving in the next section, but it should be added now that Figure 6–1 is an incomplete analysis because it fails to show all of the effects of a net reduction in saving. It simply illustrates the incentive a person has to curtail his own saving when the government promises to provide retirement benefits.

It should be noted, however, that there are some other factors that suggest that saving may not fall by so much as the preceding analysis indicates. One of these is the effect of social security on retirement; by inducing the elderly to retire earlier, the system produces a separate force tending to increase saving. An extreme example will illustrate this clearly. Suppose social security forced you to retire at age 40 on a very meager pension—because it would have to be paid for perhaps 35 years. In this case, you would have only about 20 years to accumulate sufficient assets to provide for a lengthly period of retirement. Consequently, you would increase your saving dramatically during your working years, much more so than if you were not going to retire until age 65. Although this is an extreme example, it clarifies how a lengthening of the period of retirement (fewer working years to provide for longer retirement) tends to increase saving. As we saw in the previous section, social security has had this effect for some of the elderly. The size of this offsetting effect on saving, however, is almost certain to be quite small. Recall that labor force participation among men over 65 fell from 46 percent in 1950 to 22 percent in 1974. Suppose that half of this decline is a result of social security; then the system has led to earlier retirement for 12 percent of the elderly. It is only for this 12 percent that the offsetting effect on saving previously described is relevant. Moreover, even for this group, there is no reason to suspect that the positive effect on saving of induced early retirement will offset the negative effect associated with the provision of retirement benefits. Therefore, it seems clear that the positive stimulus to saving due to induced earlier retirement will be minor in comparison to the negative effect, so the net result will still be a substantial fall in saving.

A second factor that mitigates the depressing effect of social security on saving is the fact that some people would save less than the social security tax in its absence. If a person would normally save 5 percent of his income for retirement, and the tax is 10 percent, then his saving will not fall by the amount of the tax. Saving will fall to zero, but that reduction is equal to half the tax liability. For people who would save very little in the first place, saving falls by less than tax liabilities. This is likely to be true for those with low incomes (and perhaps for those who optimistically expect to be supported by relatives when retired). Many people, however, would probably save more than the social security tax in its absence. Supportive evidence lies in the fact that large numbers of people continue to save even after paying social security taxes. The existence of people who would prefer to save very low percentages of their incomes is probably not of great importance—although it is a second reason to expect saving to fall by less than tax liabilities for some people.

On balance, the anlysis seems to suggest strongly that social security will substantially reduce saving, but what does the evidence indicate? If you have followed the analysis closely, you may be surprised to learn that saving as a percent of national income has shown only a slight decline since World War II. This, however, does not mean that social security has not strongly depressed saving. The relevant question is what the saving rate would have been in the absence of social security. If the saving rate would have increased in the postwar period without social security, then social security has significantly depressed saving by keeping the rate from rising. This is what some economists believe has happened.

There are several reasons why the saving rate would have been expected to rise in the postwar period. Not only was the retirement age falling, but also life expectancy was rising. There were also fewer working years in which to save for retirement because people were staying in school until a later age. With a trend toward longer retirement and fewer working years, saving for retirement would automatically tend to rise. In addition, rising real incomes over the period should have reinforced this tendency. Therefore, the small reduction in the rate of saving since 1945 may simply mean that social security has strongly reduced saving in a situation where otherwise there would have been a rising trend.

Recent empirical evidence tends to support this conclusion. Feldstein has estimated that personal saving was 50 percent lower in 1971 than it would have been without social security.[5] In addition, he cites evidence suggesting that countries with larger social security systems tend to have lower private saving rates, other things being equal.[6] Alicia Munnell has also found social security to have a significant negative impact on saving, although her estimates indicate a smaller effect than Feldstein's.[7] It must be stressed that this body of research remains quite controversial, and other research is currently under way. At present, indications are that there has been a significant negative effect on saving, but the exact magnitude remains in doubt.

Another piece of evidence bearing on this question should be mentioned. In 1947, when very few people received benefits under social security, families with heads over 65 had a median money income of 60 percent of the median income of all families in the United States. In 1972, after a tremendous expansion in social security benefits, the median money income of elderly families had *fallen* to 54 percent of the median income for all families. (These figures include only money incomes, not in-kind benefits such as Medicare. If Medicare were included, the percentage would probably be close to 60 percent for 1972.) How could such a massive increase in social security benefits fail to improve the relative position of the elderly? The most plausible answer would seem to be that the elderly provide less support for their own retirement as the government provides more. This could result from smaller earnings after retirement, less saving before retirement, or a combination of the two. These responses would support the theoretical analysis, although other factors may also be involved.

[5] Martin Feldstein, "Social Security, Induced Retirement and Aggregate Capital Accumulation," *Journal of Political Economy*, 92(5):905 (Sept./Oct. 1974).

[6] Martin Feldstein, "Social Security and Private Savings: International Evidence in an Extended Life Cycle Model," in M. Feldstein and R. Inman (eds.), *The Economics of Public Services*, an International Economic Association Conference Volume (New York: Halsted Press, 1977).

[7] Alicia H. Munnell, "The Impact of Social Security on Personal Savings," *National Tax Journal*, 27(4):553 (Dec. 1974).

Effects of Reduced Saving

It may not be clear why we have devoted so much attention to the way social security affects saving. If, however, social security reduces saving, the consequences are of tremendous importance for an evaluation of the system.

The act of saving, that is, consuming less than one's income, represents a reduction in the demand for consumer goods. When the funds that would have financed current consumption are put in a bank, or used to purchase bonds or stocks, they alternatively provide financing for borrowers to purchase capital goods such as factories, machines, computers, and so on. Thus, saving tends to be channeled ultimately into productive investment in real capital goods. As a result, saving tends to increase society's stock of productive capital, and this, in turn, increases the future productive capacity of the economy. The rate of saving is consequently one important determinant of the growth in real income over time.

Figure 6–2 illustrates this effect. In year 1 the production frontier relating capital goods and consumer goods output is shown as TT. Suppose that the economy operates at point E, with $0K_1$ production of capital goods and $0C_1$ production of consumer goods. Because of this level of production of capital goods in year 1, the society will have a larger stock of productive capital the following year.[8] With a larger stock of capital, the productive capacity of the economy is greater and production can take place on the new production frontier T_2T_2 in year 2. Thus, consuming less in 1 year enables society to have higher real incomes and consumption in later years by augmenting the stock of productive capital. The real before-tax rate of return on capital investment measures the quantitative tradeoff involved. If that rate is 10 percent, saving $1 today means that we could consume $1.10 a year later (or $0.10 every subsequent year) because real output is augmented to that degree.

Now consider the effect of social security. If social security is introduced in year 1, it will tend to reduce the aggregate saving in the economy. The economy operates at E' rather than E with a higher consumption of consumer goods and a smaller output of capital goods. (Taxpayers do not generally increase their consumption, of course; they reduce saving in response to the system. However, the retirement benefits financed by the taxes raise the consumption of retired persons, so total consumption rises.) A smaller output of capital goods in year 1 means the society has a smaller capital stock in year 2. Thus, the pro-

---

[8] Actually, some currently produced capital goods will simply replace that part of the capital stock that wears out during the year and so will not lead to a higher capital stock in the following year. Gross investment must exceed depreciation if the capital stock is to grow over time.

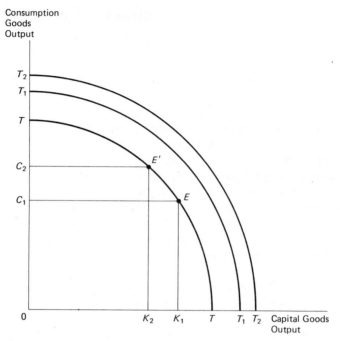

Figure 6–2. Effects of reduced saving.

ductive capacity of the economy is lower in year 2 than it would have been, and the production frontier is T_1T_1 rather than T_2T_2. Social security, by reducing the rate of capital accumulation, results in a slower rate of growth in the output of the economy. Increased current consumption tends to have a cost in the form of reduced real incomes in the future.

The effect of reduced saving is cumulative over a period of years, and the result of any one year's reduction will be quite small. The reason is that any single year's saving represents only a small increment to the accumulated capital stock of the economy. For example, the capital stock of the United States in the late 1970s may be valued at roughly $4000 billion ($4 trillion), yet saving in a single year may be only $150 billion. If social security reduced saving from $150 billion to $100 billion, the capital stock a year later would be $4100 billion instead of $4150 billion—a reduction of about 1 percent. However, social security reduces saving each year, and the cumulative effect can be very large. Indeed, Feldstein's estimates, although admittedly rough, indicate that the current capital stock would have been more than $6000 billion if social security had never been introduced. As a result, Feldstein es-

170

Table 6–3. Distributional Effects of Reduced Saving

a. Without Social Security

Year	1	2	3	4	5
Young	C250	D500	E1000	F2000	G4000
	(-25)	(-50)	(-100)	(-200)	(-400)
Middle aged	B250	C500	D1000	E2000	F4000
	(-25)	(-50)	(-100)	(-200)	(-400)
Retired	A (+50)	B (+100)	C (+200)	D (+400)	E (+800)

b. With Social Security

Year:	2	3	4	5
Tax Rate:	10%	10%	10%	10%
Young	D500 (-50)	E950 (-95)	F1800 (-180)	G3500 (-350)
Middle aged	C500 (-50)	D950 (-95)	E1800 (-180)	F3500 (-350)
Retired	B (+100)	C (+190)	D (+360)	E (+700)

timates real GNP is today 10 to 20 percent below where it would have been if social security had not reduced the nation's rate of saving.

We have been considering the effect of reduced saving on aggregate output; let's turn now to how it affects individuals under the social security system. Consider Table 6–3a. This table illustrates consumption and saving behavior in the absence of social security. Thus, individuals are saving 10 percent of their incomes during their working years and consuming the accumulated sums when retired. (It is assumed that the annual interest return on private saving is 100 percent, equal to the rate of growth of the economy.) Thus, individual C saves $25 and $50 in years 1 and 2 (and consumes $225 and $450 in these years), and consumes the accumulated sum of $200 in year 3. In this way, Table 6–3a shows what the lifetime consumption patterns of people would be in the absence of social security.

The introduction of social security reduces the rate of growth in incomes. Suppose the system begins in year 2, with individuals C and D paying taxes of $50 each to finance a retirement benefit of $100 for individual B. This does not reduce incomes in year 2, but the following year the capital stock is lower than it would have been, and the incomes of D and E are $950 rather than $1000, a reduction of 5 percent. A tax of 10 percent then finances a transfer of $190 to individual C. The reduced saving in year 3 results in the capital stock in year 4 falling farther behind what it would have been, and total incomes are then $1800 rather than $200, a reduction of 10 percent. In this way, social security gradually causes incomes to fall below the level they would have attained if saving did not fall.

Now consider how individual D fares under social security. D's consumption in years 2, 3, and 4 is $450, $855, and $360. Compare this to what D's consumption would have been without social security (from Table 6–3a): $450, $900, and $400; his lifetime consumption is lower under social security. For individual E, consumption is $855, $1620, and $700 with social security, but $900, $1800, and $800 without. Because social security causes real national income to grow less, the lifetime incomes of people are lower under this system. (The numbers in this example are based on the assumption that the real return on capital investment is greater than the rate of economic growth. Because these rates are estimated to be 10 percent and 2 percent, respectively, this is a reasonable assumption.) If Feldstein is correct, people beginning to work now will have, roughly speaking, 10 to 20 percent less income every year of their lives.[9]

Not everyone is harmed by social security; individuals B and C still clearly gain. They receive retirement benefits without having suffered a reduction in income before retirement. Individual B, for example, receives $100 in year 2, and can consume $200 in that year because he had also accumulated private saving of $100 prior to the beginning of the social security system. In general, people near retirement age when the system begins or as it is expanding rapidly in its early years (as in the 1950s) will be better off despite the slowdown in economic growth. Their lifetime consumption is still higher. Of course, exactly what groups of people fall in the category of gainers is, in reality, not clear, because this depends on the magnitude of the saving effect and its impact on real incomes. It is quite possible that all those who benefited from the system are now retired or deceased, and everyone working now and in the future will bear the cost as lower lifetime incomes.

Other Issues in Social Security

"Individual Equity" Versus "Social Adequacy"

The terms *individual equity* and *social adequacy* recur frequently in official discussions of social security. Individual equity refers to the degree to which an individual's benefits are related to taxes paid. If the retirement benefits were strictly proportional to taxes paid so that a person who had paid twice the taxes of someone else would receive twice the benefits,

[9] A reduction in saving will tend to increase the interest rate and reduce wage rates (because there is less capital per worker). Thus, there may also be some redistribution of the smaller total output from workers to investors.

then the system would embody individual equity. Social adequacy, on the other hand, refers to the welfare objective of assuring adequate benefits regardless of taxes paid.

These two objectives are competing goals and both cannot be fully realized simultaneously. If benefits are strictly related to taxes paid, low income families who had paid low taxes would receive very small benefits—a violation of social adequacy. On the other hand, if everyone received a sizable benefit regardless of taxes paid, then the goal of individual equity would be sacrificed.

As the social security system is actually structured, it represents an uneasy compromise between these conflicting objectives, with greater emphasis on social adequacy. The complicated benefit formula used to calculate retirement benefits is weighted in favor of low income taxpayers. In addition, there is a special minimum benefit paid to eligible retirees regardless of how little taxes they may have paid. Thus, benefits are a higher proportion of previous earnings for low wage earners than for high earners. This amounts to a redistribution of income among the retired, with those who had low earnings getting a higher rate of return on their taxes than those who had relatively higher earnings. Individual equity is not completely sacrificed, however, because benefits generally increase with taxes paid, but less than in proportion to taxes.

Although the intent of provisions favoring low earners is clear, some people have questioned the extent to which the system actually benefits the poor. Milton Friedman has pointed out that persons in low income classes have a shorter life expectancy and consequently receive benefits for fewer years. In addition, they generally start work at an earlier age than persons in high income classes, so they pay taxes for a greater number of years.[10] Friedman believes that these factors offset the advantages of relatively higher benefit levels so the poor do not gain significantly at the expense of the nonpoor. Most observers, however, believe that these factors only partially offset the redistributive effects of the benefit formula, but there seems to be little evidence on this point.

It is not clear how to draw a balance between individual equity and social adequacy. One recent change, however, has weakened the case for trying to achieve social adequacy through the social security system. In 1974 the federal government began a program called Supplemental Security Income, or SSI. This is a welfare program that provides cash assistance to the elderly who have little income or assets. In effect, it guarantees a minimum income, with the level of support approximately equal to the poverty line for a married couple. SSI therefore serves the welfare function of providing income support for the elderly poor. With this

---

[10] Milton Friedman, "Second Lecture," in Wilbur J. Cohen and Milton Friedman, *Social Security: Universal or Selective?* (Washington, D.C.: American Enterprise Institute, 1972).

welfare function served by a separate program specifically designed to deal with it, there is less reason for social security to be concerned with the same problem. Indeed, SSI has weakened the ability of social security to help the aged poor. Under SSI, if an elderly poor person receives a dollar more from social security, his assistance payment under SSI falls by a dollar. Raising social security benefits for those also covered by SSI therefore does not help them at all.

Treatment of Working Wives

Under present law, retirement benefits depend on marital status and prior earnings in a rather complex way. The retirement benefits for a retired, married couple in which the wife or husband did not work is 150 percent of the benefit for a single person with the same earnings. A married couple both of whom worked and paid social security taxes has a choice. Each can claim the retirement benefit based on his individual earning record, or the couple can receive 150 percent of the retirement benefit due one of them. In other words, a working wife can receive benefits based on her own earnings or a benefit equal to 50 percent of her husband's retirement benefit.

This treatment often results in working wives finding that the family's total retirement benefits are no higher than had she never worked and paid taxes at all. For a wife with low earnings relative to her husband's, total retirement benefits will be greater if she takes a benefit equal to 50 percent of her husband's benefit rather than the benefit she is entitled to based on her own earning record. Note that she would receive this 50 percent benefit even if she hadn't worked, so the social security taxes she paid did not increase the family's total retirement benefits. Many working wives view this as unfairly discriminating in favor of nonworking wives. (We are referring to work in the paid labor force; obviously, wives not in the labor force provide valuable services at home.)

Another consequence of this treatment is that retirement benefits can differ between two-person families with the same total earnings. In 1976 a family retiring in which the husband alone had worked, with average monthly earnings of $585, received monthly benefits of $546. A family with the *same* combined average monthly earnings, but with 75 percent earned by the husband and 25 percent by the wife, received monthly benefits of $455.60.[11] Outcomes like this are fairly common under the social security system. Again, they reflect a compromise between social adequacy and individual equity. Two-person families need more income

[11] *Report of the Consultant Panel on Social Security to the Congressional Research Service,* prepared for the Committee on Finance of the U.S. Senate and the Committee on Ways and Means of the U.S. House of Representatives, 94th Congress, 2nd Session (Washington, D.C.: U.S. Government Printing Office, August 1976).

than one-person families, so the goal of social adequacy suggests that they be given larger retirement benefits unrelated to taxes paid. This, however, immediately produces situations like those just discussed that are widely viewed as violating standards of individual equity. Any move to increase benefits to families with working wives must be paid for by reducing benefits to families with nonworking wives (or single individuals), thereby sacrificing social adequacy. It is easy to point out the tradeoffs involved, but it is much more difficult to make the final hard decisions. However the matter is resolved, it is clear that problems relating to the treatment of working wives have become more important in recent years because the labor force participation of married women has greatly increased. Fourteen percent of married women were in the labor force in 1940, but this figure had risen to 40 percent by 1970.

Incomplete Coverage

Not all occupations are covered under the social security system. Jobs specifically excluded from coverage include federal government jobs that provide their own pensions such as the civil service system. Members of Congress, the President, and the Vice-President are also excluded. State and local governments can select on a voluntary basis to have their employees covered by social security, and they can also withdraw from the system at any time after 7 years. Some $2\frac{1}{2}$ million federal employees and $3\frac{1}{2}$ million state and local employees did not participate in the social security system in 1975.[12] There are several other less important jobs that are not covered. In all, about one job in ten is not covered.

Incomplete coverage creates problems in part because of the frequent movement of workers between covered and uncovered jobs. A person can receive both a federal civil service pension and social security retirement benefits if he qualifies under both systems. To be eligible for social security benefits, it is only necessary to have worked in a covered job for 10 years (40 quarters). Thus, a person may work for the federal government for 30 years and receive a full pension, and also receive social security benefits by working 10 years in another job. More than half of the civil service retirement beneficiaries also receive social security retirement benefits. (Retirees receiving benefits from social security and another source are known as "double dippers.")

Double dipping often results in a windfall gain for federal as well as state and local employees. By establishing minimum eligibility for social security, they receive low retirement benefits from that system, but these benefits are often extremely high in relation to taxes paid. Recall

---

[12] *Reports of the Quadrennial Advisory Council on Social Security*, House Document No. 94-75 (Washington, D.C.: U.S. Government Printing Office, 1975), p. 34.

that the benefit formula used in calculating social security benefits is heavily weighted in favor of those at the low end of the scale. By meeting minimum eligibility requirements, a government employee gets the unusually favored treatment that was intended to help poor workers. It is clear that the government retirees are aware of this opportunity, and many have taken advantage of it. On the other hand, a former government employee may work for $9\frac{1}{2}$ years in a job covered by social security, pay taxes, but receive no benefits because he just misses establishing eligibility.

It should be noticed that this inequity (if it is that) is a direct result of the benefit formula that discriminates in favor of those who have paid relatively low taxes. Once again, it is the pursuit of social adequacy that is largely responsible for the problem. If benefits were strictly related to taxes paid, government employees would be unable to gain in this manner.

Even if the potential windfall gain did not exist, there is still a large incentive for people to opt out of the social security system if possible. Recall that the expected return on taxes paid will probably be in the neighborhood of 2 percent, and somewhat less for higher paid workers. Many private investments can be expected to yield a substantially higher return.[13] Thus, quite apart from the matter discussed earlier, it is not surprising that government employees wish to stay out of the system. Recognizing this opportunity, a number of state and local governments have elected to withdraw from the system in recent years.

What is wrong with permitting some workers to terminate coverage under social security? For that matter, why not allow anyone who wants to to withdraw? The problem is that social security is financed on a pay-as-you-go basis. If some people withdraw, taxes on remaining workers must be increased to finance current benefits. In the extreme case, if all taxpayers were permitted to withdraw, there would be no revenue to pay benefits to those already retired.

For a pay-as-you-go system to continue to function, the government must be able to collect the required taxes each year. This is impossible if people can withdraw any time they wish; mandatory coverage is an essential part of the system. Such a system can function, of course, if only certain narrowly defined groups are excluded from coverage as is now the case. The major issue involved in allowing some groups but not others to withdraw is one of equity: Is it fair for some to be required to participate in the system while others are not? A number of independent advi-

---

[13] Note that a person who withdraws from the system cannot fully avoid the cost resulting from the impact of the system on capital accumulation. Wage rates will be lower as a result of the reduced capital stock even for those who do not participate in the system.

sory panels on social security have recommended mandatory coverage of all jobs, but government employees have successfully opposed this move.

Demographic Trends and the Future

Because in a pay-as-you-go system of social security the funds are transferred from workers to those retired, the number of workers relative to the number of retired persons is an important factor. The more workers there are per retiree, the lower the tax burden per worker required to finance a given benefit level. Changes in the number of workers per retired person are heavily influenced by the pattern of birth rates—with a long lag, of course. It now appears that the number of workers per retired person will fall sharply in the first half of the twenty-first century, and this has serious implications for the future of social security.

After World War II the birth rate rose rapidly, and the total fertility rate (average number of babies born per woman during her lifetime) rose to a peak of 3.77 in 1957. This large crop of "war babies" will be retiring early in the next century. Since 1957 the total fertility rate has dropped sharply, reaching 1.9 in 1973. This rate is actually below the rate of 2.1 that would ultimately produce zero population growth. If the total fertility rate rises gradually to 2.1 by 1985 and remains at that level, we can predict with reasonable accuracy what will happen to the composition of the population. The resulting changes can be summarized in this way: Today there are about 30 retired persons per 100 workers, but by the year 2030 there will be about 45 retired persons per 100 workers.

The 1974 Advisory Council on Social Security has projected the impact of this demographic change on the future cost of social security. In addition to assuming that the fertility rate would rise to 2.1 and remain there, two other important assumptions were made. First, it was assumed that real wages would rise at 2 percent per year. (This is equal to the average annual increase from 1950 to 1973, but greater than the increase in recent years.) Second, the social security replacement rates were assumed to remain fixed at their 1975 levels. The replacement rates refer to the retirement benefit relative to previous earnings. This assumption implies that retirement benefits will rise along with increases in real incomes as the economy grows, but not faster.

The consequences of these assumptions (and several other less critical ones) are shown in Table 6–4. This table shows the tax rates required to finance the cash benefits of the system under the assumed conditions. Note the sharp jump in the tax rate in the year 2010: This is the year the "war babies" begin to retire. By 2030 the tax rate would have to

177

Table 6–4. Projected Tax Rates Needed to Finance Future Social Security Benefits

Year	Required Tax Rate
1985	11.0
1995	11.7
2005	11.8
2010	12.4
2020	14.8
2030	16.2
2040	15.9
2050	16.0

Source: Report of the Quadrennial Advisory Council on Social Security, p. 112.

reach 16.2 percent, compared to an actual tax rate of 9.9 percent in 1977.

The estimated tax rates in Table 6–4 do not include the taxes necessary to finance Medicare. The tax rate for Medicare, 1.8 percent in 1977, is expected to rise even more sharply than the rate for cash retirement benefits. Not only does the change in the age distribution push this rate up, but medical care costs are also expected to rise more sharply than the overall cost of living which produces an added upward pressure. The tax rate for Medicare is predicted to exceed 7 percent by the year 2030. If this occurs, the combined OASDHI tax rate would exceed 23 percent—nearly double its current level! And recall that this higher rate would only finance the same relative level of benefits for those retiring in 2030 as is being provided for the retired population today.

Making such long-run predictions is a hazardous undertaking, but unless the birth rate unexpectedly rises sharply in the next 10 or 15 years the age distribution of the adult population in the first part of the next century will show a marked increase in the percentage of retired persons. This is the critical factor that produces the rising tax rates.

As a result of this demographic change, workers will have to pay substantially higher tax rates, or retired persons must receive substantially lower retirement benefits than assumed, or some combination of the two. There seems little basis for predicting how the political process will resolve this issue, but because we'll be retiring about that time (2010) our interest is somewhat more than academic.

Proposals for Reform

The Feldstein Proposal

Martin Feldstein believes that the most serious disadvantage of the current system is its adverse impact on the nation's rate of saving.[14] Consequently, he has proposed a major change in the system that is designed to avoid this impact, at least partially.

Feldstein's proposal is to raise the social security tax rate substantially and use the additional resources to create a large reserve fund. Retirement benefits would not be increased (beyond already scheduled levels), so the additional taxes would not be utilized in a pay-as-you-go fashion to increase current benefits. In part the purpose of the higher current taxes is to permit a reduction in taxes in the future because the interest on the reserve fund will be used to pay part of the future retirement benefits, thereby allowing taxes to finance a smaller share of future benefits.

More importantly, accumulating capital in this way would add to the saving rate and lead to greater total output in subsequent years. For this to occur, it would not be necessary for the government to invest the reserve fund directly in real capital and thereby come to control a large share of the nation's capital. Instead, it could simply purchase outstanding government bonds. Private individuals and institutions that would otherwise have held the bonds would channel their investable funds into private investment. Therefore, accumulating a reserve fund would lead to an increase in the capital stock and higher per capita incomes.

For Feldstein's plan to operate as planned, it is important that the additional taxes not be used to finance higher benefits. If higher benefits were granted, this would simply represent an expansion in the pay-as-you-go system and would produce a further reduction in private saving. The relevant question is whether politicians could resist the political pressure to raise benefit levels once more tax revenue were available. We will ignore this problem and assume that Feldstein's plan is carried out as intended.

Not everyone would gain from this policy. A very sizable group would be substantially worse off. To see this, suppose the tax rate is increased from 10 to 15 percent for a period of 10 years. Thereafter, the rate can fall below 10 percent because interest on the accumulated fund can pay for some of the retirement benefits. Clearly, people near retirement will suffer under this arrangement. A person aged 55, for example, will pay higher social security taxes for 10 years and receive retirement benefits that are no higher than he would have received anyway. Some-

---

[14] Martin Feldstein, "Toward a Reform of Social Security," *The Public Interest*, 40:75 (Summer 1975).

one aged 50 will pay higher taxes for 10 years and then lower taxes for 5 years; he will probably also be worse off. A fairly young person will gain; the higher taxes for 10 years will be more than offset by the lower taxes for his remaining working years, and possibly his lifetime earnings will be higher because the real growth of GNP will increase as a result of higher levels of aggregate saving. The exact age at which this begins to occur depends on how long the higher tax rate remains in effect and the real rate of return on the new investment generated.

Obviously, the major group to gain is composed of future generations who do not have to pay the higher tax rate: Their taxes are lower over their entire lifetimes for the same retirement benefits. Moreover, their incomes will be higher due to the faster growth of GNP.

The consequences of Feldstein's proposal are almost the opposite of the consequences of introducing social security in the first place. As we saw, those who were relatively old when the system began were the major gainers, with all subsequent generations having lower lifetime incomes. With the accumulation of a reserve fund, those who are relatively old when the fund is being accumulated are the major group harmed, and the young and all future generations benefit.

The Friedman Proposal

Milton Friedman is concerned primarily with the infringement of individual freedom associated with the social security system; it forces people to provide for retirement in a way and on terms beyond their control.[15] He proposes that the system be terminated, but very gradually over a long period of time.

Friedman's proposal to phase out the system would work in this way. Retirement benefits already accumulated would be paid, but there would be no further accumulation of benefits in the future. People already retired would continue to receive their existing pensions (including cost-of-living adjustments). People near retirement would receive a sizable pension because they had already accumulated benefits implicitly owed them as a result of paying taxes over many years. Their pension, however, would be smaller than if the social security system continued on its present course. At the other extreme, young people just entering the labor force would receive no retirement benefits under social security because they would not have accumulated benefits as a result of paying taxes. Thus, there would be a gradual reduction in the level of retirement benefits, and after 50 or 60 years social security benefits would have fallen to zero. Note what this implies for taxes. Social security taxes would also gradually fall, but very slowly at first. Because retirement

[15] Friedman, op. cit., pp. 44–49.

benefits to those already retired were fixed, the required taxes would fall only slowly as retired persons died and were replaced by new retirees receiving lower benefits. The taxes paid after the adoption of Friedman's proposal, however, would *not* entitle one to added benefits on retirement; only taxes paid before that time would be accompanied by promises of future benefits.

Friedman's proposal would clearly increase the saving rate. Young workers would receive zero or negligible pensions under social security so they would be induced to save more to provide for their retirement, and similarly for middle-aged workers, because they too would receive smaller retirement benefits from social security under Friedman's plan. A higher rate of saving implies, of course, greater output and real incomes in subsequent years. In terms of its effect on saving and capital accumulation, Friedman's plan has the same effects as Feldstein's.

Who is benefited and who is harmed by Friedman's proposal? Future generations clearly benefit. They will have higher life-time incomes as a result of a larger real capital stock. Although beginning a system of pay-as-you-go social security harms subsequent generations, terminating that system reverses the process and leads to higher incomes in later years. Young workers will also probably benefit, but to a lesser degree. Although they will pay (declining) social security taxes over their working lives, the increasing capital stock will gradually raise before-tax incomes. Middle-aged workers are the ones most obviously harmed. They will continue to pay fairly high social security taxes until reaching retirement age, but their social security pensions will not reflect these taxes (only past taxes). Although there is also an offsetting feature from the greater capital accumulation leading to higher before-tax incomes, this offset will be small for those near the end of their working lives because it occurs only gradually over time. They are too old to receive much benefit from slowly rising before-tax incomes.

Thus, Friedman's proposal tends to harm middle-aged groups and benefit the young and future generations. Interestingly, it has the same allocative and distributive effects as Feldstein's proposal! Despite their apparent dissimilarity, these proposals produce the same broad general consequences. Although perhaps surprising at first glance, in both instances there is an increase in the saving rate, which invariably works to the advantage of the young and future generations. The only difference is that in one case the government collects additional taxes and invests them for the workers, whereas in the other case the workers are induced to save additional amounts for themselves.

An Underlying Issue

Although the broad economic effects of the two proposals are quite similar, there is one important difference. Feldstein's plan accepts the government's function to provide retirement benefits as legitimate, whereas Friedman's plan embodies the view that individuals should be allowed to provide for retirement as they wish. In choosing between these two proposals, it is important to consider the fundamental question: Should the government force people to provide for their retirement? Unless an affirmative answer can be given to this question, Friedman's plan appears superior.

One reason for compelling people to provide for their old age is paternalistic. It has been argued that people typically give too much weight to present consumption and not enough weight to future needs. Decisions to save only minimal amounts early in life may be regretted as one approaches retirement age, but by then it will be too late to remedy the situation. In this view, people must be protected from making costly mistakes by inadequately recognizing their retirement needs.

A second reason is based on protecting the interests of those who would save. If some people do not provide for their own retirement, then it is clear that the remainder of society will not let them starve. Instead, those who are prudent will feel compelled to provide for the imprudent. The imprudent, in other words, will impose a cost on those who are prudent. To avoid these costs, people may consider it reasonable to require each person to provide for his own retirement needs.

Both these positions are logically sound, but their significance depends clearly on how many people would, in fact, fail to make adequate provision for their retirement. If only 1 percent of the people would fall in this category, then these arguments are not compelling reasons to require all people to save. Unfortunately, there seems to be little evidence on this point one way or another. It should be mentioned that the fact that many retired persons today have no means of support except social security does not mean that they wouldn't have saved in the absence of social security. After all, the promise of social security benefits can be expected to lead many people not to make private arrangements for support in their old age and hence to become dependent on the system when they retire.

These two arguments for mandatory saving should be sharply distinguished from a third: Some people can't afford to save for their old age. This argument, although undoubtedly true, points out the need for a welfare program to help those who are poor, whether young or old. A welfare program or programs can and should exist to help needy people, but that is an issue that is entirely separate from the question of requiring the nonpoor to save.

If it is determined that many people would save insufficient amounts on their own, then Feldstein's proposal has the advantage of being capble of correcting the situation. (Of course, Friedman's plan could be modified to accomplish this by simply requiring that people save a certain part of their income privately.) Even if there are reasons to justify forced saving, the reasons do not imply that the government must provide retirement benefits. Furthermore, even if it is decided that the government should provide retirement benefits, that does not mean they should be provided on a pay-as-you-go basis. Feldstein's proposal reflects the view that government provision is desirable, but not on a pay-as-you-go basis because of its detrimental effect on capital accumulation.

Supplementary Readings

Boskin, Michael J. (ed.). *The Crisis in Social Security: Problems and Prospects.* San Francisco: Institute for Contemporary Studies, 1977.

Buchanan, James M. "Social Insurance in a Growing Economy: A Proposal for Radical Reform," *National Tax Journal,* 19:386–395(Dec. 1968).

Campbell, Colin (ed.). *Financing Social Security.* Washington, D.C.: American Enterprise Institute, 1978.

————, and Rosemary G. Campbell. "Conflicting Views on the Effect of Old-Age and Survivor Insurance on Retirement," *Economic Inquiry,* 14(3):369(Sept. 1974).

Cohen, Wilbur, J., and Milton Friedman. *Social Security: Universal or Selective?* Washington, D.C.: American Enterprise Institute, 1972.

Feldstein, Martin S. "Social Security, Induced Retirement and Aggregate Capital Accumulation," *Journal of Political Economy,* 82(5):905–926(Sept./Oct., 1974).

————. "Toward a Reform of Social Security," *Public Interest,* 40:75–95(Summer 1975).

Munnell, Alicia H. *The Future of Social Security.* Washington, D.C.: Brookings Institution, 1977.

GOVERNMENT AND THE DISTRIBUTION OF INCOME

CHAPTER 7

In a recent article on egalitarianism, *Business Week* reported that "the greatest single force changing and expanding the role of the federal government in the United States today is the push for equality."[1] It is probably true that a concern for the distributional consequences of government policies plays a significant role in shaping these policies. This is true not only for "welfare" programs, narrowly defined, but also for almost all government policies. Social security, for example, is not generally thought of as a "welfare" program, but clearly this policy has been designed, in part, to redistribute income in favor of those considered to be neediest among the elderly. The same thing could be said about innumerable other policies.

Examination and evaluation of the distributional impact of each policy separately can often provide a misleading picture. It is important to take a broader approach to the distribution issue because there are dozens of policies that interact and overlap, and it is the combined effect of all these policies together that is of interest. The impact of government on the distribution of income will be examined in the latter part of this chapter. The first matter to consider, however, is the justification for government to take income from some and give it to others.

Arguments Favoring Redistribution by Government

Equity

Probably the most frequently encountered rationale for government redistribution is the belief that great inequalities in income are ethically unacceptable. Why should some people have incomes exceeding

$100,000, and others struggle to exist on $5000? Compassion for those with low incomes seems to suggest that a redistribution in favor of the poor would be a fairer way to divide the total income "pie." Within this context, the equity argument is simply a value judgment that greater equality is a "good" thing. It is, however, a value judgment that many people make without hesitation.

As a value judgment, it is not susceptible to proof or disproof; it simply expresses a person's feelings. If the government takes $1000 from a wealthy man and gives it to a poor man, one person is benefited and the other person is harmed. (Some qualifications are considered later.) There is no objective way to compare the harm done to one person with the benefit received by the other, and only a subjective opinion can be expressed that the result is desirable or undesirable.

If everyone shared the same values, the equity argument would provide clear guidance as to whether and to what extent the government should redistribute income. Because people's values differ widely, however, it is clear that a general concern for equity does not provide much specific help in evaluating how much redistribution is desirable.

Public Good Element in Redistribution

Raising the incomes of the poor by making transfers to them may have the characteristics of a public good. If many of the nonpoor feel (for whatever reason) that higher incomes for the poor are desirable, then the income level of the poor is a good that simultaneously affects the well-being of many nonpoor persons. It is quite similar to national defense, because actions that raise the incomes of the poor benefit not only the poor but also some (or all) of the nonpoor. If the nonpoor have a sufficiently large demand for helping the poor, a redistribution of income from the nonpoor to the poor will benefit both groups. Under these circumstances, there is an efficiency case to be made for government redistribution.

If the nonpoor want to help the poor, however, why not make transfers individually on a voluntary basis rather than have the government perform this function? Where is the case for redistribution by government? The answer, of course, is the free rider problem. Too small a volume of voluntary transfers—just as with national defense—would be supported by private contributions. Suppose, for example, that each of 10 million nonpoor would be willing to pay $1000 if the combined incomes of the poor were increased by $5 billion. No nonpoor person would voluntarily make a transfer, because a $1000 transfer by itself could not make a dent in the extent of poverty—just as one car equipped with pollution controls would not perceptibly clean up the atmosphere. Yet all the nonpoor would be better off if the government levied a tax of

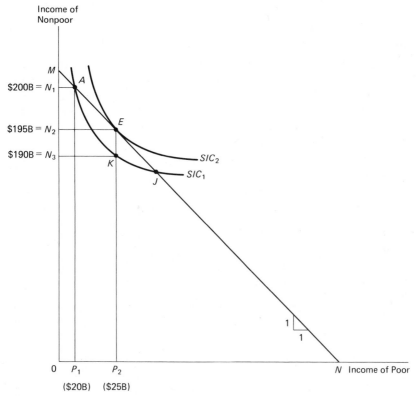

Figure 7-1. Public good aspects of redistribution.

$500 on each and transferred the revenue ($5 billion) to the poor; each of the nonpoor would obtain an outcome worth $1000 to him at a cost of $500. As this example suggests, there can be benefits to both the nonpoor and the poor from redistribution by government.

Figure 7–1 illustrates the gain to the nonpoor. Consider a distribution of income where the nonpoor have $200 billion and the poor have $20 billion; this is shown by point A. The constraint MN shows all the ways the total $220 billion in income can be divided between the two groups. SIC_1 is a social indifference curve for the nonpoor; the slope shows how much of their income they are willing to give up to achieve a higher income for the poor. (This is a social indifference curve for a public good, so its slope reflects the *sum* of the MRS's of all the nonpoor.) The slope of SIC_1 at point A shows that the nonpoor are willing to pay $10 billion to raise the income of the poor by $5 billion. Thus, a transfer of $5 billion will benefit the nonpoor: they can attain point E on SIC_2 by giving up $5 billion of their income and "purchasing" $5 billion more income for the poor. Although the indifference curve for

187

the poor is not drawn in (the *SIC* curves show the welfare effect for the nonpoor only), they will also obviously benefit from having $5 billion more income.

This analysis suggests that some redistribution may be mutually beneficial to all groups in society, but it does *not* determine what is the "best" distribution of income. Point *E* in Figure 7–1 shows the distribution preferred by the nonpoor only; the poor will clearly prefer a distribution farther down the *EN* segment of the constraint. A further redistribution (beyond point *E*) will benefit the poor and harm the nonpoor. An efficiency criterion cannot judge the merit of this further redistribution; it is akin to a movement along a utility frontier where one person or group benefits at the expense of another.

Recall that this entire analysis is based on the assumption that the nonpoor are willing to pay something to increase the incomes of the poor. It is likely that many people share this type of feeling.[2] The relevant question, of course, is how much it is worth to the nonpoor as a group to help the poor. Because "helping the poor" is a public good for those who share this feeling, the problems of determining the demand curve for a public good make it difficult to answer this question precisely. It seems fairly clear, however, that in the United States we have moved well into the *EN* portion of the constraint in Figure 7–1. (This is likely because the political process requires less than unanimous agreement to enact redistributional programs.)

Insurance

Redistribution of income to lower income groups may provide some other benefits to those who pay taxes to finance this redistribution. Even if taxpayers don't care about the poor per se, it may still be in their interest to support a system of transfers. There are several possible reasons for this. One is that the people who are currently nonpoor bear a risk that they could become poor in the future. Bad health, accidents, or technological progress that wipes out the demand for a particular skill can impoverish anyone. A system of government redistribution to the poor acts as a type of insurance for the nonpoor; if misfortune strikes, they will be eligible for financial assistance. Insurance protection is a benefit to the nonpoor even if they never receive benefits, just as health insurance is worthwhile even if you never become ill. What type of redistributional programs would be supported by this consideration, however, is not entirely clear.

---

[2] The equity argument for redistribution may be closely related to this public goods argument. If the view that equity requires a redistribution from the nonpoor to the poor is shared by many of the nonpoor, and the nonpoor are willing to pay to achieve greater equity, then the common goal of more equity is a public good.

A similar benefit for the nonpoor occurs if redistribution leads to a reduction in crime, riots, or social unrest. This consideration was stressed during the wave of riots that occurred during the late 1960s. Redistribution may be a way of buying off potential criminals and thereby purchasing security. It is not clear how quantitatively important this type of effect is. Crime has increased dramatically in recent decades at the same time that the volume of redistribution has risen enormously (not that causation should necessarily be inferred). Many scholars, notably de Tocqueville, have observed that the closer we move to equality, the more remaining inequalities are resented. If so, redistribution may not lead to a more stable society. In addition, it should be noted that there are other ways besides redistribution to deter criminal activity, and there is no reason to think that redistribution is the least costly way of dealing with crime.

Political Power

"One man, one vote" is a phrase sometimes used to describe the ideal that all people have equal political influence in a democracy. Yet it is widely felt that money can sometimes buy political favor that a mere vote cannot. Concentration of income or wealth in the hands of a few may confer political as well as economic power. Consequently, it is sometimes suggested that government should tax the wealthy heavily to deprive them of the means to acquire undue political influence. Note that this argument, in contrast to the preceding ones, emphasizes leveling incomes from the top for its own sake rather than raising incomes at the bottom of the income distribution.

As applied to wealthy individuals and familes, this argument is weak for two reasons. First, the problem identified is a weakness inherent in our political system. It would probably be simpler to redesign political institutions in a way to guard against excessive influence than to implement an equitable and efficient tax and transfer scheme to accomplish the same goal. Second, the argument ignores the free rider problem. There are many wealthy persons, thousands, or hundreds of thousands, depending on the definition. Government actions that benefit the wealthy (such as reducing the progressivity in the income tax) are like public goods for all wealthy individuals. It is, therefore, rarely in the interest of any one wealthy person to contribute money, time, and so on, in an attempt to influence legislation that will benefit not just himself but many other wealthy persons. This is one of the cases where the free rider phenomenon is a desirable influence.

Actually, the danger that money will buy political influence is more acute with labor unions and large businesses. These organizations already represent large groups of people, and the free rider phenomenon is not so much of a problem. It should be clear, however, that this issue is not closely related to questions concerning the distribution of income.

Arguments Opposing Redistribution by Government

Equity

Just as there are equity factors that favor government redistribution, there are also equity considerations that oppose it. Principal among these is the view that a person has the right to keep the income he earns. This is a value judgment, of course, and reflects the view that a competitive price system distributes rewards in a fair manner. If the system is competitive, resource prices reflect the contribution these resources make to production, that is, prices equal marginal value products. Thus, a person's income equals the contribution to the "total income pie" made by him and the resources he owns. If it is considered fair for a person to take out of the "total income pie" an amount equal to what he adds to it, then the distribution of income generated by a competitive price system would be equitable and any government redistribution would be inequitable.

Very few people subscribe to this value judgment without reservations because marginal value productivity and moral deservingness (whatever that is conceived to be) are not the same thing in the views of most people. A person with a skill or talent that is scarce relative to demand can receive a high income, irrespective of his moral worth as an individual. Conversely, a person without—for whatever reason—resources valued highly in markets will have a low income. Markets place monetary values on productive services, not on the people who perform them. Thus, the distribution of income generated by the market need not be regarded as fair unless one's sole criterion of fairness is payment according to marginal productivity.

It would probably be going too far to completely reject the market-determined distribution of income as having no connection with most people's conception of equity. After all, the market does tend to reward ambition, hard work, foresight, and perseverance and to penalize (or reward less) laziness, ineptitude, or dishonesty. This is perhaps the reason why the market system of rewards is not totally rejected.

Incentives and Economic Efficiency

Most government programs that redistribute income tend to undermine economic incentives and produce misallocations of resources. They are not, in other words, pure distortionless transfers, but involve some "leakages" that reduce the total size of the income pie. We have already seen examples of the welfare costs produced by redistributive expenditure policies in earlier discussions. The welfare costs mean that the average real income of persons is reduced by efforts to achieve more equality in the distribution of income.

An extreme example will illustrate the problem clearly. Suppose the government mandates complete equality of incomes. Every person's (or family's) income will be equal to the average, regardless of actual productive efforts. A guarantee of an income that cannot be increased or reduced by one's own actions provides no financial incentive to work, save, or bear risks. Who would work if working did not yield a higher income than not working? If no one worked, total national income would fall and average income with it. We would have equality of income, but the absolute level of income would be very low. Most, if not all, people would be worse off than with inequality but higher average incomes.

This is an extreme example, but it serves to point out the conflict between equality and efficiency in stark terms. Recognizing the consequences of complete equality, very few people advocate it as an ideal. It is still possible, however, to move part way toward greater equality without the disastrous effects hinted at earlier.

Economists tend to emphasize the efficiency implications of redistributive schemes. Pointing out that there is an efficiency loss from redistribution does not, it must be stressed, imply that the redistribution is undesirable. Efficiency is just one criterion to use in evaluating policy, and a moderate loss in efficiency may be a price worth paying for greater equality. Economics can be of assistance in evaluating redistributive policies by suggesting the likely size of the resulting welfare costs.

Political Aspects

Deciding that the market distribution of income is not ideal is not equivalent to deciding that the government should undertake to redistribute income. The political process that will determine government policy is itself an imperfect mechanism, and there is no guarantee that the policies finally implemented will bear much resemblance to the "ideal." In the context of our discussions of expenditure programs, we pointed out a few of the features in these policies that are widely recognized as inequities. Such results are to be expected; the relevant question is whether an imperfect political mechanism will be better than an imperfect market, not whether there is some conceivable distribution of income that would be better than that generated by the price system.

Resolving distributional issues places a great strain on a democratic political process because such issues are inherently divisive. For many of the services provided by government, people have a common or similar interest in seeing that they are performed well. Although not everyone will agree on the exact content of the defense budget, everyone agrees on the need for a major commitment of resources and on the goal of achieving national security. Such a limited degree of agreement is absent when redistribution is openly contemplated. Redistributive schemes inevitably benefit one group of people at the expense of another; there is no common interest because the interests of the groups are diametrically opposed. (This need not be true for a small redistribution of income if redistribution itself is a public good.) It should be no surprise if the uneasy political compromises that result are less than satisfactory for all groups concerned.

Weighing the Pros and Cons

Economics cannot demonstrate that one distribution of income is "better" than another. Indeed, the concept of an "optimal" or "best" distribution of income must be firmly rejected. Different distributions of income involve gains in well-being for some at the expense of others; to judge such changes requires relying in part on value judgments that cannot be objectively demonstrated to be true or false. This does not imply that economics cannot aid people in making better-informed decisions in this matter. There are many factual and analytical questions that can at least in part be resolved through the use of economics.

In view of the many factors to be considered, it is difficult for an individual to arrive at a well-reasoned and consistent view of what his values suggest is appropriate redistributive policy by government. In weighing the benefits and costs of redistribution, one piece of advice can be offered: Remember to evaluate these benefits and costs at the margin. The marginal benefit you perceive from the government's redistributing the first $1 billion to the poor is likely to be quite large: It could literally be a life-or-death matter. The marginal benefit of increasing the volume of redistribution from $50 billion to $51 billion will probably be much smaller. The opposite is true for the marginal costs. At low levels of redistribution, the marginal costs due to efficiency losses or inequities in government programs are likely to be small. The marginal costs of moving to complete equality will rise at increasing rates. Thus, marginal benefits fall and marginal costs rise with increased amounts of redistribution.

No suggestion is being made, however, that there is an objectively best amount of redistribution where marginal benefits and costs are equal. We are only considering what is a logical framework for an individual to utilize: The marginal benefits and costs are those factors that, according to your values, are advantages and disadvantages. Other people's will differ. Still, recognizing the importance of thinking in terms of marginal changes will forestall much unproductive speculation about whether the arguments for government redistribution are better or worse than the arguments against. The relative importance of the arguments depends on how much redistribution is being contemplated. If the government were not now redistributing any income to the poor, we suspect that virtually everyone would agree that some redistribution is desirable; marginal benefits are undoubtedly greater than marginal costs at low levels of redistribution. With the government already redistributing many billions of dollars annually, however, there would likely be much less agreement that a further increase is desirable.

This brings us to the question of how government is currently affecting the distribution of income. How unequally are incomes distributed, and how does government policy affect the degree of inequality? The remainder of this chapter is devoted to this surprisingly complex question.

Government Expenditure Policies and the Distribution of Income

Almost all government policies will have some effect on the distribution of real income because some people are benefited and others are harmed by virtually all government actions. To determine the distributional impact of all government policies is an impossible task as it would involve knowing the benefits each person receives from public goods. Consequently, we will concentrate on those policies that affect the distribution of predominantly nonpublic goods and services. In addition, our major concern will be with policies that affect the incomes of low income persons because most of the arguments imply that redistribution should favor this group. The most important way government affects the incomes of the low income population is through expenditure programs, especially those that provide either cash or in-kind transfers. Each year the Social Security Administration provides a compilation of data on what it calls "social welfare expenditures." Social welfare expenditures include spending on all programs that provide goods and services or cash to persons and families. In fiscal 1976 total social welfare expenditures by federal, state, and local governments were $331.4 billion, with the federal share equal to 60 percent of the total. This comes to an expenditure of over $1500 per person in the United States, or $6000 per family of four.

Table 7–1 gives a breakdown of social welfare expenditures in 1976 by major functional categories. The six categories designated in Table

Table 7–1. Social Welfare Expenditures, Fiscal Year 1976 ($ in billions)

Category	Total Expenditures	Expenditures from Federal Funds	Expenditures from State and Local Funds
Social insurance	$146.6	$120.8	$ 25.8
Public aid	48.9	33.2	15.7
Health and medical	19.2	9.4	9.8
Veterans' programs	19.0	18.8	0.2
Education	86.4	9.2	77.3
Housing and other social welfare	11.2	7.0	4.2
Total	331.4	198.3	133.0

Source: A. M. Skolnik and S. R. Dales, "Social Welfare Expenditures, Fiscal Year 1976," *Social Security Bulletin,* Vol. 38, No. 1 (Washington, D.C.: U.S. Government Printing Office, January 1977), Table 1.

7–1 actually include more than a hundred separate programs. For example, of the $146.6 billion spent on social insurance, $72.6 billion was spent on social security (OASDI), $17.8 billion on Medicare, $19.7 billion on unemployment insurance, and $24.4 billion on public employee retirement programs, with the remainder allocated to several smaller programs. The social insurance category accounts for the bulk of expenditures by the federal government, whereas education is the major area of expenditure by state and local government.

There are many programs included in this classification of social welfare expenditures not commonly considered "welfare" programs—social security, education, and veterans programs are obvious examples. The public aid category includes most of the programs that are designed almost exclusively to help the poor. Included in the public aid category are Medicaid, food stamps, Aid to Families with Dependent Children, and Supplemental Security Income, to name the largest. Nonetheless, it is important to consider all social welfare expenditures in an analysis of the impact of government on income distribution. Although social security, unemployment insurance, and public schools are not designed exclusively for the poor, such programs provide important benefits to at least some poor (as well as nonpoor). A poor family with two children in public schools, for example, receives services with a market value perhaps of $3000 per year. For many low income families, the public school subsidy is quantitatively far more important than the food stamp transfer.

Table 7–2 traces the growth of social welfare expenditures in recent years. In the 29-year period from 1947 to 1976, social welfare expenditures grew from $17.3 billion to $331.4 billion. Inflation is only partly responsible for this growth; 1947 expenditures stated in constant 1976

Table 7–2. Social Welfare Expenditures, Selected Years, 1947–1976*

	1976	1971	1966	1959	1947
Total social welfare	$331.4	$171.9	$88.0	$49.8	$17.3
From federal funds	198.3	92.6	45.6	23.5	9.8
From state and local funds	133.0	79.3	42.4	26.3	7.5
Total social welfare as percentage of NNP	22.3	18.5	13.5	11.3	8.3
Total government spending as percentage of NNP	37.4	35.4	31.3	31.0	20.4

Sources: A. M. Skolnik and S. R. Dales, "Social Welfare Expenditures, Fiscal Year 1976," *Social Security Bulletin,* Vol. 38, No. 1 (Washington, D.C.: U.S. Government Printing Office, January 1977), Table 1; other government documents.
* In billions of dollars; fiscal years.

dollars were $40.2 billion, so in real terms social welfare expenditures increased by a factor of more than 8 in 29 years. It is also interesting to note that state and local expenditures (mainly education) increased more rapidly until 1966; at that time federal expenditures were only slightly above the state and local share. By 1976, however, federal spending exceeded state and local spending by almost 50 percent. Note in particular the rapid growth in social welfare expenditures since 1966, especially by the federal government. Federal expenditures on social welfare programs quadrupled in the decade after 1966, a decade which saw national income only double.

Table 7–2 also compares these sums relative to other expenditure figures. Total social welfare expenditures rose from 8.3 percent of net national product (NNP) in 1947 to 22.3 percent in 1976. It took 19 years (from 1947 to 1966) for this percentage to rise by 5.2 percentage points (from 8.3 to 13.5), but in the following 10 years the percentage rose by nearly 9 points.

This massive increase in social welfare spending reflects two basic changes in government budgets. First, government spending has become increasingly important relative to net national product. Total government expenditures were only 20.4 percent of NNP in 1947 but rose to 37.4 percent by 1976. A second basic change is that a larger part of the growing government budgets—federal, state, and local—is being devoted to social welfare spending. This is particularly true for the federal government. Only 26.6 percent of total federal spending was devoted to the social welfare category in 1947, compared to nearly one half in 1976.

These figures indicate that a massive transformation has occurred in the content of public budgets since the mid-1960s. We are left now to consider how the vast increase in social welfare spending has affected the extent of inequality and the distribution of income.

The Distribution of Money Income

The most widely used estimates of the distribution of income in the United States are those published annually by the Bureau of the Census. Table 7–3 shows the Census Bureau's estimates of the percentage distribution of families by money income class for selected postwar years. As can be seen, even though more than half of all families had incomes between $10,000 and $25,000 in 1976, 3.9 percent of all families had incomes below $3000. At the other extreme, 17.8 percent of families had incomes above $25,000. Considerable inequality characterizes the distribution of money income.

In interpreting these numbers several points should be noted. First, the distribution reported in Table 7–3 is composed only of multiperson families—single-person families are not included. Second, this is a distribution of all *money* income. It includes not only wage and salary income, dividends, and interest but also government cash transfer payments such as social security, unemployment insurance, and others. Thus, the figures already reflect the impact of substantial welfare expenditures, yet 3.9 percent of all families had incomes below $3000 even after receipt of all cash transfer outlays. Third, the figures give incomes before payment of direct personal taxes such as income and social security payroll taxes.

Although it is clear that a sizable number of families had low incomes in 1976, the number was dramatically smaller than in earlier years. In 1947 nearly half of all families had incomes below $3000, whereas only 2.8 percent had incomes of more than $10,000. Since 1947 there has been a major decrease in the percentage of families with incomes below $3000, and an equally impressive increase in the percentage with incomes above $10,000. Inflation is partly responsible for the increase in

Table 7–3. Percentage Distribution of Families by Money Income Level, Selected Years, 1947–1976

Income Class	1976	1966	1960	1947
Under $3,000	3.9	14.3	21.6	48.9
$ 3,000 to $5,999	10.4	22.3	33.2	39.3
6,000 to 9,999	15.7	33.7	30.9	9.0
10,000 to 14,999	20.2	20.4	10.6	⎫
15,000 to 24,999	32.0	7.5	2.8	⎬ 2.8
over $25,000	17.8	1.7	0.9	⎭
Median income (dollars)	14,958	7,447	5,631	3,048

Source: U.S. Bureau of the Census, "Money Income and Poverty Status of Families and Persons in the United States: 1976," *Current Population Reports,* Series P-60, No. 107 (1977), Table 2.

the level of nominal money incomes; prices more than doubled between 1947 and 1976. Real incomes, however, still rose significantly; 15 percent of families in 1947 had incomes below $3000 in constant 1976 dollars, and this fraction had fallen to 3.9 percent in 1976. Median family income in constant 1976 dollars approximately doubled between 1947 and 1976. It is clear that poor and nonpoor alike have made sizable gains in real income over this period. Economic growth is, of course, the major factor responsible for this increase in real incomes. (Government cash transfers may have played some role in improvements at the bottom of the income distribution, but the impact has not been great.)

A different way of presenting these statistics is shown in Table 7–4. This table is constructed by grouping families according to whether they fall in the lowest 20 percent of the income distribution, the second 20 percent, and so on. Then the total income of all families in each fifth, or quintile, is expressed as a percentage of the total income of all families. Thus, in 1976 the lowest quintile had a combined money income of 5.4 percent of total money income for the entire population. This means that the average money income of families in the lowest quintile was 27 percent of the average income of all families. (If 20 percent of all families—a quintile—have 20 percent of all income, this implies that those families have an average income equal to the average of all families. For the lowest quintile, a percentage of 5.4 percent means that they have 5.4/20, or 27 percent of the average.) The top quintile had an average of slightly more than twice the average of all families, or 41.1/20, and the average income of families on the top quintile was 7.6 times (41.1/5.4) the average income of families in the bottom quintile.

Two characteristics of these numbers stand out. First, for each year they indicate substantial inequality in the distribution of income. This is

Table 7–4. Percentage Income Shares for Families, Selected Years

Year	Lowest Quintile	Second Quintile	Third Quintile	Fourth Quintile	Highest Quintile
1929	3.5	9.0	13.8	19.3	54.4
1947	5.1	11.8	16.7	23.2	43.3
1952	4.9	12.2	17.1	23.5	42.2
1962	5.0	12.1	17.6	24.0	41.3
1972	5.4	11.9	17.5	23.9	41.4
1976	5.4	11.8	17.6	24.1	41.1

Sources: United States Bureau of the Census, "Money Income in 1972 of Families and Persons in the United States," *Current Population Reports,* Series P-60, No. 90 (1973), Table 16, for 1947, 1952, 1962, and 1972. For 1976, U.S. Bureau of the Census, "Money Income and Poverty Status of Families and Persons in the United States: 1976," (Advance Report), *Current Population Reports,* Series P-60, No. 107 (1977), Table 4. **197**

to be expected because this table simply portrays the same data that underlie Table 7–3, but in a different form. Second, and more interestingly, there seems to have been remarkably little change in the relative distribution of income over the entire postwar years. The share going to the top quintile dropped from 43.3 to 41.1 percent, and the share of every other quintile increased only slightly. Note in particular that the share of the lowest quintile increased from 5.1 to 5.4 percent, a relative improvement of only 6 percent. Thus, although absolute incomes have risen for poor and nonpoor alike, the relative positions of the various quintiles have scarcely changed.

The lack of improvement in the relative position of the lowest quintile is a finding that has bothered and surprised many people. It is curious because low income families are thought to be the major beneficiaries of the massive growth in social welfare expenditures. Because social welfare expenditures as a percentage of national income have approximately tripled since 1947, it is reasonable to expect a significant change in the distribution of income. Why there has been no significant change is a puzzle to be considered in the following section.

One other set of statistics that is of interest in connection with the income distribution issue is the government's count of persons living in poverty. The government defines—admittedly somewhat arbitrarily— poverty levels of incomes for families with different characteristics. There are, in fact, 124 poverty levels that vary with the size of family, age of family head, and farm or nonfarm place of residence. For example, the poverty level for a nonfarm family of four, headed by a male, was $5674 in 1976. Families with incomes below their respective poverty lines are officially designated as poor. The poverty lines are adjusted upward each year to reflect increases in the cost of living.

Table 7–5 provides some interesting information about persons in families with incomes below their poverty lines. The total number of poor persons declined from 39.5 million in 1959 to 24.3 million in 1974. Note that most of this decline occurred before 1966, the year in which the rate of increase in social welfare spending began to accelerate sharply. Social welfare expenditures increased by $38.2 billion between 1959 and 1966, and then increased further by $151.3 billion between 1966 and 1974. Interestingly, the number of poor persons declined by 11 million between 1959 and 1966, but by only 4.2 million between 1966 and 1974.

Note also that the largest reduction in the incidence of poverty occurred in families with nonaged male heads. This is significant because nonaged, male-headed households is the one category that had no special cash assistance programs over the entire 1959–1974 period except for unemployment insurance. Government cash assistance programs had little to do with the impressive reduction in poverty—from 25.7 million

Table 7–5. Selected Characteristics of Persons Below the Poverty Level, 1974, 1966, and 1959 (in thousands)

	1974	1966	1959
Number of poor persons	24,260	28,510	39,450
65 years and over	3,299	5,111	5,679
Under 65 years			
Family with female head	9,891	7,841	8,115
Family with male head	11,070	15,558	25,695

Source: U.S. Bureau of the Census, "Characteristics of the Population Below the Poverty Level: 1974," *Current Population Reports,* Series P-60, No. 102 (1976), Table 1.

to 11.1 million persons—in this category. The decline can be attributed to economic growth and the higher wage rates and earnings accompanying it. By contrast, several cash assistance programs were available for the elderly and female-headed families (social security, Supplemental Security Income, and Aid to Families with Dependent Children), but these two groups taken together experienced only a slight decrease in the number living in poverty.

It should be mentioned, however, that many more persons would have been in poverty without existing government transfer programs. According to one recent estimate for 1976, 25 percent of all families had pretransfer incomes that would have placed them below their poverty lines. After receipt of transfers, however, only 12 percent of families remained in poverty.[3] In other words, about 13 percent of all U.S. families were made nonpoor by government transfer payments. Table 7–5, of course, includes only those who remained poor even after receipt of government assistance.

Nonetheless, it is somewhat paradoxical that the rapid increase in social welfare expenditures since 1966 has not led to a greater reduction in the number of poor persons. That and the unchanged relative distribution of income are paradoxes that will be resolved, at least in part, in the next section.

The Distribution of Net "Real" Income

Despite widespread use of the Census Bureau's estimates, it has become increasingly evident in recent years that these figures are inaccurate measures of relative living standards. One important defect in the Census Bureau's figures is that they measure only *money* incomes. Con-

---

[3] U.S. Congress, Congressional Budget Office, *Poverty Status of Families Under Alternative Definitions of Income,* Background Paper No. 17, January 1977, p. 27. (Henceforth cited as *Poverty Status of Families.*)

Table 7–6. Federal Outlays Benefiting the Poor, Selected Fiscal Years

	1974	1969	1964
Federal outlays ($ in billions)			
Cash payments	$11.9	$ 8.2	$6.4
Food and housing transfers	4.5	0.7	0.3
Education	2.1	1.2	0.1
Health	6.4	3.5	0.7
Manpower	2.2	1.4	0.2
Other	2.0	0.9	0.2
Total	$29.0	$15.9	$7.9
Total federal cash transfers	$11.9	$ 8.2	$6.4
Total federal in-kind transfers	$17.1	$ 7.7	$1.5

Source: United States Department of Health, Education, and Welfare, Office of the Assistant Secretary for Planning and Evaluation, Office of Program Systems, "Federal Outlays Benefiting the Poor—Summary Tables" (March 1974), Table 1.

sequently, in-kind subsidies such as food stamps are not counted as income to the recipients. Clearly, however, in-kind transfers should be counted. If a $1000 cash transfer to a poor person—who proceeds to spend it on food, housing, and medical care—reduces poverty, then so does $1000 worth of these goods provided outright or at subsidized prices. Although in-kind transfers are often worth less to the recipient than a cash transfer of the same cost, this is no reason to disregard them completely.[4]

Table 7–6 shows the importance of in-kind transfers to the poor. Total federal outlays benefiting the poor are given by program categories. The "poor" referred to in the table are those still officially "poor" *after* receipt of all government transfers. (Thus, the $6.4 billion spent on health programs in 1974 is not a measure of total federal spending in the health area, but only that portion reaching the official poverty population.) As shown in the table, there has been not only a significant increase in total federal transfers to the poor—from $7.9 billion in 1964 to $29.0 billion in 1974—but also a marked change in their composition. In-kind transfers have become increasingly important, rising by a factor of more than 11, whereas cash transfers have only doubled. The most rapidly increasing federal welfare programs have been in-kind transfers, yet these transfers do not reduce poverty or inequality as officially defined in terms of money incomes.

If in-kind transfers were counted as income, the number of poor persons would fall drastically. In 1974 the official "poverty gap" was $14 billion. This means that the total money incomes of the poor fell $14

---

[4]Estimates of in-kind transfers to the poor given in this section are based on the market value of these transfers, not the actual benefit as perceived by recipients.

billion short of their combined poverty lines. Because federal in-kind transfers to the poor in 1974 equaled $17 billion, counting these transfers as income would more than eliminate the poverty gap. In other words, the average income of officially poor families if in-kind transfers were included would actually be above the poverty line. (This does not mean that every poor family would have an income above its poverty line; some would be raised well above their poverty lines, and others would still fall short.) Moreover, these figures do not include in-kind transfers provided by state and local governments.

Two recent detailed studies of the distributional impact of selected in-kind transfers by Timothy Smeeding and by the Congressional Budget Office tend to support this conclusion.[5] These studies found that the number of poor persons fell by 50 to 60 percent with the inclusion of in-kind transfers. Because these studies do not consider education (it can be argued that in-kind benefits from education should not be counted[6]), and include only half of all the in-kind transfers, it is likely that the poverty-reducing effect of in-kind transfers is understated. Thus, according to the official definition, there is very little poverty in the United States; it only remains for our accounting procedures to be modified to record this achievement. Those who are still poor could be raised out of poverty through increased transfers financed by reducing the transfers to those who are raised far above their poverty lines.

Some people object to an emphasis on the number of poor persons as an index of the degree of poverty because poverty lines are fixed in terms of real incomes. Consequently, the poverty level of income falls as a percentage of average income when the average rises over time as a result of economic growth. This suggests that it may be better alternatively to consider what happens to the relative shares of income over time. As shown in Table 7–4, the Census Bureau reports little change in the share of income going to each quintile over the postwar period. There are, however, several significant defects in these statistics.

Just as with the definition of poverty, the Census Bureau's income distribution figures record only money incomes. If education benefits and other in-kind transfers were counted as income, as they should be, the degree of inequality would be less. (More than one half of the $331 billion in social welfare spending in 1976 fell into these categories and therefore was not counted as income by the Census Bureau.) In addition, the Census Bureau's figures measure money income before payment of

[5] *Poverty Status of Families* and Timothy Smeeding, *Measuring the Economic Welfare of Low-Income Households, and the Anti-poverty Effectiveness of Cash and Non-cash Transfer Programs*, unpublished Ph.D. dissertation, University of Wisconsin, Madison, 1975.

[6] When the poverty lines were officially formulated, public schools were already generally available to the poor. Thus, the poverty lines presuppose the availability of schools. The same is not true of other in-kind transfers.

taxes. Because the highest quintile pays about 60 percent of all income and payroll taxes, compared with 1 percent for the lowest quintile, subtracting taxes would result in greater equality in after-tax incomes. Finally, the lowest 20 percent of families actually contain less than 20 percent of the population—about 17 percent, in fact. Low income families are typically of smaller size; average family size in the lowest quintile is about 2.95 persons compared with 3.75 persons for the highest quintile. Comparing per capita incomes in the various quintiles would also indicate less inequality.

Table 7–7 gives the percentage shares of net income received by each quintile after adding in-kind transfers and education, subtracting federal income and social insurance taxes, and converting to a per capita distribution for the years 1952, 1962, and 1972. There are two striking differences between the adjusted and unadjusted (Census Bureau) estimates. First, the adjusted figures display far greater equality in each year. In 1972, for example, the share of the lowest quintile, at 11.7 percent, was more than double the official estimate. In addition, according to the Census Bureau's figures, the ratio of average money income in the top quintile to that in the bottom quintile was 7.7. After the adjustments, the ratio was less than 3. The second difference is that the adjusted figures imply a significant trend toward equality between 1952 and 1972. The share of the lowest quintile was increased from 8.1 percent in 1952 to 11.7 percent in 1972, an improvement of 44 percent in the relative position of low income families. This trend is largely the result of rapid increases in government expenditures on education and in-kind transfers.

The adjusted figures in Table 7–7 are only rough estimates. Although scholars working in this area are in wide agreement that the Census Bureau figures overstate the extent of inequality and understate the trend toward equality, the magnitude of these biases is still in dispute. Some believe, for example, that the trend toward greater equality is less pronounced than indicated in Table 7–7. The uncertainty surrounding this issue is largely (but not wholly) the result of a lack of hard data concerning how nonmoney incomes (especially government in-kind transfers) are

Table 7–7. Adjusted Percentage Income Shares for Families, Selected Years

Year	Lowest Quintile	Second Quintile	Third Quintile	Fourth Quintile	Highest Quintile
1952	8.1	14.2	17.8	23.2	36.7
1962	8.8	14.4	18.2	23.1	35.4
1972	11.7	15.0	18.2	22.3	32.8

Source: Derived from estimates presented in E. K. Browning's "The Trend Toward Equality in the Distribution of Net Income," *Southern Economic Journal* (July 1976).

distributed. In addition, there are still other omissions from the Census Bureau figures that bias their estimates in the opposite direction from those discussed. Fringe benefits to employees (e.g., employer-financed pension contributions or health insurance) are in-kind income that is not counted. Because only a small share of the lowest quintile is employed (and those who are employed are less likely to hold the types of jobs that provide large fringe benefits), including fringe benefits as income might tend to reduce relatively the income share going to the lowest quintile. Further problems in the measurement of inequality will be considered in the next section.

The recent Congressional Budget Office (CBO) study provides detailed estimates of the distributional impact of cash transfers, some in-kind transfers, and personal taxes for 1976. The major results of this study are presented in Table 7–8. First, consider the final percentage distribution of posttax/posttransfer income: The lowest quintile is estimated to have 7.2 percent of total net income and the top quintile 41.3 percent. These figures suggest substantially greater inequality than the figures for 1972 in Table 7–7. The reason is not, however, that there were any major changes in the distribution between 1972 and 1976; there probably weren't. Instead, there are two major differences in the adjustments made to the original money income distributions in comparison to Table 7–7.

The CBO report estimates the distribution of only selected in-kind transfers totaling $41 billion in 1976. Actually, there were about $165 billion in government in-kind transfers in that year; the major omission was public education ($86 billion). Although the benefits of excluded expenditure programs were not so heavily concentrated on low income families as those included,[7] there is no doubt that the final distribution would be somewhat more equal if all were counted. A second difference between the CBO estimates and those in Table 7–7 is that the CBO made no adjustment for differences in family size among the quintiles. As a result of counting an unrelated individual as a single-person family (unrelated individuals were not included in Table 7–7), the average family size in the lowest quintile is about half that in the highest quintile. The lowest 20 percent of families according to this definition of a family contain only 13.8 percent of the population. Consequently, the bottom 13.8 percent of the population received 7.2 percent of total net income, and the top 26 percent received 41.3 percent. If the CBO figures were adjusted to take account of these two defects, it is probable that the final distribution would display approximately the same degree of income equality as shown in Table 7–7 for 1972.

---

[7] The in-kind transfers that were counted in the CBO report were food stamps, child nutrition, housing assistance, Medicaid, and Medicare. All of these transfers tend to be heavily concentrated on low income groups.

Table 7–8. Distribution of Family Income, 1976 ($ in billions)

Quintile	Pretax/ Pretransfer Income	Percentage Shares, Pretax/ Pretransfer Income	Cash Assist- ance Added	In-Kind Assist- ance Added	Posttax/ Post- transfer Income	Percentage Shares, Posttax/ Post- transfer Income
Lowest 20%	$ 3.3	0.3	54.0	75.8	75.1	7.2
Second 20%	76.3	7.2	115.2	126.0	119.7	11.5
Third 20%	173.7	16.3	195.5	199.8	172.6	16.6
Fourth 20%	276.1	26.0	291.9	294.1	243.7	23.4
Highest 20%	534.1	50.2	549.1	550.9	429.7	41.3

Source: Congressional Budget Office, "Poverty Status of Families Under Alternative Definitions of Income," Background Paper No. 17, January 13, 1977, Table A-4.

The CBO's estimates also provide interesting information about the distribution of taxes and transfers by income class. The bottom two quintiles together (which contain less than 30 percent of the population) received a total of $122.2 billion in cash and in-kind transfers and paid a total of $7.0 billion in personal taxes. Thus, there was a *net* redistribution of $115.2 billion in their favor[8]—more than the total amount ($93 billion) spent on national defense. This is about $1800 per person, or $7200 per family of four. The government net redistribution alone is sufficient to move all these families above their poverty lines without including the $79.6 billion in pretax/pretransfer income received by these families! The net transfer to the lowest quintile is almost $3000 per person, or $12,000 per family of four. There is a correspondingly large net transfer away from the upper quintiles, primarily the upper two. The upper two quintiles receive cash and in-kind transfers equal to $34.8 billion, but pay personal taxes of $161.6 billion—a net loss of $126.8 billion.[9] Of this, $104.4 billion is a net transfer away from the highest quintile alone.

It is also of interest to note that the bottom quintile is almost totally dependent on government as a source of income—95 percent of its total net income takes the form of government transfers. The interpretation of this fact, however, is not obvious. Although the lowest quintile has a

[8] Actually, this figure may not measure exactly the net redistribution because of two omissions. First, some transfers were not counted, as noted already. Second, not all taxes were counted, either; only income and payroll taxes were included. It is our judgment that these two omissions—which work in offsetting directions—are of approximately equal size. If so, then the $115 billion figure measures the net redistribution fairly accurately.

[9] This is not equal to the net transfer to the lowest two quintiles for the reasons mentioned in the last footnote. In addition, not all taxes finance transfers: Some finance public goods whose benefits are not allocated in the table.

pretax/pretransfer share of only 0.3 percent, this does not mean that this quintile would have had such a small income in the absence of government transfers and taxes. The reason is that the pretax/pretransfer income for these families is likely to fall in response to redistribution. As explained in the last chapter, the government transfers many billions of dollars to the elderly, but the relative economic position of the elderly has not improved significantly because older people have responded by reducing their own sources of support, principally by working and saving less. The same type of reaction is likely to occur in other cases. For this reason, the pretax/pretransfer distribution tends to become more unequal in response to government redistribution.

Thus, a net redistribution of $115.2 billion to the lowest two quintiles does not mean that their pretransfer incomes would be raised by this amount over what they would have been in the absence of these policies. This is why some economists are dubious about how much net improvement is produced by government redistribution. Nonetheless, we think it is highly probable that there has been a significant improvement in the relative distribution of real income, although by exactly how much is an unresolved empirical question.

Other Problems in Measuring the Degree of Income Inequality

The concept of income used so far is essentially the notion of the market value of goods and services that were (or could have been) consumed during a period of 1 year. For a number of reasons, this is actually too narrow a concept on which to base ethical judgments about inequality. Differences in net (cash plus in-kind) incomes in a particular year may not imply inequality in a meaningful sense.

Consider the way differences in preferences can affect measured net incomes. For a group of people with equal *abilities* to earn incomes, there will nonetheless tend to be differences in actual incomes earned. Some people, for example, may choose to become teachers even though they could have received higher money incomes by working for a private business. In such a case, the difference in money incomes between teachers and business employees is called an "equalizing income differential." This means that inequality in money incomes is necessary to equalize the net attractiveness of the jobs, that is, to make real incomes equal. Some, but certainly not all, of the differences in money incomes reflect differences of this sort.

Another way differences in preferences can lead to differences in money incomes without implying any meaningful inequality is by producing differences in the amount of leisure time (meaning all time not spent working for money wages) that families have. Consider two people who can work at the same wage rate; one may choose to work shorter hours because he values leisure more highly (or, equivalently, dislikes work more). There would be a difference in money incomes, but most would agree that their real incomes are the same. In short, leisure time is a valuable consumption item, just as food or housing, and it should be considered a part of a person's real income. In addition to different hours of work in different jobs, two significant sources of variation in leisure time deserve explicit mention because they are frequently overlooked: the retirement decision, and the decision of several members of a family to work. Retirement is an explicit decision to sacrifice money income in return for more leisure, as is the decision of a wife to work in the home rather than for money wages in the market. Both phenomena lead to differences in money incomes in some situations where real incomes are not different.

Exactly how to place a monetary value on leisure time is a difficult theoretical and empirical problem, but it seems clear that ignoring leisure altogether will overstate the degree of inequality. Persons and families ranked lower in the distribution of money income tend to consume more leisure. For example, the average adult in the lowest quintile of families worked only 14 weeks in 1974, whereas the average adult in the highest quintile worked 39 weeks. Unfortunately, these figures fail to distinguish between part-time and full-time work; anyone who earned $1 or more during a week is considered employed. Thus, the figures should be interpreted with some care. A glance back to Table 7–8, however, supports the view that the amount of labor supplied is quite small in the lowest quintile. A pretax/pretransfer income of $3.3 billion could be earned by 750,000 people who work full time at the minimum wage. Because there are 25 million people in the lowest quintile, clearly only a small percentage work. This should come as no surprise because just under 50 percent of (multiperson) families in the lowest quintile have family heads under 24 years of age or over 65, age groups where school attendance and retirement are quite prevalent. In the highest quintile, less than 8 percent of family heads belong to these age groups.

Another difficulty with the concept of net income on which estimates in the previous section are based is the use of a 1-year accounting period for the measurement of income. Two people may have unequal incomes in a given year, but if we consider a longer time period, such as their lifetimes, their incomes may be identical. A person who goes to work after finishing high school will normally have a higher income at age 20 than a classmate who attends college, but the reverse will probably be true 20 years later. Or consider the lifetime earnings of a professional athlete and a doctor. When they are young, the athlete's income will be much higher; in later years, the reverse will be true. Although their lifetime earnings may be identical, comparing their incomes in any given year will show great inequality. In general, incomes tend to rise with age up to about age 55, and then decline. The median income in 1972 of families headed by a person aged 14 to 24 was $7447, whereas for the 45 to 54 age group the median was nearly double, $14,056. Above age 65 the median was $5968. When we look at the income distribution in one specific year, we are comparing some people at their peak earning years with others at the low point in their life cycles. Such comparisons give a misleading impression of the degree of inequality over a longer period of time.

In some cases, looking at the distributional impact of government programs in 1 year also tends to exaggerate the amount of redistribution from a longer run perspective. This is especially true of social security. In any single year, social security transfers income from earners who tend to be in the upper quintiles to retired persons who are concentrated in the lower quintiles. Thus, statistics such as those presented in Table 7–8 reflect a substantial redistribution toward lower income classes due to social security taxes and transfers. Taking a longer-run point of view, there is likely to be much less redistribution; each person pays taxes during his working years and later receives transfers when retired.

A slightly different matter concerns whether there is mobility within the income distribution. It is possible to have an unchanging relative distribution of income for two quite different causes. In one case, the same people tend to inhabit the bottom positions year after year, and likewise for the top positions. Alternatively, the overall distribution may not change significantly, but people move up and down in the distribution over time. It is proable that most people would find the latter situation more acceptable because it implies mobility and less inequality from a longer-run perspective.

Recent evidence suggests that there is a substantial amount of mobility within the income distribution. Bradley Schiller examined the earnings distribution for a sample of workers aged 30 to 34 in 1957, and compared that to the distribution in 1971 for the *same* group of workers.[10] He found that 71 percent of the workers had a relative standing in 1971 at least 10 percentiles different from their standing in 1957. The average shift was 21 percentiles! Another study examined the official poverty population from 1967 to 1972 and found that only 20 to 30 percent of those who were poor in any one year were poor for all 6 years.[11] These findings suggest substantial mobility rather than a situa-

[10] Bradley R. Schiller, "Equality, Opportunity, and the 'Good Job,' " *The Public Interest*, 43:111 (Spring 1976).
[11] U.S. Department of Health, Education, and Welfare, Office of the Assistant Secretary for Planning and Evaluation, "The Changing Economic Status of 5000 American Families: Highlights from the Poverty Study of Income Dynamics" (Washington, D.C.: U.S. Government Printing Office, 1974).

tion where people are rigidly locked into certain positions in the income distribution for their lifetimes.

All of these factors cast doubt on the reliability of any inferences that can be made about inequality in real economic positions from statistics like those discussed earlier. This does not imply that the "true" distribution of income is "really" equal: Common sense, casual observation, and the existing empirical evidence all conflict with that conclusion. Rather, it is suggested that our ethical conception of what equality is and whether it should be pursued as a goal ought to incorporate a broader range of considerations than can be summarized in simple tables like Tables 7–7 and 7–8. Out of necessity, most government redistributive plans will be based on *annual* differences in *money* (plus perhaps some types of in-kind) incomes. Equalizing annual money incomes will, in some instances, produce greater inequality in real incomes because it will ignore factors of the type we have discussed here. This is unlikely to be true for redistribution from those who are very well off (in money terms) to those who are very poor. Much redistribution, however, involves shifting money around within the broad middle income classes, and for policies that do this the possibility of some perverse effects on the degree of true equality would seem to be quite significant.

Supplementary Readings

Breit, William. "Income Redistribution and Efficiency Norms," H. M. Hochman and G. E. Peterson (eds.), *Redistribution Through Public Choice.* New York: Columbia University Press, 1974.

Browning, Edgar K. "The Trend Toward Equality in the Distribution of Net Income," *Southern Economic Journal,* 43(1):912–923(July 1976).

Okun, Arthur. *Equality and Efficiency: The Big Trade-off.* Washington, D.C.: Brookings Institution, 1975.

Smolensky, Eugene, and Morgan Reynolds. *Public Expenditures, Taxes, and the Distribution of Income.* New York: Academic Press, Inc., 1977.

Tobin, James. "On Limiting the Domain of Inequality," *Journal of Law and Economics,* 13(2):263–278(Oct. 1970).

U.S. Congress, Congressional Budget Office. *Poverty Status of Families Under Alternative Definitions of Income,* Background Paper No. 17. Washington, D.C.: U.S. Government Printing Office, January 1977.

CHAPTER 8

ALTERNATIVE POLICIES TO REDISTRIBUTE INCOME

In earlier chapters we have considered several government programs with important redistributive consequences. Food stamps, Medicaid, and social security, for example, concentrate subsidies on lower income households. We have not, however, considered all the various methods of redistribution that can be used and the types of economic effects relevant in comparing the alternatives. This chapter focuses more specifically on the most important alternatives. It emphasizes what economics can contribute to two important questions: What type of policy (or policies) shall be used to redistribute income, and what factors are important in evaluating how much redistribution is desirable? Needless to say, neither economics nor economists can determine what type of policy is best and how much redistribution is desirable, because such conclusions will ultimately reflect value judgments concerning the effects of alternative policies. Economics can, however, determine some of the effects of policies that most people would consider relevant in reaching a determination. That is what we will attempt to do in this chapter.

We will begin with a discussion of the major alternative cash transfer programs that may be used with special attention given to the negative income tax (NIT). The United States does not at this time have a comprehensive national transfer program of the NIT variety. Nonetheless, it is important to understand how an NIT works because there are a number of actual programs which are simply variants on this basic theme.

Cash Transfer Policies

The Negative Income Tax

The negative income tax, also known as a guaranteed annual income, is a program of cash transfers to families, with the size of the transfer depending on the family's income and size. The distinguishing characteristic of this program is that, for families of a given size, the transfer is larger the lower their income. The poorer the family is—at least in terms of its money income—the more assistance received. Table 8–1 illustrates how a hypothetical NIT transfer would vary with income for a four-person family. In this example, if a family's own income (pretransfer income) is zero, the transfer is $4000. At higher income levels, the transfer is smaller, ultimately reaching zero at $8000.

Considering only families of a given size, an NIT can be concisely described by its three policy variables. First is the *income guarantee,* which is the transfer received by a family with no income of its own—$4000 in Table 8–1. The *marginal tax rate* is the second policy variable. The marginal tax rate indicates how much the transfer payment declines as pretransfer income rises. Thus, the marginal tax rate is 50 percent in our example because the transfer falls by $0.50 for each $1 increase in pretransfer income. The third policy variable is called the *breakeven income* and is the level of income at which the transfer falls to zero—$8000 in Table 8–1.

An NIT can also be illustrated graphically. Figure 8–1 shows several alternative plans. In this figure, pretransfer income is measured horizontally and disposable income (pretransfer income plus the transfer) is measured vertically. The 45 degree line indicates the equality between pretransfer and disposable income in the absence of the NIT (and other

Table 8–1. Hypothetical Negative Income Tax

Pretransfer Income	Transfer	Total Disposable Income
$ 0	$4000	$4000
1000	3500	4500
2000	3000	5000
3000	2500	5500
4000	2000	6000
5000	1500	6500
6000	1000	7000
7000	500	7500
8000	0	8000

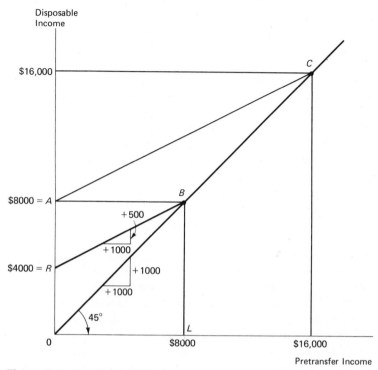

Figure 8–1. Hypothetical NIT plans.

transfers or taxes). It has a slope of 1, implying that an additional $1000 in pretransfer income adds exactly $1000 to disposable income. The line RB illustrates the relationship between pretransfer income and disposable income for the NIT just described. The transfer is the vertical distance between RB and the 45 degree line. $0R$ ($4000) is the income guarantee and BL ($8000) is the breakeven income. The slope of RB shows that disposable income rises by only $500 for each $1000 in pretransfer income under this NIT (because the transfer falls by $500). The marginal tax rate is equal to 1 minus the slope of the transfer schedule RB. The other NIT plans shown in Figure 8–1 will be considered in a moment.

The transfer received at any income level below the breakeven income can be calculated from the following simple equation:

$$T = r(B - Y_i) \qquad (1)$$

where T is the transfer payment, r is the marginal tax rate, B is the breakeven income, and Y_i is the family's pretransfer income. If r is 50 percent, then we can say that the NIT fills 50 percent of the gap between the family's income and the breakeven income. The transfer would be equal to half the "poverty gap" if the breakeven income were set at the poverty line.

The three policy variables of the NIT are not independent of each other. If the income guarantee is set at $4000 and the transfer falls by $0.50 for each $1 of pretransfer income (a marginal tax rate of 50 percent), then obviously the transfer will fall to zero at $8000. Thus, the breakeven income is already determined when the income guarantee and the marginal tax rate are set. The breakeven income equals the income guarantee divided by the marginal tax rate. This relationship is also apparent from equation (1) because, if we set pretransfer income (Y_i) equal to zero, the transfer (the income guarantee) will be equal to rB. Therefore, specifying any two of the policy variables implicitly determines the third.

The relationship among the policy variables poses a difficult policy choice. First, consider the significance of each policy variable. The income guaranteee will represent the total disposable incomes of families with no other income, so it is important that the guarantee be high enough to permit an adequate standard of living. A low marginal tax rate is desirable to preserve work incentives because a high rate means that disposable incomes will rise only slightly when earnings increase, which would give recipients little incentive to increase earnings. (More on marginal tax rates and work incentives will be presented later.) A low breakeven income appears desirable because it restricts transfers to those with low incomes and, at the same time, keeps the costs managable (because those above the breakeven income must bear the cost of financing the NIT).

It seems desirable, then, to have a high income guarantee, a low marginal tax rate, and a low breakeven income. Because of the relationship among these policy variables, however, this is impossible: A "low" marginal tax rate multiplied by a "low" breakeven income cannot equal a "high" income guarantee. The difficult tradeoff among policy variables can be clarified by reference to Figure 8–1. Suppose the poverty line is $8000 and the income guarantee is set at this level (0A) to ensure that no family is in poverty. If the breakeven income is also kept relatively low at $8000, the entire transfer schedule is AB. This implies, however, a marginal tax rate of 100 percent, because disposable income does not rise as pretransfer income increases between zero and $8000. This plan would leave no financial incentive for low income families to work because a family would have the same disposable income when it earned nothing as when it earned $8000.

How can we avoid destroying the incentives families have to support themselves? To make earning an income worthwhile, it is necessary to lower the marginal tax rate well below 100 percent. There are two distinctly different ways to do this, and each way has drawbacks. One method is to maintain the income guarantee at $8000 and lower the marginal tax rate, but this implies a higher breakeven income. For example, if the tax rate is lowered to 50 percent, the breakeven income would have to be $16,000, and the entire relationship would be shown by line AC. This program would not completely destroy work incentives, but it would weaken incentives of a much larger number of people—all those with incomes below $16,000—and many (in the $8000 to $16,000 range) would now be subject to a marginal tax rate under an NIT that excluded them before. Perhaps more important, it would be exhorbitantly costly, because it would involve transfers to about half the American people!

A second way to lower the marginal tax rate is to hold the breakeven level of income at $8000 and lower the income guarantee. With a 50 percent tax rate, an income guarantee of $4000 is implied, and we are back with the schedule shown as RB. This method of reducing the tax rate would substantially improve the financial rewards from working for low income families (as compared with the AB schedule, which removes all incentives), and it would reduce the cost of the program. However, these effects come at a cost: The level of assistance for low income groups is reduced, and the income guarantee is now only half the poverty line.

There are harsh choices that must be made in setting the policy variables of an NIT. A high guarantee and a high tax rate (implying a low breakeven income) restrict transfers to those with low incomes but weaken incentives. A high income guarantee and a low tax rate (implying a high breakeven income) produce a large number of transfer recipients and impose a high cost that must be borne by those taxpayers remaining above the breakeven income. A high tax rate must be applied to the remaining taxpayers to finance such an NIT, and this will weaken their work incentives. Alternatively, a low income guarantee and a low or moderate tax rate (say, 50 percent) keep costs down and maintain work incentives, but the level of assistance will be modest.

Given this unenviable tradeoff, why is the NIT the overwhelming favorite among economists? The answer must await a careful comparison among the alternatives available, but one point should be stressed now: The difficult choice we are considering exists in one form or another in most real-world welfare programs. It is more an inevitable consequence of scarcity making it impossible to achieve all our goals simultaneously than of the NIT per se. In fact, several existing welfare programs are variations of the NIT (the food stamp program is one of them!), and the same type of tradeoff exists for them as well. Careful attention will be given to the NIT not only because it is a hypothetical policy favored by many economists but also because in its several variations, it is already an integral part of the U.S. welfare system.

Economic Effects of the NIT. Although a seemingly simple policy, the NIT has a wide range of effects on resource allocation.

WORK INCENTIVES. Much attention has been given to the question of how the NIT would affect the work incentives of transfer recipients. In principle, any transfer program will affect work effort in two ways: first, through the "income effect" and second, through the "substitution effect." By providing a transfer to families, the NIT makes them better off and more able to afford to work less. Having a higher real income, the recipient will increase his consumption of normal goods, including leisure or time spent not working. (Recall that an increase in leisure is the same as a reduction in work effort.) This is the income effect of the NIT, and it is related to the size of the transfer payment; the larger the transfer, the greater the income effect favoring less work.

The NIT affects work incentives another way by reducing the net wage rate of recipients. Reducing the transfer received when a person earns more income has the effect of lowering the hourly compensation for work. For example, if a person is employed at $4 per hour and works an additional hour, the extra $4 in earnings will reduce the NIT transfer by $2 (assuming a 50 percent marginal tax rate), so the net increase in income is only $2 for an extra hour's work. The net wage rate is cut in half by this NIT, so a person sacrifices less disposable income by reducing his work effort. Thus, the relative price of consuming leisure—the sacrificed net income—has fallen from $4 per hour to $2 per hour, and this lower relative price encourages greater consumption of leisure (less work). This is the substitution effect of the NIT, and its magnitude is related to the marginal tax rate of the program. The higher the marginal tax rate, the lower the net wage and the greater the incentive to substitute leisure for money earnings, because leisure will cost less in sacrificed money income.

An NIT can be expected to reduce work effort both through its income effect and its substitution effect. Some consequences of this diminished incentive to work are illustrated in Figure 8–2. An individual's budget constraint relating money income and leisure in the absence of the NIT is shown as YN. YN has a slope of $4 per hour, the market wage rate of the individual. Equilibrium for the individual occurs at point E, with money income of $0Y_1$ and leisure of $0L_1$ (so work effort is NL_1).

Introduction of the NIT shifts the budget constraint from YN to YRM. $0B$ is the breakeven income, and MN is the income guarantee (both expressed here in weekly magnitudes). The vertical distance be-

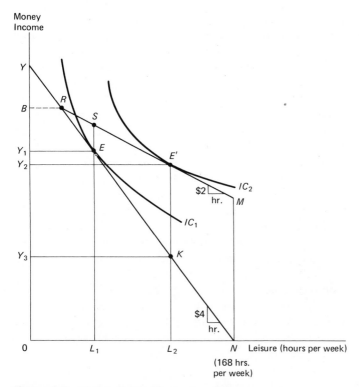

Figure 8-2. Work incentive effects of an NIT.

tween the subsidized portion of the constraint, *RM,* and the unsubsidized constraint equals the transfer. The transfer is, of course, larger when the individual works and earns less: It equals *MN* with zero work effort, *E'K* if work effort is NL_2, and *SE* if work effort is NL_1. The slope of the constraint has become flatter, $2 per hour, rather than the previous $4 per hour, reflecting the 50 percent marginal tax rate that cuts the net rate of pay in half. Note that the rotation of the constraint at point *R* lowers the price of leisure: Less money income must be sacrificed when more leisure time is consumed.

Confronted with the *YRM* constraint, the individual's preferred combination of money income and leisure occurs at *E',* where money income equals $0Y_2$ (the sum of earnings, KL_2, and the transfer, *E'K*) and leisure equals $0L_2$. The reduction in work effort from NL_1 to NL_2 shows the total effect of the NIT on work effort—the combined influence of the income effect and the substitution effect. (We will show these effects separately later.) For this particular individual, the NIT has actually led to a reduction in total money income. Although the individual is receiving a transfer of *E'K,* his own earnings have fallen by a larger amount

215

from $0Y_1$ to $0Y_3$. This need not always be the outcome; indeed, most scholars think that work effort will rarely fall by enough to reduce total money income. It does, however, indicate one reason why the work incentives question is considered important—if the recipient's own earnings fall, the goal of increasing his disposable money income will be frustrated.

Economic theory predicts that there will be some reduction in work incentives from an NIT but does not allow us to predict its size. There are a growing number of empirical studies designed to estimate its quantitative impact and its relationship to the policy variables. The empirical evidence is of two types: (1) studies of the reactions of low income families to different wage rates implicit in existing welfare programs similar in nature to the NIT, and (2) studies of the results of experimental NIT programs funded by the government.

In reviewing the nonexperimental evidence, Irwin Garfinkel concludes that the evidence supports the view that work effort will fall under an NIT. However, there is no consensus about the size of the reduction. For an NIT with a moderate income guarantee and a 50 percent marginal tax rate, the estimated reduction in work effort ranges from 3 percent to 40 percent for prime-aged married men (the group where the disincentive problem is expected to be the smallest).[1] Estimated reductions for other demographic groups are generally somewhat larger.

The NIT experiments have yielded direct information about work incentive effects. In one of the experiments, hours worked fell by 6 percent for men and 15 percent for women.[2] Because these were results of an actual field test of the NIT, they might be considered very reliable. Unfortunately, this is not the case. Technical problems in interpreting the results are quite common. For example, participants in the experiment knew the program would last only 3 years, and this could have affected their reactions. In addition, the control group not receiving the NIT transfer—that provided the basis for estimating what participants would have done in the absence of the program—could receive benefits under existing welfare programs. If the control group worked less because these other programs affected its work effort, the estimated impact on the work effort of the experimental NIT group would be too low. These and other problems concerning whether we can generalize on the basis of a small-scale experiment make interpretation of the experimental results difficult.

---

[1] Irwin Garfinkel, "Income Transfer Programs and Work Effort: A Review," *Studies in Public Welfare,* U.S. Congress, Joint Economic Committee, Subcommittee on Fiscal Policy, Paper No. 13, 93rd Congress, 2nd Session (Washington, D.C.: U.S. Government Printing Office), February 1974, pp. 11–32.

[2] Albert Rees, "An Overview of the Labor Supply Results," *Journal of Human Resources,* 9:158 (Spring 1974).

Exactly how large an effect on work effort an NIT would have, and how the effect is related to the size of the program, is still an unresolved problem.

WELFARE COST. By artificially lowering the net wage rates of the transfer recipients, the NIT will distort decisions on work effort. Consider the example of the person with a $4 market wage rate whose net wage rate is $2 under the NIT. He will give up leisure (supply labor) as long as he considers an extra $2 in income worth more than the sacrificed value of an hour of leisure time. At the equilibrium level of work effort under the NIT, leisure would have a value of $2 per hour, and the individual would be willing to work an additional hour if he received anything more than $2 in compensation.[3] Becuase his market wage rate is $4, his employer would be willing to pay $4 for additional hours of work. The marginal benefit from additional work—$4 per hour—is greater than the marginal cost—$2 worth of leisure given up—so there are efficiency gains from working longer hours. Yet under the NIT the individual will not work longer hours because his *net* wage rate is $2 per hour due to the reduction in the transfer payment that occurs when he earns the additional $4. He will be led to work too little because the marginal private benefit from working that he receives—$2 per hour—is less than the marginal social benefit of his labor services—$4 per hour.

Because the marginal tax rate makes market and net wage rates diverge, the NIT produces a welfare cost. This is illustrated in Figure 8–3, where the equilibrium under the NIT occurs at E' on the subsidized constraint YRM. To see the loss in potential welfare, imagine that the government gives the individual an unrestricted, or lump sum, cash transfer instead of the NIT transfer. Because the cost of the NIT is $E'K$, a lump sum transfer of equal cost will produce the budget constraint Y_2N_2 parallel to the original YN constraint, implying that the transfer is not reduced when more is earned; hence the net wage rate is unaffected by the lump sum transfer. This constraint permits the individual to reach a higher indifference curve, IC_3, at point L. Thus, the recipient can be made better off at no additional cost to the taxpayers.

Alternatively, a smaller lump sum transfer can make the recipient equally well off as under the NIT. If given a lump sum transfer of YY_1 (producing the constraint Y_1N_1), the individual can reach IC_2 at point T, the same level of welfare as under the NIT. Note that the cost of this lump sum transfer is only JK, or $E'J$ less than the NIT. $E'J$ is a measure of the welfare cost of the NIT: It shows that the NIT costs $E'J$ more than is necessary to permit the recipient to attain the level of welfare indicated by IC_2.

---

[3] In other words, the marginal rate of substitution between income and leisure is in equilibrium equal to the net wage rate. This is shown by the tangency in Figure 8–2 between the recipient's indifference curve and budget constraint.

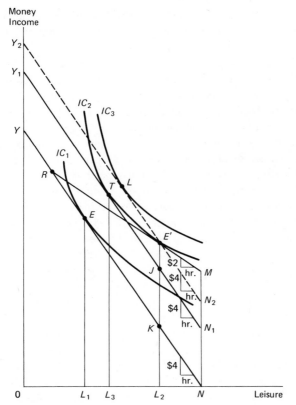

Figure 8–3. Welfare cost of an NIT.

We have seen that the recipient can be made better off with a lump sum transfer than with an NIT of the same cost, or (what amounts to the same thing) equally well off at a lower cost. The reason for this is that the NIT lowers the net wage and encourages the recipient to consume too much leisure (work too little). This distortion of the NIT is caused by the marginal tax rate that induces the recipient to substitute leisure for money income.

Figure 8–3 can also be used to show the income and substitution effects of the NIT. The income effect is the increase in leisure from $0L_1$ to $0L_3$ that results from giving the recipient enough income to attain IC_2, but without affecting the net wage rate received. The substitution effect is the increase in leisure from $0L_3$ to $0L_2$ that results from the lower net wage rate when the recipient is kept on the same indifference curve, IC_2. The welfare cost of the NIT is due to the substitution effect alone: $0L_2 - 0L_3$ measures the overconsumption of leisure. The income effect of the transfer is not a distortion; it is simply the increase in consumption of leisure—and other normal goods—that results from a pure, nondistorting change in the income distribution. That is why economists emphasize the importance of the size of the marginal tax rate of the NIT, because it lowers the net wage rate and causes the uneconomic substitution of leisure for money income.

If the welfare cost of the NIT (and other transfer programs as well) can be avoided by using lump sum transfers, why don't economists favor such transfers? That is a reasonable question, and the answer involves understanding the nature of a lump sum transfer more precisely. A lump sum transfer is one where the amount transferred does not depend on income, consumption, work effort, education, family size, or any other economic characteristic under the control of the recipient. It is simply fixed in amount, totally independent of any individual's action. By its very nature, it is impossible to restrict it to those with low incomes because, by definition, it is unrelated to any of the characteristics associated with the poor. If given only to people with low incomes, it would not be a lump sum transfer because it would give incentive to others to reduce their incomes to become eligible for the transfer and would thereby create a distortion. Thus, in the interest of *equitably* relating assistance to need we may choose to use transfers related to income despite the efficiency cost.

For this reason, lump sum transfers and taxes are not generally considered practical policy tools. Nonetheless, they serve a highly useful role in analysis as a conceptual benchmark against which to view the allocative effects of real world taxes and transfers. They provide a means of understanding how other policies may distort the allocation of resources and the factors that determine the size of these distortions. In the present context, even though the NIT produces a welfare cost, that cost may be smaller than those of alternative practical policies. This is precisely what many economists believe.

INCIDENCE OF THE NIT. One objection sometimes made to the NIT is that it will simply lead employers to reduce their wage rates. If the market wage rates of recipients fall when they receive NIT transfers, they may be no better off on balance. Actually, an NIT can be expected to affect wage rates, but in the opposite direction than implied by this argument.

In our earlier analysis, we found that the NIT would lead a recipient to reduce the quantity of labor supplied at the existing unchanged market wage rate. For the individual shown in Figure 8–2, labor supply falls from NL_1 to NL_2. Note that this is the reduction in labor supplied when the market wage rate is unchanged. The aggregate effect can be shown as a leftward shift in the labor supply curve for workers who are recipients of the subsidies. Figure 8–4 illustrates the consequences. Prior to introduction of the NIT, the equilibrium wage rate (more preicsely,

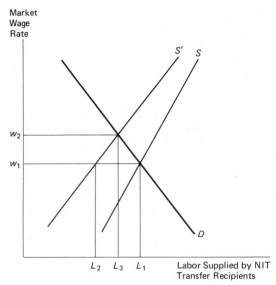

Figure 8–4. Effects of an NIT on the labor market.

this should be thought of as the general level of wage rates of low income workers) is w_1, and L_1 is the quantity of labor supplied. The NIT leads workers to desire to supply fewer manhours per year at the initial wage rate w_1. Thus, the supply curve shifts to S', where the L_1L_2 reduction in the quantity of labor supplied at the market level is the sum of reductions such as the L_1L_2 reduction shown in Figure 8–2 for one individual.

Because of the reduction in labor supply, the market wage rate is bid up to a new equilibrium at w_2. The change in the market wage rate has important implications for the distributional effects of the program. It means that recipients benefit by more than the total transfers received, that is, there is a second benefit in the form of a wage rate increase. The higher wage rate is an additional cost to the rest of society, resulting in higher prices for some products or lower prices for other factors of production, or both. Consequently, taxpayers not only pay taxes to finance the program but also bear the cost of the higher wage rate. Therefore, the redistribution accomplished by the NIT is greater than the taxes and transfers involved.

The importance of this effect on market wage rates depends on the magnitude of the reduction in labor supply. As mentioned earlier, it is not clear how large the labor response is likely to be.

OTHER ALLOCATIVE EFFECTS. Although much of the popular discussion of the NIT has centered around its potential impact on work incentives, there are also other incentives that may be affected. One is the incentive to save. If the return to saving is counted as income, as it generally is under the federal income tax, then the NIT will reduce the net return received when part of current income is set aside to provide for future consumption needs. That is, if a person elects to save for retirement, his higher retirement income (interest, dividends, and so on) will lower his NIT transfer on retirement. This will have an adverse effect on the recipient's incentive to save, and the higher the marginal tax rate, the lower the net return on saving.

A similar disincentive occurs with respect to investments associated with augmenting one's earning capacity (another way to save). Consider a person now earning $5000 under an NIT with a guarantee of $3500 and a 50 percent tax rate. If he has the opportunity to undertake a training program that will raise his earning capacity from $5000 to $7000, how much is that worth to him? Actually, it will increase his net annual income by only $1000, because his transfer will be zero with earnings of $7000 instead of $1000 with earnings of $5000. In this way, an NIT also reduces the incentive to augment one's earning capacity—whether by on-the-job training or by doing well in public school. Again, the marginal tax rate is the key to the significance of this effect.

Another set of potential effects depends on the definition of income used to determine the size of the NIT transfer. If certain types of income are excluded or certain expenditures are deductible, then the NIT acts to subsidize these items by lowering their relative prices. For example, if mortgage interest payments are deductible, a dollar in interest will cost the transfer recipient only 50 cents under an NIT with a 50 percent marginal tax rate because the transfer will rise by 50 cents for every dollar of interest payments. The consequences of these "tax loopholes" will be considered more fully when we examine the federal income tax, but it should be noted that the same problem exists in the definition of income under an NIT. And, once again, the marginal tax rate is critical in determining the incentive recipients have to convert their income into "nontaxable" or uncounted forms in order to receive larger NIT transfers.

Finally, the NIT can also affect family size and structure through the way transfers depend on family size. Consider three alternative NIT plans whose income guarantees are given by family composition in Table 8–2. Plan A gives each family an income guarantee approximately equal to the poverty line; plan B is an equal per person guarantee, $1500 per person regardless of family size; plan C sets an income guarantee of $2000 for each adult and $1000 for each child. All plans involve the same guarantee, $6000, for a family of four.

Because it costs more to support a larger family, equity calls for larger transfers to larger families, and all three plans in Table 8–2 meet this criterion. This means, however, that a family can receive a larger

Table 8–2. Alternative Income Guarantees by Family Size and Composition

Family Size and Composition	Plan A	Plan B	Plan C
1 (1 adult)	$3000	$1500	$2000
2 (1 adult, 1 child)	4000	3000	3000
2 (2 adults)	4000	3000	4000
3 (1 adult, 2 children)	5000	4500	4000
3 (2 adults, 1 child)	5000	4500	5000
4 (2 adults, 2 children)	6000	6000	6000
5 (2 adults, 3 children)	6700	7500	7000
6 (2 adults, 4 children)	7400	8000	8000

transfer by having more children. Under plan A, if family size is increased from three to four, the transfer increases by $1000. Furthermore, the "bonus" for additional children exists for all families with incomes below the breakdown level. There is a clear conflict between treating different-sized families equitably and avoiding incentives to increase family size.

An NIT can also affect family structure by creating the incentive to split families into smaller units. Under plan A, for example, a family of four with no income receives $6000, but if the husband leaves the wife and children (or *appears* to leave them) he receives $3000 as a single-person poor family and they receive $5000 as a family of three. By splitting up, the family's total transfer is increased from $6000 to $8000. Similarly, two single individuals receive a transfer of $3000 each, but only $4000 if they marry. These incentives to form smaller family units are inevitable when the guarantees are set equal to the poverty lines.

Plans B and C produce no incentives to split larger family units into smaller ones because a given number of people receive the same total transfer regardless of how many separate family units are involved. In both plans, however, the guarantee for a single individual is well below the poverty line, and this is inevitable if the guarantees are set to equal the poverty line for a family of four. Once again, a conflict between equity and incentives is apparent and a tradeoff among desirable goals is necessary. Most people have concluded that a program like plan C is the best compromise, even though this approach creates incentives to have children and also involves a transfer to a single individual that is below the poverty line for a family of one.

THE NIT AND ACTUAL WELFARE PROGRAMS. It is important to understand that many of the most important existing welfare programs are simply variations on the basic NIT theme. The food stamp program, for example, is nothing more than an NIT coupled with a requirement that at least a certain minimum sum be spent on food. Refer back to Table 4–2 and note that the food stamp subsidy declines as the monthly income of the recipient rises. Such an inverse relationship between the transfer and income is the defining characteristic of the NIT. In the case of the food stamp program, the implicit marginal tax rate on net income varies slightly from one income level to another, but it is typically in the 25 to 30 percent range.

Other welfare programs are also NIT's in disguise. Aid to Families with Dependent Children (AFDC) is a program of cash assistance paid to female-headed households with children. Because the transfer is smaller when the family's income is higher, it is essentially an NIT restricted to a particular demographic group within the population. The nominal marginal tax rate is 67 percent, but administrative practices often make the effective rate somewhat lower. Supplemental Security Income is another NIT that is restricted to a particular demographic group, primarily the aged poor, but also the blind and disabled. Its marginal tax rate is 50 percent. Some housing subsidies, such as public housing, are also similar to the NIT combined with a restriction on housing consumption.

Even social security bears some resemblance to the NIT. Although the basic pension is not related solely to low income, the earnings test reduces the pension if earnings exceed a certain amount, producing a marginal tax rate of 50 percent on earnings.

Therefore, a study of the NIT is not merely an academic exercise; it helps us understand the workings of several existing programs. For example, the AFDC program has apparently led some men to leave their wives and children because transfers are restricted to female-headed families.[4] This is just the outcome that can occur when income guarantees are related to family structure as in plan A in Table 8–2.

THE CUMULATIVE MARGINAL TAX RATE PROBLEM. One consequence of having a number of mini-NIT's in the system in addition to various taxes (such as social security and state income and sales taxes) applicable to the low income population deserves special mention. Some families receive benefits from more than one program and concurrently pay several taxes related to income. The result is often high *effective* marginal tax rates. Consider a family that receives only food stamps, with its marginal rate of 25 to 30 percent. This family is also subject to a social security tax of about 12 percent on its earnings. Thus, an additional $100 in earnings reduces the food stamp subsidy by $30 and increases the social security tax by $12. Disposable income rises by only $58, so

---

[4] Marjorie Honig, "The Impact of Welfare Payment Levels on Family Stability," *Studies in Public Welfare*, U.S. Congress, Joint Economic Committee, Subcommittee on Fiscal Policy, Paper No. 12, 93rd Congress, 1st Session (Washington, D.C.: U.S. Government Printing Office), November 1973.

the effective marginal tax rate is 42 percent.[5] In addition, state and local income and sales taxes may also be applicable, and these can raise the effective rate to 45 percent or above.

When a family receives benefits from more than one program, the situation is aggravated. If the family just described receives a housing subsidy where benefits fall by $25 for each $100 of earnings, then its effective marginal tax rate is about 70 percent. A family receiving aid under the AFDC program as well as food stamps and housing assistance is faced with a tax rate of 80 percent or more.

At present, low income families are already subject to high marginal tax rates. There is wide variation among families, of course, depending on which program or combination of programs is involved. Many low income families, however, receive assistance from several programs: In 1974, 20 percent of those who received any welfare benefits received benefits from five or more programs. The percentage of families receiving multiple benefits is certainly higher now, and, inevitably, for those families effective marginal tax rates are clearly very high.

The way in which a number of transfers and taxes can combine to produce a very high effective marginal tax rate is called the "cumulative tax rate effect." It is extremely important because it is the effective rate that is relevant in terms of economic incentives. Even if the nominal rate of each separate program is low—as in the food stamp program—piling one program atop another can often spell disaster for work (and other) incentives by producing high effective marginal tax rates.

Demogrants

Demogrants are a form of cash transfer in which all members of a demographic group receive the same transfer. Frequently, the demographic group contains the entire population. Senator George McGovern proposed such a program in the 1972 presidential campaign by suggesting that the federal government make a grant of $1000 per person to every man, woman, and child in the United States.

At first glance, it might seem that demogrants avoid the disincentive effects of high marginal tax rates. With a demogrant of $1500 per capita, a family of four would receive $6000 regardless of its income: The subsidy would not fall as income rises. A demogrant has a zero marginal tax rate. However, once the necessity of raising taxes to finance the outlays on demogrants is recognized, it becomes clear that positive marginal tax rates are required.

For simplicity, suppose that the demogrant is $6000 per family and

---

[5] Actually, the effective marginal tax rate is not exactly equal to the sum of the separate rates because the income base is defined differently under the separate programs.

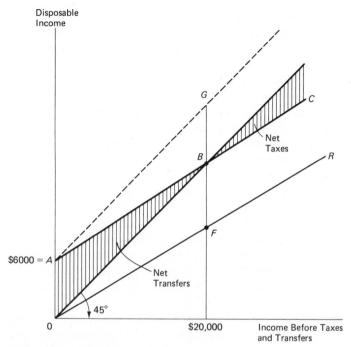

Figure 8–5. Hypothetical demogrant program.

that the average income of all families is $20,000. Then the total out-lays on demogrants would be 30 percent of total family income because the average outlay per family ($6000) is 30 percent of average family income ($20,000). If a tax on total family income is used to finance the demogrants, a rate of 30 percent applied to all income, without any exemptions or deductions, is required. The combined effect of the transfer and taxes is to produce an NIT with an income guarantee of $6000, a marginal tax rate of 30 percent, and a breakeven income of $20,000.

This is illustrated in Figure 8–5. The effect of the outlays, or demogrants, alone is shown by the dotted line parallel to the 45 degree line. The transfers add $6000 to each family's income. A proportional tax of 30 percent on family income reduces income by 30 percent at each level as shown by the schedule *OR*. The net effect on income at each level is the difference between the transfer received and the tax paid. The schedule *ABC* shows the net effect. At an income equal to the average, $20,000, the transfer (*BG* = $6000) equals the tax (*BF* = $6000), so disposable income remains unchanged. At lower incomes the transfer exceeds the tax, and disposable income is raised by the demogrant, whereas the reverse is true at higher income levels. In short, income is redistributed from families with incomes above the average to those with **225** incomes below the average. The demogrant financed by an income tax is exactly equivalent in its effects to an NIT with an income guarantee of $6000 and a 30 percent marginal tax rate, which is financed by a tax on families with above-average incomes.

Note that the net amount redistributed from above $20,000 to below that level by the demogrant plan is far less than its total outlays. Total outlays at $1500 per capita would be about $330 billion, but the net addition to disposable income for people below the average (equal to the net reduction for people above the average) would be only a small fraction of that, probably about $70 billion. The remainder simply involves giving people back an amount equivalent to the taxes they paid. Consequently, the demogrant program, involving total taxes and expenditures of $330 billion, is equivalent to an NIT with total taxes and expenditures of $70 billion. In contrast, however, the NIT makes only the net transfer and collects only the net taxes, thereby avoiding collecting taxes from the same people who receive the transfers. Although government expenditures are very different under the two programs, *the economic effects are exactly the same,* because the net effect on income at each level is what counts.

This specific example also illustrates another related but general point: The economic consequences of government expenditures are not necessarily proportional to the magnitude of total spending. The fact that the government in country *A* spends 30 percent of national income does not necessarily mean that it has a bigger impact than the government in country *B,* which spends only 8 percent of national income.

Demogrants are fundamentally a variation of the NIT, and our earlier analysis of the effects of an NIT is applicable. Again, it is interesting to note how many apparently dissimilar programs turn out on closer examination to be quite similar to the NIT. As another example, it might be mentioned that some proposals for national health insurance are simply demogrants where the transfers are made in kind rather than in cash. If everyone receives the same health insurance coverage, then the transfer per person is equal, but is given as health insurance rather than money.

Wage Rate Subsidy

There is another type of cash transfer program that is more favorable to work incentives than the NIT, namely, the wage rate subsidy (WRS). The WRS transfers income by increasing the net wage rates received by workers. Table 8–3 illustrates how it would work. The transfers take the form of supplements to the hourly wage rates, with larger supplements received by workers with lower wage rates. If, for example, a worker is paid $1.00 an hour by his employer, the government adds a subsidy of $1.50 per hour, bringing the net wage up to $2.50. At higher market

Table 8-3. Hypothetical Wage Rate Subsidy

Market Wage Rate	Subsidy	Net Wage Rate
$1.00	$1.50	$2.50
1.50	1.25	2.75
2.00	1.00	3.00
2.50	0.75	3.25
3.00	0.50	3.50
3.50	0.25	3.75
4.00	0	4.00

wage rates the subsidy per hour is reduced, but not by the full amount of the increment in the market wage. This ensures that workers with higher market wage rates also receive higher net wage rates, which in turn gives recipients incentive to increase their market wage rates.

Under a WRS, recipients can receive larger total transfers by working longer hours. There is no incentive to stop work altogether because the transfer is zero when hours worked are zero. It does not necessarily follow, however, that recipients will work longer hours than if they received no transfer. The WRS increases the recipient's net wage rate, but whether a higher wage rate leads to more or less work effort depends on whether his labor supply curve is upward sloping or backward bending. The net effect on work effort is indeterminant, because the income effect of the subsidy favors less work effort but the substitution effect encourages more work.

Although a WRS may either increase or reduce work effort when compared to no transfer at all, the more relevant question is how it affects work incentives when compared to alternative transfer programs such as the NIT. In comparison to the NIT and similar programs, the WRS promotes greater work effort. Because both transfers have income effects that favor less work effort, the difference between the programs lies in their substitution effects. Because the substitution effect of the lower net wage rate of the NIT favors less work and the substitution effect of the higher net wage of the WRS favors more work, the net effect of the wage rate subsidy is to lead to greater work effort than the NIT.

This means that, for a given cost to taxpayers, a WRS will lead to a higher money income for recipients than will an NIT, because total transfers are the same but earnings will be higher under the wage subsidy program. This does not imply, however, that recipients will be better off under the WRS. They will have more money income, it is true, but they will be working longer hours (consuming less leisure), so the net effect on welfare is uncertain. Whether the taxpayers who would finance the WRS would prefer the work incentive effects of the WRS depends on whether they are more interested in raising the money incomes of the poor or their leisure. Judging from most discussions of poverty—always expressed as a lack of money income alone—and the importance attached to the work incentives question, it is probable that the general public would prefer a welfare program that encourages more work effort.

There are other factors, however, to be considered in evaluating the WRS. One important problem is that, unlike the NIT, the WRS will not always concentrate transfers on the poorest families. People with low wage rates receive large subsidies, but low wage rates do not necessarily imply low family incomes. If a husband works full-time at a wage of $4.00 an hour and his wife works at $2.00 an hour, their combined salaries would be $12,000 a year—far above the poverty line. Yet the wife would receive $2000 a year from the plan described in Table 8–3 (2000 hours at a subsidy of $1 an hour). Similarly, younger people working part-time at low wages would be subsidized, regardless of the incomes of their parents. The difficulty of confining the subsidy to the poor stems from the fact that poverty is generally considered in terms of the family unit and total income from all sources. If this is the appropriate way to regard poverty, then the distributional effects of the wage rate subsidy are not so favorable as those of some alternative programs.

Another problem concerns the administration of a wage rate subsidy. Because the total transfer a person receives depends on both the wage rate and the hours worked, accurate information on these variables is needed. For many, this information would be difficult to obtain. Waiters, or self-employed persons such as the operator of a small farm, are typical of people who do not work at a fixed hourly wage rate. In addition, how could we deal with two housewives who swap chores and pay each other $0.25 an hour?

Perhaps the most important problem with the WRS is its inability to provide for those unable to work. There is no income guarantee in the program, yet clearly some provision must be made for those who cannot work or perhaps can work only part-time. This suggests the necessity of a companion program to deal with these cases. If people could easily be categorized "able to work" and "unable to work," there would be no problem. The WRS could be used for those "able to work" and an NIT or something similar for those "unable to work." Unfortunately, people are not so easily categorized, and there would be numerous in-between cases. Consequently, there would be some difficult problems in coordinating a companion program with a wage rate subsidy.

Although a wage rate subsidy would be more favorable to work incentives than an NIT, it seems inferior in a number of other respects. Obviously, it is not easy to formulate a welfare program with no defects!

Cash Versus In-Kind Transfers

A basic question in the design of a system to redistribute income is whether the transfers should be in cash that can be spent as the recipient wishes or in the form of a subsidy to particular goods and services. As emphasized in the last chapter, subsidies of particular goods and services—in-kind tranfers—have grown significantly in recent years. Today, there are large subsidies to education (and job training), medical care, food, and housing. Other goods consumed by low income households receiving somewhat smaller subsidies are child care centers, legal aid, and transportation. Subsidies for energy consumption have recently been proposed. Given the magnitude of in-kind programs, it is important to consider whether there is a more convincing rationale for this type of program than for a program of cash transfers.

Traditionally, economists have argued that cash transfers are preferable because the recipients will be better off if they can spend the subsidy as they wish.[6] We explained why recipients would prefer a cash transfer in connection with food stamps, but the same principles apply to other in-kind transfers as well. Proponents of in-kind transfers, therefore, must argue that there are other factors besides the well-being of recipients that need to be taken into account.

Two general arguments have been offered in support of in-kind programs. One is paternalistic and holds that, if given cash, the poor would spend too much of it on nonessential goods like liquor and cigarettes, and too little on medical care, food, housing, or education. This argument rejects the well-being of recipients, as judged by the recipients themselves, as a criterion for evaluating transfer policies. A second argument is based on the belief that consumption of particular goods by the poor generates external benefits for the taxpayers: "Taxpayers don't want to give the poor money; they want to give them housing (or medical care, education, etc.)." Although intangible, such a preference by taxpayers means they derive benefits from expanded consumption of particular goods by the poor. As we saw earlier, when external benefits accompany the consumption of particular goods, the result is inefficiency in the form of underconsumption of that good (and overconsumption of other goods). A cash transfer would not achieve an efficient allocation because the recipient would consume a quantity where his marginal benefit would equal the price. Efficiency would require the recipient to consume at a level where his marginal benefit plus the marginal external benefit of other people would equal the price of the product. An in-kind

---

[6] This argument does not mean that cash transfers like the NIT have no welfare cost. However, it is generally believed that the welfare cost of an NIT—which distorts labor supply but not the consumption mix—will be smaller than that of an in-kind transfer, which generally distorts labor supply and the consumption mix.

Table 8–4. Percentage Distribution of Family Expenditures, by Income Class, 1960

	Money Income Class		
Category	Under $3000	$5000 to $7499	$15,000 and over
Food	29.4	24.7	20.1
Housing*	34.4	29.1	29.1
Transportation	8.6	16.0	14.9
Medical Care	8.5	6.6	6.1
Clothing	7.1	9.9	12.2
Recreation	2.3	3.8	4.7
Tobacco	2.1	2.0	1.1
Alcohol	1.0	1.5	1.9
Other	6.6	6.4	9.9

Source: Consumer Expenditures and Income: Survey Guidelines, Bureau of Labor Statistics Bulletin 1684 (1971), pp. 104–105, Table B-17.
*Includes shelter and other home-related expenses.

transfer is potentially more efficient than a cash transfer in this setting because it can be designed to lead to greater consumption than the recipient would choose if he were free to spend the transfer independently.

Both of these arguments have in common the contention that the poor spend too little of their incomes on some goods and (therefore) too much on other goods. Proponents of these positions, however, have failed to present any evidence concerning what is considered the appropriate level of consumption of various goods or whether actual in-kind programs work to achieve desired consumption levels. Consequently, a careful appraisal of these arguments is difficult. Nonetheless, data concerning consumption patterns by income level cast some doubt on the significance of these views. Table 8–4 shows how families at different income levels spent their incomes in 1960. For our purpose, 1960 is a good year to use because in-kind programs were not prevalent then, and the expenditure patterns may be taken to reflect the actual preferences of families.

Note that families with incomes below $3000 (about 20 percent of all families in 1960) were devoting 72 percent of their budgets to food, housing, and medical care. If clothing and transportation are included, the percentage rises to 88 percent. These figures lend little support to the contention that low income families indulge in frivolous consumption. In fact, higher income groups devote smaller percentages to food, housing, and medical care—60.4 percent in the middle income range and 55.3 percent at the highest income level. Middle and high income groups spend a larger portion of their budgets on alcohol, tobacco, and recreation than the lower income group.

These figures do not, of course, necessarily dispose of the arguments for in-kind transfers. They suggest, however, that the poor would not in any flagrant way "waste" the taxpayers' money if given cash. It may be that popular support for in-kind programs reflects an inappropriate generalization based on a few notorious and atypical cases where cash transfers were used in ways that offended the average taxpayer.

There are still other factors to consider. Although the externality and paternalistic arguments imply that *some* type of in-kind transfer may lead to a better consumption pattern for the poor than a cash transfer, they do not imply that *any* in-kind transfer is better. For example, the evidence that education and housing subsidies have reduced consumption of the subsidized goods for some recipients raises questions about the effectiveness of actual programs. In addition, administrative costs are generally higher for in-kind programs. Administrative costs for the food stamp and public housing programs have been estimated at 11 and 7 percent, respectively, in comparison to an estimated administrative cost for an NIT of 3 percent. If these figures are representative of cash and in-kind programs, they mean that cash transfers can provide 4 to 8 percent more resources to the recipients at no additional cost to taxpayers. Once this difference in administrative costs is recognized, there is no longer any theoretical presumption that an in-kind transfer can be more efficient than a cash transfer, even granting that external benefits exist. Instead it becomes an empirical question of whether the efficiency gain from a better consumption pattern, if any, is larger than the higher administrative costs involved.

Perhaps the most important problem with arguments for in-kind programs is that they must be invoked to defend subsidies for a large number of different goods. Recall that arguments for in-kind transfers hold that poor people would spend too little on some goods and too much on others if given cash. Because the poor spend 88 percent on necessities anyway, there is little scope for significantly increasing this share by using several in-kind programs. At best, the effect of in-kind programs (in comparison to cash transfers) is to increase the portion of any given budget that is devoted to selected goods, such as food, housing, and medical care, and to reduce the portion devoted to other goods. When most of the budget is already spent on the selected goods, there is little room for increasing the share of these goods in the budget, and the maximum potential advantage of subsidizing selected goods is small. Since most of a cash transfer would be spent on necessities anyway, why use several in-kind programs that would probably have a combined effect that differs very little from a cash transfer that lets the recipient spend the transfer as he wishes? Thus, arguments for in-kind transfers are not so convincing when they are used to defend in-kind transfers for several goods that would normally occupy a major share of recipients' budgets.

The paternalistic and externality arguments for in-kind transfers represent logically plausible defenses of this approach in principle. They do not appear so persuasive, however, as a defense of existing in-kind programs that subsidize most of the goods that would be heavily consumed by the poor in any event. It should be mentioned that not all economists share this judgment. In particular, some economists believe that externality considerations do provide substantial justification for existing in-kind transfers.

Public Employment Programs

In recent years there has been growing interest in the possibility of using some form of public sector employment program in combination with cash and/or in-kind assistance as a strategy for welfare reform. (President Carter's 1977 proposal for welfare reform placed great emphasis on a public jobs program.) The rationale for this approach is based on the premise that it is possible to classify all needy families into two groups: those who cannot (or should not be expected to) work, and those who are able to work but cannot earn an adequate income. For those who are unable to work, a cash assistance program with a high income guarantee *and marginal tax rate* can be used without reducing work incentives for those able to work (because they would be ineligible for the cash assistance program). For those who can work and are unable to find suitable employment in the private sector, a government job at a fixed wage rate will be provided. Thus, those who are needy but are able to work will be required to do so. At first glance, this dual program approach holds out the promise of avoiding the difficult tradeoff involved when a single cash assistance program must be designed to apply to all low income groups.

Let's consider a hypothetical public employment program that is typical of recent proposals. Each eligible family is to be guaranteed *one* public sector job. To be eligible, a family's other income (exclusive of wages on the guaranteed job) must fall below its poverty line (or other specified income level). The wage rate for the guaranteed job would be $3.50 per hour for 40 hours per week, or $7200 per year for full-time employment. Other poor families would be ineligible for the jobs program because they are not expected to work, such as the elderly or female-headed families with children. These groups would be eligible for cash assistance, as they are now.

A basic problem with a program of this nature is the need to classify individuals and families into three mutually exclusive groups: those eligible for cash assistance (who need not work); those eligible for a public sector job (who must work); and those ineligible for either welfare program. Can families be classified in these three groups fairly? It is difficult to see how a classification scheme that permits only three alternatives can be fair. There is enormous variation among people in terms of family size, age, other sources of income, health, productivity, work-leisure preferences, and so on. Can having the same job guarantee for all those considered eligible possibly be fair?

Consider a few examples. Is it fair for a family with one child to have the same job guarantee as a family with five children? Is it fair to exclude childless couples? Is it fair that an elderly couple over 65 can receive cash assistance without working, and a poor couple without children aged 60 is ineligible for any assistance at all? Is it fair that a family whose other income falls $1 short of its poverty line receives the same job guarantee (so its total income will be far above the poverty line) as a family with no income at all?

These examples are not meant to suggest that such problems could not be satisfactorily resolved, but they are indicative of the range of issues that must be faced in implementing such a program. The basic issue here is whether the distribution of benefits under a program of guaranteed public jobs can meet minimum standards of equity. Actually, in practice it would be impossible to ascertain the distribution of benefits. For a participant in the program, it is necessary to distinguish between the part of his total pay that is payment for services rendered and the part that is welfare assistance. For example, a person's productivity in whatever public job he is assigned may justify a salary of $4000 a year, but he will receive $7200. In this case, $3200 of his total pay should be viewed as a welfare grant and the remaining $4000 as unsubsidized earnings.

Clearly, people of widely differing productivities will be participating in a public jobs program. The labor services of some will be worth $3000, some $4000, and others $6000, yet all will receive $7200 a year for full-time work. This means that the welfare component of the recipient's pay is reduced by a dollar for every dollar increase in productivity. For those who participate and work full time, the jobs program is akin to an NIT with an income guarantee of $7200 and a marginal tax rate of 100 percent, reducing benefits (the welfare component of the pay) by a dollar for each dollar increase in real earnings. If this type of subsidy were paid explicitly, it would be viewed by most people as highly inequitable.

Turning now from the issue of equity to the issue of incentives, it is frequently held that a public employment program avoids the work disincentive effects associated with a program of cash transfers. In a trivial sense this is true: A person can receive the welfare component of his public sector pay only by working, so he gains nothing by refusing to work. The incentives issue in welfare reform, however, is far more involved, and a jobs program produces a number of undesirable incentive effects of its own. Let's consider four.

First, the program has a strong work disincentive if it is available only to families whose other income falls below some fixed level. Consider a family of three, where the husband earns $6000 and the wife $3000. Because their $9000 joint income is above their $4400 poverty line, they are currently ineligible for a public job. If, however, the husband works less and earns only $4399, and the wife quits her job, their total income falls below their poverty line, and they become eligible for a public sector job. If the wife takes the guaranteed job, the family's total income is $11,599, a considerable increase from the initial $9000. In this case, the husband has a strong incentive not to earn over $4400 so that his wife is eligible for the public sector job. (This example also shows how many people who are not needy can receive benefits under a public employment program.)

Second, there is little incentive for workers to put forth their best efforts. If jobs are guaranteed at a fixed rate of pay, why should workers strive to do a good job? They get paid even if they slack off. Would it be politically possible to discharge poor but unproductive or uncooperative workers from their "guaranteed" jobs?

Third, administrators in the public jobs program are likely to assign workers to the wrong jobs. Workers should be assigned the tasks where they are relatively the most productive if the total output of the public jobs program is to be as large as possible. Administrators have little incentive to do this, and political pressures ("No one should have to do menial or dead-end work") make efficient assignment of jobs within the program unlikely.

Fourth, the program may induce many workers to seek jobs in the public sector although they are more productive in the private sector. A person who can earn $6000 in a private job has incentive to take a public sector job paying $7200 even if his productivity in the public job is only $2000. In this case, there would be a net loss in total output of $4000: $6000 in sacrificed private sector output with only a $2000 increase in public sector output. Only if the labor services of all participating workers were more valuable in public sector jobs than in private jobs could this loss be avoided, and this is certain to be untrue (especially in view of the disincentives mentioned previously).

Now consider the cost to taxpayers of providing assistance to low income families by financing public jobs. Consider a worker whose annual labor services are worth $4000 in either a private or a public job. He would then prefer to work in the public sector at a salary of $7200, $3200 of which is a welfare subsidy and the remaining $4000 a payment for labor services. What is the cost to taxpayers of increasing his income by $3200 above his earnings in the absence of the program? The cost to taxpayers of financing the $7200 job is greater than $7200 because of administrative and overhead costs. It is not clear how large a cost this will be, but a figure of 15 percent of the wage cost would probably not be too large to assume. (President Carter's proposal allows for a cost of nearly 30 percent of the wage cost.) If this is the case, the administrative cost of a $7200 job is $1080, so the burden on taxpayers will be $8280. Moreover, the administrative cost should be compared with the welfare assistance component of the $7200. In our example, the actual welfare assistance to the worker is $3200, and to provide that aid necessitates an administrative cost of $1080, or about 33 percent of the aid transferred. If these figures are representative, they suggest that the administrative cost of supplying welfare assistance through a jobs program is quite high. Recall that it has been estimated that cash assistance programs can generally be administred at a cost of less than 5 percent of the welfare assistance that reaches recipients.

It seems clear that a public employment program would be quite inequitable and inefficient when considered as a welfare program. The jobs approach involves using one type of policy that has impacts on the attainment of three different government goals: (1) welfare assistance to the poor, (2) an efficient allocation of resources between the public and private sectors, and (3) a high level of aggregate employment. Jumbling these functions together produces unavoidable conflicts. For example, suppose that it is desired to reduce employment in the public sector (for efficiency reasons) and at the same time to increase welfare assistance. Under a jobs approach, this cannot be accomplished; reducing public sector employment requires lowering the guaranteed public sector wage, but that in turn would reduce welfare assistance. In contrast, using a cash assistance program and continuing to pay public employees in accordance with their productivities avoid this type of dilemma.

Despite the defects of a public employment program, it does eliminate the possibility of gross malingering. That, in addition to the fact that its harmful effects—its inefficiencies and inequities—are well hidden, difficult to explain, and hard to document, may help to explain its political appeal. Moreover, a well-designed program might avoid some of the difficulties mentioned.

Redistribution and Marginal Tax Rates

Determining whether to use cash or in-kind transfers is a question of what type of redistributive policy to use. In that context, questions concerning *whether* to redistribute income or *how much* to redistribute need not be raised. Now we turn to an examination of how much to redistribute. Obviously, economics cannot fully resolve this question. People will disagree over whether it is desirable to take $10 billion from the non-poor and give it to the poor. In part, disagreement results from different values regarding equality, the rights of people to keep what they earn, freedom, and so on. But judgments about what volume of redistribution is desirable also partly depend on the economic consequences resulting from the policies undertaken. By clarifying these consequences, economics can contribute to resolving the question.

The most important economic limitation to redistribution is its adverse effect on incentives. Redistribution tends to dampen incentives to produce and thereby may reduce the total income available to be divided among the population. For small amounts of redistribution, this effect may be of trivial size; unfortunately, it is not known at what level of redistribution adverse incentive problems become quantitatively significant. We do know, however, that productive incentives tend to be related to the level of marginal tax rates. As we saw with the NIT and other programs of a similar nature, work incentives (and other incentives) are weakened by using higher marginal tax rates. This is also true for taxpayers who must be subjected to higher rates to raise additional revenue needed for transfers to lower income families. Thus, it is important to know how marginal tax rates of recipients and taxpayers are influenced by the volume of redistribution.

It is obvious that additional redistribution will generally result in higher marginal tax rates for both transfer recipients and taxpayers. It is far from obvious, however, exactly how large the impact is and how it is related to the type of program used. It turns out that seemingly small amounts of redistribution can often have a sizable effect on marginal tax rates. An example will make this clear. Suppose an NIT is used to transfer income to families with incomes below $6000, and the average pretransfer income of these families is $4000. If we use an NIT that makes an average transfer of $2000 to each family, the average post-transfer (disposable) income of these families will be raised to $6000. This means we could bring each family exactly up to $6000. We could transfer $6000 to families with zero pretransfer income, $4000 to families with $2000 in pretransfer income, $500 to families with $5500 in pretransfer income, and so on. Note that this describes an NIT with a marginal tax rate of 100 percent, a program that would leave no incentive to work at all. When we try to concentrate a moderate volume of resources exclusively on a relatively small number of very low income families, the impact on marginal tax rates is surprisingly large. The reason is that the transfer must be reduced rapidly as income increases to make sure the transfer is zero at the low breakeven income level.

This could be avoided by giving every family an equal transfer of $2000, implying a zero marginal tax rate between zero and $6000. Consider, however, what happens between $6000 and $8000. A family with an income of $7000 would receive no transfer, but if its income fell to $6000 it would receive the $2000 transfer. Thus, the family would have a higher disposable income by reducing its earnings, and this would be true for all families with incomes between $6000 and $8000. The incentive problem is not avoided in this way; instead, it is just shifted into a higher income range. The abrupt reduction in the transfer from $2000 when income is $6000 to zero when income is $6001 creates a "notch" problem—a discontinuity in the relationship between pretransfer income and disposable income.

To avoid such a notch problem, the transfer must be gradually reduced until it reaches zero at the breakeven income level, and this gradual reduction is what produces the marginal tax rate in the program. We now see why concentrating seemingly moderate transfers exclusively on low income families will produce very high marginal rates—or a notch problem, which is just as bad.

The preceding numbers are hypothetical and are intended only to illustrate why marginal tax rates can be very sensitive to the volume of redistribution. Let's now turn to the actual relationships. In the following discussion, we will assume that any additional redistribution is carried out through an NIT program. In addition, for simplicity the tax revenue is assumed to be raised by taxing income above the breakeven level of the NIT at a constant marginal tax rate. In other words, we will consider programs that redistribute income from above a certain level (the breakeven level) to below that level, and determine the impact on the marginal tax rates for both recipients and taxpayers.

Table 8–5 summarizes the results.[7] All the figures for marginal tax rates are for a redistribution of 1 percent of national income (about $14 billion) from above to below the breakeven income. Thus, if we concentrate $14 billion in transfers on families with incomes below $7000, marginal tax rates for these low income families will rise by 30 percentage points. This gives the increment in marginal tax rates that must be considered in addition to already existing rates. Recalling that rates are typically very high for low income families—perhaps averaging about 60 percent—redistributing an *additional* 1 percent of national income will increase their effective marginal tax rates by 30 points—to about 90 percent on average. The adverse impact on incentives would probably be considerable.

If instead of concentrating all transfers on families below $7000 we use a breakeven income of $10,000, the transfer can be tapered off more slowly so the effect on marginal tax rates will be smaller. One percent of national income redistributed to families with incomes below $10,000

---

[7] These are rough estimates.

Table 8–5. Redistribution of 1 Percent of National Income

Breakeven Income	Increment in Marginal Tax Rate for Recipients	Increment in Marginal Tax Rate for Taxpayers
$ 7,000	+30	+2
10,000	+15	+3
15,000	+ 5	+5

will cause the marginal tax rates of those families to rise by 15 percentage points. Alternatively, if a breakeven income of $15,000—average family income—is used, the increment is 5 percentage points.

The opposite pattern is apparent for families above the breakeven income: the higher the breakeven income, the greater the increment in marginal tax rates needed to raise the additional revenue equal to 1 percent of national income. With a higher breakeven income, not only are there fewer families to bear the tax burden, but also, more importantly, the average taxable income per family will be smaller because only income in excess of the breakeven income is taxable.[8] (With a breakeven income of $15,000, the taxable income of a family with $20,000 is $5000. If $1000 in revenue is required to finance the NIT, a marginal tax rate of 20 percent on taxable income must be imposed.) Thus, the total income in excess of $15,000 of families earning above that level equals only one fifth of national income, and so a rate of 5 percent is required to raise revenue equal to 1 percent of national income. With a lower breakeven income, the tax base is larger and the required increment in marginal tax rates is smaller.

Under any program of redistribution, marginal tax rates must rise substantially to redistribute just 1 percent more of national income. With a breakeven income of $7000, marginal rates on low income families would clearly rise to unacceptable levels. This means to redistribute substantially more than we now are to low income families, a breakeven income higher than $7000 must be used. For instance, we might use a breakeven income of $15,000. Then marginal tax rates of all families would rise by 5 points, but only half the transfer would go to the really poor families (below $7000), because families in the $7000 to $15,000 range would receive about half of the total transfers. Thus, this plan would redistribute only 0.5 percent to low income families. If we wanted to get 1 percent of national income to these families, we would have to redistribute 2 percent of national income, with 1 percent going to the $0 to $7000 range and the other 1 percent to the $7000 to $15,000 range. This would require marginal tax rates to rise by 10 per-

[8]Taxing the total incomes of those above the breakeven income would result in a "notch" problem.

centage points (twice the increment shown because twice as much is re-distributed) for recipients and taxpayers alike.

There are some harsh tradeoffs implied by the figures in Table 8–5. Because marginal tax rates are already very high for low income families, we would like to avoid pushing them much higher. But even using the program with the $15,000 breakeven income, the rate would rise sharply—by 10 points if 1 percent of national income were added to their current income. Concurrently, to finance the transfer, the increase in rates on taxpayers would push most families nearly to, or above, an *effective* marginal tax rate of 50 percent.[9] No one knows how large an impact such a program would have on productive incentives, but it is easy to believe it would be substantial.

Figure 8–6 depicts the programs with the $7000 and $15,000 break-even incomes in a different form. Schedule *ABC* shows the transfer-tax schedule for an additional 1 percent redistribution using a breakeven income of $7000. Schedule *DEF* shows the relationship when the break-even income is $15,000. Note the different distributional effects involved. Using the lower breakeven income generates substantially larger transfers for the lowest income families (for example, $2100 for a family with no income), but marginal tax rates for these families would rise sharply. A higher breakeven income produces more modest rate increases, but the transfers to the lowest income families are much smaller, and the rate increases for upper income families are larger. Again, more difficult tradeoffs.

Unless we are prepared to accept the effects of marginal tax rates approaching 100 percent for low income families, substantial additional redistribution must utilize a program with a relatively high breakeven income. Even this option produces significant increases in marginal tax rates, and it also poses a difficult equity problem. With a breakeven income of $15,000, approximately half of the redistribution involves transfers within the broad middle income ranges. In other words, money would be transferred from those just above the average to those just below. There would be greater equality within the range from half the average to double the average income—a range that includes about 70 percent of all families. Ignoring incentive questions, is this redistribution equitable?

There are many reasons why shifting money around in the middle income ranges is difficult to defend as equitable. Recall our discussion in the last chapter explaining why a family's money income in one particular year is not a good indication of its standard of living, especially if a longer-run (more than 1 year) perspective is adopted. Taking income

[9] Effective marginal tax rates of most taxpayers are already close to or above 40 percent because of the combined effect of federal income, state income, social security, and sales taxes.

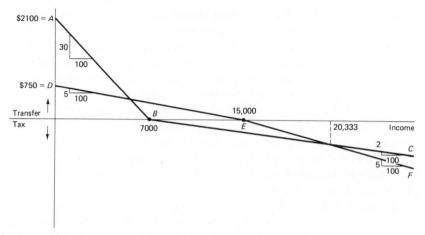

Figure 8–6. Distributive effects of two NIT programs.

from the $18,000 level and transferring it to the $12,000 level would mean in some cases shifting income from a middle-aged laborer at the peak of his earning years and helping a young college graduate just starting out. For this and other reasons, redistribution within the middle income range is not obviously a move toward greater equality in a meaningful sense. Yet redistribution of this type is unavoidable if we are going to transfer significantly more income to low income families without greatly increasing their marginal tax rates.

Both efficiency and equity considerations are therefore involved in a decision to increase or reduce the volume of redistribution. The efficiency consideration relates to the incentive effects of changes in the level of marginal tax rates. The equity considerations relate to whether greater equality in incomes is ethically desirable. Choices concerning the volume of redistribution are among the most difficult and controversial of all policy decisions, and it is easy to see why.

Proposal for Reform: The NIT

Over the past decade, a number of economists of widely differing political persuasions have advocated an NIT as a replacement for most, if not all, federal welfare programs. At issue is whether a single transfer program with uniform nationwide standards would be more equitable and efficient than the current system, which is composed of several separate—but overlapping and interacting—programs. (Actually, there are at least 168 federal expenditure programs that aid the poor, but most of these involve outlays of only a few million dollars.) Given the complexity of the existing system and the numerous factors that are relevant, arriving at a balanced judgment is difficult. Nonetheless, the major advantages and disadvantages of an NIT are fairly clear.

At the outset it should be emphasized that we are considering an NIT of total cost equal to the programs it replaces. Thus, there would be no increase in the cost to taxpayers. The volume of redistribution is considered fixed, so we can focus on different ways of effecting this redistribution. As we saw in the last section, adding an NIT to the present system to increase substantially the amount of redistribution would be difficult. Here we are concerned with welfare *reform*, not with an *expansion* in the system.

The principal advantages of an NIT as a replacement for existing programs include the following:

1. Assistance would be in the form of cash; as shown earlier, recipients would generally be better off according to their own preferences if they could spend the transfers as they saw fit. This advantage supposes that the NIT would replace the in-kind transfer programs now in use. Although recognizing that there are several arguments favoring in-kind transfers, proponents of the NIT find them generally unconvincing.

2. Administrative and compliance costs of an NIT would be lower. Although there is little firm evidence on this point, it seems generally agreed that the cost of administering a single, fairly simple program would be lower per dollar of transfer than for the present system composed of many potentially overlapping programs. In addition, costs borne by recipients in the form of filling out forms, establishing and maintaining eligibility, and so on, would probably be lower under the NIT. Smaller administrative and compliance costs mean that more resources can be made available to the poor at no extra cost to taxpayers.

3. Assistance would be objectively and uniformly related to need. Under the present system, there are wide differences in the level of assistance given to families with the same incomes. These differences reflect in part the fact that current programs grant assistance primarily to the poor who are elderly, in female-headed families, unemployed, and so on. What this means, for example, is that a poor person aged 65 can receive assistance under Supplemental Security Income, but an equally poor elderly person aged 64 may receive no assistance. Proponents of the NIT view disparities of this sort as inequitable; these disparities would be avoided by an NIT because a low income—for whatever reason—would entitle an individual to assistance. Families of the same size and income would receive equal transfers.

4. The NIT would concentrate transfers on those with low incomes. Recall that under the present system many programs confer a large share of their benefits on the nonpoor. Unemployment insurance, where over 80 percent of the benefits go to families in the upper four fifths of the

income distribution, is an example. Under an NIT, larger transfers would go to those with lower incomes. Although some of the transfers under the NIT would probably go to the nonpoor, depending on where the breakeven income is set, these transfers would be small compared to those received by lower income families.

5. The NIT would be easier to understand than the present system. Not only would it be simpler to determine how much is being transferred and who is benefiting from it (which is quite difficult to determine with current programs), but the various tradeoffs among the policy goals would become more apparent. Existing programs require tradeoffs of much the same type as the NIT, but this is often not understood because of the number of interacting programs involved. It is clear that neither the public nor Congress comprehends the present system sufficiently well to make informed decisions about changes in or additions to the system.

A clear example of the type of problem created by the lack of simplicity in the current system of overlapping programs occurred in 1970 when the House of Representatives actually passed a type of NIT, President Nixon's Family Assistance Plan (FAP), which would have resulted in marginal tax rates exceeding 100 percent for millions of low income people.[10] (The FAP later failed in the Senate.) The reason for this unintended outcome was that the FAP, with its own 50 percent marginal tax rate, was simply added to the existing programs. But the important point is that the complexity of the present system makes it difficult to understand the tradeoffs that must be made, and the interaction of overlapping programs. Although it is necessary to make difficult decisions in setting the policy variables of the NIT, the relationships are easy to understand, and it is to be hoped that the unavoidably hard choices that must be made will be based on an informed consideration of the factors involved.

It will be noticed that many of the advantages claimed for the NIT simply reflect perceived disadvantages of the present system. Proponents of the NIT view current programs as constituting a "welfare mess," with severe inequities in the distribution of transfers among the poor, avoidable distortions in consumption patterns, high administrative costs, and a complexity that makes rational decision making impossible. Although the NIT is not presented as a panacea, it is viewed as an improvement over the status quo.

There are, at the same time, a number of disadvantages to substituting an NIT for existing programs. These disadvantages should be reviewed.

[10] Milton Friedman, "Welfare: Back to the Drawing Board," reprinted from *Newsweek* in Friedman, *An Economist's Protest* (Glen Ridge, N.J.: Thomas Horton and Co., 1972), pp. 136–138.

1. Money income is not always an accurate indication of need. We have already emphasized the inadequacies of annual income as a good measure of a family's standard of living. Because transfers under the NIT would be based on money incomes, they would not necessarily be related to "need." For example, a family may have a child who requires expensive medical treatment and be poorer in a meaningful sense (unless they have insurance) than another family with an equal money income. Of course, an NIT could allow medical expenses to be deducted, but the more special circumstances it tries to take into account the more complex it becomes. In any event, the relevant question is whether standards under existing programs constitute a better definition of need than would the income measure employed by an NIT—not whether the NIT's measure is imperfect. Opinions on this point differ.

2. Work incentives would be impaired by the NIT. This contention is far from obvious because we are using the NIT as a replacement for existing programs that already imply high effective marginal tax rates. On average, marginal tax rates need not rise under the NIT when it replaced other programs. What would happen is that marginal rates would rise for some low income families and fall for others. Those families currently facing very high rates would generally have a lower rate under the NIT, whereas the opposite would be true of families with unusually low rates now. Whether the net effect would be a reduction in work effort is therefore unclear, but it obviously could be.

3. The NIT would treat the symptoms but not the causes of poverty. It would give money to the poor, but do nothing to help them become more self-supporting. This argument is usually advanced by those who advocate job training and educational subsidies to increase the earning capacity of the poor. It is true that the NIT would do nothing directly to increase earning capacity, but it would provide the means to finance job training if the recipient chose to use his subsidy in that way. It can be argued, however, that this is not enough. Unfortunately, evidence from the several manpower training and compensatory education programs that have been tried in the past leaves considerable doubt about the effectiveness of such policies.

4. Many poor families would find their benefit levels reduced under an NIT. No one likes the thought of reducing assistance to needy families, but it is clear that some low income families would be worse off under an NIT. Families receiving unusually large benefits under the present system would have lower benefits under the NIT, just as those with unusually low benefits now would receive larger benefits. The average benefit level would go up somewhat because of the saving in administrative costs, but some would still be worse off. The real question is whether existing differences in benefit levels for families with equal incomes are equitable or inequitable. If these differences are inequitable, **243**

some people are getting too much and others too little now, and a move to the NIT would seem fair. In other words, would the distribution of benefits under the NIT formula be more or less fair than under the present system? The answer probably depends on whether the income definition of the NIT corresponds to one's view of need, as mentioned earlier.

5. It is sometimes argued that the taxpayers would not support so large a volume of redistribution under the NIT as they now do under present programs. Taxpayers, it is argued, are willing to pay taxes if the funds are used to subsidize obviously needy groups (the elderly poor, female-headed households) or support consumption of necessities (food, housing, medical care). They might not, however, be willing to bear so large a tax burden when cash transfers are made to all with low incomes. This argument is difficult to evaluate because we do not understand precisely how the political process functions. Some have expressed the opposite concern: that, by making the redistribution open and aboveboard, political pressures would push benefit levels of an NIT up. After all, recipients vote, too. It is certainly possible that the politically determined volume of redistribution could differ under an NIT, so this is a legitimate concern in evaluating the proposal.

Replacing the current system with an NIT therefore raises a number of issues. Although we, along with many other economists, find considerable merit in the proposal, it is important to consider both its advantages and disadvantages.

Supplementary Readings

Aaron, Henry J. *Why Is Welfare So Hard to Reform?* Washington, D.C.: Brookings Institution, 1973.

Browning, Edgar K. *Redistribution and the Welfare System.* Washington, D.C.: American Enterprise Institute, 1975.

Campbell, Colin (ed.). *Income Redistribution.* Washington, D.C.: American Enterprise Institute, 1977.

Congressional Budget Office. *The Administration's Welfare Reform Proposal: An Analysis of the Program for Better Jobs and Income.* Washington, D.C.: U.S. Government Printing Office, April, 1978.

Congressional Budget Office. *Welfare Reform: Issues, Objectives and Approaches.* Washington, D.C.: U.S. Government Printing Office, 1977.

Danzinger, Sheldon, Robert Haveman, and Eugene Smolensky. *The Program for Better Jobs and Income—A Guide and Critique.* Washington, D.C.: U.S. Government Printing Office, Joint Economic Committee, October 17, 1977.

Okun, Arthur. *Equality and Efficiency: The Big Trade-off.* Washington, D.C.: Brookings Institution, 1975.

PUBLIC CHOICE

Public choice theory is the study of the processes through which government policies are determined and implemented. To this point we have been examining how existing (or proposed) policies affect resource allocation, which involves analyzing the way private markets respond to incentives inherent in policies. We have not, however, considered how the policies themselves are determined. They are, of course, determined politically, and public choice theory provides a limited basis for understanding the way the political process functions.

Is there an "invisible hand" in political decision making that leads to the enactment of efficient and equitable policies? This is clearly one of the most important questions that can be posed. The price system is a mechanism for allocating resources and distributing income; the government is simply an alternative or supplementary mechanism that also has an impact on resource allocation and income distribution. The price system works well in some situations but poorly in others (e.g., externalities, monopoly). Presumably, the same is true of government, but a theory is needed to explain how various forces interact in the political process before we can determine how well the government functions. That is what public choice theory tries to supply.

After about two hundred years of study, economists have a fair understanding of how the price system works. Unfortunately, the same cannot be said of their understanding of the political process. It has been seriously studied only for the past two or three decades. Although many important insights have been gained, we are still a long way from a moderately complete understanding of the decision-making process in government. Therefore, this chapter will provide no pat answers or no general model that can be easily applied in all situations. Instead, we will consider some of the components research suggests are likely to be integral parts of a general model. Their relative importance, however, is unknown.

Voting and Resource Allocation

Direct Majority Voting

Many political decisions emerge from a process of majority voting. We will begin by analyzing majority voting directly by citizens as a method of determining the total outlay to be made for the production of a public good. In reality, citizens seldom have the opportunity to determine the output of a public good directly by their votes, but it is still convenient to consider how such a process would work. Moreover, although our assumptions are unrealistic, the results of the analysis may be applicable to more realistic settings. In other words, the outcomes of citizens' first electing representatives who then vote on policies may be quite similar to the outcomes of citizens' voting directly on the policies themselves. We will consider whether this relationship holds later.

Assume for simplicity that we have a three-person community composed of individuals A, B, and C. By majority voting, they must determine how much output of a public good to finance through taxes. Suppose that the citizens have decided to divide the total cost of the public good equally among themselves. If the marginal cost for each unit of the good is $30, then each citizen will pay $10 per unit of the good produced. The number of units of output to be produced (and hence each citizen's total tax liability) will be determined by majority voting.

Figure 9–1 can be used to illustrate the voting process. The demand curves of the three voters are shown as d_A, d_B, and d_C; these curves indicate the marginal benefits to each voter from different levels of output. It is assumed that in deciding how to vote, each voter compares the benefits he would receive from a change in output with the change in the cost he must bear. The tax costs are summarized in the line TP_i, indicating the *tax price* per unit of the public good for each voter. Because we are assuming that the public good costs $30 per unit and the voters will share the costs equally, the tax price per unit of output for each taxpayer is $10. Total tax liability will depend on the number of units produced. As shown in the diagram, A prefers 4 units of output, B prefers 10 units, and C prefers 12 units. Majority voting will be used to determine a unique level of output.

The process of majority voting can be thought of as proceeding in this way. Beginning at a zero level of output, suppose a proposal is made to provide publicly, say, 2 units, with the costs divided as shown. Each voter compares benefits to tax costs; if he is better off with 2 units of the public good provided *and* paying taxes of $20 compared to no tax and none of the public good, he votes in favor of the proposal. If a majority of the citizens vote in favor of the proposal, it passes. Even if a proposal for 2 units passes, however, this may not be the *equilibrium* level of output under the voting process. Other proposals to increase or reduce output can be made and voted on. An equilibrium occurs at a level of output where any proposal to either increase or reduce output would be opposed by a majority.

Figure 9–1 allows us to identify the equilibrium in the simple setting depicted there. If output is initially zero, all three voters will support a proposal to increase output to 2 units, because the marginal benefits of the first 2 units exceed marginal costs (the tax price) for all three voters. Similarly, a proposal to expand output to 4 units will pass unanimously. At 4 units, however, a proposal to increase output to 5 units will be favored by *B* and *C* but opposed by *A*. Because a majority prefer 5 to 4, output will be increased. The process does not stop here, however, because both *B* and *C* will vote in favor of increasing output to 10 units. Ten units of output is, in fact, the equilibrium level of output. To see why, note that a majority of voters (*A* and *B*) will oppose any increase beyond 10 units and a different majority (*B* and *C*) will oppose any reduction below 10 units. Hence, a proposal to provide 10 units can defeat any other proposal; this is characteristic of an equilibrium under majority voting. Ten units of output will be provided, and each voter will be assigned a $100 total tax liability to cover the $300 cost of providing the good.

Figure 9–1. Majority voting process.

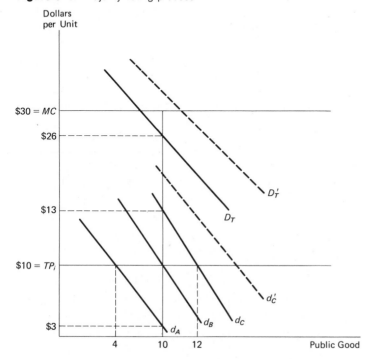

A basic implication drawn from this analysis is that the *median* preferred quantity of voters will be selected by majority voting. Of the three preferred quantities (4, 10, and 12), 10 is the median preferred quantity, with the same number of voters favoring a larger and smaller output. This result generalizes for any number of voters.

Although the model is quite simple, it helps us understand a number of important characteristics of political decision making by majority vote. First, note that the median voter, here individual *B,* is the only voter fully satisfied with the politically determined level of output—everyone else prefers either more or less output. (Of course, in the unlikely case where everyone had the same demand for the public good, all voters would unanimously agree.) It is *not* accurate to say that majority voting "gives the majority what it wants," because "the" majority that supports any given proposal will seldom agree among themselves.

Second, it is possible to see why so many people feel that government is not responsive to *individual* wants. By its very nature, the political process responds to an individual's wants only when they are in agreement with those of a substantial number of fellow voters; voters with preferences that are quite different from those of the bulk of voters are likely to remain dissatisfied.

Third, majority voting is likely to be unresponsive to *changes* in individual wants. Suppose individual *C*'s demand curve shifts to d_C'. Despite the fact that individual *C* wants a larger quantity of output, the equilibrium level of output remains unchanged. This characteristic is sometimes described by saying that majority voting ignores *intensity of preferences.* All a person can do is vote yes or no, and an impassioned yes carries no more weight than a weak yes. Only if the median preferred quantity changes is the actual outcome likely to vary.

Finally, there is no inherent tendency for majority voting to produce efficient policies. Recall from Chapter 2 that the efficient level of output is where the summed marginal benefits equal marginal cost. In Figure 9–1, the individual benefits for taxpayers *A, B,* and *C* at 10 units of output are $3, $10, and $13, so the combined marginal benefit is $26. ($D_T$ is the vertical summation of the three individual demand curves.) Because marginal cost is $30, the tenth unit of output is worth less than it costs. Nonetheless, an output of 10 units is the equilibrium under majority voting. In this case, majority voting produces too large an output. The opposite, however, is also possible. If individual *C*'s demand were d_C' instead of d_C, summed marginal benefits would be given by D_T', and the equilibrium level of output (still 10) would be less than the efficient level. Thus, there is no inherent tendency for efficient outcomes to be produced through majority voting; whether they are depends on the exact distribution of demands around the median.[1]

---

[1] Under all real-world tax institutions, the same tax price does not confront all voters. For example, under a proportional income tax, a voter with twice the income of another

Logrolling

The process of majority voting will sometimes lead to the approval of policies that are actually opposed by a majority of voters. One way this can occur is through a process known as logrolling. Logrolling is a process of trading votes to achieve a majority. A simple example will indicate why it occurs.

Suppose we have three voters, A, B, and C. Only one voter, C, favors the subsidization of college construction. Only one voter, B, favors subsidization of hospital construction. At first glance, it would appear that the proposals for both subsidies would fail under majority voting because each program is opposed by two of three voters. This, however, may not be the outcome. Individuals B and C could agree to exchange votes to secure passage of their favored proposals. In other words, C could agree to vote for a hospital subsidy (which he really opposes) if B in turn will agree to support the college subsidy that C wants. Depending on how strongly each party wants a particular subsidy, the exchange of votes may be to their mutual advantage. If the exchange takes place, both subsidies secure the needed majority, although each subsidy is really opposed by a majority of voters.

Figure 9–2 illustrates the effects of the logrolling process in more detail. Assume that the marginal cost of constructing hospitals and colleges is \$30 each, and the costs are assumed to be divided equally among the voters. The horizontal axis indicates the level of output of a composite good composed of one college plus one hospital; the marginal cost of this composite good is \$60. Output is measured in this way because logrolling forces voters to consider several proposals simultaneously. Thus, when C votes for a college subsidy, he knows he must also vote for a hospital subsidy; the relevant question concerns C's demand for both programs together. In Figure 9–2, d_C indicates C's demand for the composite good; it may, of course, be that he only really benefits from the college subsidy, just one part of the composite good. As drawn, d_B and d_C will coincide. The reason for this is that the terms of trade in the logrolling agreement—here one college for one hospital—will be negotiated until both agree on what quantity of one to exchange for the other. In terms of the composite good, both B and C agree that 8 is the appropriate output, although they will have different demands for the colleges and hospitals.

The votes on college and hospital subsidies are taken separately, but now B and C trade votes and an output of 8 hospitals and 8 colleges is determined. In this case, logrolling has worked to produce a larger-than-

would pay twice as much in taxes and hence face a tax price per unit of government output that is twice as high. Although the diagrammatic analysis becomes more complicated, the general conclusions derived in the text remain valid. **249**

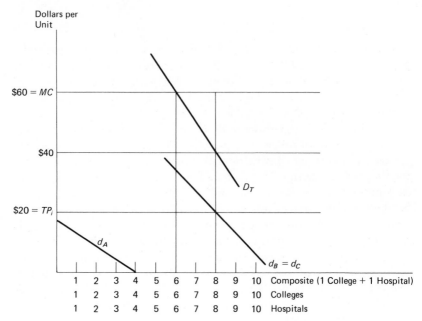

Figure 9–2. Logrolling process.

efficient output of both goods. This can be seen by comparing total marginal benefits and costs at the equilibrium level of output. At an output of 8 units of the composite good, the marginal benefit to B and C is $20, whereas the marginal benefit to A is zero. Total marginal benefits are $40 as shown by the vertically summed demand curve D_T. Because marginal cost is $60, 8 units of output represents too large an output.

Intuitively, the reason why logrolling produces too large an output in this case can be easily seen. Only a majority of voters are needed to achieve passage of the relevant bills. Under logrolling, the majority trade votes on terms that lead them to favor the *same* quantity of the composite good. Put differently, the majority who agree will vote to increase expenditures up to the point where their marginal benefits equal the marginal costs they must bear. (Without logrolling, only the median voter's marginal benefits and costs are equal.) There will be a minority, however, who are made worse off, that is, who bear net marginal costs; thus, the combined marginal costs of all the voters exceed combined marginal benefits. Too much is produced when the preferences of all the voters are considered.

An important question is whether logrolling always tends to produce an overexpansion in government spending. Insofar as logrolling agreements arise in order to secure passage of expenditure bills, the preceding analysis suggests that overexpansion is the result.[2] It is possible, however, that logrolling could occur to block the passage of bills that would, without logrolling, pass. In that case, too low a level of spending would result. Although logrolling to expand expenditures seems more typical, logrolling to reduce expenditures is a theoretical possibility.

The process of logrolling is often defended as a means of protecting minority interests. On a particular issue, a minority of voters may passionately favor a particular policy, but under majority voting without logrolling their interests will be ignored, implying a "tyranny of the majority." Logrolling, however, provides a method by which minorities can secure favorable legislation by agreeing to support other policies. Although logrolling can in this way protect minority interests, the relevant question is whether it leads to overrepresentation of minority interests. According to the preceding analysis, when logrolling occurs, it leads to inefficiency because it ignores the minority of voters who are not a party to the logrolling agreement. Too much weight is given to minority preferences by logrolling.

A final point should be made. Logrolling among individual voters is not likely to occur when there are large numbers of voters (or with a secret ballot). In national elections, for example, there is little incentive for individual voters to exchange votes for senators and congressmen because it would have no perceptible impact on the final outcome. Logrolling is most likely to occur when a vote trade will have a significant impact on the outcomes of the votes, and that will generally be true only when a relatively small number of votes is required to achieve a majority. Decision making by representatives within legislative bodies apparently involves a small enough number of voters for logrolling to be effective, because it is quite common in such settings.

Electing Representatives

In the United States, candidates of the two major political parties run against one another for political office, and majority voting generally determines which candidate will serve.[3] Our general approach can be used to shed some light on the likely outcomes of such elections. Begin by assuming that candidates are distinguishable only in terms of a liberal-conservative spectrum. In other words, candidates will be classified according to how far left or right their policy positions are. Further assume that voters will support the candidate whose position is closest to their

---

[2] James M. Buchanan and Gordon Tullock, *The Calculus of Consent* (Ann Arbor: University of Michigan Press, 1962).

[3] When more than two candidates are running, the one with the most votes (not necessarily a majority) wins. This is called plurality voting.

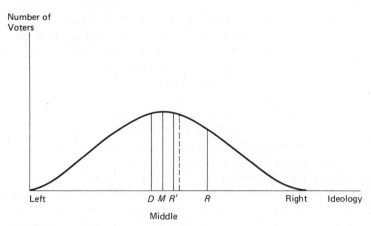

Figure 9–3. Middle-of-the-road politics.

own. Thus, the voter's choice is narrowed to a single issue. Although this is perhaps an oversimplified example, it serves to make some simple but important points.

The distribution of voters according to political ideology is shown by the bell-shaped curve in Figure 9–3. The line drawn at point M separates the total electorate in half; half the voters have positions to the right of this middle-of-the-road position, and the other half have positions to the left. Now consider an election between two candidates, a Republican and a Democrat. If the candidates take positions shown by R and D, who will win the election? Clearly, the Democrat will win because a majority of the voters have political beliefs closer to his than to the Republican's. A dotted line can be drawn halfway between R and D, and we will assume that all voters with beliefs to the left of the dotted line will vote for the Democrat and those to the right will vote for the Republican. Voters will then be supporting the candidate whose views are *closer* to their own position.

Faced with this likely outcome, it is in the Republican candidate's interest to modify his position to the left. By doing this, he can attract some votes near the middle without losing any support to the right. For example, if he takes the position at R', where M is half way between D and R', he will get exactly half the votes. If he takes a position a little to the left of R', he will get a majority. Of course, the Democrat can also change his position. In the limit, both candidates have incentive to move to the middle-of-the-road positions at M. Voters will be indifferent between the candidates, and the likely outcome will be a tie vote.

Of course, candidates do not take identical positions, and elections rarely end in ties. The analysis indicates, however, the tendency for politicians to adopt middle-of-the-road positions as they seek voter support.

Because they do not have complete and accurate information about voter preferences, this is only a general tendency, but it accords well with political realities. (As casual evidence to indicate the importance politicians place on discerning voters' preferences, recall the extensive use of polls in recent national primaries and elections.) When a politician has the courage (?) to stake out a position far from M, he is usually defeated. This happened in the presidential election in 1964 when Goldwater took a position like that at R, offering voters "a choice, not an echo," and was soundly defeated. It happened again in 1972 when McGovern took a position well to the left of M and suffered a similar fate. Such occurrences are relatively rare because politicians are astute enough and sufficiently interested in winning to stay fairly close to the middle.

This is simply another example of the importance of the median position in majority voting, because M is the median. It does, however, serve to indicate why it is generally correct for voters to feel they are not offered much choice at election time. Insofar as the lack of real choice is a result of politicians' successfully locating the median preference, this is not necessarily bad. In any event, it is what one should expect from competition among politicians for votes.

In many respects, this model is an oversimplified representation of reality. When there are hundreds of policies on which politicians must take positions, it is not possible to compress all choices into a single left-to-right continuum. As we shall see, politicians do not always have incentive to take the median position on every issue (even if they can locate the median).

The Cyclical Majority Phenomenon

There are some situations in which there is no equilibrium under majority voting. No matter what policy is chosen, there is another policy that is favored by a majority. Sound impossible? Consider the situation described in Table 9–1. There are three voters, A, B, and C, and there are three possible policies: a small budget (S), a medium budget (M), and a large budget (L). The ranking of these alternative policies for each voter is given. Thus, A's first choice is the medium budget, his second choice is the small budget, and his least preferred alternative is the large budget. Confronted with two alternatives, each voter will vote for the higher ranked alternative.

If majority voting is used to select among the three alternatives, the choices must be considered on a pairwise basis. M can be pitted against S, and the winner of that vote can be pitted against L. In a selection between M and S, M will win, because voters A and B prefer M to S. When M is run against L, L will prevail, because B and C prefer L to M. It appears that L is the winner until we notice that if L is run against

S (which was defeated by M in the first vote), then S wins, because A and C prefer S to L. To summarize the outcomes: S can defeat L, L can defeat M, and M can defeat S. There is no equilibrium because every policy can be defeated by one of the others. No matter what is chosen, something else is preferred by a majority. This is called the cyclical majority phenomenon because policy choices can cycle from M to L to S to M and so on indefinitely.

Understanding how this phenomenon can occur is simple, but appreciating its general significance is more difficult. To some, it has shaken their faith in democracy and majority rule; to others, it is only a theoretical curiosity of little practical relevance. What is really at issue is how often the phenomenon actually occurs in political decision making.

Clearly, there are some situations in which the cyclical majority phenomenon would not occur. In Table 9–1, if C's ranking were SML instead of SLM, then M could defeat both L and S and represent a stable equilibrium. The cyclical majority phenomenon occurs only when the rankings of voters bear a certain relationship to one another. How likely is it that voters' rankings of alternatives will produce no stable equilibrium? If it is assumed that all possible combinations of rankings are equally likely, then the cyclical majority phenomenon would occur in about 11 percent of the cases. Some scholars, however, have argued that this overstates the probability of its occurrence because the rankings that produce the cyclical outcomes are inherently unlikely. As an example, consider C's ranking in Table 9–1: SLM. C prefers both extremes—the large and the small budget—to the intermediate position—the medium budget. Although this is conceivable, it is odd, because generally the intermediate position would be preferred to at least one of the extremes. This, for example, is true of the situation shown in Figure 9–1. For any three levels of output that are specified, no voter will prefer both the largest and the smallest output to the one in between. The rankings of voters implied by Figure 9–1 will produce a stable equilibrium: 10 units of output.

This argument implies that when voters are determining how much to spend on one particular project, and when the costs are prorated in advance, a stable equilibrium is likely to result. Many political decisions, however, do not fit this description, and it is our view that the cyclical majority phenomenon is quite common in more realistic settings. Let's begin by using an example to illustrate how it might occur. Suppose the government is going to divide $1000 among 100 voters and initially proposes to give each voter $10. Then someone proposes that the entire amount be divided among 51 voters. The second proposal would defeat the first because 51 voters, a majority, would prefer it. Next, a third proposal is introduced: Give a still larger amount to two members of the original 51 member majority (to induce them to change

Table 9–1. Cyclical Majority Phenomenon

Voters	A	B	C
Ranking	M	L	S
	S	M	L
	L	S	M

sides) and divide the remainder among the 49 who receive nothing under the second proposal. The third proposal would defeat the second one. In short, no matter how the $1000 is divided among the voters, it is always possible to design another proposal that would give less to a minority and more to a majority, and that proposal would be favored by a majority. In this situation, there is no proposal that could consistently defeat all others under majority voting. This example is characteristic of real-world situations when voters select among politicians who take stands on a variety of issues. The reason is that alternative combinations of policy issues have different effects on the distribution of income (that is, on who benefits and who loses) just as in the preceding example.

For example, a politician might favor higher social security benefits, higher tariffs, and higher price supports for agricultural products. The combined impact of these three policies might redistribute income in favor of a majority, so the politician could secure majority approval. A second politician, however, might propose a policy package composed of higher food stamp subsidies, higher subsidies to college students, and even higher (than proposed by the first politician) tariffs. The combined impact of these three policies might benefit a majority when compared to the proposals of the first politician, so the second politician could defeat the first. No matter what combination of policies is proposed, it is always possible to design another combination that would benefit a majority because it is always possible to use government policies to redistribute income in favor of a majority. When all government policies are considered as a package—which is what happens when we choose among political candidates—there is no combination of policies that represents a stable equilibrium under majority voting.

The nonexistence of a stable equilibrium does not mean that we would expect to see constant cycling among alternatives, with no decision ever being reached. Decisions are made simply because when a vote is taken on one issue, or in one election, one of the two alternatives being voted on will necessarily win (barring ties). What the absence of an equilibrium means is that the political decisions actually reached are not favored by a majority over all other alternatives.

There are at least two important insights to be obtained from an understanding of the cyclical majority phenomenon. First, one should expect underlying inconsistencies in government policies. Minimum wage laws that create unemployment coexist with job training programs to put the unemployed to work. Farm price supports raise the cost of food to the poor, but food stamps lower the cost. Some subsidies (such as aid to colleges) tend to benefit the relatively affluent, others benefit the poor, and still others benefit middle income families. It is not possible to examine actual policies and infer a consistent set of "social priorities," because choices through the political process should be expected to be inconsistent. The group of voters who form an effective coalition favoring farm price supports is different from the group favoring food stamps. Because the preferences or priorities of the different groups and individuals differ, there is no reason to expect political choices to be consistent. Some political choices reflect the dominance of the views of one group, and others reflect the dominance of a different set of values.

Second, one should expect an underlying instability in government policies. No matter what the government does, an astute politician can always find a new policy package that will secure majority approval. This means that government will provide no stable framework of laws, taxes, and expenditures within which individuals can confidently plan their lives. Frequent change can be predicted. Of course, if voters believe a stable framework is important, they may place limits on the types of policies governments can enact. Presumably, this feeling underlies the views of those who favor constitutional limitations on the power of government.

We must be cautious of attaching too much importance to the cyclical majority phenomenon. It may be that voters' underlying preferences effectively limit the range of issues over which cycling can theoretically occur, or it may be that actual political institutions operate to make the phenomenon occur more rarely than theoretical considerations would suggest. At this stage in the development of public choice theory, the significance of the problem is unknown.

Participants in the Political Process

Many different groups of people influence government decisions: voters, politicians, government employees, lobbies, judges, the media, intellectuals, and so on. Examining the incentives confronting some of these participants and their likely behavior can contribute to a broader understanding of the political process.

Voters

It is appropriate to begin by considering citizens in their role as voters. The voting public elects many government officials and thereby empowers them to make and enforce government policy. The voting decisions of the public therefore determine who will run the government and indirectly influence the policies enacted. Given the importance of the role played by voters, it is instructive to examine their behavior to ascertain if they have incentives to seek out and support political candidates who favor efficient and equitable government policies.

Many factors influence a person's vote: a candidate's personality, spouse, wit, honesty, and ethnic, religious, and regional background. Naturally too the candidate's position on policy will likely be important. Other things equal, voters will favor the candidate whose policies they believe will yield them the greatest net benefits (or smallest net costs). Voters will cast votes in an attempt to further their self-interest. This is not necessarily bad; recall that the pursuit of self-interest in a competitive price system generally tends to produce socially desirable outcomes. It is, in fact, this characteristic of voters that gives political candidates incentive to formulate policies that benefit the public.

The basic question is whether voters will tend to favor policies that are efficient, that is, policies that have total benefits in excess of costs. In answering this question, it is helpful to distinguish between two different cases in which a policy will benefit a specific voter. In one case, a policy benefits voter A *and* involves total benefits in excess of total costs when the effects on all persons are considered. In this situation, the policy is an efficient one and the voter will support it (and the candidate who favors it, other things equal). In the second case, a policy benefits voter A *and* involves total costs greater than total benefits. This policy is inefficient, yet voter A will still support it because it benefits him.

There is no inherent tendency for voters to support efficient government policies. Even the most inefficient policies generally benefit some groups of voters (although at greater costs to the rest of the public), and those who benefit will support them. Thus, we could expect producers to support higher tariffs on competing imported products, dairy farmers to support higher milk price supports, coal miners to support taxes on oil, the elderly to support greater social security benefits, and college students (and professors) to support higher subsidies to colleges. We do not mean to prejudge all of those policies as necessarily inefficient or inequitable (although some probably are), but only to suggest the importance of the pursuit of personal gain in motivating voters. People are not narrowly *self*-interested in their market behavior and then *public*-interested in the voting booth; they strive to obtain whatever goals they have through both processes.

257

Actually, voters are seldom given the opportunity to express a preference on a single policy. Instead, they must choose among candidates offering different bundles of policies. In this setting, it is easy for a voter to justify supporting a candidate who favors a policy greatly in the voter's interest. A college student is likely to support a candidate who will halve college tuition. Although this clearly augments the student's wealth at the expense of the general taxpayers, the candidate also favors a multitude of other policies that benefit other groups. The student, in rationalizing his vote, can claim that his candidate has "something for everyone" and that the tuition subsidy simply indicates his candidate's broad concern for college students as well as other groups. Most voters no doubt believe they act "in the public interest," but people have an amazing capacity to believe (like General Motors) what benefits them is good for the country. Sometimes it may be true, but not always.

The behavior of voters is strongly conditioned by another influence, the tendency of voters to be rationally ignorant of the consequences of their political choices. "Rational voter ignorance" is one of the most important forces operating in the political process, and it has far-reaching effects. Rational voter ignorance can best be understood as the hypothesis that voters will be relatively less informed about their political decisions than about comparable private market decisions. It does not mean that people have perfect information in the market place and zero information about activities in the public sector. Because acquiring information involves costs, people will seldom be perfectly informed about any choices they make.

To see why voters are rationally ignorant, let's consider the extent of information collected (and the relative costs) by a person considering the purchase of private health insurance in contrast to his selection of a national health insurance plan. To make a wise choice about private health insurance, a person would like to obtain a great deal of information: the types of illnesses covered by the policy, the costs of different parts of the policy, the probabilities of contracting the illnesses covered, the costs of being treated for all these illnesses, and so on. Clearly, few people will acquire all the needed information, and this behavior is rational, given the cost of acquiring information.

To evaluate national health insurance proposals, however, much more information is required. To make an informed decision, a person would need to know not only all of the above facts about alternative proposals but also how much of a tax burden he would bear (not an easy matter to determine), the likely impact of alternative national health insurance schemes on medical care and other prices, how the cost controls in the plan will actually affect him, and so on. In short, the voter needs a great deal more information to make a wise decision about the government policy, and the additional information is of a different nature, because it is more like knowledge that requires scientific research to substantiate.

The higher information cost is one reason to expect voters to be relatively uninformed in their political decision-making. There is, in addition, a second reason that is perhaps of even greater importance. The gain that a person can realize from acquiring political information is much less than the gain from acquiring information about goods purchased privately. Suppose a person spends several months researching national health insurance; what benefit does he get? He can patriotically cast a better-informed vote, but because his is one vote among millions, it will have no perceptible effect on the outcome. The same national policy is almost certain to be enacted regardless of whether any single person is well informed. Consequently, people have little incentive to obtain information about the operation of the government, the action of politicians, or the effects of government policies. In contrast, the purchase of private goods is different. If a person becomes better informed about alternative private health policies, he gets the benefits of choosing the one better suited to his needs. His private choice is decisive in influencing the outcome, which contrasts sharply with his voting decision. In the marketplace, the benefits associated with becoming better informed are greater, the costs of information are lower, and the consumer will acquire more information.

It should be stressed that relative ignorance is rational. Observers often bemoan the lack of knowledge and interest on the part of voters, but no amount of cajoling is likely to effect a change. It is far more important for most people to obtain information of use in their daily lives than to engage in scientific research on social problems.

The existence of rationally ignorant voters has important repercussions for the workings of the political process because the political process caters to voters as they actually are, not as they would be if they were fully informed. For example, rational voter ignorance accounts for the generally low level of political discourse. Political speeches (as well as newspaper editorials) often rely on slogans, oversimplifications, inadequate theories, and misleading facts. Appearances and plausibility count for more than truth. Voters lack the necessary information to evaluate the assertions made by politicians, which in turn gives politicians little incentive to achieve accuracy and balance in their views.

Although voters will generally be rationally ignorant about most government policies, some voters will be relatively more informed on certain issues. Dairy farmers are likely to know more about how milk price supports affect them than are the remainder of the public. Where the consequences of a policy for some voters are desirable or disastrous and involve large benefits or costs, the affected voters are more likely to realize whether or not they benefit. In these cases, the benefits of acquiring more information exceed the costs, and the affected groups will be better informed. Often voters will base their voting decisions on a small subset of policies that affect them strongly. It may be rational for a college student to favor the candidate who wants higher tuition subsidies. The student knows he will directly benefit from that policy but finds it difficult to determine what the net effect of all the other policies favored by his candidate would be for his welfare. This type of reasoning often leads voters to evaluate political candidates almost wholly on the basis of a few issues that affect them directly. As we shall see, this is one reason for the prevalence of special interest legislation.

As a final example, voter ignorance is the explanation for the frequently noted tendency of politicians to emphasize the obvious and short-term effects of policies while ignoring the hidden, long-term consequences. It is well known that an incumbent President is extremely concerned with the state of the economy just before the election. Reducing the unemployment rate by November may be a good strategy even if the cost is a higher rate of inflation several months later. Voters may not be aware of the long-run costs of reducing unemployment quickly, nor will they make the connection later.

Politicians

Those who seek office and those who hold elected offices play a role in politics similar to the role of businessmen in private markets. Businessmen are the moving force in markets: They make the actual decision concerning what to produce and in what quantities. Similarly, politicians—at least successful ones—determine what government does; their voting and logrolling activities determine the broad outlines of government policy. To stay in business, businessmen are led to take account of consumers' interests by virtue of having to produce a product consumers want. Likewise, politicians are led to take account of voters' interests by having to offer a policy "package" that attracts enough voters to stay in office. In both the political and the market spheres, the process used to make decisions gives us some reason to believe that the public's interest will be served.

The analogy between political and business entrepreneurs cannot be pressed too far, because there are important differences. A businessman does not require approval of a majority of the public to operate his business, yet a politician frequently does. A businessman cannot force any consumer to purchase his product, but a politician's programs are financed by taxes levied on many who opposed the programs. A businessman offers wares for sale, one at a time, day after day, in competition with numerous other competitors, whereas a politician sells a package of hundreds of policies once every several years, and generally in competition with only one other candidate. These differences are not intended to imply that one process is any better than the other, but only that the market and political processes differ.

In trying to understand the behavior of politicians, public choice specialists have found it useful to assume that politicians behave in a way they believe will maximize the votes they receive at the next election.[4] This is not a cynical assumption, but a realistic one. Elected officials will remain in office only if they continue to attract enough voter support. Political survival requires that politicians pay attention to the vote-gaining and vote-losing effects of their actions just as business survival demands attention to the profit picture. Successful politicians—the ones who actually make government decisions—will be the ones who are best at attracting votes. Politicians may believe they are acting "in the public interest" (and indeed may be, according to their own conception of the public interest), but they would not be successful unless their actions *also* attracted votes.

The important question is: What type of government policies will result from an attempt by politicians to maximize votes? This is a complex question, and one to which public choice theory provides no complete or simple answer. In trying to determine an answer, two points should be recalled. First, politicians are elected on the basis of their positions on many issues; it is the overall "package" offered in comparison to competing politicians that counts. Politicians thus need not please the majority on each separate issue. Second, the voters are rationally ignorant of much of what politicians stand for, their past actions, and the likely consequences of their proposed policies.

The importance of these points can be illustrated by looking at some examples. Consider a politician who must take a position on the three policies listed in Table 9–2. Each program benefits only 20 percent of the voting public. Yet a politician who opposes all three policies could be defeated by another who favors them. The reason is that each group benefits by one of the policies and may secure benefits in excess of the harm done to it by the other two policies. Farmers, for example, may believe the higher taxes they would pay to finance the college and welfare subsidies will be less than the gain they receive from higher price supports; in their view all three policies are better than none. If all three groups feel this way, they will vote for a politician favoring all three policies when the alternative is a politician opposing all three.

This example illustrates how special interest legislation may be passed even though a large percentage of the public is harmed. Special interest

---

[4] Alternatively, it might be assumed that they will just attempt to achieve a majority of the votes cast. In most cases, it would make little difference which assumption is made.

Table 9–2. Implicit Logrolling

Policy	Favored by	Opposed by
Farm price supports	20%	80%
Welfare assistance	20%	80%
College tuition subsidy	20%	80%

legislation can be thought of as policies that yield large individual benefits to a small proportion of the public coupled with small individual costs falling on a large proportion of the public. For example, a policy may grant benefits of $1000 a year to 2 percent of the voters at costs of $25 a year to the remaining 98 percent. A politician may gain votes by favoring this policy. He is almost certain to gain the votes of the 2 percent who are benefited, regardless of his position on other issues (at least, in comparison to an opponent who opposes this policy). Moreover, he may not lose much support among the remaining 98 percent even though this policy harms them because the damage done is small and may be offset by benefits under other policies he supports.

In effect, special interest legislation that enables a politician to put together an overall majority by combining numerous programs that benefit separate minorities is an example of *implicit logrolling*. As noted earlier, logrolling makes voters consider different policies simultaneously, and that is exactly what must be done when voters choose among candidates offering different policy packages. In this way, voters are led to support a politician who favors some policies they don't want to get the one they do want.

Rational voter ignorance often increases the incentive of politicians to favor special interest legislation. The harm done to each member of the majority by one policy is quite small and in many cases difficult to estimate. (What annual cost do you bear from milk price supports or subsidies to airports?) Voters are often rational in not making an attempt to estimate the damage done from hundreds of policies affecting them only slightly and often indirectly. Instead, they concentrate on policies that have large and obvious effects on their own well-being, that is, on special interest legislation that benefits or harms them.

Rational voter ignorance has still other effects on the behavior of vote-maximizing politicians. Any policy has both costs and benefits, but the visibility of these effects (that is, how obvious they are to voters) varies widely from policy to policy. Some consequences of policies are more hidden and difficult for the average person to perceive than others; a policy with hidden benefits but apparent costs is unlikely to be favored by politicians because voters underestimate the true benefits. The political process is consequently biased against policies with hidden benefits and visible costs. Conversely, it is biased toward policies with highly visible benefits and hidden costs.

Consider a policy of subsidizing medical research out of general income taxes. The benefit is an increased probability of finding a cure for some disease, but many voters who might benefit in the future if a cure is found are likely to be unaware of this benefit (some would not even be born). The tax costs, on the other hand, are quite obvious. If voters sufficiently underestimate the benefits, politicians may be led to oppose the policy even if it is efficient. As another example, social security involves two large hidden costs: the impact on capital accumulation and the half of the tax that is nominally levied on employers (but almost certainly reduces workers' take-home pay). Social security's benefits—pensions for the retired—are fairly apparent. Politicians may be led to overexpand a policy with such hidden costs but visible benefits.

In fact, politicians may have incentives to design policies in ways that make benefits clear to those who benefit and costs difficult to perceive for those who are harmed, if it is possible. The most obvious costs are generally taxes, but even these can often be levied in a way to obscure their burden. Taxes that are nominally paid by businesses often are actually borne by consumers or workers, but the ones who bear the final burden may be unaware of it. Corporate income taxes, excise taxes, customs duties, the employer portion of social security taxes, and deficit finance are all methods of financing expenditures that depress disposable incomes of people who are probably unaware of it. It is probably no accident that nearly 50 percent of all federal expenditures were financed by these methods in 1976.

Although it is impossible to be very precise in this matter, it seems clear that vote-maximizing politicians are sometimes led to favor genuinely efficient policies and sometimes to favor highly inefficient policies. *All other things the same,* the greater the total benefits relative to the total costs of some policy, the more votes a politician can gain by supporting it. This is the positive aspect of the incentives political institutions give politicians. Other things, however, are not always the same, and politicians can sometimes gain votes by favoring policies that benefit some voters but impose greater (possibly hidden) costs on others.

Bureaus and Bureaucrats

Congressional actions can be thought of as expressing a collective *demand* for public services, but there is also a need for an institution to design and implement policies. Government agencies or bureaus are generally empowered to carry out the policies enacted by Congress. Recent research has suggested that bureaus do not simply passively respond to the dictates of Congress, but instead take an active role in the decision-making process and exercise some degree of power in determining policy.

The term *bureaucracy* is often used to refer to any large organization, but it is necessary to recognize important differences between public and private bureaus. Private bureaus are usually part of a business organization that is operated for a profit, so the activities of private bureaus are subject to a market test: They must produce something that people are willing to purchase. Government bureaus are nonprofit organizations that do not sell their services directly to the public. In a sense, they sell their services to Congress, but they do not set a price per unit and allow Congress to determine quantity. Instead, they obtain an annual lump sum appropriation to cover the total costs of all the services provided. In addition, public bureaus, as distinct from private bureaus, are generally monopolies. The Department of Health, Education, and Welfare, for instance, is responsible for almost all policies dealing with medical care; there are no other bureaus competing with it to obtain funds from Congress in this area.

Given these differences between public and private bureaus, it is to be expected that the bureaucratic supply of public services will produce different results than the private supply. To see how the results are likely to differ, let's begin by considering what goals motivate the top-level bureaucrats. Bureaus are not allowed to operate at a profit, so we cannot assume that they try to maximize profits. Alternatively, however, bureaucrats can attempt to maximize the total size of their budgets.[5] A larger budget will generally mean higher salaries, more power, and more prestige for top-level bureaucrats. In addition, the internal advancement of personnel virtually assures that those who reach the top will consider the activities of the bureaus highly beneficial and worthy of enlargement. As a piece of casual evidence, have you ever heard of a bureaucrat trying to convince Congress to cut his budget?[6]

Assuming that bureaucrats attempt to maximize their budgets is not equivalent to assuming that they are successful. (Recall that competitive firms are assumed to maximize profits, yet they end up with zero economic profits.) Congress, after all, must approve budget requests. Bureaus, however, may be in a favorable bargaining position to realize their goals. From observing congressional action over a period of years, bureaus have a fairly good idea of the maximum budgets Congress will approve. By proposing a budget of this size on a take-it-or-leave-it basis,

[5] William A. Niskanen, Jr. *Bureaucracy and Representative Government* (Chicago: Aldine-Atherton, Inc., 1971).

[6] Robert McNamara, Secretary of Defense under Presidents Kennedy and Johnson, did propose budgets to Congress that he defended against decreases *and* increases. This type of behavior was sufficiently rare to attract public attention.

the bureau may secure approval of a budget larger than Congress would actually prefer.

If the proposed budget is larger than Congress desires, why doesn't Congress just appropriate a smaller amount of money? The answer is that the entire legislative body is not knowledgeable of the actual costs associated with various programs through the bureau. Legislators have to oversee thousands of different programs, and lack the time or the incentive (because their constituents are rationally ignorant) to become knowledgeable about program costs and options in each area. Congressmen must rely heavily on what the experts (from the bureaus!) tell them about costs and benefits. In this setting, the typical Congressman has little option but to either approve or disapprove the bureau's proposed budget. He may vote to approve a budget that is larger than the one he would support if aware of the relevant alternatives. The all-or-nothing nature of the choice confronting Congressmen, together with lack of information, makes it possible for bureaus to secure overlarge budgets.

This analysis suggests that the interaction between Congress and government bureaus has a tendency to produce budgets that are too large. There are factors, however, that may limit this tendency. For example, Congress may take a more active and informed role in determining bureau policy, perhaps by employing its own experts (e.g., the Congressional Budget Office) to help formulate policy alternatives. In addition, the tendency toward overexpansion probably does not operate with equal force for all bureaus. If the policies being administered are sufficiently simple and easy to understand, Congress will not have to rely so much on the bureau for advice and can more effectively monitor the bureau's activities. Simplicity, then, from the bureau's point of view, may have its drawbacks; bureaus may be led to make the policies so complicated that they can be understood only by the bureau's own experts.

Bureaus may also have incentive to produce a different type of service than would be provided by competitive firms under identical cost and demand conditions. C. M. Lindsay has observed that the "product" of a bureau is usually a complex good with different characteristics that can be produced in different proportions.[7] For example, hospital care can be provided in lavish rooms with little attention from doctors, or vice versa. Lindsay argues that some characteristics are more visible and easily monitored than others. Just as voter ignorance may lead politicians to neglect policies with hidden benefits, ignorance on the part of politicians may lead bureaus to provide highly visible and easily measured services

[7] Cotton M. Lindsay, "A Theory of Government Enterprise," *Journal of Political Economy*, 84:1061 (Oct. 1976).

at the expense of other, possibly more important, services. As evidence supporting this hypothesis, Lindsay examined the operation of Veterans Administration hospitals and found that they provide small quantities of "invisible" services (e.g., the quality of services) but relatively large quantities of highly "visible" services (e.g., average lengths of stay for patients in hospitals).

To see how this concept of relative visibility may sometimes give bureaucrats perverse incentives, consider the Food and Drug Administration (FDA). Amendments in 1962 gave the FDA the authority to withhold drugs from the market until they were proven safe. A bureaucrat administering this program can impose costs on the public in two quite different ways. First, genuinely effective drugs can be withheld too long, causing suffering and death because of the unavailability of the drugs. Alternatively, dangerous drugs can be approved for sale, causing suffering and death from their use. These two errors differ greatly in their "visibility." Those who become ill or die because drugs are not marketed are unlikely to know enough to blame the FDA for the delayed introduction of the drug. If, alternatively, the FDA mistakenly approves a dangerous drug such as thalidomide, the subsequent suffering will be readily connected with its cause. Faced with these alternatives, which type of mistake would you expect the FDA to make more often? It seems likely that the FDA would be overly cautious and delay the introduction of drugs for longer periods of time than the public's interest requires to avoid the disastrous effects of an error. Empirical evidence suggests that this has, in fact, been true.[8]

Pressure Groups and Lobbies

Perhaps the most maligned villains in politics are the organized lobbies, which actively attempt to influence legislators' votes on pending legislation as well as the content of bills brought to a vote. The American Medical Association, agricultural interests, the National Rifle Association, labor unions, the Sierra Club, Common Cause, and many more groups finance lobbies that attempt to influence legislation. To many people, the successes of these organizations exemplify what is wrong with the political process.

Before considering the impact such organizations have on policy determination, we should begin by asking why lobbies exist in the first place. Groups of people often have a common interest in influencing legislation of a certain type, but that does not explain how such lobbies can be financed. A lobby that pushes for a certain type of legislation simulta-

---

[8] Sam Peltzman, *Regulation of Pharmaceutical Innovation* (Washington, D.C.: American Enterprise Institute for Public Policy Research, 1974).

neously helps all those who will benefit from the legislation; in effect, it provides a *public good* for those who favor the legislation (and a *public bad* for those who oppose it). Thus, the free rider problem will hinder the voluntary formation of lobbies. After all, each one of us has an interest in promoting (or opposing) hundreds of different policies, but we rarely donate money to support lobbies in these areas.

Compared to the hundreds of thousands of "special interests" affected by government policy, the few hundreds of active lobbies are more noticeable for their relative scarcity than anything else. The free rider problem explains why there are not more lobbies, but how can we explain the ones that do exist? One explanation is that lobbies arise when there are relatively few parties greatly affected by a particular type of policy. When small numbers are involved, the free rider problem can be overcome; this probably accounts for the way businesses in a concentrated industry are able to lobby for policies like tariffs. Alternatively, Mancur Olson has developed a theory to explain the existence of lobbies in some large numbers settings.[9] Often a lobby results as a by-product of an organization that is formed to further some nonpublic good type of interest. Workers often pay dues to labor unions, for example, not to obtain favorable labor legislation from lobbying efforts but rather in order to obtain employment (a private good). Unions can use part of the dues to finance the public good, lobbying, for its members; thus, lobbying activities are actually a by-product of union membership. Olson shows how this "by-product theory" can explain the way many important lobbies representing the interests of thousands of people obtain financial support. Nonetheless, the difficulties of overcoming the free rider problem are apparently severe enough that there are relatively few powerful lobbies.

Given the existence of lobbies, are they able to secure favorable legislation? Actually, it is not at all obvious how lobbies will be able to influence legislation. Politicians are interested in the vote-getting potential of their actions, and the members of unorganized groups (with no lobbies) can vote just as easily as the members of organized groups.[10] To mention an obvious example, Congress passed dozens of pieces of legislation in the 1960s benefiting the poor and elderly, but these groups were not represented by professional lobbies. This legislation was passed because members of these groups represented large voting blocs. Members of groups with lobbies also vote, but they can cast no more votes by vir-

[9] Mancur Olson, Jr., *The Logic of Collective Action* (New York: Schocken Books, 1968).

[10] Richard E. Wagner makes this point in his review of Olson's book, "Pressure Groups and Political Entrepreneurs: A Review Article," *Papers on Non-market Decision Making* (Charlottesville, Va.: Thomas Jefferson Center for Political Economy, 1966), pp. 161–170.

tue of having a lobby than they could without one. How then do they represent a stronger political force than an unorganized group?

Once the prevalence of rational ignorance on the part of voters and politicians is recalled, it is possible to understand how a lobby can have an impact greater than an unorganized group of the same size. Politicians do not have full knowledge of the interests of their constituents: A lobby can inform a politician that there are x thousands of voters with a deep interest in a particular issue. Voters often don't know what politician is most likely to further their interests, but their lobby can inform them, and once informed they are more likely to vote. In a world of rational ignorance, lobbies can probably mobilize more voters and bring these votes to the attention of the relevant politicians more readily than if the group were unorganized. So lobbies may exercise some independent influence on legislation decisions.

Although lobbies can have a differential impact for these reasons, their power is probably much less than popularly supposed. We have already explained why the political process can produce special interest legislation even without lobbies. Lobbies perhaps accentuate the tendency for special interest legislation, but most of it would exist even in their absence.

Is Government Too Big?

Whether the political system is biased toward producing too much or too little government intervention is a question that has attracted considerable attention over the years.[11] This is understandable because not only is it an important question on which people hold strong preconceptions, but also it seems that public choice theory should logically culminate by answering it. Interestingly, economists have been able to find support for quite different positions on this issue by using public choice theory. The political process is a highly complex mechanism that contains numerous conflicting forces within it, and the quantitative importance of the various forces is as yet unknown.

Anthony Downs, in a well-known article, has argued that government spends too little because of rational voter ignorance.[12] He contends that voters typically underestimate the benefits of government expenditures (because they are often "remote" and "uncertain"), and consequently support smaller budgets than they would if they were fully in-

---

[11] See Anthony Downs, "Why the Government Budget Is Too Small in a Democracy," *World Politics* (July 1960); Buchanan and Tullock, op. cit.; R. Amacher, R. Tollison, and T. Willett, "Budget Size in a Democracy: A Review of the Arguments," *Public Finance Quarterly* (Apr. 1975).

[12] Downs, op. cit.

formed. Although Downs recognizes several biases in the opposite direction, he feels that they are not as powerful as the tendency for voters to underestimate benefits. John Kenneth Galbraith provides a complementary argument by stressing that private advertising may lead people to be more aware of the advantages of consuming private goods than of consuming government-provided services.[13]

Alternatively, there are several forces that probably introduce a bias toward overlarge budgets. Buchanan and Tullock have argued that logrolling often produces larger-than-efficient spending programs, especially for programs that confer large benefits on a small proportion of the public but with costs spread more thinly over the remaining population.[14] The use of hidden taxes by government may lead voters to underestimate the true burden and thus approve too much spending. Activities of government bureaus and organized lobbies may also work in this direction.

Balancing these considerations to determine their net effect is a difficult task. Our knowledge of the strength and prevalence of these forces in the political process is not yet adequate to permit a clear-cut answer to the question of whether political forces generally produce too much government. In fact, the question itself is perhaps not well put. There are thousands of different government expenditure policies, and it seems likely that some are too large and some are too small. In other words, the numerous political forces that have been discussed do not operate with equal force for each individual program. In some cases, the forces that produce too much government spending may predominate in determining one policy, whereas the reverse may be true for a different policy. Downs may be correct that, for expenditures where a large portion of the benefits are unperceived, too little will be spent. Many programs, however, do not have large hidden benefits, and some expenditure programs have large hidden costs. Although it is still interesting to consider whether, in some aggregate sense, government spends too much or too little, we should not interpret our answer to mean that all we need do is expand or contract all policies.

Significance of "Government Failure"

For many years economists have studied the functioning of private markets. Circumstances under which markets function well and under which they function poorly are now understood. When markets function to produce inefficient results, "market failure" is said to occur. Monopolies,

[13] John K. Galbraith, *The Affluent Society* (Boston: Houghton Mifflin, 1958).
[14] Buchanan and Tullock, op. cit., Chapters 9 and 10.

externalities, and public goods are now familiar examples of market failure.

Only in relatively recent years have economists (and other social scientists) begun to study how the political process *actually* functions (as distinct from how it would function in some nonexistent utopia). The result of this inquiry is the emerging theory of public choice. It has become clear that there is such a thing as "government failure": government's enacting policies that produce inefficient and/or inequitable results as a result of the rational behavior of participants in the political process.

The public choice approach to the analysis of political decision making should lead to a major alteration in the way government is viewed. Thirty years ago, it was not uncommon for economists, observing that Congress had passed a housing subsidy, to make a statement like "We, the people, through our elected representatives, have decided that housing should be subsidized." (Unfortunately, many noneconomists—and some economists—still make similar statements.) As a *partial* description of the forces that shape actual government decisions, which emphasizes the positive aspects of democratic processes, this statement may be adequate. It is, however, incomplete and naive. Just as we should not think that private markets always function efficiently, it is equally incorrect to picture government as always operating to reflect accurately the public's interests.

Public choice theory, with its implication of occasional government failure, is significant for two somewhat different reasons. First, it must be kept in mind when we evaluate the market and find it not functioning too well in some area. Although one frequently hears the argument "The market has failed; therefore, the government *should* intervene," this is a logical non sequitur. Both the market and the political system are processes for allocating resources and distributing incomes, and each has defects. The fact that the market is inefficient does *not* imply that government will do any better. It is always possible that government intervention will make a bad situation worse. The converse of this non sequitur is also logically invalid. In situations where the government has performed poorly, it does not follow that the market will necessarily function better. Consider this argument: "The influence of the military-industrial complex has led to great waste in the defense budget; therefore, we should rely on the market to provide national defense." The fallacy is clear. Both types of arguments are still far too common.

In deciding whether the market or the government will produce better results, it is necessary to choose between two imperfect mechanisms. The forces that shape both market and government outcomes must be understood in order to make wise decisions. Unfortunately, public choice theory is not sufficiently developed to identify the areas in which government is likely to be relatively inefficient, but it raises the proper questions, and future research may provide the answers.

There is a second reason why the public choice approach is important. It emphasizes how governmental decisions depend on procedures and institutions in the political process, and on the incentives created for participants in the process. These institutions and procedures are not sacrosanct; they can be changed. Reform of the governmental decision-making process may lead to better government policies being selected. Although our emphasis in this chapter has been on the way current political institutions function, public choice theory can also be used to compare alternative methods of making and enforcing government policy.

In recent years, there have been several highly publicized reforms in the political process: Lowering of legal voting age, easier voter registration requirements, and limits on campaign contributions are examples. As should be clear from the analysis in this chapter, these "reforms" are unlikely to have any significant impact on actual policy making. They do not in any way modify the important factors we have identified in the political process. They are largely window dressing, exactly the types of reforms we would expect to emerge from current political processes and institutions.

What would a reform that would have major repercussions look like? Consider, for example, the following:

1. Members of Congress shall be determined by a process of random selection from among the general public.
2. Some types of legislation shall require a three-fourths majority, rather than a simple majority, to pass.
3. Decisions on major policy proposals shall be made by direct majority voting by the general public rather than by Congress.
4. Every expenditure proposal shall be linked to a (visible) tax increase so that individual voters can easily determine their share of the cost.

Clearly, these reforms would have far-reaching effects. We do not mean to imply that we think these reforms would necessarily improve the public choice process, but they illustrate substantive proposals for meaningful reform. (The reader will find it an instructive exercise to apply the approach of this chapter in an effort to determine the advantages and disadvantages of these proposals.) Even if we can identify desirable reforms, the sticky question remains: How can we expect the imperfect political process to adopt these reforms?

Supplementary Readings

Amacher, R. C., R. D. Tollison, and T. D. Willet. "Budget Size in a Democracy: A Review of the Arguments," *Public Finance Quarterly* 3(2):99–121(Apr. 1975).

Borcherding, Thomas E. *Budgets and Bureaucrats: The Sources of Government Growth.* Durham, N.C.: Duke University Press, 1977.

Breton, Albert. *The Economic Theory of Representative Government.* Chicago: Aldine Publishing Co., 1974.

Buchanan, James M. *Public Finance in Democratic Process.* Chapel Hill: University of North Carolina Press, 1967.

Buchanan, James M., and Gordon Tullock. *The Calculus of Consent.* Ann Arbor: University of Michigan Press, 1962.

Downs, Anthony. *An Economic Theory of Democracy.* New York: Harper & Row, Publishers, 1957.

———. *Inside Bureaucracy.* Boston: Little, Brown and Company, 1967.

———. "Why the Government Budget Is Too Small in a Democracy," in Edmund S. Phelps (ed.), *Private Wants and Public Needs,* Revised Edition. New York: W. W. Norton and Company, Inc., 1965.

Mueller, Dennis C. "Public Choice: A Survey." *Journal of Economic Literature* 14(2):395–433(June 1976).

Niskanen, William A., Jr. *Bureaucracy and Representative Government.* Chicago: Aldine Publishing Co., 1971.

Riker, William H., and Peter C. Ordeshook. *An Introduction to Positive Political Theory.* Englewood Cliffs, N.J.: Prentice-Hall, Inc., 1973.

Yeager, Leland. "Economics and Principles," *Southern Economic Journal,* 42(4):559–571(Apr. 1976).

PRINCIPLES OF
TAX ANALYSIS

CHAPTER 10

To a large extent, the analysis of taxes parallels the analysis of expenditures. Our major concerns remain how the policy affects the pattern of output of goods and services (allocative effects) and who bears the cost (distributive effects). As with expenditures, the exact consequences depend on the particular tax employed, but there are nonetheless some general principles that are helpful to keep in mind.

Tax Incidence

The questions "Who pays the tax?" and "Who bears the burden of the tax?" can have quite different answers. Determining who pays the tax is a simple matter of tax liability as defined by the tax statutes. Locating the economic units responsible for writing the checks covering the tax is not of much interest to economists because these units may not be the ones that actually bear the burden of the tax. Everyone knows this, of course, and realizes, for example, that the federal excise tax on liquor, although paid by liquor producers, is actually passed on to consumers in the form of higher prices. Tax incidence theory is concerned with determining who bears the real burden of taxation. More generally, the incidence of a tax refers to its effects on the distribution of income.

All taxes ultimately result in a reduction in the real disposable incomes of some people. It is potentially misleading to refer to "business" or "property" bearing the burden of a tax, because businesses and property are owned by individuals, and it is these individuals who *may* suffer reductions in their real incomes as a result of business and property taxes. (Whether or not these individuals actually *do* bear the burden of these taxes is, of course, a question of locating the actual incidence of the taxes.) Do not be misled, therefore, by references to "businesses pay-

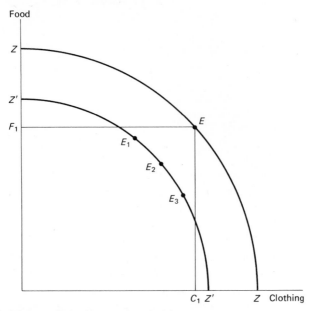

Figure 10–1. Nature of tax incidence.

ing their fair share" of taxes because businesses per se do not bear the burden of any tax. It makes more sense to ask whether business *owners* bear a fair share of the tax burden.

Before proceeding, it is necessary to consider the meaning of incidence more carefully; it is not as unambiguous a concept as might be thought at first glance. Possible ambiguity results from the necessity of accounting for what the government does with the tax revenue raised. The consequences of any tax obviously depend to some degree on how the government uses the revenue, because the government may tax individuals and then use the revenue to provide goods and services that benefit those who originally paid the taxes. Two different concepts of incidence are widely used by economists; these concepts differ in what is assumed to happen to the tax revenue.

Balanced-Budget Incidence

Balanced-budget incidence refers to the distributional effects of a tax combined with the expenditure program it finances. In other words, it considers how the opportunity cost of a given spending policy is distributed among the public by the tax. Figure 10–1 can illustrate this concept of incidence. ZZ is the production frontier relating the outputs of food and clothing, assumed for simplicity to be the only two goods produced by the private sector. Initially, equilibrium is at point E, with outputs of food and clothing equal to F_1 and C_1.

Now let the government undertake an expenditure program to provide a public good. Because productive resources must be employed to produce the public good, a smaller quantity of resources will be available to produce food and clothing. The resources remaining in the private sector can produce the output combinations shown by $Z'Z'$. Suppose an excise tax on clothing is used to finance the expenditure, and the final equilibrium on $Z'Z'$ occurs at point E_1.

The balanced-budget incidence of the tax-and-expenditure program compares the distribution of private income (here just food and clothing) at points E and E_1. Of course, Figure 10–1 does not show how the lower private income of the community at E_1 is divided among persons: We must go beyond the aggregate effects shown in the diagram to determine this. When we do so, however, we will be comparing the distributions of income implied by points E and E_1.

Balanced-budget incidence seems to be what most people think of as the incidence of taxation: It tells us how the cost of spending programs is divided among the population. It has the defect, however, of making the incidence of a tax depend on how the revenue is spent.[1] In other words, there is no such thing as *the* balanced-budget incidence of a particular tax because the final effects depend on how the revenue is spent. In addition, it is usually impossible to say that a particular tax finances a particular spending program when the government utilizes many different taxes. For example, what expenditure does the federal excise tax on liquor finance? It is not possible to say, because the revenue goes into a general fund along with the revenue from dozens of other taxes, and thousands of spending programs are financed out of the general fund.

Despite these difficulties in applying balanced-budget incidence, this concept is useful in many contexts. It has the advantage of cautioning us to remember that taxes are the way we pay for government expenditures, and therefore a balanced view often requires that both policies be considered together.

Differential Incidence

The concept of differential incidence assumes that government expenditures are held constant and then compares the distributional effect of substituting one tax for another. In other words, it compares alternative ways to finance a given government expenditure. Figure 10–1 can also illustrate differential incidence. As we just saw, point E_1 shows the equi-

[1] A change in the expenditure program financed by the tax will normally have an effect on consumer demand. Thus, the point on $Z'Z'$ that will be an equilibrium under a given excise tax on clothing will depend in part on how the revenues are spent.

librium with an excise tax on clothing used to finance the expenditure on the public good. If an income tax were used instead of the excise tax, equilibrium would be at E_2. The differential incidence of the income tax relative to the excise tax involves a comparison of the distributions of disposable income implied by the alternative equilibria at points E_1 and E_2. The alternative method of financing could include more than two taxes; for example, E_3 might be the equilibrium under an excise tax on food.

Differential incidence avoids the necessity of considering the effects of expenditure programs by assuming that expenditures remain unchanged as one tax is substituted for another. It is still not an entirely unambiguous concept because the differential incidence of a tax depends on what other tax it is compared to. There is no such thing as "the" differential incidence of an excise tax, because the effects differ depending on whether it is compared to an income tax or a property tax. Generally, when this concept is employed, some tax is selected as a benchmark against which all other taxes are compared. A proportional tax on income is frequently used as the reference point.

Differential incidence and balanced-budget incidence are the two major concepts of incidence used by economists. Although neither concept is entirely unambiguous and without problems, they force us to be careful in defining clearly what is meant by the burden of a tax. Which concept to use depends largely on the purpose of the study. For example, if you are concerned with tax reform or with determining the "best" (according to some criteria) method of financing an expenditure, then the use of differential incidence is dictated by the subject of the investigation. On the other hand, if you are concerned with the impact of government on the distribution of income, balanced-budget incidence is the natural selection.

Incidence of Excise Taxes

The nature of tax incidence analysis can be illustrated by examining the effects of excise taxes. Although excise taxes are only moderately important as sources of revenue (in 1976 only $20 billion out of a total of $300 billion in federal revenue came from excise taxes), they permit many important principles to be illustrated. The incidence of the personal income tax and the corporate income tax, two more important sources of tax revenues, will be examined in later chapters.

Let's consider the effect of a per unit excise tax on margarine. Assuming that the margarine industry is a constant cost competitive industry, the pretax equilibrium is shown in Figure 10–2 by the intersection of the supply and demand curves at a price and quantity of P_1 and Q_1. An

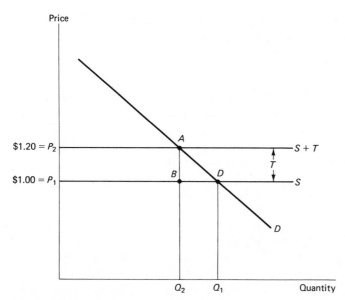

Figure 10-2. Incidence of an excise tax.

excise tax of 20 cents per unit of output is levied on all firms in the industry. This means that firms will be willing to supply any given quantity of margarine at a price to consumers 20 cents higher than before.
Thus, the supply curve confronting consumers shifts vertically upward
by 20 cents to $S + T$, and a new equilibrium is established at a price of
$1.20 and quantity of Q_2.

With a constant cost industry, the price to consumers ultimately rises
by the amount of the tax per unit. In this case, the tax is said to be
shifted forward to consumers because they bear the burden of the tax in
the form of a higher price. In the final equilibrium, firms are receiving
an after-tax price of $1 just as before the tax. Consequently, factors of
production engaged in producing margarine bear no tax burden.[2] Total
tax revenue received by government is shown by the rectangle P_2ABP_1.

The term *shifting* refers to the process by which markets adjust to a
tax. It is this process that may permit the incidence of the tax to differ
from the point of legal liability. In the present example, firms are legally
liable for the tax, but the actual burden has been shifted to consumers
through a higher price. Unless the tax leads to a change in some market
price or prices (including input prices), it cannot be shifted. If it is not
shifted, the economic units legally liable for the tax will also bear the in-

---

[2] Here we are considering the long-run effects of the tax. In the short run, an excise
tax may lead to a temporary reduction in the net price received by producers even in an
industry where the long-run supply curve is horizontal.

cidence of the tax. Thus, the determination of the incidence of a tax is really a question of determining if and how market prices change in response to the tax.

Shifting a tax is not a conscious process that occurs only because the firms wish to avoid the tax. Of course, firms as well as all other tax-payers would like to avoid the burden of taxation, but whether or not they can depends on the nature of the market as well as the type of tax. Consider an excise tax levied on only one firm in a competitive industry. If this one firm raises the price, its consumers will simply purchase from other untaxed firms, so the taxed firm must leave its price unchanged. Although the taxed firm would like to shift the tax to someone else, it is unable to do so. The situation is entirely different when all firms are taxed, as in Figure 10–2. Therefore, shifting does not occur just because someone wants to avoid a tax.

The analysis depicted in Figure 10–2 is not a complete analysis of the reaction of the economy to the tax. It is a partial equilibrium analysis that emphasizes the effects in the market directly affected by the tax and ignores secondary effects that may occur in other markets. Because markets are interdependent, there will of necessity be effects in other markets. For example, a tax that raises the price of margarine will increase the demand for butter (because butter and margarine are substitutes), and this may also increase the price of butter. Secondary effects such as this are also relevant in determining the incidence (distributional effects) of the margarine tax but are generally ignored because they are thought to be of much less importance than the direct effects in the market where the tax is levied. Incidentally, a higher price of butter is not a *net* cost to the public because the higher price paid by consumers benefits the producers. It is a redistribution of income from butter consumers to butter producers. By contrast, the higher price paid by margarine consumers because of the tax does *not* benefit producers, so in this case the higher price does reflect a net cost on the public.

We have referred to the incidence of the tax on margarine as falling on margarine consumers, but exactly what concept of incidence is being used here? Actually, the partial equilibrium analysis of an excise tax can be made consistent with either balanced-budget or differential incidence if appropriate assumptions are made. To interpret the analysis as balanced-budget incidence, it is necessary to assume that the revenue is not spent in a way that affects the supply or demand curves of margarine. To interpret the analysis as differential incidence, it is necessary to assume that the reduction in the other tax that the margarine tax replaces has no effect on the supply or demand for margarine. In making either of these assumptions, we are clearly ignoring some conceivable secondary effects, but that is inevitable if we are to make the problem manageable. As a first approximation, then, the analysis of Figure 10–2 is probably accurate enough for most purposes.

Incidence and Elasticities of Supply and Demand

Our conclusion that an excise tax leads to an increase in price equal to the tax per unit is valid when the industry is a *constant cost* competitive industry. In general, the extent to which an excise tax leads to a higher price depends on the price elasticities of supply and demand, that is, on how responsive consumption and production are to a change in price. As we shall see, an excise tax may not always be passed on to consumers in the form of a higher price.

In Figure 10–3(a) we have the supply and demand curves for an increasing cost (upward-sloping supply curve) industry, with an initial equilibrium at P_1 and Q_1. A per unit excise tax shifts the supply curve to $S + T$, but in this case as firms cut back output, the reduced demand for productive resources leads to lower input prices. Thus, costs fall as output is reduced, and the price does not have to rise by the full amount of the tax to cover the now lower unit costs of production. The final equilibrium is at Q_2, with a price to consumers of $1.15, but with an after-tax price of $0.95 to producers. The final consumer price is higher than production cost by $0.20, the per unit tax, but production costs have fallen from the original equilibrium. In this case, the tax is said to be partially shifted forward to consumers (their price is $0.15 higher) and partially shifted backward to producers (their price is $0.05 lower). In this instance, the incidence of the tax falls on both consumers and producers.

Figure 10–3(b) shows what happens if the industry supply curve is perfectly inelastic, that is, vertical. Under this condition, firms will not reduce output if taxed. The same level of output placed on the market will fetch the same price, so the price to consumers does not rise. Producers simply accept the reduced after-tax price and continue producing at the same level of output. Formally, this is shown by the fact that a vertical upward shift in a vertical curve does not alter the supply curve ($S = S + T$ in the diagram), so the market price remains unchanged at P_1. This result can perhaps be seen more easily by imagining that the tax is paid by consumers (which does not affect the final incidence but in this case makes the diagram easier to follow). An excise tax on consumers shifts the demand curve downward to $D - T$, where the $D - T$ curve indicates the after-tax price that consumers are willing to pay for the product. As far as the firms are concerned, demand has simply fallen, but with a vertical supply curve a reduced demand leads to a

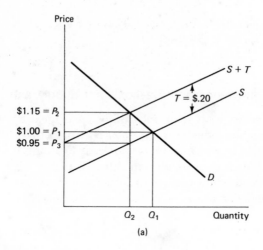

(a)

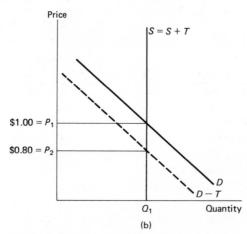

(b)

Figure 10–3. Incidence of an excise tax with different supply elasticities.

lower price and no change in output. An excise tax on a good with a vertical supply curve therefore is borne entirely by producers.

This analysis suggests an important general principle: The more inelastic the supply curve (with a *given* demand curve), the greater the share of the tax that will be borne by producers of the good. This is a significant proposition, and it explains why economists believe that taxes on wages and salaries tend to be borne largely by workers (because labor supply is very inelastic), whereas taxes on particular products are often shifted forward to consumers (because product supply curves are generally highly elastic). A similar analysis can be made to show how the incidence depends on the elasticity of demand: The more inelastic the demand curve (with a given supply curve), the greater the share of the tax that will be borne by consumers of the good. Taking these two principles together allows us to state that the incidence depends on the relative elasticities (or slopes)[3] of the demand and supply curves.

Significance of Tax Incidence

Determination of the incidence of taxation is important for a very simple reason: We want to know whether a tax leads to a just division of the cost of government expenditures. To determine whether the tax burden is shared fairly, we need to know the real burden placed on various economic groups by the tax. That, of course, is the subject of incidence analysis.

Economics cannot ascertain whether a tax is fair, because "fairness" must reflect a value judgment about the incidence of the tax. Economics can, however, help us make more informed value judgments by determining the actual incidence of taxes. On the other hand, many economists have attempted to formulate and refine the value judgments that are widely used to evaluate the fairness of the incidence of taxes. Our discussion of incidence would be incomplete without at least a brief mention of the criteria commonly used to evaluate the incidence of taxes.

Taxation According to Benefit Received. Because the government expenditures financed by taxes provide benefits to people, the magnitude of these benefits could be used to determine the size of the tax burden various people should bear. To say that taxes should be levied in accordance with benefits received is to explicitly make a value judgment about the proper division of the tax burden.[4] The great advantage of the benefit principle is that it emphasizes the essential two-sidedness of government tax-expenditure decisions. If people do not receive benefits commensurate with their tax burden, then perhaps the expenditure should not be undertaken at all.

Even if we make this value judgment (and clearly not everyone would), its practical application in most cases is virtually impossible. As

---

[3] Formally, the division of the burden between consumers and producers depends on the ratio of the slopes of the demand and supply curves, but this is exactly equal to the ratios of the elasticities of the curves. See John F. Walker, "Do Economists Ever Agree? The Case of the Teaching of Excise Tax: Shifting and Incidence," *National Tax Journal,* 27:351–356 (June 1974).

[4] The "benefit principle" holds that people should be taxed according to the *marginal* benefits they receive from government spending. Taxation according to *total* benefits would mean that taxpayers would receive no *net* benefit as a result of government spending and taxation. The discussion on pp. 29–30 of Figure 2–1 indicates how the taxes financing a public good should be divided among taxpayers according to the benefit principle.

we have repeatedly emphasized, there is no way of determining the benefits to specific people from expenditures on public goods such as national defense. In addition, application of this principle would be in some instances self-defeating. For example, if some people are taxed to provide funds to redistribute to other people, we cannot then tax the recipients according to the benefits they receive, for that would completely negate the effects of the redistribution.

Despite these practical problems in applying the benefit principle universally, there are cases where people seem to approve of its selective application. Highway finance through taxes on gasoline is a case in point. Because the benefits of highways are probably correlated fairly well with gasoline use, this is an example (admittedly crude) of taxation according to benefits.

Taxation According to Ability to Pay. The principle that taxes should be levied in accordance with the taxpayer's ability to pay is often considered the basic criterion of justice in taxation. It suggests that those who have equal ability to pay should bear the same tax burden and those who have greater ability should bear a heavier tax burden. In general, this principle is often applied only to taxes and not to expenditures.

Although "ability to pay" provides a convenient slogan, to implement it we must be more precise about its meaning. Under what conditions do two taxpayers have equal ability to pay? In practice, many economists have assumed that income is the best measure of ability to pay. (As we will see, however, the definition of income is not exactly uncontroversial.) If this assumption is granted, then an equal tax burden for those equally able to pay (sometimes called *horizontal* equity) means that those with the same income should bear the same tax. By making these value judgments, we arrive at a criterion that can actually be applied as a benchmark to judge a tax. With reference to our earlier example, we can see that an excise tax (constant cost case) would fail the test of horizontal equity except in the unlikely event where all those with the same income purchase the same quantity of the taxed good.

What constitutes vertical equity—the treatment of those with different abilities to pay—is even more controversial. Although it is generally agreed that those with higher incomes have a greater ability to pay and should therefore bear a heavier tax burden, the principle does not tell us how much heavier the tax burden should be. (For example, if we decide to use an income tax to finance government expenditures, should a proportional or a progressive tax be used? In both cases, taxpayers at higher income levels pay a larger tax than taxpayers with lower incomes, but with a progressive rate the higher income individuals pay relatively as well as absolutely more.)

Note that the ability to pay principle is simply an attempt to make an explicit value judgment about the distributive effects of taxes. Insofar as our concern is with the distribution of income, however, we should not forget that expenditure policies also have a major impact on the distribution. Yet the ability to pay principle—ambiguous as it admittedly is—is seldom applied to government expenditures.

Partial Versus General Equilibrium Analysis

We employed partial equilibrium analysis in our examination of the incidence of an excise tax. Partial equilibrium analysis refers to the study of a specific market, such as the market for the output of some industry. It examines the direct effects of the tax within this market and tends to ignore the secondary effects occurring in other markets. For example, we saw that the output of the taxed industry tends to fall. This means that productive resources leave the untaxed industry and find employment in other industries, thereby increasing output and possibly depressing prices in other sectors. This secondary effect on other industries is ignored in a partial equilibrium analysis, which concentrates only on the taxed industry. Why we do employ an analysis that ignores some effects? Basically, it is because economists believe these secondary effects are usually sufficiently small, uncertain, and spread over so many other industries that we may legitimately concentrate on the taxed industry where the effects are likely to be most significant. More importantly, the secondary effects are unlikely to have a feedback effect on the taxed industry that would upset our conclusions concerning that market.

Partial equilibrium analysis provides an appropriate framework for the analysis of many problems, but there are some cases where its application is inappropriate. For a policy that directly affects one industry or market, it gives reasonably accurate results, but for a policy that directly affects many or all markets it can be misleading. We will give one example to show why that is so. A general sales tax is a tax on the sale of all goods and services in the economy; that is, it is an excise tax applied to all goods.[5] It is tempting to generalize on the basis of the results of our earlier partial equilibrium analysis of one excise tax in order to infer the effects of a general sales tax. If we did this, we might conclude that a general sales tax tends to raise all product prices and is therefore borne by consumers. This, however, is unlikely to be so. Our analysis of one excise tax in effect assumed that other industries were not taxed; when other industries are taxed—as with a general sales tax—the effect in any given market can be quite different.

Let's examine the effect of a general sales tax within a broader framework that can take account of what happens in several industries. We

---

[5] To qualify as a general sales tax, the tax must be the same percentage of the market price for all goods and services.

will assume that the economy produces two products, X and Y. An excise tax is applied to both products, so the sales of both goods, X and Y, are taxed. We will consider the balanced-budget incidence of this tax. To be specific about how the revenue is spent, we will assume that the government simply returns the revenue to people in the form of unrestricted cash transfers. This simplifying assumption makes it plausible to suppose that the demand curves for X and Y are not affected because the public has the same total purchasing power after the tax-plus-transfer as before. All productive resources will continue to be employed in the production of X and Y; no public good is being financed by the sales tax. The initial (before tax and transfer) supply and demand curves in the two markets for X and Y are shown as S_Y, D_Y, S_X, and D_X in Figure 10-4. Initially, equilibria in the two markets are at outputs of Y_1 and X_1, with prices of P_Y and P_X. To examine the effects of the general sales tax, we proceed by assuming that the tax is applied in two steps: First, an excise tax is applied to X, and then one is applied to Y. A tax per unit of T_X shifts the supply curve of X up to $S_X + T_X$ in Figure 10–4(b), so the quantity of X falls from X_1 to X_2. The tax on industry X also has an effect on industry Y because a smaller quantity of productive resources is now employed in X. There is an increase in the supply of resources to industry Y, which leads to lower wage rates, land rents, and so on. Thus, costs of production fall in Y, which is reflected by the shift in the supply of Y to S_Y' in Figure 10–4(a). Consequently, output is higher and price is lower in Y, with the opposite true in the taxed industry.

In a partial equilibrium analysis, the effects shown in Figure 10–4(a) for industry Y are generally ignored. When there are many nontaxed industries, these effects will be quite small, but when all industries are taxed the effects will be significant.

At this point the economy has adjusted to a tax on X. Now if we add a tax on Y, both products will be taxed, and we will have a general sales tax. A tax of T_Y on Y shifts the supply curve of Y from S_Y' to $S_Y' + T_Y$, with this latter curve coinciding with the initial supply curve, S_Y.[6] Output falls from Y_2 to Y_1, and price rises to P_Y. The opposite occurs in industry X: The increase in the supply of productive resources to X shifts the supply curve (net of the tax on X) from S_X to S_X', and the supply curve, including the tax on X, becomes $S_X' + T_X$. Output therefore increases from X_2 to X_1, and price falls to P_X.

Consider carefully the final equilibrium under the general sales tax. Note that the price and output of both goods are the same as before the tax! The sales tax has not led to higher product prices. (Thus, we would

---

[6] Of course, S_Y and $S_Y' + T_Y$ coincide only if the tax on Y is the same percentage of the final market price as the tax on X.

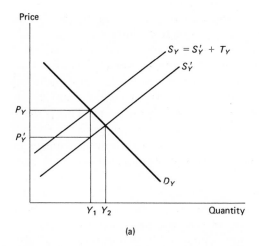

(a)

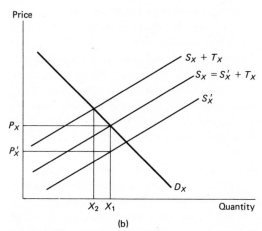

(b)

Figure 10–4. Incidence of a general sales tax.

be seriously misled if we generalized on the basis of our analysis of a single excise tax where prices rise.) If consumers do not bear the burden of the tax, however, then who does? Consider Figure 10–4 again. Although consumers pay P_Y and P_X, firms receive net (after-tax) prices of P_Y' and P_X'. Consequently, they have lower revenues to pay factors of production. The prices received by factors of production (wage rates, and so on) are lower, so factor incomes are lower. The incidence of the tax lies with owners of productive resources who receive less compensation for supplying services. (Although wage and salary incomes are lower, people can still purchase the same quantities of X and Y because we have assumed that the government returns the tax revenue to the public as cash transfers.)

There is still another way to approach the analysis of a general sales tax. Assume that the tax is initially applied to all industries. The immediate effect is to reduce the funds firms have to pay for productive resources, so the demands for labor, land, and so on fall. Because all industries are taxed, productive resources cannot avoid the consequent fall in resource prices by moving to another industry. Hence, rather than be unemployed, resources are employed at lower factor prices. This perhaps overly concise analysis leads to the same result, but we prefer the preceding two-step analysis because it illustrates more clearly what happens in each industry separately and why partial equilibrium analysis in the general sales tax case leads to the wrong conclusion.

It has been implicitly assumed in this analysis that the same quantities of productive resources will be placed on the market at the lower resource prices. In other words, we are assuming that the aggregate supply curves of labor, land, and capital to the economy are perfectly vertical. Economists believe that this is often a plausible assumption, at least as a first approximation. The possible effects of taxes on the overall supply of resources will be examined in later chapters.

The two-sector diagram in Figure 10–4 is not really a full-fledged general equilibrium model. (General equilibrium analysis refers to an analysis that takes full account of all the interdependencies among markets.) It does, however, include more relationships among markets than the usual single market approach. Basically, it is designed to illustrate the nature and importance of the broader framework that must be used in the analysis of certain problems.

It is not possible to lay down an ironclad rule concerning when it is appropriate to use partial and when to use general equilibrium analysis. Ideally, we would like to be able to trace out all the effects in any analysis, but no general equilibrium model has been developed that is capable of accomplishing such a gargantuan task. Instead, we try to use the simple partial approach when it seems plausible that the secondary effects are not likely to upset our conclusions. As we have just seen, however, there are some taxes where a broader framework is necessary. Corporate income taxes, value-added taxes, and personal income taxes are other taxes that affect many parts of the economy simultaneously, and where the single industry approach is likely to be misleading.

Equivalence of Major Broad-Based Taxes

There are four taxes that have a tax base essentially equal to national income:

1. General sales tax: A tax levied on the sale of all final goods and services in the economy.

2. Individual income tax: A tax levied on all personal income in the form of wages and salaries, interest, dividends, royalties, rents, and any other payments for the services of productive resources.
3. Value-added tax: A tax levied on firms according to the value added by each firm. Value added is simply the firm's gross receipts minus the cost of intermediate goods that have already been taxed at an earlier stage of production.
4. Expenditure tax: A tax levied on the total outlays of households on goods and services.

These taxes are "broad-based" taxes because the tax base includes all of national income. Income and sales taxes are, of course, well known in the United States, and value-added taxes are used in a number of European countries. Expenditure taxes are very rare.

Now we can state a proposition that is remarkable: All four of these taxes have identical economic effects. This is a proposition concerning the differential incidence of these taxes and means that substituting a (say) general sales tax for an income tax leaves the real disposable incomes of all people unchanged. After our analysis of a general sales tax, this can be understood easily. Recall that a sales tax tends to reduce wage rates and other resource prices. If an income tax is substituted for a sales tax, the wage rates paid by firms to workers would be higher, but the workers would have to pay part of their wages to the government. The workers' *net* wage rates would thus be reduced by either an income tax or a sales tax, and similarly for other resource prices.

Actually, this proposition of equivalence is simply an application of the result obtained earlier in our discussion of excise subsidies, only now this result is applied to the tax side of the policy: It makes no difference on which side of the market (buyers or sellers) the subsidy (or tax) is levied. The tax base of all four of these broad-based taxes is national income, but each tax is levied at a different point in the circular flow of income. Figure 10–5 illustrates this point with the familiar circular flow diagram for a simple economy composed of households and firms. At point 1, national income is measured by the total sales of goods and services; a general sales tax is imposed at this point. At point 2 national income is measured as the sum of wages, rents, interest, and other factor payments; an income tax is imposed here. At point 3 national income is measured as the sum of value added by all firms; a value-added tax is levied on this sum. At point 4, national income is measured as the total expenditures of households on goods and services; an expenditure tax is levied on this base. Thus, all four of these tax bases are equal to national income, but the taxes are simply collected at different points in the circular flow.

It should be stressed that these taxes can be shown to be *perfectly*

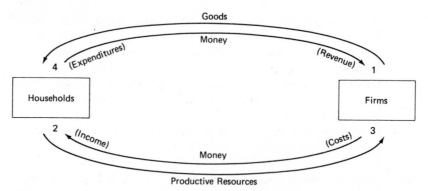

Figure 10–5. Equivalence of major broad-based taxes.

equivalent to one another *only under certain strong assumptions*. It is necessary, for example, that the tax base be defined in a consistent way. Clearly, an income tax with numerous "loopholes"—deductions or exclusions—will not be equivalent to a general sales tax that strikes all goods and services. In addition, the equivalence holds only for taxes levied at a flat rate on each tax base. A progressive income tax using graduated rates will not be equivalent to a sales tax using a uniform rate.

In view of these and other qualifications that could be mentioned, it is clear that real-world taxes of these types will not be identical. Nonetheless, recognizing their general similarity is very helpful. It allows us to see, for example, that there is little if any difference between a sales tax and a value-added tax in terms of their economic effects.

The Welfare Cost of Taxation

All methods of financing government expenditures, including taxation, result in a burden, because they are part of the process that diverts control over resources to the government. In some cases, however, a tax will produce a burden that is larger than necessary to raise a given amount of tax revenue. This additional burden occurs because the tax leads to a misallocation of the resources that remain in the private sector. This welfare cost of taxation is also frequently referred to as the *excess burden* of taxation to emphasize that it is a cost in addition to the direct burden as measured by the revenue.

It is important to distinguish clearly between the welfare cost of a tax and its direct cost as reflected in the withdrawal of resources from the private sector. This distinction can be seen most clearly with an example. Suppose an excise tax is levied on vacuum cleaners, but the tax is set at such a high level that the output of vacuum cleaners falls to zero.

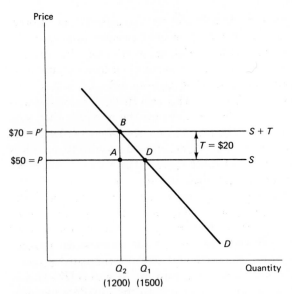

Figure 10–6. Welfare cost of an excise tax: constant cost industry.

In this case there is no direct cost due to the tax because no tax revenue is collected, but there is clearly a burden due to the tax. Resources are misallocated: Too few vacuum cleaners are produced and too much of other goods. We know that consumers would prefer to have more (than zero) vacuum cleaners and less of other goods because they chose that pattern of production through their purchases in the absence of the tax. Thus, consumers are worse off (they bear a burden) with the resource allocation produced by the tax. Note that this welfare cost exists even though there is no tax revenue (no direct cost), so the two types of burdens are conceptually quite different.

When an excise tax is levied at a rate that yields some positive amount of tax revenue, there is *both* a direct cost and a welfare cost. We can examine this case with the aid of Figure 10–6, where it is assumed that the vacuum cleaner industry is a constant cost competitive industry. An excise tax of $20 per vacuum cleaner raises the supply curve to $S + T$, so output falls from Q_1 to Q_2 and price rises from P to P'. Tax revenue—the direct cost of the tax—is equal to $PP'BA$. Note that the price to consumers ($70) is now above the true marginal cost of production ($50), and this is the source of the misallocation of resources that causes the welfare cost. The tax has driven a wedge between the price that guides consumer decisions and the price (net of tax) that guides producer decisions.

The welfare cost is reflected in a misallocation of resources involving

too low an output of vacuum cleaners and too large an output of other goods. The reduction in the output of vacuum cleaners from Q_1 to Q_2 means that consumers sacrifice cleaners that are worth more than the cost of producing them. The reduction in vacuum cleaner consumption means a loss of benefits equal to BDQ_1Q_2—simply the sum of the marginal value of units from Q_1 to Q_2. This area BDQ_1Q_2 is *not* the welfare cost because it is not a *net* loss in welfare. The resources that were producing the $Q_1 - Q_2$ units can be used to produce more of other goods. Thus, the tax restricts production of the taxed good and diverts resources to other uses so we get more of other goods. The value of the other goods produced, however, is less than the loss in value due to the smaller output of the taxed good. The resources that produced the $Q_2 - Q_1$ units have a market cost of ADQ_1Q_2, which is a measure of how much these resources are worth in the production of other goods. Thus, consumers sacrifice BDQ_1Q_2 in benefits due to restricted production of vacuum cleaners but gain ADQ_1Q_2 due to stimulated production of other goods. The loss exceeds the gain by the area BAD: This is a measure of the net loss or welfare cost due to the misallocation produced by the excise tax. It is simply the difference between the demand curve (giving marginal value) and the supply curve (giving marginal cost) over the range of the output restriction due to the tax.

An excise tax leads to an inefficient restriction in output of the taxed good. This distortion in resource allocation is, as we have mentioned, a cost that is additional to the direct cost as measured by the tax revenue. The nature of this welfare cost can be further clarified by considering the effect on a single consumer's welfare. In Figure 10–7, MN is the initial budget constraint, with vacuum cleaner consumption measured horizontally and consumption of other goods measured vertically. Before the tax, the consumer was in equilibrium at point E. An excise tax raises the price of cleaners and pivots the budget constraint to MN'. The consumer's most preferred point on MN' is at point E_1, consuming q_2 units of the taxed goods. Total tax revenue is equal to E_1R.

To show that there is a welfare cost due to this tax, we must show how the *same* tax revenue could be raised by another type of tax and yet leave the consumer better off. To do this, we will assume that the tax revenue is raised with a lump sum tax. A lump sum tax is a tax with a total tax liability that is fixed and independent of the taxpayer's consumption pattern, income, or wealth. For example, the taxpayer might be assigned a tax of $1000 that must be paid—it cannot be avoided by not earning income, not consuming vacuum cleaners, and so on. Governments typically do not use lump sum taxes, and they are used in our analysis only as a benchmark against which to compare the other taxes. They are a particularly good benchmark because they have no welfare

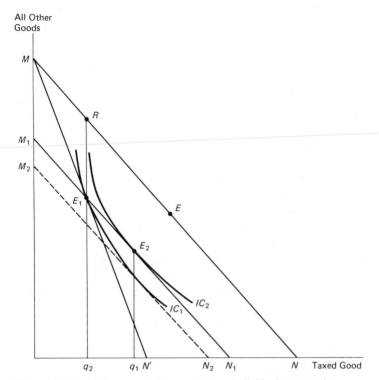

Figure 10–7. Welfare cost of an excise tax: individual perspective.

cost: They do not interfere with the operation of any market by driving a wedge between prices on the two sides of the market.

A lump sum tax that raised the same revenue as the excise tax (equal to E_1R) would shift the original budget constraint, MN, parallel and downward to M_1N_1. It simply reduces the income of the consumer by MM_1 (equal to E_1R) but does not affect the relative prices of goods. Confronted with the M_1N_1 constraint, the consumer would be in equilibrium at point E_2, consuming more vacuum cleaners and less of other goods. Note in particular that the consumer is better off (on a higher indifference curve) with the lump sum tax even though the tax revenue is the same as with the excise tax. The same amount of revenue raised by the excise tax would be obtained without harming the consumer as much. The extra loss in welfare (the difference between IC_2 and IC_1) due to the excise tax is the welfare cost.

The size of the welfare cost in dollars can also be shown in this diagram. A lump sum tax that produces the same level of welfare as the excise tax for the consumer is shown by the dotted constraint M_2N_2

291

(tangent to IC_1). This tax yields MM_2 in revenue, and MM_2 is a measure of the total (direct plus welfare) cost of the excise tax. Because the direct cost (tax revenue) of the excise tax is only MM_1, the difference, M_1M_2, is the welfare cost of the excise tax. In more advanced courses, the conditions under which M_1M_2 in Figure 10–7 (summed over all consumers) is equal to the area BAD in Figure 10–6 are spelled out. For our purposes, it is sufficient to note that both diagrams show the same distorting effect of the tax, but from different points of view. The q_1q_2 restriction in consumption shown in Figure 10–7 corresponds to the Q_1Q_2 restriction shown in Figure 10–6.[7]

Our analysis has been confined to an excise tax levied on a constant cost competitive industry. The welfare cost for an increasing cost competitive industry is shown as the area BAD in Figure 10–8. It is still, of course, measured by the area between the original demand and supply curves over the output restriction. Note in particular that the welfare cost is not equal to the area BAC—a fairly common error.

An excise tax therefore produces a hidden cost in the form of a misallocation of resources that remain (after the tax) in the private sector. The total sacrifice borne by people is greater than would be anticipated by considering only the tax revenue. This is also true of all other real-world taxes. Note, however, that this analysis says nothing about whether the expenditures financed are worthwhile. It might be that the expenditures provide benefits that are greater than the sum of the direct and welfare costs of the taxes. We are now restricting our attention to the tax side of the budget in an attempt to understand the nature of the costs of taxation.

One significant qualification to the analysis should be mentioned: It was implicitly assumed that the taxed market was efficient in the absence of the tax. When this is not true, the analysis becomes more complex. For example, an excise tax levied on a good whose production generated external costs might not produce a welfare cost. In fact, in this setting, as we saw in Chapter 2, a tax might actually improve resource allocation. On the other hand, an excise tax on a monopoly would be doubly inefficient because it would restrict production of a good already being produced in too small a quantity.

---

[7] The careful reader will note that the q_1q_2 reduction in consumption in Figure 10–7 is not the difference in consumption before the tax and after the tax. It is instead the difference in consumption under the excise tax and under an equal yield tax that does not distort the consumer's decisions. For Figure 10–6 to be perfectly consistent with this, the demand curve must be constructed on the assumption that consumers continue to pay the same total tax burden at all points on the demand curve. Such a demand curve is called a "compensated" demand curve and is the relevant one in estimating welfare costs. In most cases, this complication is a theoretical subtlety that has little practical significance; in the case of an income tax, however, it is of some importance, as will be seen in the next chapter.

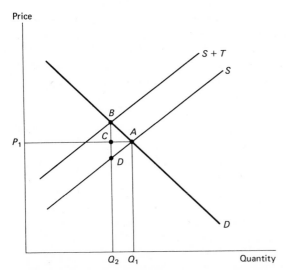

Figure 10–8. Welfare cost of an excise tax: increasing cost industry.

Other Sources of Welfare Cost

Economists usually emphasize the distortions in resource allocation that taxes produce by driving a wedge between buying and selling prices in one or more markets. There are, however, other types of welfare costs that can be important on occasion.

Adminstrative Costs. Government administrative costs are a type of welfare cost because these costs serve to reduce the *usable* revenue received by government. If the government collects $100 billion in revenue, but $1 billion must be spent in keeping records, auditing, printing and mailing forms, and so on, then the government will have only $99 billion to spend. It will thus cost the public $100 billion (plus the other welfare costs) to provide $99 billion in revenue that can be used to finance desired expenditures. The size of the administrative costs will vary from one tax to another. For all federal taxes taken together, the administrative cost of the Internal Revenue Service typically runs at only 0.5 percent of tax revenues.

Compliance Costs. Administrative costs recorded by the government do not include all collection costs because individual taxpayers bear significant costs in complying with tax laws. Compliance costs include the time used in reading, understanding, and filling out tax forms; using tax lawyers and accountants; keeping records in order to fill out (and possibly defend) the tax forms; mailing the completed returns; and using the banking system to transfer funds. These costs all serve to make the burden on the public greater than the revenue received by government. Unfortunately, there is no evidence concerning how large these costs are. It seems fairly clear, however, that they are larger than the administrative costs recorded by the government.

Lobbying Costs. A more subtle from of welfare cost occurs when some people devote resources in an attempt to change the tax laws. Lobbying also involves costs that do not generate revenue. The free rider problem probably operates to diminish the significance of these costs.

It is not known how large these welfare costs are compared to the welfare costs produced by the price-distorting effects of taxes. We will be able to form a better judgment after considering what factors determine the magnitude of this latter type of welfare cost.

The Magnitude of Welfare Costs

We have discussed the nature of the welfare cost produced by the "tax wedge." It is also important to understand under what conditions this welfare cost will be large. In other words, what determines the size of the welfare cost? Two important determinants will be considered here.

Price Elasticities of Supply and Demand

In Figure 10–9, the original demand and suppy curves are D and S. As we have seen, a tax of $20 per unit produces a welfare cost that can be measured by the triangular area BAD. Now suppose we keep the tax per unit fixed and see what happens to the welfare cost if the price elasticity of demand for the taxed good is greater. A more elastic demand curve— which implies the same before-tax price and quantity—is shown by D'. With this demand curve, the tax would reduce output to Q_3, and the welfare cost would be equal to area KLD. Note that KLD is larger than BAD: Both triangles have the same height ($KL = BA = $ tax per unit), but the base of KLD (LD) is greater than the base of BAD (AD). (Recall that the formula for the area of a triangle is one-half the base times the height.)

This illustrates an important proposition: the more elastic the demand curve for the taxed good, the greater the welfare cost of a given per unit tax. In other words, taxing goods in inelastic demand will produce a smaller welfare cost. An inelastic demand simply means that consumption is *less responsive* to the higher price, so the reduction in output produced by the tax will be smaller. Thus, resource allocation is less dis-

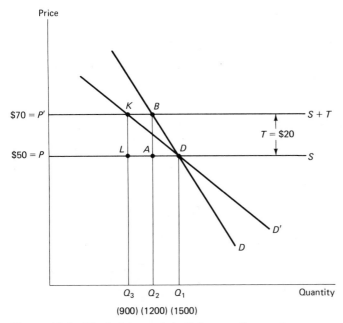

Figure 10-9. Effect of demand elasticity on welfare cost.

torted because it depends to a smaller degree on relative prices in this case.

Other things equal, then, taxes on goods with inelastic demand are to be preferred. Unfortunately, other things are not always equal. Goods with inelastic demands are often "necessities" that are consumed heavily by low income households. Cigarettes, for example, are in inelastic demand, but a tax on cigarettes would place a relatively heavier burden on low income smokers compared to high income smokers. In short, we must be concerned with the distributional effects (incidence) of taxes as well as their welfare costs, and this frequently involves unpleasant tradeoffs.

On the supply side, a similar analysis can be employed to show that the welfare cost of a given per unit tax will be smaller the more inelastic is the supply curve of the taxed good. (The reader may wish to verify this.) Thus, goods in inelastic demand or supply are good bases for taxes. Because labor supply (in the aggregate) is thought to be very inelastically supplied, a tax on labor income would produce a relatively small welfare cost. Indeed, the belief that the supply of productive resources (land, labor, and capital) is relatively inelastic is in part the basis for support among economists for broad-based taxes such as income taxes. Because the demand and/or supply elasticities of specific goods are generally high relative to the elasticity of supply of (say) labor, econo-

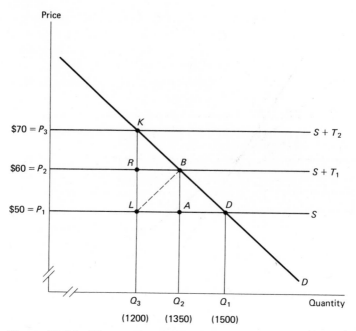

Figure 10–10. Effect of tax rates on welfare cost.

mists believe that broad-based taxes will produce smaller welfare costs than excise taxes.

The Tax Rate

By now it is probably obvious that the welfare cost will be greater the larger the tax per unit (with given demand and supply curves). The exact relationship, however, is not obvious and requires careful consideration.

In Figure 10–10, the welfare cost of the $10 per unit tax is equal to area BAD. Now consider a larger tax per unit of $20. This tax shifts the supply curve to $S + T_2$, and equilibrium is established at Q_3 and P_3. The welfare cost is equal to area KLD. Triangle KLD can be decomposed into four triangles of equal size: KRB, RBL, LBA, and BAD. Thus, the welfare cost of the $20 per unit tax is 4 times as great as the welfare cost of the $10 tax per unit. *Doubling* the tax per unit *quadruples* the welfare cost.

The reason why the welfare cost increases faster than the tax rate can be understood by considering what happens as the tax is gradually increased. Raising the tax curtails consumption that is increasingly worth more than its cost. The additional (marginal) welfare cost is equal to the excess of the marginal value of curtailed consumption over its marginal cost. For example, if the tax is $10 per unit and increased slightly, the 1350th unit will not be produced (consumed). This unit has a marginal value of $60 and a marginal cost of $50, so foregoing this unit of output causes a *net* loss of $10. If the tax is $20 per unit, a small increase will lead to the 1200th unit's not being produced, and that unit is worth $20 more than its cost. In other words, increasing the tax chokes off additional consumption that has a higher and higher net benefit (excess of demand over supply price). The marginal damage done by the tax increases with the tax rate, which implies that the total welfare cost increases more than in proportion to the tax per unit.

One implication of this conclusion is that a number of low rate taxes can produce the same revenue at a lower welfare cost than one tax levied at a higher rate. Instead of doubling one tax rate (and quadrupling the welfare cost), we can use a second tax and raise the additional tax revenue by only approximately doubling the welfare cost. As we tax more goods at low rates, we begin to approach a broad-based tax like a general sales or income tax. Thus, this analysis also suggests that broad-based taxes are likely to have a smaller distorting effect than a high tax levied on a few goods.

Estimation of the Welfare Cost of Taxation

Our analysis of the determinants of the magnitude of the welfare cost of an excise tax can be summarized by deriving a general formula for estimating the welfare cost. Referring back to Figure 10–6, we can express the welfare cost of a per unit excise tax on a constant cost competitive industry as

$$W = \tfrac{1}{2} T\Delta Q \tag{1}$$

where W is the total welfare cost (area BAD), T is the tax per unit, and ΔQ is the reduction in quantity caused by the tax. The quantity reduction depends on the elasticity of demand, and we can express the ΔQ term in terms of the demand elasticity. Recall that the price elasticiy of demand is defined by

$$\eta = \frac{\Delta Q/Q}{\Delta P/P} \tag{2}$$

By solving equation (2) for ΔQ, we get

$$\Delta Q = \frac{\eta \Delta PQ}{P} \tag{3}$$

297

which shows how the change in quantity depends on the elasticity of demand and the change in price. For an excise tax on a constant cost competitive industry, the change in price caused by the tax (ΔP) is equal to the tax per unit (T), so the right side of equation (3) can be rewritten as $\eta TQ/P$. Substituting this for ΔQ in equation (1), we get

$$W = \tfrac{1}{2}\left(\frac{\eta T^2 Q}{P}\right) \tag{4}$$

This formula shows that the welfare cost varies in proportion to the elasticity of demand and with the square of the tax per unit, conclusions we have already explained. Equation (4) has been derived for a per unit excise tax; actually, most excise taxes are ad valorem, levied as a certain percent of market price rather than as a fixed sum per unit of output. Equation (4) can easily be modified to yield the formula for an ad valorem tax. The tax rate of an ad valorem tax (t) is equal to the tax per unit (T) divided by the price, or $t = T/P$. Thus, we can substitute tP for T in equation (4) to obtain

$$W = \tfrac{1}{2}\,\eta t^2 PQ \tag{5}$$

Equation (5) is the most commonly used formula for estimating the welfare cost of an excise tax. As we now understand, the welfare cost depends on the demand elasticity, the tax rate, and the total expenditures on the taxed good (PQ). Variations of this formula have been used to estimate the welfare costs of monopolies, tariffs, and other taxes: It is quite a general formula and well worth understanding thoroughly.

The derivation of equation (5) was based on the assumption that the taxed good was produced under constant cost conditions. For an increasing cost industry—one with an upward-sloping supply curve—the formula is slightly different because the welfare cost depends on both supply and demand elasticities. The formula is[8]

$$W = \tfrac{1}{2}\left(\frac{\eta\epsilon}{\eta+\epsilon}\right)t^2 PQ \tag{6}$$

where ϵ is the price elasticity of supply. Equation (5) is the one most frequently used because constant costs are thought to be common.

Now let's apply equation (5) to a few hypothetical examples to get a feeling for the likely quantitative significance of the welfare cost of an excise tax. Suppose an ad valorem excise tax of 20 percent were applied to a good with total expenditures (PQ) of $1 billion and a demand curve of unitary elasticity. By applying equation (5), $W = \tfrac{1}{2}(1)(0.2)^2 \cdot \$1$ billion, or $20 million. Because the tax revenue would be $200 million,

---

[8] For a derivation of this formula, see David N. Hyman, *The Economics of Governmental Activity* (New York: Holt, Rinehart and Winston, Inc., 1973), pp. 169–171.

the welfare cost in this example would be 10 percent of tax revenue. For a tax rate of 40 percent, the welfare cost would be $80 million, equal to 20 percent of the tax revenue. Whether or not these welfare costs are considered large depends on one's viewpoint, but they are far from insignificant. (Recall too that the formula does not measure the welfare costs due to administrative and compliance costs.)

Incidentally equation (5), or (6) if appropriate, can be used to estimate the welfare cost due to externalities. In this case, the term t in the formula is interpreted to be the marginal external effect at the market equilibrium as a percent of market price. For example, suppose the marginal external benefit is 10 percent of the market price of some good. If total expenditures on the good are $1 billion and the demand elasticity[9] is 1, then $W = \frac{1}{2}(1) \cdot (0.1)^2 \cdot \$1$ billion, or $5 million. The welfare cost is only 0.5 percent of the $1 billion size of the market. This suggests that small external effects are probably not worth trying to correct by government policy. (This is especially true when we recall how difficult it is to design an appropriate corrective policy.) On the other hand, large external benefits will have large welfare costs because the welfare cost here also varies with the square of the marginal external benefit.

Importance of the Welfare Cost of Taxation

The welfare cost of taxation is significant for the analysis of two quite different problems. First, it is useful in comparing taxes with one another to determine what tax or taxes can raise a given revenue at the smallest welfare cost. Although all real-world taxes produce welfare costs, the distortions produced by different taxes are likely to vary considerably. For example, both theory and evidence suggest that an income tax produces a smaller welfare cost than an excise tax yielding the same revenue.[10] Unless distributional considerations suggest otherwise, this analysis implies that an income tax is better than an excise tax.

The welfare cost of taxes is significant for another, probably more important reason. It is necessary to consider the welfare cost of taxation as part of the cost involved in carrying out government expenditures. If the government spends $1 billion on some project, the cost to the public is the direct cost of sacrificing $1 billion in tax revenue *plus* any welfare costs resulting from the taxation. If the welfare cost is $200 million, then the total cost borne by the public is $1.2 billion when the govern-

[9] The demand elasticity relevant for this computation is the elasticity of the social demand curve, including the external benefits, not the consumers' private demand curve.

[10] Arnold C. Harberger, "Taxation, Resource Allocation, and Welfare," in his *Taxation and Welfare* (Boston: Little, Brown, 1974).

ment spends the $1 billion. Unless the government expenditure of $1 billion produces benefits greater than $1.2 billion, the expenditure policy will be inefficient.

In our earlier discussions of government expenditures, the welfare cost of taxation was ignored. Figure 10–11 illustrates how to incorporate the welfare cost of taxation into an analysis of government spending. Government spending is measured on the horizontal axis, and the marginal benefits and costs per dollar of expenditure are measured on the vertical axis. The marginal cost of spending is the direct cost ($1 in tax revenue per $1 of expenditure) *plus* the marginal welfare cost of raising revenue. If taxes that produced no welfare costs (i.e., a lump sum tax) were used, the marginal cost of spending $1 would be $1, and MC_D would be the relevant curve. In this case, the efficient rate of government spending would be S_2, where the government spends up to the point where the marginal benefit equals $1.

When the government uses taxes producing welfare costs, the marginal cost of spending $1 is greater than $1. This is shown by the

Figure 10–11. Efficient level of government expenditures financed with distorting taxes.

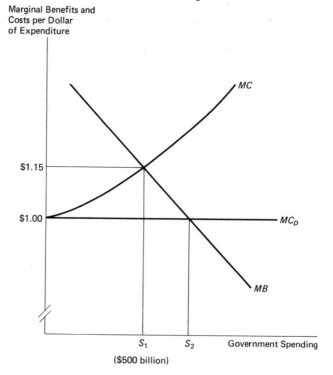

MC curve, where the difference between MC and MC_D ($1) equals the marginal welfare cost of taxation. The MC curve slopes upward because the marginal welfare cost of taxation rises with the level of taxation. Recall that the total welfare cost of taxation varies with the square of the tax rate. Thus, each successive increase in the rate (and hence revenue) costs more than the one before, so the MC curve slopes upward.

With the upward-sloping MC curve, the most efficient level of government spending is at S_1. At this rate of spending, marginal benefits of $1.15 are equal to marginal costs ($1 in direct costs plus $0.15 in marginal welfare cost). Even though there are spending projects available that would produce benefits of more than $1 for each $1 spent—as shown over the S_1S_2 range—these projects should not be undertaken. Note that this means it is not efficient for the government to correct all inefficiencies in resource allocation. The fact that marginal benefits of spending in the S_1S_2 range exceed the direct costs implies that some inefficiency in resource allocation will remain. However, spending to correct these inefficiencies would produce an even greater inefficiency through the greater welfare cost of the taxes needed to finance the spending.

An example will indicate how potentially important this point is. Figure 10–12 shows a competitive industry in which production (or consumption) of the product generates external benefits. DD is the private demand curve of the consumers, and the market equilibrium occurs at a price of $1 and an output of 800 units. D_TD shows the social demand curve obtained by adding the marginal external benefit curve (not shown separately) to the private demand curve. Its intersection with the supply curve indicates that the efficient rate of output is 1000. The welfare cost associated with the competitive underproduction of the good is measured by the area BAL. In this example, the welfare cost is $25, or about 3 percent of total expenditures on the good. This welfare cost of $25 is also the *maximum potential welfare gain* possible from increasing output to the efficient level with, say, a subsidy.

We emphasize that this is only a *potential* gain. It can be realized only if the sole costs of increasing output to 1000 are the costs of resources required to produce the additional units of output, as given by the area $BCEA$ in the diagram. Any other costs will make the *actual* gain less than $25. Suppose, for example, that an excise subsidy of 20 cents per unit is used to lower the price to consumers to $0.80 and induce them to purchase 1000 units. This subsidy involves a total outlay of $200, and raising this amount of revenue results in additional costs in the form of marginal welfare costs of taxation (taken to include administrative and compliance costs). In addition, there will be administrative and compliance costs associated with the subsidy itself. If the sum of these costs exceeds 12.5 percent of the total cost of the subsidy, or $25, then this

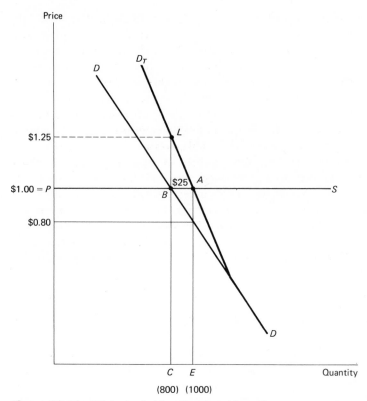

Figure 10-12. Efficient subsidy with external benefits.

subsidy actually produces a less efficient outcome than the original market equilibrium. It would then be better not to introduce the subsidy at all.

Note that we are considering a fairly substantial misallocation caused by the externality: The efficient output is fully 25 percent above the market equilibrium output. Nonetheless, a subsidy is likely to make matters worse when all the costs involved are taken into account. This suggests that market misallocations must be quite severe before we can realistically expect an improvement through the use of government spending. Small inefficiencies in the market allocation of resources are best left alone—it would cost more than it is worth to try to correct them.

In short, when the government uses taxes that produce welfare costs, government expenditures must produce substantially larger benefits than would be generated if the taxpayers spent the same sums as they wanted. Otherwise, the expenditures will reduce welfare. In evaluating expenditure programs, it is therefore important to consider the marginal welfare costs of taxation.

Supplementary Readings

Barzel, Yoram. "An Alternative Approach to the Theory of Taxation," *Journal of Political Economy,* **84** (6): 1177–1198 (Dec. 1976).

Blum, Walter J., and Harry J. Kalven, Jr. *The Uneasy Case for Progressive Taxation.* Chicago: University of Chicago Press, 1953.

Break, George F. "The Incidence and Economic Effects of Taxation," in Alan S. Blinder et. al., *The Economics of Public Finance.* Washington, D.C.: Brookings Institution, 1974.

Mieszkowski, Peter. "Tax Incidence Theory: The Effects of Taxes on the Distribution of Income." *Journal of Economic Literature,* 7 (4): 1103–1124 (Dec. 1969).

Musgrave, Richard. *The Theory of Public Finance.* New York: McGraw-Hill Book Company, 1959.

THE FEDERAL
INDIVIDUAL INCOME TAX

From the standpoint of its contribution to revenue, the federal individual income tax is the most important tax in the United States. Revenues from this tax totaled $179 billion in 1978, or 44 percent of total federal revenue. Levied as a direct tax on incomes, it is the only direct contact most Americans have with the federal tax collection process. Although reform of this tax has been considered a major political issue for several years, it is still widely considered to be potentially the fairest and most efficient method of raising tax revenue. This and the following chapter will be devoted to an analysis of the federal income tax.

What Is Income?

The popularity of the income tax as a revenue source stems from the wide agreement that income is the best measure of a person's ability to pay taxes. The credibility of income as a measure of taxpaying capacity depends critically on the way it is defined. Any definition of *income* is of necessity somewhat arbitrary, but the most widely accepted definition is the following: Income is the monetary value of consumption plus any change in net worth over a period of time (usually taken to be a year).[1]

Nothing in this definition links income to its source. Funds received as wages and salaries, dividends, interest, rents, royalties, or gifts are all considered income because they will either finance consumption or be saved (thereby affecting net worth). Hence, this definition of income accords with common usage of the term. Further examination of the definition will show, however, that other, less obvious items are included as income.

---

[1] An early case for the use of this general definition was made by Henry Simons, *Personal Income Taxation* (Chicago: University of Chicago Press, 1938).

Although income, according to our definition, is measured in monetary units it need not be received as cash. Fringe benefits provided by an employer, such as free lunches, health insurance, or contributions to pensions, are income, just as are wages paid in cash. Fringe benefits are an example of income in kind rather than cash. Government in-kind transfers (as well as cash transfers) also count as income because the source of income is irrelevant.

There are other important types of income in kind. A person who owns a home consumes housing services, and the monetary value of these housing services should be treated as income. Similarly, goods and services that are produced and consumed within the home also qualify as income. Food preparation, growing of foods at home, housecleaning, and child-rearing provided by the husband or wife all constitute services that have a monetary value to the family and hence are income. Even leisure can be considered a consumer good and thus part of income.

The second dimension of our definition of income concerns changes in the value of capital assets. If the value of an individual's home rises from $50,000 to $52,000 over a year, the $2000 increase in value (or capital gain) is income because it represents an increase in net worth. Note that the home need not be sold for this capital gain to be considered income. Thus, our definition counts income as it *accrues,* not when it is realized through a market sale. The accrued capital gain augments one's capacity to consume without depleting net worth.

The definition of income will be explored further in the next chapter. Before proceeding, however, it should be stressed that the definition discussed here is not the one embodied in current tax laws. Instead, we have developed a broad and comprehensive concept of income that can be used as a benchmark against which the actual definition of taxable income in the tax laws can be compared. There are two reasons why a broad concept of income is important. One is to ensure that the tax is equitable. Income, broadly defined, is a comprehensive measure of the resources available to pay taxes; it is also a primary determinant of an individual's standard of living. Unless income is broadly defined, people who receive income in nontaxable forms will pay lower taxes, and that will be unfair.

A second reason to use a broad measure of income is to promote economic efficiency. If certain types of income are not taxed, people will have incentive to convert their income into these nontaxable forms, and such a reallocation of resources, induced by tax considerations, will be inefficient. As we explained in the last chapter, a broad-based tax leaves few avenues that allow tax liabilities to be reduced by rearranging the use of resources, and therefore the welfare cost of the tax is likely to be small.

We will have a great deal more to say about equity and efficiency considerations later on. Although equity and efficiency criteria seem to favor a broad definition of income, there are other factors to be considered. In particular, in some cases it is administratively difficult to tax some forms of income. This is especially true when the goods or services consumed are not purchased in the market and therefore have no easily measured monetary value. Consider the value of the services of a stay-at-home spouse: How much are they worth? Although these services have a monetary value, it would be difficult and costly, if not impossible, for the tax collector to measure accurately. In such cases, the cost of measurement and the inequities and inefficiencies resulting from incorrect measurement make exclusion of some items from the tax base the wisest course of action. Thus, our comprehensive definition of income is not intended to be an assessment formula but instead a guiding principle to be considered along with other factors.

Definition of Taxable Income in Practice

The Internal Revenue Code does not explicitly define income; instead, it enumerates items to be included and excluded from the tax base. As a result of its numerous provisions, taxable income in 1972 was only $446 billion out of a possible $945 billion in personal income. Obviously, this figure falls short of representing a comprehensive measure of the incomes of persons and families. Table 11–1 shows in summary form how various provisions in the tax law affect the size of measured taxable income.

The first line gives total personal income, which equaled $945 billion in 1972. This figure is not available from income tax statistics; rather, it is the most comprehensive measure of income of persons and families available from the National Income and Product Accounts. Even this

Table 11–1. Derivation of Taxable Income, 1972

1.		Personal income	$945 billion
2.	Plus	Miscellaneous additions	64 billion
3.	Minus	Exclusions	211 billion
4.	Equals	AGI	$798 billion
5.	Minus	Nonreported AGI and AGI on nontaxable returns	80 billion
6.	Equals	AGI on taxable returns	$718 billion
7.	Minus	Deductions	143 billion
8.	Minus	Exemptions	128 billion
9.	Equals	Taxable income	$446 billion

Source: Derived from various government publications.

measure, broad and comprehensive as it is, excludes some items that would be considered income according to the definition discussed in the last section. For example, it fails to include leisure or in-kind income produced at home. Nevertheless, personal income provides a fairly good idea of the potential tax base available if income was defined fairly comprehensively.

Taxable income, however, is only $446 billion, or 47.2 percent of personal income. The difference between the two figures represents the net effect of a multitude of special provisions in the tax laws. For example, after adding several miscellaneous items and subtracting excluded items, we arrive at adjusted gross income (AGI). AGI is the broadest measure of income available from the income tax statistics; it goes on the top line of each family's Form 1040. Exclusions from AGI are not reported on the tax forms, although they generally constitute income according to our definition. For example, government transfer payments ($103 billion) are the most important excluded item. Other exclusions include imputed income from owner-occupied homes, employee fringe benefits, interest on municipal bonds, and several other less important items.

Two further major adjustments to AGI are made before taxable income is determined. First, each member of the family is allowed a personal exemption of $750. Thus, a family of four is granted exemptions totaling $3000 that are subtracted from AGI. Second, various deductions from AGI are permitted. The taxpayer has the option of taking a standard deduction or itemizing allowable deductions. The standard deduction or "zero bracket" amount was $3200 in 1977 for a family of four. The taxpayer will normally choose to itemize if his total allowable deductions are greater than the zero bracket amount. This is generally the case for higher income taxpayers. The most important itemized deductions are mortgage interest and interest on consumer loans, certain state and local taxes, charitable contributions, and medical care expenses (above a minimum).

Taxable income is determined by subtracting deductions and exemptions from AGI. The relevant tax rate schedule is then applied to taxable income to obtain each taxpayer's liability.

Tax Rate Structure

Any tax can be described by defining the tax base (taxable income in the case of the federal income tax) and the tax rate, or structure of rates, that is levied on the base. Before describing the rate structure of the federal income tax, it is important to identify the different types of rate structures that may be used. There are three major alternatives: proportional, progressive, and regressive. The difference between these rate structures depends on how the average tax rate (total tax liability divided by the tax base) varies with the tax base. If the average tax rate is the same at all levels of the tax base, the tax is proportional; if the average tax rate rises with the tax base, the tax is progressive; and if the average tax rate falls as the tax base increases, the tax is regressive.

In Table 11–2, there are examples of each type of rate structure. The proportional tax is levied at a flat rate of 10 percent on taxable income. The average tax rate is 10 percent at all income levels. The marginal tax rate—the rate applicable to additional taxable income—is also constant at 10 percent. Under the progressive tax, tax liability is a higher percentage of taxable income at higher income levels. Note this implies that the marginal tax rate is above the average at each income level (beyond the minimum level). When taxable income rises from $2000 to $3000, or by $1000, the tax goes up by $250, so the marginal rate is 25 percent over this range—greater than the average rate. To achieve a rising average tax rate—a progressive tax—it is an arithmetical necessity for the marginal rate to be above the average rate. Under the regressive tax, tax liability is a lower percentage of taxable income at higher income levels. A falling average tax rate implies that the marginal rate at each income level is below the average rate.

Some additional points concerning this classification of tax rate structures should be mentioned. First, note that the absolute size of the tax liability is larger at higher income levels under all three taxes. At least this is true of the hypothetical examples in Table 11–2; it is possible for a regressive tax to impose a higher absolute tax liability at lower income levels, although no real-world taxes do this. Thus, it is somewhat misleading to view a regressive tax as one where "the poor pay more"

Table 11–2. Tax Rate Structure

		Taxable Income			
		$0	$1000	$2000	$3000
1. Proportional	Tax	$0	$ 100	$ 200	$ 300
	Average Tax Rate	—	10%	10%	10%
	Marginal Tax Rate		10%	10%	10%
2. Progressive	Tax	$0	$ 50	$ 150	$ 400
	Average Tax Rate	—	5%	7.5%	13.3%
	Marginal Tax Rate		5%	10%	25%
3. Regressive	Tax	$0	$ 150	$ 200	$ 250
	Average Tax Rate	—	15%	10%	8.3%
	Marginal Tax Rate		15%	5%	5%

despite the common use of this description. The poor would pay a higher percentage of their income as taxes under a regressive tax, but generally not higher taxes in an absolute sense.

Second, the rate structure influences the distribution of after-tax income in a particular way. The more progressive the rate structure, the more equal the distribution of after-tax income. (A possible exception arises when the incentive effect of the tax changes the before-tax distribution of income. For the moment, this will be ignored.) Under a proportional tax, if taxpayer A has twice the taxable income of taxpayer B before the tax, he will have twice the disposable income of taxpayer B after the tax. In this sense, a proportional tax leaves the relative distribution of income unchanged. In contrast, with a progressive tax, taxpayer A will have less than twice the after-tax income of taxpayer B. Therefore, a progressive tax makes the relative after-tax distribution more equal. The opposite happens under a regressive tax because taxpayer A will end up with more than twice the income of taxpayer B.

Third, and perhaps most important, the technical distinction between rate structures is defined in terms of the average tax rate and the tax base. A flat rate tax of 30 percent on the price of cigarettes is a proportional tax, as is a 4 percent sales tax or a 2 percent tax on property values. In this technical sense, there are no regressive taxes in the United States: All taxes are either proportional or progressive with respect to their own tax bases.

These terms, however, have come to be used in a different, but not necessarily incorrect, way to refer to tax burdens in relation to income (regardless of the legal bases). For example, if the tax burden of a consumer under an excise tax is considered relative to his income (rather than to his purchases of the taxed product), then a tax that is proportional with respect to its own base might be either regressive or progressive with respect to income. Consider the excise tax on cigarettes. Cigarette expenditures are a higher fraction of the incomes of low income families, so an excise tax proportional to cigarette consumption will be regressive relative to income.

There is no reason why the terms *progressive, proportional,* and *regressive* should not be used in this way; indeed, most economists, as well as other interested persons, typically use this designation, so perhaps this is the strongest indirect evidence that income is considered a good tax base. If people did not feel that income was the most appropriate tax base, why compare tax burdens under nonincome taxes with income? If income is considered the best possible tax base, however, why bother to use any other tax? If we wish to have tax burdens bear a definite relationship to income, there is only one way to accomplish this with certainty, and that is by taxing income explicitly rather than indirectly, through the use of excise, sales, and other taxes.

Having explained the different types of rate structures, let's now look at the rate structure of the federal individual income tax. Table 11–3 shows the rate structure for married taxpayers filing joint returns for 1977. The rates are expressed as marginal rates applying to different income brackets. For example, taxpayers with taxable incomes up to $3200 paid no taxes. A taxpayer with taxable income of $3700 paid 14 percent of the income in excess of $3200 or $70 in taxes. When taxable income was $4700, the tax was 14 percent of the first $1000 plus 15 percent of the next $500, or $215 in total. The marginal tax rates ranged from 14 percent in the lowest bracket to 70 percent on all taxable income in excess of $200,000.[2] Consequently, the average tax rate rises with taxable income, at least beyond the lowest bracket, so the tax is progressive relative to taxable income. The marginal tax rate is above the average at each income level, again beyond the first bracket.

Note that the average and marginal rates as they apply to *taxable income* are given in Table 11–3. As explained in the last section, taxable income is much smaller than the comprehensive measure of income we defined earlier. Thus, if average tax rates were expressed as a percent of a more inclusive measure of income, the average rates would be lower. For example, in 1977 a family of four with an income of $7200 actually paid no federal income tax: Its average tax rate relative to its total income is zero because exemptions plus deductions and tax credits equaled its total AGI, and taxable income was therefore zero. To put this in perspective, total federal income taxes are only about 10 percent of personal income in the United States, despite the use of tax rates ranging from 14 to 70 percent. The reason, of course, is the existence of many exclusions, deductions, and exemptions that make taxable income roughly half of total personal income.

Incidence and Welfare Cost

Proportional Tax on Labor Income

Incidence. In examining a proportional tax on income, we need to consider where the actual burden, or incidence, of the tax falls and whether the tax distorts the allocation of resources resulting in a welfare cost. The average person tends to believe his tax liability under the federal income tax measures his actual tax burden. As indicated in Chapter 10, the person responsible for paying a tax may not be the economic unit that actually bears the burden: The true incidence of the tax may differ

---

[2] Since 1969, earned (wage and salary) income has been subjected to a maximum rate of 50 percent. Rates in excess of 50 percent are applicable only to income from capital (such as dividends).

Table 11–3. Federal Income Tax Rate Structure, 1977

Taxable Income	Marginal Tax Rate	Tax at Mid Bracket	Average Tax Rate (Tax as Percentage of Taxable Income at Mid Bracket)
$ 0– 3,200	0%	$ 0	0%
3,200– 4,200	14	70	1.8
4,200– 5,200	15	215	4.6
5,200– 6,200	16	370	6.5
6,200– 7,200	17	535	8.0
7,200– 11,200	19	1,000	10.9
11,200– 15,200	22	1,820	13.8
15,200– 19,200	25	2,760	16.0
19,200– 23,200	28	3,820	18.0
23,200– 27,200	32	5,020	19.9
27,200– 31,200	36	6,380	21.8
31,200– 35,200	39	7,880	23.7
35,200– 39,200	42	9,500	25.5
39,200– 43,200	45	11,240	27.3
43,200– 47,200	48	13,100	29.0
47,200– 55,200	50	16,060	31.4
55,200– 67,200	53	21,240	34.7
67,200– 79,200	55	27,720	37.9
79,200– 91,200	58	34,500	40.5
91,200–103,200	60	41,580	42.8
103,200–123,200	62	51,380	45.4
123,200–143,200	64	63,980	48.0
143,200–163,200	66	76,980	50.2
163,200–183,200	68	90,380	52.2
183,200–203,200	69	104,080	53.9
203,200 and above	70	—	—

Note: Bracket rates above 50 percent apply only to capital income; labor income above $47,200 is taxed at a maximum rate of 50 percent. Taxable income is determined after subtracting $750 for each personal exemption claimed; Table 11–3 shows tax liabilities before application of the $35 tax credit for each dependent.

Source: U.S. Treasury, Internal Revenue Service, *1977 Federal Income Tax Forms,* p. 37.

from the point of legal liability. A federal income taxpayer who pays $3000 in income taxes may therefore not bear such a large burden. If the income tax affects before-tax incomes—say, by causing a reduction in labor supply, which increases wage rates—then a person's tax liability will tend to overstate his actual tax burden because part of the total burden is shifted to others in the form of a higher wage rate.

It is clearly *possible* for an income tax to be shifted in this way, but the relevant question is whether it *actually* is shifted. To examine this question, we will consider the effects of a proportional tax on labor income.

(The federal income tax hits other sources of income, not just labor income. Labor income is, however, by far the major type of income, generally accounting for 90 percent of AGI.) A proportional tax on labor income (e.g., wages and salaries), wherever earned, is a broad-based tax that cannot be avoided by workers' moving from one industry to another. In contrast, recall the method of shifting in response to an excise tax on one industry—where productive resources move to untaxed industries. With an income tax, workers can reduce their tax liabilities only by reducing the quantity of labor supplied, that is, by working and earning less. Leisure is not taxed, only money income is, so workers might be led to consume more leisure and less money income in response to a tax on money income.

Consider a flat 30 percent tax on labor income. As a first approximation, this reduces a worker's net rate of pay by 30 percent. If the worker's market wage rate is $5 per hour, a 30 percent tax means that his net, or take-home, wage rate will be $3.50, because the government receives $1.50 of every $5 earned. The primary question is whether a lower net rate of pay will lead workers to reduce the quantity of labor services supplied. According to economic theory, the answer is unclear. A reduction in the net wage rate influences labor supply decisions in two opposing ways. One is through the income effect: Workers are made poorer and thus will tend to work more to partially offset the income loss due to the tax. The other influence is the substitution effect: The net rate of pay is lower, so consuming leisure (working less) involves a smaller sacrifice in income. The income effect of an income tax thus favors more work whereas the substitution effect favors less work; hence, the net effect is uncertain.

The net effect of a change in effective wage rates on the quantity of labor supplied is reflected in the slope of the labor supply curve. If the income effect of a lower wage rate exactly offsets the substitution effect, the labor supply curve is vertical. In this case, a proportional income tax does not change the quantity of labor supplied and therefore has no effect on market wage rates. The income tax will not be shifted, and the final incidence will fall on workers whose take-home pay falls by exactly the amount of the tax.

Figure 11–1 illustrates this case. D_L is the market demand for labor services: It shows the maximum rate that employers are willing to pay for alternative quantities of labor. S_L is the supply curve, drawn as vertical under the assumption that income and substitution effects exactly offset one another in the aggregate. Before the tax, $5 is the market wage rate. A proportional tax of 30 percent can be analyzed in one of two equivalent ways: an upward shift in the supply curve or a downward shift in the demand curve. With a vertical supply curve, it is simpler to view the tax as shifting the demand curve. Thus, D_L' shows the max-

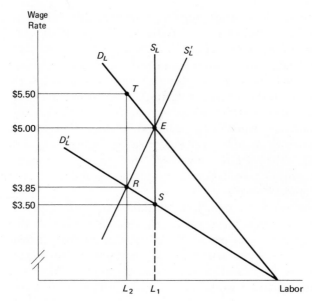

Figure 11-1. Proportional tax on labor income.

imum net (after-tax) rate of pay associated with alternative quantities of labor. The net rate of pay is 30 percent (rather than a fixed amount) lower than the market wage rate at each quantity, so D_L' is determined by pivoting the original demand curve downward rather than by a parallel shift. The new equilibrium under the income tax occurs where S_L intersects D_L', because workers make labor supply decisions in response to their net rates of pay. With the vertical supply curve, the quantity of labor is unchanged, and the effect of the tax is to reduce the net rate of pay from $5 to $3.50. Employers, of course, are still paying $5 ($1.50 of which goes to the government), so their productive activities are not influenced by the tax. When the supply curve is vertical, the incidence of a proportional tax on labor income falls on workers who bear the full burden of the tax in the form of lower net rates of pay.

If the supply curve is upward sloping, which will be true if substitution effects outweigh income effects, market wage rates will rise and workers would not bear the full burden of the tax. In Figure 11–1, if the supply curve is instead the upward-sloping S_L' curve, equilibrium under the tax will occur at point R. In this case, workers reduce their labor supplied, so with labor scarcer it commands a higher market wage rate, $5.50. With an upward-sloping supply curve, the incidence of the tax lies only partially with workers because their net rate of pay does not fall by the full amount of the tax. Unless labor supply is quite elastic, however (that is, unless the quantity of labor falls sharply with a change in net pay), the major part of the tax is still borne by workers.

Economists generally believe that the quantity of labor supplied is fairly insensitive to moderate changes in net wage rates. Empirical evidence (to be considered later) as well as common sense suggests that this is plausible. Many factors other than the monetary return influence work effort decisions (such as prestige, a desire to get away from home, to avoid boredom, or to associate with congenial coworkers), and it may be that the independent effect of the wage rate is relatively modest. If this is true, then the assumption of a vertical supply curve is reasonably plausible, and the incidence of a proportional income tax falls on workers. This is an important conclusion, and it strengthens the case for using an income tax because it means that the true burden of the tax can be divided among people according to a reasonable, comprehensive measure of their taxpaying capacity, namely, their income. On the other hand, if an income tax is shifted capriciously through the economic system, it would be difficult to use it and achieve an equitable distribution of the true tax burden by this means.

The preceding analysis has considered highly aggregated effects of the income tax. It should not be inferred, however, that the income tax has no relevant effects. It is possible that different workers, as well as different industries and occupations, may respond differently to the tax. For example, some workers may work more and others less; there may be an increase in labor supply to some occupations and a reduction elsewhere. Unfortunately, it is not possible to make any firm predictions because so much depends on the actual preferences of the workers, the nature of different jobs, and so on. Although it is generally agreed that the total quantity of labor supplied will not be significantly affected, there may be offsetting changes concealed within that total.

Welfare Cost. Now let's consider the welfare cost, or excess burden, of a proportional tax on labor income. It is sometimes argued that an income tax will have no welfare cost if it leads to no changes in the quantity of labor supplied. This is untrue. As indicated earlier, an unchanged quantity of labor reflects two equal offsetting and opposing influences: an income effect that stimulates more work effort and a substitution effect that stimulates less. Any tax will have an income effect because it reduces after-tax income; this is not an excess burden, however, but rather an unavoidable effect of the tax. It is the substitution effect of the tax that is responsible for the excess burden, and this exists even if the net effect of the income and substitution effects together is zero.

Figure 11–2 illustrates this point. The budget constraint relating money income and leisure before the tax is YN, and the worker is initially in equilibrium at point E, working NL_1 hours and earning EL_1. A

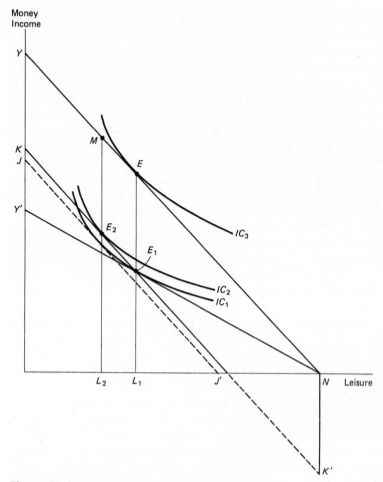

Figure 11–2. Welfare cost of a tax on labor income.

proportional tax lowers the net wage rate, confronting the worker with the $Y'N$ constraint. Assuming that this worker prefers to work the same number of hours, his new equilibrium is at point E_1; he is still working NL_1 hours, but with a lower after-tax income of E_1L_1 and tax liability of EE_1. The move from point E to point E_1 reflects the combined effect of the income and substitution effects of the tax.

To show the welfare cost, assume that a lump sum tax is used instead to raise the same amount of revenue. A lump sum tax equal to EE_1 dollars shifts the budget constraint downward to KK', parallel to the original constraint but lying below it at all points by the amount EE_1. The KK' constraint passes through point E_1, but it is steeper than the $Y'N$ constraint produced by the income tax because the net rate of pay (at the margin) is not reduced by a lump sum tax. With the KK' constraint, the taxpayer's preferred point is E_2, where KK' is tangent to indifference curve IC_2. At point E_2, the taxpayer is working more and is better off despite paying the same tax ($ME_2 = EE_1$) as under the income tax. Thus, it is possible to raise the same revenue as the income tax without harming the taxpayer so much; the income tax has a larger burden (an excess burden) than necessary to generate any given amount of revenue. The size of the welfare cost is measured by the difference in welfare under the income tax (IC_1) and under an equal-yield nondistorting tax (IC_2), equal to KJ measured in dollars.

An income tax distorts labor supply decisions by leading taxpayers to work less (NL_1 rather than NL_2) than is economically efficient. Even though work effort may be the same before and after the tax (comparing points E and E_1), the relevant comparison is between work effort under the income tax and under an equal-yield nondistorting tax such as a lump sum tax. Work effort and welfare will always be greater under a lump sum tax, and this is an indication of how the income tax stifles productive labor effort.

The reason why an income tax produces a welfare cost is that work effort decisions are guided by the after-tax return to working, whereas the actual productivity of working is indicated by the higher before-tax return. If a person's market wage rate is $5 an hour, this is a measure of the value of his labor services. With a 30 percent tax, he will work up to the point where $3.50 just compensates for giving up the last hour of leisure (at point E_1 in Figure 11–2). The marginal cost of working an additional hour is then $3.50 (the value of the leisure sacrificed), and the marginal social benefit is $5. Even though the marginal social benefit of greater work effort exceeds marginal cost, the worker will not work longer hours because, as a result of the tax, he receives only $3.50 for his efforts, not a wage equal to the $5 marginal social benefit. Thus, taxpayers are led to undersupply labor services with the income tax because of the "tax wedge" that separates market and net wage rates. (Compare this analysis to our discussion of the welfare cost of the NIT: Note that both a positive and a negative income tax produce the same type of welfare cost.)

Progressive Tax on Labor Income

The qualitative analysis of a progressive tax on labor income is quite similar to that of a proportional tax. In both cases, the tax reduces the net rate of pay to workers, and so may influence the quantity of labor supplied. Just as with a proportional tax, a progressive tax has opposing income and substitution effects, so the net effect is uncertain on theoretical grounds. If a progressive tax does not lead to a change in the quan-

317

tity of labor supplied, then market wage rates will be unaffected, and the incidence of the tax will be borne by workers, just as with the proportional tax.

In considering a progressive tax, however, it is important to understand the roles played by the marginal and average tax rates. Under a proportional tax, the marginal and average rates are equal, and, furthermore, they are equal for all taxpayers. Under a progressive tax, the marginal tax rate exceeds the average tax rate, and the rates vary from one taxpayer to another (because they vary with income). This is significant because the size of the income effect depends on the average tax rate, whereas the size of the substitution effect depends on the marginal tax rate.

The average tax rate of any type of income tax for a taxpayer indicates how large a share of income is sacrificed to the tax collector. The greater the share of income paid in taxes, the larger the incentive to work more to recoup some of the loss. Hence the income effect favoring more work is related to how much tax is paid, and this depends on the average tax rate. The marginal tax rate determines the reward associated with changes in work effort and is therefore related to the substitution effect. Welfare costs reflect substitution effects, and so are dependent on the marginal rate of tax.

Table 11–4 will clarify these remarks. Assume we have a taxpayer with an income of $10,000 and we want to compare three alternative ways of raising $2000 in tax revenue. One way is to use a proportional tax of 20 percent. A second way is to use a progressive tax that exempts the first $5000 in income and taxes income in excess of that amount ($5000 for a taxpayer with a total income of $10,000) at a rate of 40 percent. A third way is to use a progressive tax that exempts the first $7500 in income and taxes income above that amount ($2500 for our taxpayer) at a rate of 80 percent.

A taxpayer with $10,000 in income will pay $2000 in taxes under all

Table 11–4. Taxpayer with $10,000 Income

Tax Structure	Tax	Average Tax Rate	Marginal Tax Rate	Sacrificed Disposable Income If $1000 Less Is Earned
1. Proportional: 20% on all income	$2000	20%	20%	$800
2. Progressive: exempt $5000; 40% tax on income above $5000	$2000	20%	40%	$600
3. Progressive: exempt $7500; 80% tax on income above $7500	$2000	20%	80%	$200

three taxes. This loss in income implies an income effect to work more, with the size of the effect roughly equal for all three taxes because they have the same average tax rate. The substitution effects will differ greatly among these taxes, however. The marginal tax rate determines how any change in earnings affects disposable income. Under the proportional tax, if the taxpayer earns $1000 less, disposable income falls by $800 (taxes fall by $200). Because disposable income will have fallen by $1000 with the same reduction in earnings in the absence of the tax, the tax lowers the cost of reducing earnings (working less) by $200 from $1000 to $800. It becomes less expensive to consume leisure rather than work; this is the reason for the substitution effect favoring less work. Note, however, that the relative cost of earning less is even lower under the progressive tax alternatives. With the most progressive tax, the taxpayer sacrifices only $200 when he earns $1000 less, because the *marginal* rate of tax is 80 percent. It is clear that the taxpayer will be more likely to work less under the progressive taxes because the net rate of pay for work at this margin (in the neighborhood of $10,000) is lower, so the incentive to substitute leisure for money income is greater.

These remarks do not prove that people will work less under a progressive tax, because there is still an income effect favorable to work effort. Instead, we are only pointing out the respective roles of the average and marginal tax rates. The size of the marginal tax rate governs the strength of the incentive to work less (as well as the other adverse incentive effects of the tax to be considered later). Because marginal tax rates are above average tax rates for a progressive tax, adverse incentive effects due to the substitution effects of the tax are likely to be of greater significance. Still, in comparison to a no-tax situation, the income effect on work effort might be (and probably is for many taxpayers) large enough to produce no change in work effort.

Comparison of Progressive and Proportional Taxes

In general, it is not possible on theoretical grounds to make a prediction regarding relative levels of work effort under a progressive tax and a proportional tax. Although it is true that the higher marginal tax rates are, relative to average rates, the more likely work effort is to fall, we cannot be certain of the net effect of opposing income and substitution effects. Somewhat more can be said when we compare a progressive tax to an equal-yield proportional tax.

Figure 11–3 illustrates this analysis. The budget constraint under a progressive tax is shown as the truncated line Y_1BN. The constraint becomes flatter as the taxpayer works more, indicating that disposable money income rises by successively smaller amounts as the taxpayer works (and earns) more and moves into successively higher marginal rate

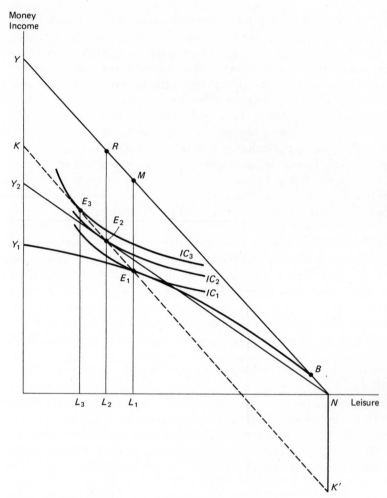

Figure 11–3. Comparison of proportional and progressive taxes on labor income.

brackets. Equilibrium under the progressive tax occurs at point E_1, where IC_1 is tangent to Y_1BN. Tax liability equals ME_1, the difference between gross earnings and after-tax disposable income. Line KK' shows the budget constraint produced by an equal-yield lump sum tax. The taxpayer would be in equilibrium at point E_3, working more on a higher indifference curve under the lump sum tax. The fact that the taxpayer is better off under the lump sum tax illustrates the welfare cost of the progressive tax, which is qualitatively similar to a proportional tax.

A proportional tax that raises the same revenue is shown by the constraint Y_2N. Confronted with Y_2N, the taxpayer is in equilibrium at point E_2, where IC_2 is tangent to Y_2N. Note that point E_2 also lies on KK', indicating that tax revenue is the same as under the progressive tax. (Tax revenue under the proportional tax equals RE_2, which is equal to ME_1.) The only difficulty in making this comparison is that one must imagine varying the tax rate under the proportional tax (rotating Y_2N about point N) until an equal tax yield equilibrium is found. A little experimentation will confirm that there must be such an equilibrium somewhere between E_1 and E_3 on KK'. Exactly where this occurs doesn't matter for the qualitative conclusions.

An equal-yield proportional tax leads to more work effort and a higher level of welfare than a progressive tax. Greater welfare under the proportional tax means that it has a smaller (but not zero) welfare cost than the progressive tax. Although the diagram may seem complicated, the reason for these findings is simple. Because both taxes are designed to yield the same revenue, the income effects are the same. Marginal tax rates are higher under the progressive tax, however, so the incentive to work less is greater. And recall that the marginal tax rate is the key to the work disincentive effect (consider Table 11–4 again). The higher the marginal tax rate for any given amount of revenue, the greater the labor supply distortion. (In fact, the reason a lump sum tax has no welfare cost is that its marginal tax rate is zero—tax liability doesn't increase if a person earns more.)

The conclusion that work effort is greater under a proportional tax of equal yield cannot be fully generalized for a group of taxpayers with different incomes. Figure 11–3 shows that one taxpayer *who pays the same tax under the two alternatives* will work more under a proportional tax. If a flat rate tax on all taxpayers is used instead of a progressive tax, some taxpayers will pay larger taxes under the proportional tax, and others will pay smaller taxes. (Refer to Table 11–2.) For example, higher income taxpayers pay larger taxes under a progressive tax, so substituting a proportional tax will lower their marginal and average tax rates. A lower marginal tax rate gives incentive to work more, but a lower average tax rate gives incentive to work less, so the net effect on this income group is uncertain. For some groups of taxpayers, therefore, we cannot state definitely that total work effort will be greater under a proportional tax. Only for taxpayers who have lower marginal and the same or higher average tax rates under a proportional tax can we be reasonably sure that work effort will be greater than under a progressive tax. It may be greater for other taxpayers (if the substitution effect is larger than the income effect), but we cannot demonstrate that on theoretical grounds.

Empirical Evidence

As we have seen, on theoretical grounds an income tax may either increase or reduce the quantity of labor compared to a hypothetical situation with no tax. Empirical evidence is needed to determine the direction and magnitude of the effect. Unfortunately, this turns out to be a difficult problem to grapple with empirically. Basically, this is because the income tax is of universal coverage, so there is no group of workers whose behavior can be interpreted as reflecting what work effort would be in the absence of the tax. Furthermore, variations in labor supply can take a variety of forms, some very difficult to measure: longer vacations, earlier retirement, less overtime, less labor force participation by married women, or less intense work while on the job. Despite these difficulties, there are some studies that consider labor supply effects of income taxes.

The bulk of empirical work dealing explicitly with income taxes is based on interviewing workers and questioning them concerning the determinants of their work effort. Generally, these surveys have concentrated on high income workers (such as lawyers, accountants, and business executives) who are in high marginal tax brackets.[3] Without exception, these studies have concluded that income taxes have very little effect on work effort. A majority of people typically report no effect on work effort, 10 to 20 percent report they work less, and a somewhat smaller percentage report they work more. This conclusion, if correct, suggests that income effects tend to approximately offset substitution effects on average, but with some people responding differently than the average.

Survey methods in economics are, however, notoriously unreliable. People frequently underestimate the actual impact of some change in economic incentives when simply asked how they think they would respond. In addition, questioning people who have high incomes is subject to a significant bias. Higher income taxpayers have already demonstrated a strong preference for income over leisure; their current income levels indicate that they feel higher earnings are worth the greater work effort; consequently, it would be understandable if the impact of taxation on these workers were modest. Workers who could have achieved high earnings but decided it wasn't worth the effort should also be considered. Having noted this, however, we should not disregard the evi-

---

[3] George Break, "Income Taxes, Wage Rates, and the Incentive to Supply Labor Services," *National Tax Journal* 6:333 (Dec. 1953); T. H. Sanders, *Effects of Taxation on Executives* (Boston: Graduate School of Business Administration, Harvard University, 1951); R. Barlow, H. E. Brazer, and J. N. Morgan, *Economic Behavior of the Affluent* (Washington, D.C.: Brookings Institution, 1966); Daniel M. Holland, "The Effects of Taxation on Effort: Some Results for Business Executives," *1969 Proceedings of the National Tax Association* (Columbus: National Tax Association, 1970), pp. 428–516.

dence from these surveys; it seems unlikely that income taxes could have had a very large effect without some indication in these interviews.

Recent econometric studies also provide indirect evidence by estimating the effect of changes in the net wage rate on labor supply.[4] These studies have generated a wide range of somewhat contradictory estimates. On balance, they seem to suggest rather modest effects on labor supply, with possibly more significant effects for certain demographic groups such as the elderly and married women.

Although the evidence is far from conclusive, it suggests that income taxes probably have relatively small effects on the aggregate quantity of labor supplied. In other words, the labor supply curve is probably quite (if not perfectly) inelastic, so the incidence of income taxes is largely borne by the workers themselves. As we pointed out, this does not mean that the tax is without any distorting effects on labor supply. A vertical supply curve can result from offsetting income and substitution effects, whereas it is only substitution effects that are relevant for welfare costs. One advantage of some recent econometric studies is that they provide separate estimates of income and substitution effects. The estimates of substitution effects are useful in determining how large the welfare cost of an income tax is likely to be, as we shall see later.

Other Effects of Income Taxation

Occupational Choice

An income tax may not affect the total quantity of labor supplied yet may still have a significant impact on resource allocation. Workers may continue to work 40 hours a week, but tax considerations may lead some workers to enter a different occupation or job, thereby increasing the supply of labor to some occupations and reducing it to others, with subsequent effects on wage rates. The reason occupational choices can be affected by an income tax is that the tax is levied only on the monetary compensation of a job, not on nonmonetary returns. Some jobs are intrinsically more attractive to workers than other jobs; they may be more secure, less hazardous, offer greater flexibility of hours, involve more interesting work, and so on. The nonmonetary compensation of more attractive jobs is greater than others, and consequently the market equilibrium will involve lower monetary pay for the more attractive jobs.

[4]Glen G. Cain and Harold W. Watts (eds.), *Income Maintenance and Labor Supply* (Chicago: Rand McNally, 1973), contains several studies dealing with the responsiveness of labor supply to marginal tax rates in taxes and transfer programs. In particular, see their article "Towards a Summary and Synthesis of the Evidence."

Differential monetary pay is necessary to make the real (combined monetary plus nonmonetary) compensation of attractive and unattractive jobs equal. Thus, a market equilibrium might involve $12,000 salaries for college graduates beginning a business career and $10,000 for those entering teaching, if teaching is considered intrinsically more attractive.

Because an income tax applies only to monetary compensation, it tends to make jobs with lower money pay but large nonmonetary advantages more attractive. Consider the case where "business" pays $12,000 and teachings pays $10,000. The $2000 difference measures the market difference in nonmonetary advantages of the jobs. A proportional tax of 25 percent makes the net monetary pay for the jobs $9000 and $7500, an after-tax difference of $1500. This lowers the monetary sacrifice required when one enters teaching so some workers will be induced to shift from business to teaching, tending to raise salaries in business and lower them in teaching. This shifting of labor will continue until the net monetary pay differential once again becomes $2000 to compensate accurately for the nonmonetary differential—perhaps when business pays $12,334 and teaching pays $9666 (after-tax wages of $9250 and $7250). A progressive income tax, with higher average tax rates on higher money incomes, would require a greater reallocation of workers to reestablish a net differential of $2000.

This analysis must be interpreted carefully. Not all differences in monetary compensation for different jobs reflect nonmonetary advantages or disadvantages. Some jobs may pay more than others in part because the required abilities are very scarce (e.g., neurosurgeons, nuclear engineers, professional athletes), and not because people consider them intrinsically less attractive. Our analysis applies to occupational choices by groups of workers whose abilities, aptitudes, or training are roughly similar. Even so, most workers are able to choose among a number of jobs involving different monetary compensations, and these choices are likely to be influenced to some degree by tax considerations. Therefore, income taxation can affect resource allocation by changing the relative supplies of labor to different occupations, quite apart from its effect on total labor supply. Some economists believe that the effects on relative labor supplies may be more important than effects on total hours worked, but there seems to be virtually no evidence to support (or reject) this conjecture.

Saving

The rate of return to private saving is part of income and is also taxed. Whether this return occurs in the form of interest on savings accounts, dividends, or capital gains (which are treated somewhat differently), it is subject to taxation. Income taxation may reduce saving by lowering the return a person can realize by saving. For example, suppose the interest rate is 8 percent; in the absence of the income tax a person can, by saving $1 now, consume $1.08 a year from now. If this $0.08 in interest income is subject to tax at a marginal rate of 25 percent, $0.02 in taxes must be paid, leaving only $1.06 to be consumed. In other words, income taxation at a marginal rate of 25 percent reduces the return to saving from 8 percent to 6 percent. This makes present consumption less expensive compared to future consumption: Without the tax, consuming $1 now means sacrificing $1.08 in consumption a year later (or $2 in consumption 9 years later), whereas, with the tax, only $1.06 is sacrificed next year to consume $1 now. Confronted with a lower net return to saving, the taxpayer has a greater incentive to consume rather than save.

The quantitative impact of income taxation on saving is not known. It is generally thought that the supply curve of saving is, like the labor supply curve, very inelastic because of the opposing income and substitution effects associated with a change in the net rate of return. If this is so, the quantitative impact on saving is not likely to be significant. Despite the fact that saving levels may be unchanged in the aggregate, there is still a welfare cost. The welfare cost reflects only the substitution effect of the tax, and that unequivocally distorts saving decisions by leading to less saving than an equal-yield lump sum tax.

One important form of saving that is frequently overlooked should be mentioned: investment in human capital. A person can save and increase his future income by undertaking training or schooling in a way that increases his productivity. Spending $20,000 attending college[5] might result in earnings of $4000 more per year thereafter. This increment in earnings, however, is also subject to tax. If the marginal tax rate is 25 percent, the effect of increasing gross earnings by $4000 is to increase disposable income by only $3000. The incentive one has to augment earning capacity is therefore diminished in the same way as is the incentive to save in other ways.

Tax "Loopholes"

Up to this point our theoretical analysis has assumed that all types of income (except leisure) were subject to tax, and that a person's tax liability did not depend on how income was spent. The federal income tax, however, contains numerous exclusions and deductions, and these provisions in the tax law—which we call "loopholes," intending this in a non-pejorative way—have economic effects of their own. These provisions

---

[5] Earnings that are sacrificed while attending college should also be considered as part of the cost of increasing productivity through schooling.

will be considered in more detail in the next chapter, but here we wish to make one basic point: These loopholes act as indirect excise subsidies.

For simplicity, assume that we have a proportional income tax levied at a rate of 50 percent. If there are no exclusions, exemptions, or deductions, a person with a total income of $10,000 will pay $5000 in taxes. Now suppose expenditures on good X can be deducted from total income; the 50 percent rate applies to taxable income, which is now defined as total income less expenditures on good X. If our taxpayer spends nothing on good X, his taxable income is $10,000 and his tax is $5000 so he will have $5000 remaining after taxes to spend on other goods (than X). If, on the other hand, he spends $1000 on good X, his taxable income is $9000, and his tax liability only $4500. Spending $1000 on good X reduces taxes by $500, so the net cost to the taxpayer of consuming $1000 of good X is only $500 (i.e., the cost of X minus the tax saving). For every $1 spent on the deductible item, taxable income falls by $1, so taxes fall by $1 times the (marginal) tax rate (in this case, 50 percent). This lowers the net cost of consuming the deductible item, just as an excise subsidy does.

To develop this analysis more fully, consider Figure 11–4. The before-tax budget constraint relating consumption of good X and other goods is MN. It has a slope of $1, assuming the market price of X is $1 per unit. A 50 percent proportional income tax with *no* deductions shifts the constraint to M_1N_1, parallel to MN but $5000 below it. (This parallel shift does not mean that the income tax is a lump sum tax. Rather, we are taking work effort and hence before-tax income as given, and examining the effects on consumption of various goods with after-tax income. An income tax does not affect the relative costs of consuming different goods, so the M_1N_1 constraint is parallel to MN.) When no deduction is permitted, the taxpayer must give up $1 in other goods to consume a unit of X, and the slope of M_1N_1 is $1. His equilibrium is at point E, consuming X_1 units of X.

If expenditures on good X are deductible, the constraint becomes M_1N. Because tax liability falls by $0.50 for each unit of X consumed, the net cost of consuming X falls from $1 to $0.50, and the slope of M_1N is $0.50. The tax liability now depends on how much X is consumed. If no X is consumed, the taxpayer will be at point M_1, consuming $5000 worth of other goods and paying taxes of $5000 (equal to MM_1). At the other extreme, the taxpayer can consume 10,000 units of X and pay no taxes; he will then be at point N. In general, the tax liability equals the vertical distance between MN and M_1N. Confronted with a lower net price for X, the taxpayer increases his consumption. Equilibrium occurs at point E_1, where M_1N is tangent to indifference curve IC_2. At this point, he is consuming 4000 units of X and $3000 of other goods, with a total consumption of $7000. His tax liability is

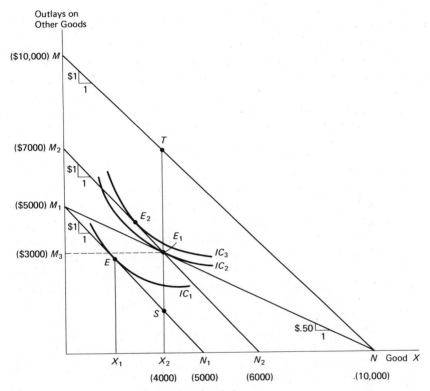

Figure 11-4. Economic effects of tax loopholes.

$3000, equal to TE_1, in the diagram. His taxes are therefore $2000 lower than if the deduction had not been allowed. This tax savings is equal to E_1S because in the absence of the deduction his taxes would have been TS (= MM_1, or $5000) whereas with the deduction they are only TE_1.

Note that the effect of the deduction is the same as when the government grants an excise subsidy to good X. If the deduction weren't permitted, the government would have $5000 in revenue and the taxpayer would have the constraint M_1N_1. If the government then pays half the unit cost of X, the consumer would have the M_1N constraint, and the cost of the subsidy would be $2000 ($E_1S$). The taxpayer would end up at the same point (E_1), and the government would still have $3000 to finance other expenditures. It makes no difference whether the government permits the deduction, or doesn't permit it and uses part of the greater tax revenue to subsidize consumption of good X. This is why the tax saving, E_1S, due to the deduction is sometimes called "tax expenditures" by economists: The deduction has the same effect on resource

327

allocation as an outright excise subsidy of the same magnitude. The only difference between subsidizing explicitly and subsidizing indirectly with a deduction is in the size of the government budget. With the deduction, the tax revenue is $3000, whereas with an explicit subsidy it is $5000 ($2000 of which is spent subsidizing good X). Politically, therefore, it may be a wise tactic to use tax "loopholes" rather than explicit subsidies because the cost does not appear in government budgets.

Because the government permits expenditures on certain goods to be deductible, taxpayers have incentive to devote more of their incomes to purchasing these goods, because the tax makes their net prices to taxpayers lower. The same general analysis applies when some types of income are excluded from the tax base. Because fringe benefits of employment are excluded, workers have incentive to have employers provide health and life insurance (among other items) for them because it is untaxed. If an employer provides a worker with $1000 in health insurance, it is not taxed; however, if the $1000 is paid in cash, taxes must be paid. If his marginal rate is 30 percent, the worker will be able to purchase only $700 in health insurance; however, at the same cost to the employer, $1000 can be provided as a fringe benefit. This is one reason for the rapid growth in fringe benefits in the last several decades.

Returning to Figure 11–4, when the deduction is used, tax revenue is equal to $3000, or 50 percent times taxable income of $6000 ($10,000 minus $4000 expenditure on X). This same revenue could be raised by taxing *total* income, $10,000, at a rate of only 30 percent. This is what much of the tax reform debate is all about: Is it better to use lower rates on a more comprehensively defined tax base, or to use higher rates on a smaller tax base? Figure 11–4 can help us understand one factor relevant in making that choice. A tax rate of 30 percent on total income would produce an after-tax budget constraint M_2N_2, lying $3000 below the before-tax constraint. This constraint passes through point E_1, the equilibrium when the deduction is allowed, because TE_1 equals $3000. Although the same tax revenue is raised, the taxpayer is better off under this tax without the deduction: he is in equilibrium on indifference curve IC_3 at point E_2. He is better off with a more comprehensive tax base and a lower tax rate. The reason is that the tax deduction distorts the taxpayer's choices by artificially lowering the price of X and leads to overconsumption of X. The broad-based income tax does not distort choices among different ways of spending income and is therefore more efficient.[6]

Note that this analysis is identical to the comparison made earlier be-

---

[6] This conclusion does depend on the plausible assumption that work effort will be the same whether or not a loophole is used.

tween an excise subsidy and an unrestricted cash transfer in Chapter 3 (see Figure 3–7). The same general principle is involved. The conclusion that a broad-based income tax is more efficient, however, depends on the assumption that there are no external benefits associated with consumption of goods given preferential tax treatment. In addition, there are factors other than efficiency to take into account. These issues and others relevant to loopholes will be considered more fully in the next chapter.

Inflation and Income Taxation

The rate brackets of the federal income tax are specified in nominal money units. Because the rate structure is progressive, inflation tends to increase automatically the real burden of the tax, even without any change in legislated tax rates on real incomes. Consider an inflation that doubles the price level over a period of years. A person with a money income of $10,000 before the inflation would have, if his real before-tax income remained constant, a money income of $20,000 after the inflation. Because the tax rate structure is progressive and designated in money terms, the average rate of tax is higher on a $20,000 income. For instance, the average rate might be 20 percent for a $10,000 income and 25 percent for a $20,000 income. Our taxpayer's after-tax income in the 2 years would then be $8000 and $15,000. His after-tax income has less than doubled with a doubling of the price level and his before-tax income; his real disposable income has fallen. Conversely, the real yield of the tax has gone up because the money yield has more than doubled.

Inflation causes real tax burdens to increase because the average rate of tax rises with money incomes. Increased real government spending can therefore be financed out of income tax revenues without increasing rates. This may create a political bias toward increased real government budgets during inflation. Recognizing this, some economists have advocated that the rate structure be designed in terms of real incomes, deflated by inflation.[7]

Growth in real incomes also affects the tax burden. Average rates of tax also rise with real economic growth. In the preceding numerical example, if the increase in money income occurred because real incomes rose as the economy grew over time, the real burden of the tax would rise proportionally more than the increase in incomes. Income tax revenue would more than double, again rising from $2000 to $5000 with a doubling in real income. Thus, an unchanged progressive tax structure

[7] See William Fellner, Kenneth W. Clarkson, and John H. Moore, *Correcting Taxes for Inflation* (Washington, D.C.: American Enterprise Institute for Public Policy Research, 1975).

automatically increases the share of money income going to government as money incomes increase over time, regardless of whether the increase is due to price increases or increases in real income.

As a result of this facet of progressive income taxation, periodic tax cuts are necessary if it is desired to keep the average tax rate unchanged over time. (Tax cuts are also necessary to keep the degree of progression unchanged.) Despite major tax cuts in 1964 and 1969, income tax revenue as a percent of personal income was the same in 1975 as in 1954, 10 percent. On balance, these tax cuts did no more than offset the automatic growth in average tax rates that would have occurred with an unchanged rate structure.

It should be noted that these implications are uniquely related to progressive taxation. Under a proportional tax, increases in money incomes caused by inflation do not increase its real burden: Money tax revenues will double with a doubling of money incomes, but the greater nominal tax revenue will represent the same control over goods and services. When money incomes rise as a result of increases in real incomes (prices unchanged), the absolute amount of real tax revenue rises under a proportional tax but only in proportion to the increase in income, leaving average rates of tax unchanged.

Estimation of Labor Supply Distortion of Income Taxes

Knowing that the income tax produces a welfare cost is not enough. It is also relevant to consider how quantitatively important the welfare costs are likely to be. We used indifference curve analysis earlier in the chapter to explain how an income tax distorts labor supply decisions. Figure 11–5 shows the same analysis but in a form more convenient for developing a formula to estimate the size of the welfare cost.

An individual taxpayer's supply of labor is shown as the upward-sloping curve S, and his market wage rate is w. With an income tax levied at a *marginal* rate of m_i, the net rate at the margin is $w(1 - m_i)$. Recall that it is the marginal tax rate that causes too little labor to be supplied (see Figure 11–3). The after-tax equilibrium occurs at L_2 units of labor supplied. If a lump sum tax (with a zero marginal tax rate) were used to raise the same revenue, the taxpayer would work L_1 units, where his supply price equals the market wage rate. Additional earnings for the L_2L_1 increase in labor would equal BAL_1L_2, but in earning that income the taxpayer would give up leisure time worth DAL_1L_2 to him. The difference, area BAD, is the money measure of how much better off he would be under a lump sum tax, which is the same as the extra cost or welfare cost of using the income tax instead of the nondistorting lump sum tax.

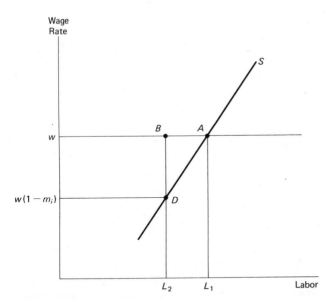

Figure 11–5. Labor supply distortion of the income tax.

As we pointed out earlier, welfare costs reflect substitution effects. Consequently, the supply curve in Figure 11–5 is not the same as the type shown in Figure 11–1 (that included substitution and income effects), but rather one that involves only the substitution effect associated with changes in wage rates. Such a "compensated" supply curve is relevant for measuring welfare costs, and it is always upward sloping (because the substitution effect of a higher wage rate induces more work effort) regardless of the slope of the more common supply curve. Income effects are kept out of the supply curve by keeping total tax liability unchanged. Thus, point A does not represent work effort in the absence of *any* tax, but work effort under a lump sum tax raising the same revenue as the income tax. Point A in Figure 11–5 therefore corresponds to point E_2 in Figure 11–2 (for a proportional tax), whereas point D corresponds to point E_1 in Figure 11–2.

Following steps like those outlined in the last chapter, we can derive a formula for estimating area BAD, the welfare cost due to an income tax with a marginal tax rate of m_i[8]:

$$W = \tfrac{1}{2}\eta\,(m_i)^2 wL \tag{1}$$

[8] Arnold C. Harberger presents the derivation of this formula in "Taxation, Resource Allocation, and Welfare," *The Role of Direct and Indirect Taxes in the Federal Revenue System* (Princeton, N.J.: Princeton University Press for the National Bureau of Economic Research and the Brookings Institution, 1964), pp. 25–80.

where η is the elasticity of the compensated supply curve, m_i is the effective marginal rate of taxation, w is the market wage rate, and L is the quantity of labor supplied. (Thus wL is total before-tax earnings.)

To use this formula to estimate welfare costs, it is necessary to know total earnings, effective marginal tax rates, and labor supply elasticities. The first two variables needed can be obtained with reasonable accuracy, but we have no conclusive evidence concerning η. Existing econometric studies provide rough estimates; based on these studies, we shall assume that an elasticity of 0.2 is a reasonable weighted average of the elasticities of different persons.[9] This implies that a taxpayer in a 30 percent marginal rate class would work 6 percent more (ηm_i) if he paid a lump sum tax instead of a tax that reduced the net return from working by 30 percent. This seems quite plausible, but the possibility that η could be somewhat higher or lower cannot be ruled out.

Two other points regarding the application of equation (1) should be mentioned. First, the federal income tax uses graduated rates, so it is necessary to consider each rate bracket separately because the marginal tax rate (m_i) varies from one bracket to another. Second, the labor supply distortion depends on the *effective* marginal tax rate on earnings, not just the rate from the federal income tax alone. A taxpayer in a 20 percent federal tax bracket who also is subject to a 12 percent social security tax and a 5 percent state income tax is in an effective 37 percent bracket,[10] and 0.37 should be entered for m_i in equation (1). Our estimate will apply to all taxes on earnings together, not just the federal income tax alone.

Table 11–5 shows the calculations for 1974. For each federal marginal bracket[11] (column 1) we have total earnings of taxpayers whose incomes are subject to that tax bracket (column 4). Column 2 shows the additional rates that result from social security, sales, excise, and state and local income taxes: These rates tend to be lower at higher federal brackets because of the ceiling on taxable earnings of the social security tax as well as the deductibility of state and local taxes on federal returns. Column 3 gives the effective marginal tax rate. The welfare cost for each bracket can be calculated from the information in columns 3 and 4, together with the assumption than $\eta = 0.2$. Thus, the welfare cost for the lowest bracket is $\frac{1}{2}(0.2)(0.34)^2 \cdot \$27.6$ billion, or $319 million. Performing this calculation for each bracket and summing over all the

[9] Cain and Watts, op. cit.

[10] This example does not take account of the fact that state income taxes are deductible in computing federal taxable income and that the employer portion of the social security tax is not taxed. Taking these factors into account, the effective rate is somewhat less than the sum of the separate rates.

[11] Since the Tax Reform Act of 1969 there has been a maximum tax rate on earned income equal to 50 percent, so the table shows no higher federal brackets because we are concerned with the effect on labor supply.

Table 11–5. Welfare Cost of Taxes on Labor Income in 1974

Marginal Rate in Federal Income Tax (m_i^F) (%) (1)	Increment Due to Other Taxes (%) (2)	Effective Marginal Tax Rate (m_i) (%) (3)	Wage and Salary Income in Class ($ millions) (4)	Total Welfare Cost by Rate Class ($ millions) (5)
14	20	34	27,603	319.1
15	20	35	17,443	213.7
16	20	36	20,430	264.8
17	19	36	24,485	317.3
18	19	37	5,405	74.0
19	19	38	146,828	2,120.2
21	18	39	21,782	331.3
22	18	40	148,265	2,372.2
23	18	41	3,857	64.8
24	17	41	21,340	358.7
25	17	42	121,023	2,134.9
27	16	43	8,577	158.6
28	16	44	59,426	1,150.5
29	15	44	4,688	90.8
31	15	46	3,858	83.6
32	14	46	32,469	687.0
34	14	48	1,705	39.0
35	13	48	224	5.2
36	13	49	18,884	453.4
38	12	50	936	23.4
39	12	51	10,556	274.6
40	11	51	1,098	28.6
41	10	51	67	1.7
42	9	51	7,066	183.8
45	8	53	5,446	153.0
48	7	55	3,403	103.3
50	6	56	24,842	779.0
Total	. . .	. . .	741,706	12,786.8

Source: Edgar K. Browning, "The Marginal Cost of Public Funds," *Journal of Political Economy,* 84 (2) (April 1976), 283.

brackets yields $12.8 billion as our estimate of the total welfare cost due to labor supply distortions of income taxes.

A welfare cost of $12.8 billion is sizable, equal to about $200 per federal tax return. Nonetheless, it should be viewed in relation to the tax revenue generated. Because the combined revenue from these taxes was about $287 billion, a welfare cost of $12.8 billion was under 5 percent of total revenue. This is actually relatively modest, at least in comparison with other taxes. Most economists believe that income taxes are probably less distorting that other alternatives because labor supply elasticities (η) are thought to be quite low so that resource allocation is not affected to any great degree. A proportional income tax structure, because of its lower marginal rates, would probably involve a welfare cost less than half as large as the $12.8 billion. Of course, efficiency is not the only criterion; proportional taxes will place a heavier burden on the lower rate classes and lead to a different distribution of after-tax income.

This estimate of a $12.8 billion welfare cost does not include all of the welfare cost imposed by income taxes; it includes only the distortion in the quantity of labor supplied. Administrative and compliance costs are not included; nor are effects on occupational choices and saving or effects due to tax loopholes. It seems likely that the total welfare cost of income taxes including all these effects would probably be at least twice the size of the labor supply distortion alone. Even so, the welfare cost would then be only about 10 percent of tax revenues.

As emphasized in the last chapter, the marginal welfare cost of taxation is also important. Using the same assumptions as above, it turns out to be from 9 to 16 percent (the exact figure depending on how progressive the change in the tax rate structure is). Government expenditures financed by income taxes involve costs of $1.09 to $1.16 per dollar of spending. These estimates, however, just as the total welfare cost estimate, consider only the effect on labor supply.

Supplementary Readings

Aaron, Henry J. (ed.). *Inflation and the Income Tax.* Washington, D.C.: Brookings Institution, 1976.

Browning, Edgar K. "The Marginal Cost of Public Funds." *Journal of Political Economy,* 84(2):283–298(Apr. 1976).

Fellner, William J., Kenneth W. Clarkson, and John H. Moore. *Correcting Taxes for Inflation.* Washington, D.C.: American Enterprise Institute, 1975.

Goode, Richard. *The Individual Income Tax.* Washington, D.C.: Brookings Institution, 1976.

Harberger, Arnold. *Taxation and Welfare.* Boston: Little, Brown and Company, 1974.

Musgrave, Richard A. *The Theory of Public Finance.* New York: McGraw-Hill Book Company 1959.

Pechman, Joseph A. *Federal Tax Policy,* 3rd edition. Washington, D.C.: Brookings Institution, 1977.

Simons, Henry. *Personal Income Taxation.* Chicago: University of Chicago Press, 1938.

FEDERAL TAX REFORM

The issue of tax reform is a recurrent one, particularly in election years. In a recent poll, a majority of Americans expressed strong dissatisfaction with the current tax system. President Carter in the 1976 presidential campaign called the U.S. tax system a "national disgrace." Several years ago, a Secretary of the Treasury predicted a "taxpayers' revolt" unless the tax laws were reformed. Over time Congress has tinkered with the tax system, but no comprehensive reform has been successfully undertaken. More recently, Congress has directed its efforts toward adjusting taxes to reduce the impact of inflation—all in a rather haphazard fashion. Some tax loopholes have been eliminated, but they have been quantitatively small in terms of the additional revenue produced by their removal; meanwhile, new loopholes have been created. Overall, Congress has had little success at comprehensive or logically consistent tax reform. Tax reform is a complex issue, and one for which there is no agreed-on solution, no doubt in part because of the distributional issues involved.

To most people, reforming the federal tax system (particularly the individual income tax) is synonymous with closing tax loopholes. The elimination of tax preferences is seen primarily as a way of reducing their own taxes. It is widely believed that tax loopholes permit wealthy persons to avoid paying their "fair share" of taxes, thereby requiring that a heavier tax burden be placed on the average person. Basically, the issue is viewed in terms of vertical equity—how tax loopholes affect the fairness of the system by influencing the distribution of the tax burden for people at different income levels. It must be stressed that this is a fundamentally incomplete view of the significance of tax loopholes. If one is concerned only with the distribution of the tax burden, this can be altered most simply by changing the structure of tax rates—by more heavily taxing those at whatever income (however defined) levels are thought to be too lightly taxed.

This is not to deny that tax loopholes have some bearing on the vertical equity of the tax system. Some loopholes disproportionately benefit persons with high incomes (e.g., treatment of capital gains), whereas others disproportionately benefit taxpayers with low incomes (e.g., exclusion of government transfers). It is important, however, to recognize that these are two potentially quite separate issues. One is how to define the tax base, and the other is what rate structure to apply to that base. The latter issue, basically how progressive the rates should be, concerns vertical equity. The former issue, what to include and exclude (i.e., permit as a "loophole") in the tax base, primarily involves horizontal equity. (Both issues also involve efficiency considerations.) The basic problem is to arrive at a definition of taxable income that will rank people equitably in terms of whether they have the same or different (higher or lower) taxpaying capacity.

Therefore, we will proceed by first considering the issues surrounding the definition of the tax base. Later in the chapter the progressivity of the rate structure applied to that base will be examined, along with some basic proposals for tax reform.

Tax Loopholes

Tax preferences, or special treatment accorded to certain types or sources of income or to certain uses of income—popularly called "loopholes"—are the focus of most discussions of tax reform. The ability of the taxpayer to deduct certain expenditures or to exempt or exclude certain types of income reduces the tax base. One can view the quantitative importance of tax loopholes in several different ways. One emphasizes how much smaller the actual tax base is in comparison with the potential tax base. For example, taxable income under the individual income tax is only about half of personal income (a broad measure of income). Alternatively, it is sometimes stressed that the Treasury loses revenue because of loopholes: If the same tax rates were applied to a larger tax base, more revenue would be generated. Similarly, if a larger tax base were employed, lower tax rates could be used to generate the same revenue.

We can begin by considering briefly the major types of provisions in the tax law that are frequently referred to as tax loopholes; they can be grouped into five major categories: deductions, exclusions, exemptions, tax credits, and the preferential treatment of capital gains.

Deductions

As noted in Chapter 11, a taxpayer may either itemize certain expenditures and deduct them from AGI (Adjusted Gross Income) or take the standard deduction. The most important itemized deductions are state and local taxes (income, property, and sales taxes); mortgage interest payments; medical expenses (medical expenses in excess of 3 percent of AGI and prescription drug costs in excess of 1 percent of AGI are deductible, along with a minimum of 50 percent of health insurance premiums); and charitable contributions. Other less important deductions include casualty losses (in excess of $100), household and child care expenses, and business expenses (moving, travel, and entertainment expenses, union dues, educational expenses, and so on.) In 1975 itemized deductions removed $121.9 billion from taxation; the standard deduction removed $100.9 billion.

Exclusions from Income

Certain types of income are excluded from the tax base and hence from tax liability. Major items that fall into this category include cash and in-kind transfers; interest income on state and local bonds; the first $100 of dividend income ($200 on joint returns); employer contributions to employee retirement plans, employer-financed life and health insurance; fringe benefits (employer-provided meals, transportation, lodging, and so on); interest income from life insurance; and imputed rents on owner-occupied housing. Note that exclusions, as distinct from deductions, are not counted in AGI and so are never reported on federal tax returns.

Personal Exemptions

The personal exemption under current law permits taxpayers to deduct $750 for the taxpayer, spouse, and each dependent; in addition, a special exemption is allowed for each taxpayer or spouse who is 65 or older or blind. The rationale behind the personal exemption is to free from taxation some level of income that is needed by the individual for minimum existence and that does not constitute taxable capacity. The personal exemption is the single largest source of tax revenue loss in the federal income tax; in 1975 it freed $158.9 billion from taxation.

Tax Credit

Tax credits are a relatively new device. Taxpayers are allowed a credit against their tax liability of some specified amount. In 1977, for example, instead of increasing the personal exemption, Congress voted to allow a tax credit of $35 for each taxpayer and family member, or a credit equal to 2 percent of taxable income up to a ceiling of $180, whichever is larger. The tax credit is then subtracted from taxes owed. In addition, tax credits are available for low income families (the earned income tax credit), for the elderly, and for child care expenses. To many, tax credits are a preferred alternative to itemized deductions. The absolute value of a deduction rises with income; for instance, a deduction of $1000 saves a taxpayer $300 in taxes if he falls into a 30 percent marginal tax bracket, and $700 in taxes if he is in a 70 percent marginal bracket. A tax credit, in contrast, has the same tax-saving value regardless of income. Consequently, many reformers have urged the replacement of itemized deductions with tax credits.

Preferential Treatment of Capital Gains

When assets held longer than 12 months are sold or exchanged, and the taxpayer realizes a profit, that profit is called a capital gain. For example, if a taxpayer bought a house for $40,000 and sold it 2 years later for $60,000, the capital gain would have been $20,000—the difference between what the taxpayer paid for it and its selling price 2 years later. Under present tax law, only half the gain is subject to tax; the remaining half is excluded. Capital gains are treated in this way to take into account the fact that these gains in income may have accrued over a period of several years, but the tax is paid in 1 year. If all capital gains were taxed in the year they were realized, it is argued that the taxpayer would bear too large a burden because of the progressivity of the tax.

Significance of Tax Loopholes

Taken together, deductions, exclusions, exemptions, credits, and the preferential treatment of capital gains remove about half of all personal income from taxation. (Recall from Chapter 11 that personal income is the broadest measure of income in the national income accounts; even so, it is less comprehensive than the definition of income discussed earlier.) Table 12–1 illustrates the relationship between personal income, AGI, and taxable income over a 25-year period. Note that taxable in-

Table 12–1. Relationships Among Personal Income, Adjusted Gross Income, and Taxable Income, 1950–1975 ($ in billions)

Year	Personal Income (PI)	AGI	Taxable Income (TI)	AGI as Percentage of PI	TI as Percentage of AGI	TI as Percentage of PI
1950	$ 226.1	$179.9	$ 84.9	79.6%	47.2%	37.5%
1960	399.7	316.6	171.6	79.2	54.2	42.9
1970	801.3	632.0	401.2	78.9	63.5	50.1
1975	1249.7	948.1	595.6	75.9	62.8	47.7

Source: Calculated from the IRS *Preliminary Statistics of Income 1975* and *The Economic Report of the President 1977*.

come as a percentage of AGI and personal income had been increasing until the early 1970s. (In the 1970s the increase in the personal exemption and tax credits reversed this trend.) The increase in income subject to taxation from 1950 to 1970 was not principally the result of tax reform; instead, it was primarily the result of increasing real incomes and inflation, which have pushed a larger share of reported income above the personal exemptions levels. Nevertheless, a large portion of income is not subject to tax. In 1975, for example, taxable income was only $595.6 billion out of a possible $1249.7 billion, or 47.7 percent.

Table 12–2 shows the relative importance of loopholes, as well as the size of income tax liabilities for different income classes. (Note that families are ranked by AGI in this table, not by the more comprehensive definition of personal income. Unfortunately, the distribution of taxes by personal income classes is not available.) Contrary to popular impression, a smaller share of AGI is taxed at lower income levels. Only 16.7 percent of income in the under-$5000 AGI class is subject to tax, and taxes are only 1.7 percent of AGI. (Recall that AGI does not include transfer payments; if these were included, the share of income subject to the tax in the lowest income class would be less than 10 percent.) By contrast, in the highest AGI class nearly 80 percent of income is taxed.

The major loopholes that exempt most income at the bottom end of the income scale from taxation are the personal exemption, standard deduction, and exclusion of transfer payments. These items are very large percentages of total income among low income households. At higher income levels, they represent a much smaller percentage of total income. Some writers prefer not to refer to these tax preferences as

Table 12–2. Adjusted Gross Income, Taxable Income and Tax Rates, 1975 Returns ($ in billions)

AGI Class	AGI	Taxable Income	TI as % of AGI	Taxes	Taxes as % of AGI	TI
$0–4,999	$ 60.0	$ 10.0	16.7%	$ 1.0	1.7%	10.0%
5,000–9,999	146.4	72.2	49.3	10.8	7.4	15.0
10,000–14,999	185.7	113.7	61.2	19.0	10.2	16.7
15,000–19,999	179.0	117.5	65.6	21.2	11.8	18.0
20,000–24,999	124.4	87.0	69.9	17.0	13.7	19.5
25,000–29,999	74.4	53.8	72.3	11.4	15.3	21.2
30,000–49,999	100.0	74.8	74.8	18.2	18.2	24.3
50,000–99,999	51.5	40.1	77.9	13.4	26.0	33.4
100,000 and above	32.8	25.9	79.0	12.4	37.8	47.9
All returns	948.1	595.6	62.8	124.8	13.2	21.0

Source: Calculated from the IRS *Preliminary Statistics of Income 1975.*

"loopholes" because they obviously disproportionately benefit the poor, but they are types of income that go untaxed.

Estimates of the quantitative significance of tax loopholes differ because analysts disagree about what constitutes a "loophole." Some studies, for example, include transfer payments, and others do not, despite the fact that transfers fit the generally agreed-on definition of income discussed in the last chapter. Some consider the standard deduction and the personal exemption loopholes, whereas others do not. Despite these differences, it is generally agreed that the revenue loss to the Treasury from tax preferences is substantial.

One of the most widely cited studies of the effects of tax loopholes on the tax base is by Pechman and Okner, who calculated the potential revenue gain associated with the elimination of selected (but not all) tax preferences.[1] Their results are summarized in Table 12–3. Overall, Pechman and Okner estimate that the elimination of the ennumerated loopholes would have increased AGI by $138 billion and taxable income by $166 billion in 1972. Tax revenues would have risen from $102.9 billion to $180.1 billion, or by 75 percent. To put this in a different perspective, each marginal tax rate could have been cut by 43 percent if these loopholes had been removed. It should be noted that Pechman and Okner considered only small reductions in personal exemptions and the standard deduction; consequently, their definition of taxable income still falls far short of a comprehensive measure of income.

The single largest increase in tax revenue comes from the addition of transfer payments. When Pechman and Okner include $79.7 billion in cash transfers, an additional $13 billion in tax revenue is produced. (Note that Pechman and Okner have not included in-kind transfers, which were about $25 billion in 1972.) Because transfer payments are heavily concentrated at the lower end of the income distribution where marginal tax rates are low, the resulting revenue gain is relatively small. The inclusion of capital gains and homeowners' preferences (imputed rents and the mortgage interest deduction) also results in sizable revenue gains, $9.6 billion and $9.3 billion, respectively. The last column in Table 12–3 provides a good reference for the relative importance of specific tax loopholes in terms of potential revenue gains. The importance of certain tax preferences also varies with the nature of the loophole for different income classes. For lower income groups the exclusion of cash and in-kind transfers and the personal exemption are quite important. For middle income taxpayers, deductions for state and local taxes, mortgage interest deductions, medical deductions, and the imputed rent on

---

[1] Joseph A. Pechman and Benjamin A. Okner. "Individual Income Tax Erosion by Income Classes" (Washington, D.C.: Brookings Institution, Reprint No. 230, 1972), p. 23.

Table 12–3. Revenue Gain from Removal of Major Tax Preferences, 1972 ($ in billions)

	AGI	TI	Revenue Gain
1. Present law additions	$776.1	$478.2	$102.9
2. Elimination of rate advantages of income splitting			21.6
3. Preferences (total)	138.2	166.0	55.8
a. One half realized capital gains	17.2	16.5	9.3
b. Constructive realization of gain on gifts and bequests	10.4	9.5	4.4
c. Tax exempt state and local bond interest	1.9	1.9	1.2
d. Dividend exclusion	2.2	1.9	.7
e. Life insurance interest	9.9	9.0	2.7
f. Homeowners' preferences	15.5	28.7	9.6
g. Other preference income	1.2	1.1	.6
h. Transfer payments	79.7	55.1	13.1
i. Personal exemptions and deductions		42.2	14.2
Equals: Comprehensive income tax	914.3	644.2	180.1

Source: Pechman and Okner, "Individual Income Tax Erosion by Income Classes," p. 23.

owner-occupied homes play major roles. For higher income classes, the preferential treatment of capital gains and the interest exclusion on state and local bonds are the most important preferences.

Economic Effects of Tax Preferences

Shifting and Incidence of Tax Preferences

Do the benefits of tax preferences always accrue to the taxpayers who claim them on their tax returns? Although it is often assumed that they do, actually the relative elasticities of supply and demand for the items given preferential treatment play an important role in determining who benefits. Suppliers may also gain from the preferential tax treatment of certain goods, and this fact explains much of the pressure for loopholes emanating from the supply side of the market. In some cases, virtually all of the benefits may accrue to the supply side and not to taxpayers per se.

Consider, for example, the exclusion of state and local bond interest from taxable income. To illustrate, assume for simplicity that a 50 percent flat rate tax on income is levied and that initially no exclusion for interest income from any source is allowed. If the pretax yield on all assets is 10 percent, with a 50 percent tax on income, the posttax yield is 5 percent. Now suppose an interest exclusion is permitted for state and local bonds; in the short run, individuals could earn a 10 percent return on municipals compared to a net return of 5 percent on all other assets. As a consequence, people will shift to state and local bonds, bidding their price up and their interest rate down to the point where the lower yield just offsets the subsidy—that is, until the yield on municipals equals the yield on other bonds. In other words, the interest rate on state and local bonds will fall to 5 percent; at that rate they return the same *net* yield as other (taxable) assets with a pretax yield of 10 percent. (This assumes that the state and local bond market is a small part of the total market for interest-bearing assets so that the return on taxable assets is unaffected.) Who, then, benefits from this exclusion?

In this case, the benefits of the exclusion accrue entirely to state and local governments (and state and local taxpayers), which are able to borrow funds at lower rates of interest. The taxpayers who own the tax exempt municipal bonds receive the same return as they would if they had purchased a corporate bond, because the tax-free return equals the posttax return on the corporate bond. Of course, under the present progressive tax system (in contrast to the proportional tax used in the example) not all benefits accrue to state and local governments; some tax savings remain to benefit taxpayers in the higher income brackets. Nevertheless, the interest exclusion is a boon to state and local governments, which can borrow at interest rates well below corporations of comparable risk.

In cases where the market can respond to tax preferences, much of the advantage of the loophole may be eliminated by changes in relative prices. The more inelastic the supply, the more prices will rise, and the more suppliers will benefit from the loophole, just as with any excise subsidy. For this reason, it is not a simple matter to determine who actually benefits from a tax loophole. In situations where market prices are not significantly affected by the loophole, which may well be true in the majority of cases, it would be correct to assert that the taxpayers utilizing the deduction would derive the entire benefit. In other cases, this would not be true, as in the example of state and local bonds where the interest rate is strongly affected.

The Welfare Cost of Tax Preferences

As indicated in the previous chapter, many tax loopholes can be treated analytically as ad valorem excise subsidies that lower the effective prices of deductible or excluded items to taxpayers. This is particularly true for itemized deductions and most of the exclusions in the tax laws. For itemized deductions and exclusions, their net price falls by $p(1-m)$, where p is the market price of the good and m is the taxpayer's effective marginal tax rate. For example, if the price of medical care is $1 per unit, and the taxpayer's marginal tax bracket is 30 percent, the net cost to the taxpayer for $1 worth of medical care is $0.70. By lowering the price of the deductible or excluded item, tax loopholes induce a substitution in favor of items that receive preferential treatment, which in turn results in a welfare cost (unless there are externalities or other distortions present—a possibility that will be discussed later in the chapter).

To identify the welfare cost, consider Figure 12–1. The effective price of the deductible or excluded items is measured on the vertical axis, and the quantity of the deductible or excluded items on the horizontal axis. Output is assumed to be supplied at a constant cost of $1 per unit. Let dd_{30} be the demand for all taxpayers in the 30 percent marginal tax bracket and dd_{70} be the demand for all taxpayers in the 70 percent marginal tax bracket. At the intial equilibrium, when no deductions or exclusions are permitted, the quantity q is consumed by taxpayers in the 30 percent marginal tax bracket, and q^* is consumed by those in the 70 percent group. Now if deductions and exclusions are allowed, the effective price of the subsidized items would fall in proportion to the taxpayers' marginal tax brackets—in this case by 30 and 70 percent. To reflect changes in relative prices due to the subsidy, we may either shift the supply curve down to reflect the lower price or pivot the demand

Figure 12–1. Welfare cost of tax loopholes.

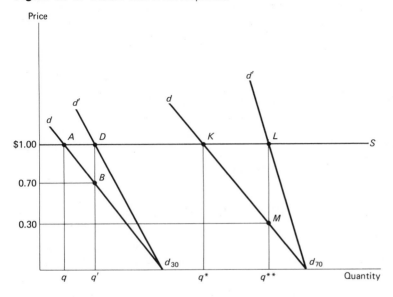

curve upward and to the right. In this case, the latter method will be used; for taxpayers in the 30 percent marginal tax bracket, the demand curve pivots to $d'd_{30}$, reflecting the absolute decrease in price, or the tax saving (in this example $0.30) associated with the loophole. (Note that the vertical distance between the two curves increases as the price increases; for example, if the price of the deductible item were $10 instead of $1, the tax saving would be $3.) The same applies for taxpayers in the 70 percent marginal tax bracket. At the lower prices, q' and q^{**}, respectively, are consumed.

To determine whether the new equilibrium levels of consumption are efficient, the relative costs and benefits associated with providing and consuming the additional output must be compared. For taxpayers in the 30 percent marginal tax bracket, the cost of providing the additional output, qq', is equal to the incremental area under the supply curve, or $qADq'$. The benefit to the same group is equal to the incremental area under the demand curve, $qABq'$. In this case, the costs exceed the benefits by the triangular area BAD. Similarly, costs are greater than benefits for taxpayers in the 70 percent marginal tax bracket by the triangle KLM. These two triangles represent the welfare cost of tax loopholes for two specific tax brackets; that is, they measure the inefficiency resulting from the loophole-induced overconsumption of deductible and excluded items.

The areas of both triangles can be estimated by the formula

$$W_i = \tfrac{1}{2}\eta_i m_i^2 Z_i$$

where W_i is the welfare cost for the ith marginal rate bracket (in this case the 30th and 70th percent marginal rate brackets, respectively), η is the price elasticity of demand for the deductible or excluded items for the ith bracket, m_i is the effective marginal tax bracket (or rate of subsidy), and Z_i is the total expenditures of the subsidized goods for the ith bracket. (Note that this formula is the same one derived to measure the welfare cost of an excise tax in Chapter 10—in both cases the welfare cost derives from the fact that the net price the consumer adjusts to differs from the marginal cost of producing the good.) Thus, with appropriate data, the welfare cost associated with tax preferences for the 30 and 70 percent marginal tax brackets can be calculated, as can the welfare cost related to the remaining marginal rate brackets. Finally, these results can be summed for all tax brackets, that is,

$$W = \tfrac{1}{2}\sum \eta_i m_i Z_i$$

to determine the aggregate welfare cost produced by this distortion. This cost was estimated to be $7.9 billion or 6.7 percent of tax revenues under the federal income tax in 1974. Note that this loss is in addition to the one due to effects on labor supply that was considered in the last chapter—here we are assuming that labor supply is fixed and examining how special provisions in the tax law lead to a misallocation of resources.[2]

Because the welfare cost of tax preferences rises with the square of the marginal tax rate, the distortion is larger at higher income levels because the effective rate of subsidy (the marginal tax rate) is greater at high income levels. This outcome is the result of a progressive tax with loopholes; if a proportional tax were used with loopholes, the welfare cost would be smaller because the same rate of subsidy would apply to all taxpayers regardless of income levels.

Other Types of Welfare Costs

In addition to the welfare cost due to the price-distorting effects of tax preferences discussed in the last section, there are other types of welfare costs that should be included in our discussion. When tax preferences are viewed as subsidies to taxpayers, a reduction in a person's taxes through the use of a loophole can be considered a transfer from the government to the taxpayer. Consequently, any use of resources to increase this transfer (reduce taxes) can be considered a welfare cost. The transfer itself is not a cost, but the resources devoted to obtaining a transfer are. Similarly, the costs incurred by the government to administer the tax system also involve a welfare cost because they represent a difference between the tax burden on the public and *usable* revenue received by the government. Although some of these costs are present in any type of tax system, they are probably higher under the current system because of the complexity of the tax laws, the progressive nature of the tax, and the existence of numerous tax loopholes. These other sources of welfare cost include:

Administrative Costs. The administration of the tax system involves informing taxpayers of the requirements of the law, assisting taxpayers in complying with the tax laws, auditing tax returns, collecting unpaid taxes, and investigating and prosecuting tax evaders. In 1975 the Internal Revenue Service processed about 82 million individual tax returns and approximately $124.8 billion in tax payments.[3] The cost of administering the tax system has been estimated at 0.5 percent of tax revenues, which, when compared to the cost of administering other govern-

---

[2] Jacquelene M. Browning. "Estimating the Welfare Cost of Tax Preferences," *Public Finance Quarterly,* forthcoming.

[3] Internal Revenue Service, *Preliminary Statistics of Income 1975* (Washington, D.C., 1977), pp. 9 and 11.

ment programs, is a source of continued pride to the IRS. These costs would, of course, tend to increase with the complexity of the tax and the degree of enforcement.

Compliance and Information Costs. Compliance costs include the time spent by taxpayers in completing and mailing tax returns, and the costs borne by employers in recording employees' salaries and in withholding part of their income for tax purposes. Information costs involve costs incurred by taxpayers to obtain information to reduce their taxes. Judge Learned Hand once argued that

> there is nothing sinister in so arranging one's affairs as to keep taxes as low as possible. Everyone does so, rich or poor, and all do right. Nobody owes any public duty to pay more than the law demands: taxes are enforced extractions, not voluntary contributions.[4]

President Carter's example to the contrary (he owed no taxes on his 1976 income but paid the IRS several thousand dollars anyway), most taxpayers appear to agree with Judge Hand's observation on the limits of their taxpaying obligations. Each year taxpayers spend millions of dollars on professional tax assistance to acquire information to minimize their taxes. More may be involved, however, than a simple desire to reduce taxes. The complexity of the tax laws may force many taxpayers to seek professional help. In 1976 over half of all taxpayers used professional tax preparers (e.g., H & R Block, tax accountants, and tax lawyers). Among taxpayers with only an elementary school education, 92 percent required professional assistance; by contrast, 57 percent of the college-educated taxpayers did their own returns.[5]

The complexity of the tax laws is not just a problem confined to nonprofessionals. Judge Hand, after a reading of a tax law, was compelled to note that the words of the tax law seemed to

> dance before my eyes in a meaningless procession . . couched in abstract terms that offer no handle to seize hold of . . . [they] leave in my mind only a confused sense of some vitally important, but successfully concealed purpose, which is my duty to extract, but which is in my power if at all, only after the most inordinate expenditure of time.[6]

Not only did the Judge have trouble in understanding the tax laws, but so does the IRS. If the IRS helps a taxpayer with his return, it will not guarantee its work. One taxpayer took his return to three different IRS offices for help and got three different calculations of the taxes he owed.

---

[4] Judge Learned Hand: *Commissioner* v. *Newman,* 159 F. 2d 848 (1947).
[5] Nancy Ross, "Tax Return Industry Growing," *Washington Post* (Mar. 16, 1975), F1.
[6] Judge Learned Hand, quoted by Joseph Goulden, *The Super Lawyers* (New York: Weybright, 1972), p. 308.

A few years ago the IRS tested its agents on their knowledge of the tax laws; there was a failure rate of nearly 80 percent. Altogether the tax laws and regulations, and interpretations based on them, total 40,000 pages—a sum that has doubled in the past 15 years.

Regardless of whether their motive is to minimize taxes or to seek help in understanding the tax laws, taxpayers are devoting a large quantity of resources to the acquisition of tax saving information. Taxpayers may incur costs (either professionally or personally—by studying the tax laws themselves) to collect information to find ways of timing future income and expenditures to minimize taxes; or taxpayers may bear similar costs to acquire tax saving information to take advantage of loopholes, given their past income and expenditure patterns. In either case, these actions involve a welfare cost. In 1975 the professional tax service industry grossed $700 million, but this figure alone is an incomplete measure of the welfare cost because it fails to include the value of the time spent by taxpayers who do their own returns. Musgrave and Musgrave estimate compliance and information costs together to be between $3 billion and $4 billion a year.[7] It should be noted, too, that information costs are likely to be greater under a progressive tax than under a proportional tax because the tax saving increases with higher marginal tax brackets; if the expected gains associated with acquiring tax saving information are greater for higher income taxpayers, they will probably invest more resources to acquire it. (Finding a loophole that allows a $100 deduction saves a taxpayer $30 in taxes if he is in a 30 percent marginal tax bracket, and $70 if he is in a 70 percent marginal bracket.) Therefore, those in higher brackets will probably be willing to spend more to locate loopholes they can use.

Costs Incurred by Special Interests to Secure Preferential Treatment. Because the creation or extension of preferential tax treatment involves tax saving, resources will be allocated to various lobbying activities to obtain (and protect) tax concessions. Frequently when taxpayers are unable to use existing tax laws to reduce their tax obligations, they will invest resources in political activities to gain preferential treatment in other ways. This may involve pressuring Congress to interpret tax laws in a special way to benefit certain individuals or groups, to pass a tax bill favoring specific taxpayers, or to legislate some special provision that benefits certain segments of the population.

Tax amendments or special provisions added to tax bills are frequently used methods of providing tax relief to certain individuals or special interests. Probably the most infamous tailormade bill was enacted in 1951

---

[7] Richard A. Musgrave and Peggy B. Musgrave, *Public Finance in Theory and Practice* (New York: McGraw-Hill, 1976), p. 460.

to benefit Louis B. Mayer, former head of MGM, and another studio executive, which saved Mayer about $2 million in taxes. The bill permitted a $2.75 million lump sum payment received by Mayer on retirement to be treated as capital gains rather than ordinary income. Moreover, the bill was written in such a way that no one else could have taken advantage of it.[8] There is really no way to judge, however, how pervasive or effective these activities are.

A closely related problem concerns the spread of tax preferences. Once preferential tax treatment is given to one group, it becomes very difficult to deny it to others. Often it appears that, as one critic of tax loopholes noted, "old loopholes never die, they just get bigger."[9] When Congress enacts a loophole benefiting one group and excluding others, the excluded group may step up lobbying activities, anticipating that Congress will broaden the preferential treatment. To cite a few examples, consider the spread of the depletion allowance in the corporate income tax. Percentage depletion for oil and gas was introduced under the Revenue Act of 1926 and extended to other minerals in varying percentages in 1932. The percentage depletion allowance permits firms to write off their investments—sometimes many times over. It was originally designed to encourage the discovery of more sources of energy and other minerals by making them attractive investments. Through 1940 to 1954, the depletion allowance was granted to other industries with rather dubious claims to be "users of scarce natural resources which are limited in supply and difficult to discover," or whose production warranted special tax treatment in the "national interest." Nevertheless, the depletion allowance was extended to clay, gravel, mollusk shells, peat, sand, shale, and slate.

To see the inevitability of such a spread once the preference is initially granted, consider the argument that the National Sand and Gravel Association presented to Congress in 1951. Witnesses testifying for the Association noted that (1) percentage depletion had already been granted to nonmetallic minerals and (2) sand and gravel were nonmetallic minerals; therefore, it seemed "unreasonable discrimination against our industry to continue to be denied the benefit of taxation policy already extended to other members of the nonmetallic minerals family." Evidently, Congress concurred. Sand and gravel were awarded a 5 percent depletion allowance, but the Association was not satisfied. It came back 3 years later ar-

---

[8] Philip Stern, *The Rape of the Taxpayer* (New York: Random House, 1973), pp. 42–43. For a more complete discussion of special tax bills enacted for the benefit of influential taxpayers and special interests, see William L. Carey, "Pressure Groups and the Internal Revenue Code," *Harvard Law Review* 68:745 (1955), and Stanley S. Surrey, "The Congress and the Tax Lobbyists," *Harvard Law Review,* 70:1147, 1176 (1957).

[9] Stern, op. cit., p. 295. For a more complete discussion of the following examples (and others), see Stern, pp. 295–306.

guing that sand and gravel were sold in competition with limestone (which had been granted a 15 percent depletion allowance) and that the 5 percent rate granted to sand and gravel was inadequate to "eliminate this competitive inequality." (It is noteworthy that limestone received its 15 percent rate by arguing that it had to compete in road building with other products such as rock asphalt, which enjoyed a 15 percent depletion allowance.)

Pressure to expand the depletion allowance continued and perhaps reached new heights (or depths—depending on your point of view) when a 76-year-old lawyer requested that he and his wife be granted a depletion allowance on their bodies. The U.S. Court of Appeals, however, decided against them, holding that "bodies and skills are not among the 'other natural deposits' for which the Internal Revenue Service allows a deduction for percentage depletion." Similarly, silent screen actress Gloria Swanson told the House Ways and Means Committee that aging actresses should qualify for depletion allowances, and, with similar reasoning, the National Football League Players Association appealed to the Senate Finance Committee to grant tax concessions to the professional athlete "who depletes his natural resources of physical ability and muscular strength while earning a high income on which he is heavily taxed." As yet the depletion allowance has not been extended to include bodies, but no doubt interested groups will keep trying.

In a similar way, Congress gradually extended capital gains treatment to many sources of income. In 1942 lump sum payments from pension, profit sharing, and stock bonus plans received by employees on death or retirement were granted capital gains treatment (which effectively decreased the tax rates by half). A year later, Congress allowed royalty or other income from the cutting of standing timber to be taxed as capital gains. In 1950 capital gains treatment was extended to inventors who sold or licensed their patents (although the income of artists, writers, and composers for the sale or license of their copyrights is still taxed at ordinary income rates).

In 1951 the sale of livestock used for breeding, draft, or dairy purposes and the sale of unharvested crops (sold at the same time as the land on which they were located) were singled out for capital gains treatment. Turkeys were also included in the original definition of "livestock" in the first draft of the bill. Former Minnesota Senator Edward Thye, however, felt that if turkeys received capital gains treatment, chickens should too, and he proposed an amendment to that effect. At that point, the following memorable exchange ensued on the Senate floor:

> Senator Douglas: Would the Senator from Minnesota consider the possibility of adding ducks, angora cats and dogs to his amendment?
> Senator Thye: There would be some justification for adding the duck, though ducks are not equal in importance to either turkeys or chickens with

respect to national income. The Senator has an argument there, but when one goes too far down the ladder . . . he may get into a category which causes someone possibly to look upon the proposition as ridiculous.

Senate Finance Chairman Walter George, fearing that the Senate might indeed look ridiculous, argued "I cannot [accept] the chicken amendment . . . I cannot conceive that Congress ever had in mind [giving capital gains treatment] to assets that are purely transitory." But when another Senator tried to amend the tax bill to deny capital gains treatment to *all* livestock, arguing that livestock was transitory, Senator George quickly backtracked, noting that it "would be a dangerous thing indeed to say that the whole [livestock capital gain] section should be impaired" by a chicken or a turkey. (The turkey amendment passed the Senate but was eliminated by a House-Senate Conference Committee; the remainder of the livestock provision passed.)

Not to lose sight of the point being made earlier, we should note again that discussions and debates of this type are encouraged by the possibility of obtaining or extending preferential treatment. Resources devoted to obtaining and enlarging tax preferences constitute a welfare cost because they produce no services valued by consumers.

Litigation Costs. Each year about 1.8 million tax returns are audited. In many cases, taxpayers peacefully submit to increased tax assessments; others do not, and challenge the decisions of the IRS. Although not all of these challenges reach the tax court or federal court, many do. Claims under $1500 are handled in the small claims section; claims in excess of this amount are settled in the tax court or federal courts (on appeal). Because the probability of an audit increases with incomes and if a taxpayer itemizes, higher income taxpayers are more likely to have their returns challenged. It is also more likely that these taxpayers will be willing to incur larger litigation costs because their expected tax saving is higher (recall that the tax saving value of a deduction is worth more to taxpayers in higher marginal tax brackets). Moreover, the performance of the IRS in tax court is notably unremarkable; the IRS won only 4 percent of its trials in tax court! (In contrast, it won 77 percent of its cases in small claims court.) There are currently 79,000 lawyers and CPAs who practice before the tax courts (and their fees are tax deductible).[10] Unfortunately, there are no estimates available on litigation costs, but they too represent a welfare cost associated with the current tax system.

Although it is clearly impossible to estimate precisely, the combined welfare costs of tax preferences must be several billion dollars a year. Some of these costs would exist even if there were no special tax preferences in the tax laws, but it seems clear that a substantial part of these

[10] Ross, op cit., p. F1.

costs can be traced to a complex tax code with innumerable special provisions.

Rationales for Tax Preferences

In the previous sections, the inefficiencies associated with certain types of tax loopholes have been discussed. To obtain a more balanced view, however, we should consider whether there are offsetting advantages from tax preferences that should be weighed against their inefficiencies. Consequently, our next chore will be to examine and evaluate the rationales for loopholes.

Equity

In the last chapter, we discussed what economists consider to be a comprehensive definition of income: consumption plus change in net worth. If income is to serve as the basis for taxation, we would like it to be a reasonable index of the taxpayer's ability to pay taxes. The question is, do persons with equal incomes (defined in this way) actually have equal taxpaying capacity, or is there some alternative definition of income that will be more equitable? Although in the bulk of cases most persons agree that income is a good measure of taxpaying capacity, it is possible that equity may be improved by occasionally departing from this definition.

To see why this may be so, consider medical expenses. It is widely felt that medical expenses should be deductible from total income in the interests of equity, and the present tax law permits this to some degree. The effect of allowing a deduction can be seen by first considering family *A,* who has a total income of $10,000 and $2000 in medical expenses. If no deduction is allowed, family *A* will be taxed the same amount (other things equal) as family *B* with an income of $10,000 and no medical expenses. If the deduction is allowed, family *A* will have a taxable income of only $8000, and it would then pay the same taxes as family *C* with an $8000 income and no medical expenses. The question is this: Should families *A* and *B* be considered to have equal taxpaying capacity (as when no deduction is allowed), or should families *A* and *C* be considered equal (as when the deduction is allowed)?

To answer this question it is necessary, of course, to make a value judgment. Many believe that it is more equitable to permit the deduction, arguing that medical expenses are a burden on people and do not constitute any taxpaying capacity. This view is strongest when applied to catastrophic medical expenses and becomes less plausible when extended to certain types of medical care that are voluntarily chosen and in part consumption items. For example, a person can deduct the cost of installing air conditioning if a doctor will certify that it is necessary to relieve allergy symptoms. In this case, there are nonmedical benefits not only for the allergy sufferer but for other family members as well. Should the cost of the air conditioning be fully deductible, partially deductible, or not deductible?

Many medical expenses are of this complex type, reflecting in part voluntarily chosen outlays that are not just uncompensated costs on households. Whether, on balance, the existing deductions make a net contribution to equity is questionable, but the underlying principle involved seems widely accepted, although often difficult to apply in many actual situations.

There are relatively few important loopholes where this type of equity argument can be made. Personal exemptions are another possible case. Allowing an exemption of $750 per person means that a two-person family with an income of $10,000 is considered to have the same tax-paying capacity as a three-person family with an income of $10,750. Does having a child reduce one's taxpaying ability by $750? There are costs associated with raising children, of course, but the decision to have children is largely a voluntary one. Some economists such as Henry Simons have argued that children are consumption items and that couples should not receive tax benefits because they decide to have children and spend part of their income raising them. Others feel that equity requires taxing larger families more lightly than smaller families with the same incomes.

Obviously, arriving at a definition of the tax base that is generally agreed to be more equitable than total income is not simple. There are certain general areas such as medical expenses that intuitively appear to be good candidates for deductions, but whether the definition of taxable income as it actually exists contributes to equity is a moot question. As already mentioned, very few important loopholes have been seriously defended on equity grounds.

Externalities

Another rationale for the existence of certain types of tax preferences is the "advancing of socially important objectives,"[11] that is, the use of tax loopholes to subsidize certain externality-generating activities. A good example is the deduction for charitable contributions; similar arguments have been made for the health insurance deduction (many claim that this deduction encourages better health, but is this an *external* benefit?) and

[11] Richard Goode, *The Individual Income Tax,* revised edition (Washington, D.C.: Brookings Institution, 1976), p. 161.

the deductions related to home ownership (encourages a more stable home environment, but again does this constitute an externality?).

Previous analysis of tax loopholes showed that tax preferences, by lowering the effective prices of certain goods, resulted in too large a production and consumption of these items. This analysis, however, ignored the possible presence of externalities. When external benefits are associated with the consumption of specific goods, the competitive equilibrium is potentially inefficient, that is, too little of the good is being consumed. Consequently, some form of subsidy to increase consumption may be appropriate, and a more efficient allocation of resources could result. In Chapter 2, external benefits were examined along with types of remedial policy. Recall that when external benefits are present a flat rate per unit subsidy equal to the size of the marginal external benefit at the efficient quantity of consumption can be used to attain an efficient allocation (see Figure 2–2). As we pointed out, many tax loopholes can be viewed as this type of subsidy because they lower the net cost to taxpayers of consuming the deductible or excluded item. Thus, it is sometimes argued that loopholes may contribute to the efficiency of the tax system by encouraging consumption of goods with external benefits.

As shown in Chapter 2, there are many difficulties with designing a subsidy that will improve resource allocation, even when external benefits exist. As a justification for certain tax preferences, the externality argument encounters two further problems. First, the rate of subsidy implicit in a tax loophole is the taxpayer's marginal tax rate. If a taxpayer is in a 25 percent rate bracket, a deduction or exclusion lowers the price by 25 percent. Only by coincidence will the marginal tax bracket be the correct rate at which to subsidize externality-generating activities.

A second problem arises from the graduated rate structure of the income tax. Taxpayers are in different marginal tax brackets, so the implicit subsidy rate of a loophole varies among taxpayers. Thus, the net cost of giving a dollar to charity is $0.30 for a taxpayer in a 70 percent marginal tax bracket and $0.80 for someone in a 20 percent bracket (and $1 for taxpayers who don't itemize deductions). If there are external benefits, such a subsidy would be efficient only if the marginal external benefit were $0.70 per dollar for the taxpayer in the 70 percent marginal tax bracket, $0.20 per dollar for one in the 20 percent bracket, and so on. This is unlikely to be the case: Why is $1 given to charity more valuable to society when donated by someone in a 70 percent bracket than when given by someone in a 20 percent bracket? In general, the externality argument for a subsidy calls for the same rate of subsidy for all consumers, and loopholes violate this condition. (There are exceptions to the rule that the rate of subsidy must be the same for all individuals, but they generally involve subsidies to poor persons and appear to have little relevance for tax loopholes.)

Overall, these remarks suggest that the externality argument for tax loopholes is rather weak. This is not to deny that external benefits may exist, but, if they do, an outright subsidy is probably more capable of improving resource allocation than a tax loophole.

Administrative Costs

Some types of income are excluded because it is argued that their inclusion would be too costly on practical grounds. Income must be valued in money terms to be taxed, and it is difficult to place a monetary value on some types of income. A clear example is provided by household services (such as food preparation, child care, and housekeeping) provided by the taxpayer. These services are income, but what is their monetary value?

The issues here are, in principle, clear-cut. If any type of income is not taxed, there will be an equity and efficiency cost. But the process of placing a money value on some types of income also has a cost that must be weighed against the equity and efficiency gains of taxing all income equally. In addition, the difficulty of placing an accurate money value on items such as household services can also lead to inequities. These factors must be weighed against one another in each separate case.

Types of income to which this rationale for exclusion from the tax base has been applied include unrealized capital gains, household services, imputed rent on owner-occupied housing, and some in-kind transfers. Experts differ on the validity of this argument in specific cases; many feel that imputed rents, in-kind transfers, and some types of unrealized capital gains could be included at moderate cost. Whatever the merits of this argument in specific cases, it is valid in principle, and it warns against trying to apply the theoretical definition of income as the sole criterion in defining the tax base. Some types of income are too costly to tax.

Concessions to State and Local Governments

The deduction of state and local taxes (income, property, and sales taxes) and the exclusion of interest income on state and local bonds are, in effect, subsidies to the operation of state and local governments. In analyzing this policy we should consider whether the activities of state and local governments should be subsidized; if so, by how much (the state and local tax deduction is the largest single deduction, amounting to $44.1 billion in 1975)[12]; and, if a subsidy is required, are special provisions in the federal tax system the best way to accomplish it?

[12] *Preliminary Statistics of Income 1975,* op. cit., pp. 11 and 26.

If state and local governments produced public goods that generated geographic spillovers, the output of these goods in the absence of a subsidy might be too small. Efficient output could require an expansion in the quantity of the public goods produced. For example, if community A successfully undertook a pollution abatement program that reduced the pollution level not only for community A but also for residents in neighboring community B, then A's pollution abatement project would produce interlocality spillovers. Residents in community B would benefit, but would pay no taxes to support the program. Without a subsidy, perhaps, the project might be scrapped or undertaken on a smaller scale that yielded no benefits for community B. If B's residents could be taxed by A, a larger quantity of pollution abatement would be produced, but when this is impossible a subsidy may be the only way to produce the optimal amount of the public good. To argue successfully, however, that tax deductions and interest exclusions are an efficient way of taking geographic spillovers into account would require that *all* services produced by state and local governments generate geographic spillovers. Surely the possibility of this being true is remote.

Again, we are discussing externalities, but this time in a nonmarket setting, and that adds new wrinkles. State and local taxes are deductible only if the taxpayer itemizes deductions, and not all taxpayers itemize. (In 1975 only 31 percent itemized.)[13] Suppose there is a community whose local government produces a public good generating geographic spillovers. Yet if less than a majority of taxpayers itemize (perhaps the community is a relatively low income one where few itemize), the tax deduction might have no effect on the quantity of the public good provided. In our earlier analysis of tax preferences, the effects of tax subsidies were examined in competitive markets; in this setting the lower price typically caused consumption of the deductible or excluded item to rise. In a nonmarket situation, however, the outcome is uncertain. Taxpayers who itemize will face lower net prices for public services, and will demand more. Taxpayers who do not itemize will continue to want the same quantity of public services because they receive no subsidy. The eventual outcome depends on the relative voting strengths of the two groups. In contrast to tax deductions, the interest exclusion on state and local bonds lowers the cost of public goods financed in this manner to *all* taxpayers in the community, and this will cause an expansion in the quantity of public goods financed by tax exempt municipals.

Both tax deductions and the interest exclusion subsidize the operation of state and local governments. Although a case can be made that some of these activities should be subsidized on the basis of geographic spillovers, the use of loopholes seems inappropriate. Instead, direct expendi-

[13] Ibid., p. 26.

tures earmarked for certain activities seem a more effective and less costly method of achieving the same result.

The general weaknesses of the arguments for tax preferences have led many economists to advocate the elimination of most, or all, loopholes and the use of a broad-based tax instead. Before turning to the design of a more broadly based tax, however, we should consider the rate structure of the present tax.

Progressivity in the Rate Structure

The widespread support of our progressive tax system implies a general acceptance of the belief that progressive taxation is necessary to maintain a proper relationship among the tax burdens of individual taxpayers. Whether a progressive tax system can be justified on objective grounds is, however, another question. Over time the use of progressive taxes has been rationalized by many arguments, and the most important ones will be presented and evaluated; afterward, arguments against progressive taxation will be examined.[14]

The Case for Progressive Taxation

Benefit Theory. The benefit theory of taxation implies a specific method for distributing the tax burden—taxes should be allocated on the basis of benefits received from government expenditures. If it can be shown that benefits increase faster than income, then a compelling case for progressive taxes can be made. Note that it is not enough to argue that wealthier persons receive more benefits from government expenditures: If a taxpayer with an income of $30,000 derives twice the benefits of a taxpayer with an income of $15,000, this only justifies a proportionate tax.

No doubt, the value of some benefits increases with income; for example, police and fire protection are probably more important to wealthier people with more property to protect. It is unlikely, however, that this will be true for all government-provided goods and services (especially social welfare expenditures), and not only must these benefits increase with income to justify graduated rates, they must also increase more rapidly than income. In addition, there is the problem of placing a value on the benefits received on which to base the tax. And last there is the question of how to redistribute income under such a system—if low income taxpayers were taxed on the basis of benefits received from transfer programs, the effect of the transfer would be negated. For these

[14] This section draws on Walter J. Blum and Harry J. Kalven Jr., *The Uneasy Case for Progressive Taxation* (Chicago: University of Chicago Press, 1953).

reasons, few people have argued that progressive taxation is called for on benefit grounds.

Ability to Pay. A second type of argument for progression considers the ability of taxpayers to pay taxes. If the benefits associated with government-expenditure programs are ignored, the problem of taxation becomes a question of allocating the total tax burden in the most equitable way. This approach requires inflicting an "equal sacrifice" on each taxpayer, and, within this context, it is argued that a dollar has less "value" to a wealthy taxpayer than to a poor person; if this is the case, then the wealthier taxpayer should pay more taxes than a poorer person. To justify a progressive tax system, this argument must be taken further—it must be argued that the ability to pay taxes (or make sacrifices) increases faster than income; that is, if one taxpayer has twice the income of another, the wealthier taxpayer has *more* than twice the ability to pay taxes.

The ability-to-pay theory rests on two crucial assumptions. First, it is assumed that it is possible to make interpersonal comparisons of utility between taxpayers to know that higher income taxpayers are increasingly more able to pay taxes (bear sacrifices). Second, it is necessary to assume that the marginal utility of money income declines in a certain way as income rises. We know that there is no objective way to make interpersonal comparisons of utility; moreover, there is no evidence to suggest that the marginal utility of income declines when income increases. In fact, a declining marginal utility of income is also consistent with the use of proportional and regressive taxes—to justify progressivity on this basis, very specific assumptions must be made about the rates at which utility declines. Ability to pay is probably the most widely accepted justification for progression, but its acceptance seems to be based more on faith than on logic. Blum and Kalven, after a careful review of the arguments for and against progressive taxation, conclude that the popularity of ability-to-pay arguments must stem from "fallacies that have frequented the theories and not their truths which . . . would not support any firm conviction about the validity of the progressive principle."[15]

Equality. Because a progressive tax system places a relatively greater burden for funding government expenditures on higher income taxpayers, a graduated-rate structure is a means of redistributing income in comparison to a proportional tax. If the top 20 percent of families have (say) 40 percent of total before-tax income, a proportional tax (which lowers all absolute incomes in the same proportion) will leave them with 40 per-

---

[15] Ibid., p. 68.

cent of total after-tax incomes. A proportional tax does not affect the relative distribution of income. In contrast, a progressive tax produces a more equal distribution of after-tax income. If the top 20 percent of families have 40 percent of before-tax income, they will have less than 40 percent of after-tax income if a progressive tax is used, and the lowest income class ends up with a higher percentage of after-tax income. Therefore, progressive taxation tends to produce greater equality in the distribution of income. If it is thought that government should attempt to equalize incomes, then progressive taxation is yet another method to do it.

A relevant question is how much of an equalizing effect is produced by using progressive taxation. More specifically, what contribution do graduated rates make to producing greater equality? Currently, rate brackets rise from 14 to 70 percent—a highy graduated rate structure. Yet a flat rate tax of 21 percent applied to the same base would yield the same revenue.[16] Note that this 21 percent tax is not a proportional tax since it does not apply to all income, only to taxable income as now defined in the tax laws. In effect, this is a form of taxation similar to that known as degressive taxation. A degressive tax is a flat rate applied to all income in excess of some exempted level. Such a tax implies that tax liabilities rise as a percentage of *total* income as we move up the income scale. Thus, this is a form of progressive taxation, but it uses only one marginal tax rate for all taxpayers rather than graduated rates.

Who benefits and who loses, and by how much, from using existing graduated rates instead of a flat 21 percent rate? Table 12–4 provides the answer by calculating the tax liabilities for a family of four at different income levels under the two alternative tax structures. As can be seen, families with incomes under $23,100 pay lower taxes under the present system than under a flat 21 percent tax, whereas the opposite is true for higher income families. Two facts should be noted. First, the biggest gainers from the graduated rate structure are not those with very low incomes, but instead are middle income families. The family with $15,000 (about median income) saves $253 or 1.7 percent of its total income under the present graduated rate system. Second, at no income level do the beneficiaries gain more than 1.7 percent of income.

What these facts suggest is that the use of graduated rates is a boon mainly to middle income families, but even for them the gain is very small. It is difficult to see how such a modest gain for families that are not particularly needy can serve as a persuasive justification for a system of graduated tax rates. Of course, the use of exemptions significantly

[16] Note that this flat 21 percent tax is not a proportional tax because it is applied to the same tax base as the present rate structure. The flat 21 percent is more akin to a degressive tax (a flat rate above an exemption), a form of progressive tax that does not use graduated rates.

Table 12–4. Distributional Effect of Shift to Degressive Tax

AGI	Present Tax	Degressive Tax	Tax Saving	Tax Saving as % of AGI
7,000	$ 0	$ 0	$ 0	—
8,000	124	168	44	0.6%
10,000	450	588	138	1.4
12,000	827	1008	181	1.5
15,000	1385	1638	253	1.7
20,000	2536	2688	152	0.8
23,100	3339	3339	0	0.0
30,000	5425	4788	− 637	−2.12
40,000	9226	6888	−2335	−5.8

benefits families with low incomes by exempting them from income taxation; personal exemptions then are easier to defend as a redistributive device than is the application of graduated marginal rates above the exempted level.

The Case Against Progressive Taxation

Complexity. Progressive rate structures tend to lead to complex tax laws and to the proliferation of loopholes. For a variety of reasons, progressive rates produce what appear to many to be numerous inequities and inefficiencies that call for special tax treatment (loopholes), thereby complicating the law. For example, a taxpayer who earns $50,000, $5000, and $5000 over a 3-year period will pay a much higher tax than a taxpayer with the same total income but who receives $20,000 a year for 3 years. This seems unfair and has led to provisions in the tax law that permit the averaging of income over several years. These provisions are quite complex and somewhat arbitrary, and their justification depends entirely on the existence of a progressive tax system. Under a proportional tax, the two taxpayers would pay the same tax: Tax liabilities would not depend on the pattern of receipt of income over time. Thus, with a proportional tax there is no need for an income-averaging provision.

The special treatment of capital gains is an even more important instance of a controversial loophole spawned largely by the use of a progressive tax system. One strong argument for taxing realized capital gains at lower rates is that these gains may have accrued over several years but are taxed in 1 year. When realized (as when someone sells a home), they would push the taxpayer into a much higher bracket—and the tax liability would be higher than if the gains were taxed (at lower marginal rates) over the years they were accruing. In effect, capital gains treatment can be defended as a crude form of income averaging. Of course, under a proportional tax (and, to a slightly lesser degree, under a degressive tax) this would not be a valid argument for special treatment of capital gains, and this complex provision would be unnecessary.

Another set of problems created by progressivity centers around the treatment of the taxpaying unit. If the family is defined as the taxpaying unit, then a two-person family with an income of $40,000 will pay more tax under a progressive tax than two single persons with incomes of $20,000 each. If instead the income earner is the appropriate unit, a two-earner family, each earning $20,000, will pay the same tax as two single persons each earning $20,000—but then the two-earner family will pay less tax than a one-earner family with an income of $40,000. There are obviously difficult and largely unresolvable ethical questions involved. Currently, there are four different rate schedules applicable to single persons, married couples filing joint returns, married couples filing separate returns, and other heads of households. Single persons now pay more tax than married couples with the same income, but at the same time some married couples pay more than if they were unmarried. This latter situation exists for two-earner families where each earner has nearly the same income. The "marriage penalty" is about $1200 in taxes for a couple with separate incomes of $20,000 each, that is, their taxes would be $1200 less if they were unmarried.[17] Some married couples have reacted by getting divorced at the end of December and remarrying in early January to end the year as single taxpayers. (Some enterprising travel services even offer tax-divorce junkets to Mexico.)

Under a proportional tax, these ethical questions concerning how to treat the taxpaying unit would not arise. All income would be taxed at the same rate whether earned by a single person, a married couple, or persons living together in the same household.

Another more indirect way that progression leads to loopholes is through its higher marginal tax rates. Because the tax saving from a loophole depends on the marginal tax rate, the higher marginal rates (for most taxpayers) under progression give them greater reason to politically support and lobby for special tax concessions.

Writing more than 15 years ago, Blum and Kalven noted: "It is remarkable how much of the day to day work of the lawyer in the income tax field derives from the simple fact that the tax is progressive. Perhaps, the majority of his problems are either caused or aggravated by that fact."[18] This observation is even more pertinent today. As already pointed out, complexity has significant costs in the form of administra-

[17] U.S. Treasury, *Blueprints for Basic Tax Reform* (Washington, D.C.: January 17, 1977), p. 174.
[18] Blum and Kalven, op. cit., p. 15.

tion, compliance, and information costs. Although no tax system can completely avoid costs of this sort, it seems likely that these costs would be lower under a proportional tax.

Political Repercussions. Another objection that can be raised to progression is that it is an irresponsible political formula where a majority of taxpayers can impose higher tax rates on a wealthy minority than they are willing to pay themselves. There is no rule or principle underlying progression, and there is the danger that the low and middle income majority will not show restraint in the tax rates they vote for those with higher incomes. This raises questions of fairness and of efficiency, because the higher rates will be applied to the most productive members of society.

Inefficiency. The impact of taxes on work and saving incentives and the resulting welfare costs have been discussed earlier. We should recall that the marginal tax rates are critical, and a graduated rate system imposes increasingly higher marginal tax rates (up to 70 percent under the present law). The welfare cost rises with the square of the marginal tax rates, so higher marginal tax rates produce disproportionately larger distortions. Although marginal tax rates are present with a proportional tax or a degressive tax, they would not be so high for most taxpayers, and the resulting distortions would be smaller. On the other hand, no one knows exactly how quantitatively important these costs are; proponents of progression generally hold that they are not too great a cost to pay.

Reforming the Income Tax

There are many important issues in tax reform, and most are extremely complex. Several of the major elements in tax reform will now be discussed, but the list is by no means exhaustive or precisely detailed.

Comprehensive Tax Base

Because of the inefficiencies and inequities associated with the present tax system, proposals to use a more comprehensive definition of income have received a great deal of attention. Suggested reforms have ranged from a selective elimination of tax preferences to a comprehensive broadening of the definition of taxable income to approximate a broad definition of income. Using the latter approach, some items would still be excluded from income because of high administrative costs (such as imputed rents), but the preferential treatment given most items would be eliminated. Consequently, a comprehensive tax base (CTB) would tax all income regardless of its source (transfer payments, wages, interest income, and so on) or its use (consumption or saving); a CTB would also tax gains in net worth whether they result from factor earnings or transfers (either public or private), whether they are expected or unexpected, regular or irregular, accrued or realized, from business or accident, and so on. (The treatment of changes in net worth, i.e., capital gains, raises some administrative problems, but many of these would be eliminated by the integration of the corporation income tax and the personal income tax as discussed in a later section; unrealized capital gains not generated in the corporate sector could be taxed at ordinary rates after appropriate adjustments have been made for inflation.)

If income is defined comprehensively (say, equal to personal income in the national income accounts), then the tax base would be nearly twice as large as at present. On this larger base, a flat rate (proportional) tax of 11 percent would raise the same revenue as the current 14 to 70 percent rates. Alternatively, the comprehensive tax base could be taxed at graduated rates at much lower levels than at present and still yield the same revenue. Thus, a CTB could be used with either a progressive, degressive, or proportional rate structure.

Because a CTB can be used with any rate structure, it might be useful to compare the three alternatives. In doing this, it is important to consider the distributional impact of the tax, the efficiency of the tax, and the allocative effects of tax preferences.

CTB and Progressive Taxation. Because marginal tax rates will be lower under a CTB than under the present tax, the inefficiency produced by the effect of marginal tax rates on work and saving incentives will generally be smaller. If the tax is truly comprehensive, tax loopholes (except those administratively impossible to eliminate) will be almost eliminated, and the welfare cost associated with them will nearly disappear. Horizontal inequities produced by loopholes will also be eliminated. These benefits have led many economists to favor a CTB with graduated rates. The justification for the graduated rates themselves is, of course, a separate issue. The relevant question here is whether the income tax is an appropriate mechanism to use in an attempt to redistribute income or whether a system of transfer payments would be preferable. In addition, there is some question about whether it is politically possible to have a comprehensive tax base and graduated rates. As pointed out earlier, progression in the rate structure creates ethical problems that many feel require special tax provisions; moreover, the generally higher marginal tax rates create a greater demand for loopholes on the part of taxpayers because the tax saving is larger. For these reasons, the combination of a comprehensive tax base and graduated rates may be difficult to achieve.

CTB and Proportional Taxation. A CTB used with a flat rate tax avoids the defects of progressive rates that were discussed earlier. In practice, quite a low rate is capable of raising the same revenue as the present graduated rate structure. If the tax base is defined as personal income that is twice as large as taxable income under the federal income tax, a flat rate tax of only 11 percent will raise the same revenue as the current tax. Note that this rate is lower than the lowest marginal tax rate in the present system (14 percent), so all taxpayers will pay lower marginal rates except those who now pay no income taxes.

Perhaps the major objection to this type of tax is its effect on the poor. Low income families for the most part pay no federal income taxes; under the CTB with a flat rate tax on all income, they will give up 11 percent of their income to the federal government. Even so, government transfers will still be more than 5 times as large as the total taxes paid, so the overall tax and transfer system will remain highly redistributive in favor of low income households. Although a proportional tax is not itself redistributive, it can be used to finance expenditures that benefit lower income classes. The fact that the poorer households pay some taxes under this arrangement is therefore not a decisive objection: Transfers can be adjusted to avoid undue burdens.

CTB and Degressive Taxation. A degressive rate structure such as the one illustrated in Table 12–4 strikes a middle ground between progressive and proportional tax rates. It exempts a certain level of income for all taxpayers and then levies a proportional tax on income in excess of the exempted level. For example, if income is defined comprehensively but each person is allowed a $1000 exemption, a flat rate tax of about 14 percent would be required. Many low income taxpayers would be exempt from taxes because their incomes would be less than the exempted level; those with incomes slightly above the exempted level would pay very low average tax rates.

A degressive tax is, of course, a form of progressive tax because the average rate rises with income. It does not, however, use graduated marginal rates, and that may be a significant advantage. Some of the disadvantages of using a progressive tax with graduated rates stem from the sharply increasing marginal brackets and not from the fact that average tax rates rise. A degressive tax would avoid these disadvantages because it uses only one marginal rate above the exemption. To some experts, a degressive tax appears to have most of the significant advantages claimed for progression but avoids or mitigates many of the disadvantages. Of course, the marginal rate required is higher than under a proportional tax, so distortions in labor supply, saving, and so on would be somewhat greater, although probably smaller than under a graduated tax rate.

363

Integration of the Corporation and Personal Income Tax

Up to now, our discussion has focused on the federal individual income tax. The federal government also taxes the net income of incorporated businesses with the corporation income tax. This tax will be discussed in some detail in the next chapter, but it is worth pointing out here the way in which this tax relates to the concept of a comprehensive tax base.

Under present law, corporate income can be taxed at three levels. First, a tax on corporate income is levied up to rates of 48 percent. Second, net corporate income, if it is distributed to stockholders as dividends, is taxed a second time at the effective marginal tax rates of the shareholders. Third, any retained income (corporate profits not distributed as dividends) that gives rise to increases in the value of the corporations' stock is taxed at capital gains rates (if the stock is sold after 12 months it qualifies for long-term capital gains rates, which lowers the tax rate to half the tax rates applied to ordinary income). Because capital gains are taxed only on realization (i.e., when the stock is sold), there is an additional tax saving—a gain equal to the amount of interest on the deferred taxes for the length of time the sale is deferred. For capital gains held for a long period, this saving could be quite large; moreover, if gains on assets are never realized by the shareholder but instead are transferred at death, the stock escapes capital gains taxation.

According to any of the accepted concepts of equity, this system of taxation is highly inequitable. The taxation of corporate income in no way accords with notions of ability to pay or horizontal or vertical equity. All corporations are owned by individuals, so the income of corporations belongs to the shareholders. Taxing corporate income is an indirect means of taxing individual income—but with no attempt to adjust the tax to the taxpaying capacity of the individuals ultimately being taxed. Consider the tax liabilities of two taxpayers, A and B, with equal before-tax incomes of $5000 a year, but with different sources of income. Taxpayer A receives his income in the form of dividends (perhaps a retirement pension); his share of *gross* corporate earnings is $5000, but after a corporate income tax of, say, 50 percent is paid on gross earnings, his net earnings are $2500. (In this discussion of equity, we are assuming the corporate income tax is borne by shareholders, but this is not entirely correct; the incidence of the corporation income tax will be discussed more fully in Chapter 13.) In contrast, taxpayer B receives his income in wages and pays no taxes (he falls into the zero rate bracket). Consequently, two individuals with equal before-tax incomes pay vastly different taxes because their sources of income differ; this, of course, violates horizontal equity.

The higher tax rates imposed on corporate income also have distorting allocative effects. Dividends are usually taxed twice (once as corporate income and again as personal income), so distributed corporate income is taxed at higher rates than ordinary income. On the other hand, corporate income that ultimately receives capital gains treatment may often be taxed at lower rates than ordinary income. On balance, however, it is believed that corporate income is taxed at higher rates than any other type of earned or investment income, and this has two important allocative consequences. Because the rate of return on capital invested in the corporate sector falls because of its tax treatment, capital is artificially attracted into the noncorporate sector. (This is discussed in much greater detail in the next chapter.) Another consequence is that corporations will tend to raise new capital by debt finance rather than by issuing new stock, because interest is a deductible expense and dividend payments are not. As a result of this increased "leverage," corporations have less of a cushion if earnings decline and are more likely to go bankrupt, with subsequent impacts on economic stability.

The most widely accepted resolution to the problems posed by the tax treatment of the corporation income tax is to integrate the corporation and personal income taxes. Corporate shareholders would continue to pay taxes on dividends received, but dividends would be "grossed up" to include the amount of corporation income tax paid. If, for instance, the corporation income tax were 50 percent, a dividend payment of $50 would be "grossed up" to indicate that it was necessary to earn a pretax income of $100 (at a 50 percent tax rate) to produce $50 in income after taxes. In addition, corporations could allocate retained earnings among stockholders; stockholders would include retained earnings as taxable income, again on a grossed-up basis. Under this plan, stockholders would receive credit for the corporation income tax paid on any earnings against their total tax liability. In this way, the corporation income tax would serve as a withholding device. Adoption of this proposal would result in the taxation of corporate income at the same rates as ordinary income; it would eliminate the double taxation of dividends; and it would be equivalent to taxing long-term capital gains as ordinary income on an accrual basis because gains in the value of the stock due to retained earnings would be taxed as they accrued rather than when they were realized.

The progressivity of the tax structure would be altered by the integration of the two taxes, but this could be adjusted by changing tax rates to achieve desired levels.[19]

---

[19] For a more detailed discussion of these points, see Charles E. McLure, Jr., "Integration of the Income Taxes: Why and How," *Journal of Corporate Taxation,* 2(4):429 (Winter 1976).

The Consumption Tax

To this point in our discussion of tax reform, it has been implicitly assumed that income is the best tax base. Lately, however, several economists have advocated the view that consumption rather than income is a more appropriate base. A consumption tax taxes income according to its use—income used for consumption purposes is taxable; income saved is not. (Recall that saving plus consumption equals income.) Suppose, for example, that a taxpayer earned $12,000 a year and saved $2000 of his wages. Under a consumption tax, his taxable income would be $10,000. Any saving (contributions to savings accounts, purchase of stocks or bonds, or gifts or bequests to others) would not be taxed, but withdrawals from saving (proceeds from the sales of stocks and bonds that are not reinvested) and gifts or bequests received would be included in the tax base. A consumption tax is a broadly based tax that could be used with progressive, proportional, or degressive tax rates and could permit certain deductions or exemptions from the base—although the more loopholes permitted, the farther we move from a broad-based tax.

The case for a consumption tax rests on three main advantages. First, it is a simpler tax. The consumption tax avoids many of the more difficult problems of measurement present with a CTB—depreciation, inflation adjustments, allocation of undistributed corporate income, and so on—because all forms of saving would be excluded from the tax base.

Second, a consumption tax is more likely to maintain intertemporal equity—that is, to maintain the relative income positions of taxpayers over their lifetimes. Under an income tax, two taxpayers with identical lifetime earnings would have different lifetime tax burdens depending on their consumption and earning patterns. Consider two taxpayers, A and B, who have equal lifetime earnings but different earning patterns. Assume that over their "lifetime," a 2-year period, taxpayer A earns $10,000 per year in year 1 and year 2. Meanwhile, taxpayer B earns $19,524 in year 1 and nothing in year 2. (The wage, $19,524, is the total of $10,000 plus the amount that would have to be invested at a 5 percent rate of return to make $10,000 available to him in year 2.) Each individual consumes the same amount in both years, that is, $10,000 per year. (In year 2, B consumes out of his saving from year 1.) Under an income tax, even one with proportional rates, B will pay a higher lifetime tax than A. This occurs because the interest income B receives on his saving, which finances his consumption in year 2, is taxed, whereas A, who has no saving in either year, is not taxed. This "double taxation" of saving—once when the income is earned and again on the interest earned on the income—can be quite large if a long period of time is involved. In contrast, a consumption tax will impose an equal tax on both taxpayers because their consumption is equal in both years.

Taxpayers with equal incomes and the same present value of future income are treated equally with a consumption tax.[20]

Third, by eliminating the taxation of saving, a consumption tax will not distort the choice between present and future consumption (assuming that all income is eventually consumed) and will lead to higher aggregate levels of saving and investment.

Although a consumption tax has these advantages, it must first be decided whether consumption or income is the best index of a taxpayer's ability to pay taxes. Some economists hold that two taxpayers with equal incomes have the same capacity to pay taxes even if one chooses to save a different fraction of income. In addition, the allocative advantage of the consumption tax in distorting saving decisions less must be weighed against the increased distortion in the income-leisure choice produced by the tax—because saving is not taxed under the consumption tax, the lost revenues must be made up by levying higher tax rates on income used for consumption.

Concluding Observations

Overall, there seems to be a strong consensus among economists that the present tax system requires far-reaching, substantive reform. Leaving the question of the rate structure aside, there is also agreement that this change should take the form of a comprehensive tax base in the form of either a consumption tax or a comprehensive income tax. Although some would prefer to leave more loopholes in the system than others, economists generally concur that the present tax laws are inefficient and inequitable.

On the question of the rate structure, there is less agreement. A progressive tax is often advocated because of its redistributive impact, but that must be weighed against the distorting effects of higher marginal tax rates. A proportional tax avoids or lessens some of the misallocative effects of a progressive tax but has no redistributive impact. A degressive tax falls somewhere between a progressive and proportional tax; it is mildly redistributive but probably more distorting than a proportional tax. Largely, the choice of a rate structure is a question of whether the tax system should be used solely as a means of raising revenue or whether its taxing function should be combined with that of redistributing income. If, however, an effective transfer system can be designed, the tax system need not be used to redistribute income. There still remains, though, the question of vertical equity and how the tax burden

[20] For a more comprehensive discussion of this example and other issues involving a consumption tax, see *Blueprints for Basic Tax Reform,* op. cit., pp. 113–143.

should be distributed among different incomes classes—the answer to that is, of course, partly a value judgment.

Supplementary Readings

Blum, Walter J., and Harry J. Kalven, Jr. *The Uneasy Case for Progressive Taxation.* Chicago: University of Chicago Press, 1953.

Break, George F., and Joseph A. Pechman. *Federal Tax Reform: The Impossible Dream.* Washington, D.C.: Brookings Institution, 1975.

Browning, Jacquelene M. "Estimating the Welfare Cost of Tax Preferences," *Public Finance Quarterly,* forthcoming.

Buchanan, James M., and Mark V. Pauly. "On the Incidence of Tax Deductibility." *National Tax Journal,* 23(2):157–167 (June 1970).

Freeman, Roger A. *Tax Loopholes: the Legend and the Reality.* Washington, D.C.: American Enterprise Institute and the Hoover Institution on War, Revolution, and Peace, 1973.

Goode, Richard. *The Individual Income Tax,* Revised Edition. Washington, D.C.: Brookings Institution, 1976.

McLure, Charles E., Jr. "Integration of the Income Taxes: Why and How," *Journal of Corporate Taxation,* 2(4):429–464 (Winter 1976).

Pechman, Joseph A. *Federal Tax Policy,* 3rd Edition. Washington, D.C.: Brookings Institution, 1977.

Ruskay, Joseph A., and Richard A. Osserman. *Halfway to Tax Reform.* Bloomington: Indiana University Press, 1970.

Stern, Philip. *The Rape of the Taxpayer.* New York: Random House, Inc., 1973.

Surrey, Stanley. *Pathways to Tax Reform.* Cambridge, Mass.: Harvard University Press, 1973.

U.S. Treasury. *Blueprints for Basic Tax Reform.* Washington, D.C.: U.S. Government Printing Office, January 17, 1977.

CHAPTER 13

OTHER MAJOR REVENUE SOURCES

In this chapter four more sources of government revenue will be considered: the corporation income tax, the social security payroll tax, property taxation, and deficit finance. Each method of financing government expenditures will be discussed briefly, with an emphasis on the broad issues of incidence and welfare cost. The appendix to this chapter brings together various parts of the tax system to examine the combined incidence of all taxes.

Corporation Income Tax

Description

The federal corporation income tax yielded $40.6 billion in revenue in 1975, making it the third largest source of revenue for the federal government. Before 1968, it was the second largest revenue source, but in that year the rapidly increasing social security tax surpassed the corporation income tax in yield. In addition to the federal government, most states use corporation income taxes, although at substantially lower rates than the federal tax. In 1975 corporate tax receipts by subnational levels of government were less than $7 billion.

Corporation income taxes are generally described as a tax on the profits of incorporated businesses. In the sense that accountants use the term *profits,* this is correct, but the tax base is not pure profit, at least not as the term is used by economists. In the federal tax statutes, the tax base is defined as the total receipts of the corporation minus certain allowable expenses, or revenues minus costs, for short. Not all economic costs, however, are treated as deductible in the tax law. Although wage and salary outlays, depreciation on capital invested, and interest paid on loans are counted as costs, a normal return for invested capital is not included as a cost. This means that the tax base is really equal to the normal return to capital invested plus any economic profits.

An example will clarify this important point. Consider a corporation with $1 million invested in plant and equipment. In one year, its sales revenues equal $2 million, and it pays out $1.9 million in wages. Its taxable net income under the corporation income tax is $100,000, but this is not economic profit. If the going interest rate is 10 percent, the $1 million invested in this corporation could have been loaned out and earned $100,000 elsewhere. Thus, the $100,000 realized on the investment in the corporation has an opportunity cost—sacrificed earnings if the capital had been invested elsewhere—of $100,000. In this case, the $100,000 "profit" of the corporation is really only the normal return to capital invested, yet that return is subject to the corporation income tax. To avoid confusion, we will refer to the tax base of the corporation income tax as the net income of equity capital rather than as "profits."

The tax rate structure of the federal corporation income tax is slightly progressive. The first $25,000 in net income is taxed at a rate of 20 percent, the next $25,000 at 22 percent, and all net income in excess of $50,000 is subject to a tax rate of 48 percent. The effective marginal tax rate for most corporate net income is 48 percent because the bulk of the tax base is generated by firms with net incomes above $50,000. In 1975 the total net income of corporations (before taxes) was $102 billion, so the $40.6 billion in revenue raised represented an overall average rate of about 40 percent. When corporation income taxes levied by states are included, the average rate was about 46 percent.

Incidence

One of the most difficult and controversial issues in tax analysis is to determine who bears the burden of the corporation income tax. Because the tax applies to all corporations and not just to one industry, it is necessary to use a general equilibrium analysis to examine its incidence. That is difficult enough, but matters are complicated further by the fact that industries within the corporate sector are of various degrees of competitiveness. In our analysis, it will be assumed that the corporate sector, taken as a whole, is generally competitive enough for the competitive model to yield reasonably accurate results. Not all analysts agree with this assumption, but unfortunately there is no general equilibrium model of an imperfectly competitive economy to provide an alternative basis for the analysis.

The corporation income tax is applied to the net income of capital invested in the corporate sector of the economy. There is also a noncorporate sector of the economy that employs capital, but the return to capital in this sector is not subject to the corporation income tax. In competitive markets, the net return to capital invested in all uses will be equal. Investors will invest capital where it yields the greatest return; if the return is higher in some uses, investors will shift capital to (increase investment in) those uses, thus driving down the rate of return until it is equal to the return in alternative uses. The tendency for capital to be allocated in such a way that the net return is equalized in all sectors is the basic equilibrating force of the economy adjusting to a tax on the return to capital in the corporate sector.

In the absence of the corporate tax, suppose that the rate of return on capital is 8 percent in both the corporate and noncorporate sectors. Now assume that a 50 percent tax is levied on net income (the return to capital) in the corporate sector. The immediate or short-run effect is to tax away half the return of investors in the corporate sector, leaving them a net yield of only 4 percent on their investment. This will not be a final equilibrium, however, because the net (after-tax) return on capital is now 4 percent in the corporate sector and still 8 percent in the noncorporate sector. Therefore, investors have the incentive to shift capital into the noncorporate sector where it will earn a higher net return. As investors reduce the supply of capital to the corporate sector, its gross return there rises, while increasing the supply to the noncorporate sector drives down the return there. This process continues until the net return is the same in both sectors. Assume finally that an equilibrium occurs when the net return is 6 percent in both sectors.

Note carefully what this equilibrium implies. Because of a reduction in capital employed in the corporate sector, its gross (before-tax) return is now 12 percent, which yields a net return of 6 percent after the corporate income tax. Because the return was previously 8 percent, investors in the corporate sector are receiving a return 25 percent below their earlier return. This is also true for investors in the noncorporate sector; their return is now 6 percent compared to 8 percent before the tax even though the tax does not apply to noncorporate investments. In this way, the corporate tax places a burden on *all* owners of capital regardless of whether their capital is employed in the corporate sector. The net return to all investors has fallen from 8 percent to 6 percent.

We have traced the effects of the corporation income tax on owners of capital, but other persons will also be affected. Because corporations must pay a higher gross return on capital as a result of the tax, the prices of products produced by corporations will rise and their consumption will fall. The opposite occurs in the noncorporate sector; output will rise and price will fall as capital in this sector becomes less expensive. Does this mean that consumers bear a burden because of higher prices of corporate sector products? Not necessarily; corporate prices are higher, but noncorporate prices are lower, and there is no reason for the overall or average price of goods and services to be affected. Only consumers who spend a greater than average percentage of their incomes on corporate products (where prices have risen) will be worse off. On average, consumers are not burdened.

This analysis is a good illustration of a general equilibrium analysis of tax incidence. In a general equilibrium approach, we emphasize not only what happens in the taxed sector but also the repercussions in the nontaxed sector. In addition, attention is given to how the tax affects individuals through changes in input prices (the return on capital in this case) and through changes in output prices that occur in all sectors of the economy. In the case of the corporation income tax, the analysis suggests that owners of capital, wherever their capital is employed, will be heavily burdened by the tax.

Diagrammatic Analysis

A diagrammatic presentation of this analysis as it pertains to capital markets should prove helpful. Figure 13–1(a) shows the effect of different allocations of a given quantity of capital between the corporate and noncorporate sectors on the rate of return in the two sectors. The curve D_{KC} indicates the productivity of capital employed in the corporate sector, expressed as a rate of return. For example, if $O_C K_2$ is employed, the return will be 12 percent, whereas a larger quantity of capital, $O_C K_1$, yields a return of 8 percent. The curve D_{KN} shows the productivity of capital in the noncorporate sector, but it is drawn relative to the origin at O_N. Thus, if $O_N K_1$ is employed in the noncorporate sector, the return is 8 percent, whereas if more is employed, $O_N K_2$, the return is 6 percent. (The curve D_{KN} is just a reversed demand curve drawn so that the origin lies at the right.) The horizontal dimension of this boxlike diagram, $O_C O_N$, measures the total amount of capital to be allocated between the two sectors. Any point on the horizontal axis indicates the distribution of capital between the sectors. Thus, point K_1 means that there is $O_C K_1$ capital in the corporate sector and the remainder, $O_N K_1$, is in the noncorporate sector. A movement to K_2 means that $O_C K_2$ is now in the corporate sector and $O_N K_2$ is in the noncorporate sector; hence a movement from K_1 to K_2 means that there is $K_1 K_2$ less capital in the corporate sector that has been reallocated to the noncorporate sector.

Before proceeding with the analysis, it may be worthwhile to explain more fully what is meant by capital "moving" from one sector to another. Capital refers, of course, to productive resources such as factories, machinery, and trucks. But how can factories and equipment designed to produce automobiles, for example, in the corporate sector "move" to the agricultural industries in the noncorporate sector and produce food?

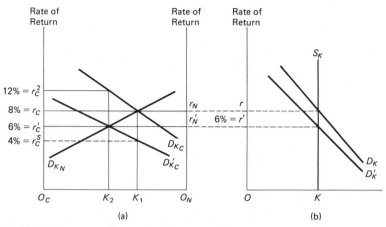

Figure 13–1. Incidence of the corporation income tax.

In general, they seldom can move in this sense, but that creates no problem for the analysis. Over a period of time the same result—more capital in agriculture and less in automobiles—will occur. Factories and equipment in the automotive industry can be allowed to wear out while new investment expands the capital stock in agriculture. Thus, the passage of time allows the capital stock to be reallocated *in effect* by channeling more new investment toward the sector with the higher net return and less toward the sector with the lower net return. Although we shall continue to refer to capital moving from one sector to another, it should be understood that this is a shorthand expression for the process described above.

Returning now to Figure 13–1, in the absence of the corporation income tax, the equilibrium allocation of capital is at K_1, where D_{KC} and D_{KN} intersect, with $O_C K_1$ in the corporate sector and $O_N K_1$ in the noncorporate sector. With this allocation, the returns to capital in the two sectors, r_C and r_N, are both equal to 8 percent. When the corporate tax is imposed at a rate of 50 percent the net return to capital in the corporate sector is reduced by half; the new schedule showing the net (after-tax) return is D'_{KC}. In the short run, before enough time has elapsed for capital to "move," owners of capital in the corporate sector bear the full burden of the tax and receive an after-tax return of r_C^S, or 4 percent. The allocation at K_1, however, is not a long run equilibrium because capital in the untaxed noncorporate sector is earning a higher net return of 8 percent. Owners of capital will move capital from the corporate to the noncorporate sectors until the net returns are equalized. The net returns are equal where D'_{KC} and D_{KN} intersect, with $O_C K_2$ capital in the corporate sector and $O_N K_2$ in the noncorporate sector. Thus, the corporation income tax produces a reallocation of $K_1 K_2$ capital from the corporate sector to the noncorporate sector as investors seek a higher return in the untaxed sector. The final equilibrium is where the net return to all owners of capital is at 6 percent, down from its original 8 percent level. All owners of capital suffer a loss of 25 percent of their pretax capital income, regardless of whether they are stockholders in corporations.

The preceding analysis is based on the assumption that capital income in the noncorporate sector is untaxed. Actually, income in the noncorporate sector is subject to tax under the federal individual income tax and property taxes levied by local governments. The effective rate of tax on capital income in the corporate sector, however, is much higher because of the corporation income tax, and differences in tax rates between sectors are all that is necessary for the validity of the preceding analysis to hold. Because capital income in the corporate sector is more heavily taxed than in the noncorporate sector, there is incentive for the reallocation of capital previously described to occur.

To say that all owners of capital bear a burden from the corporation income tax does not necessarily imply that they bear the entire burden (equal to tax revenue raised). The final incidence depends on whether the total *gross* return to capital (the return of capital income in both sectors) is altered by the reallocation of capital produced by the tax. If the total gross return is unchanged, then capital owners bear the entire burden. For example, if before-tax capital income is $160 billion (8 percent times $O_C O_N$) and gross (before-tax) capital income after the tax (12 percent times $O_C K_2$ plus 6 percent times $O_N K_2$) is still $160 billion, the after-tax capital income will be less than $160 billion by the amount of the tax [($r_C^2 - r_C'$) times $O_C K_2$]. Capital owners then bear the entire burden of the tax. Whether or not this is exactly true depends on a number of underlying elasticities in production and consumption. After examining a number of plausible relationships, Arnold Harberger (on whose seminal work this analysis is based)[1] concluded that, in all likelihood, owners of capital bear approximately the entire burden of the tax.

One implicit assumption in the analysis now deserves consideration. It was assumed that the corporation income tax did not reduce the total stock of capital, but merely affected the allocation of a given capital stock between the two sectors. This is equivalent to assuming that the supply of capital to the economy does not depend on the net rate of re-

---

[1] Arnold C. Harberger, "The Incidence of the Corporation Income Tax," *Journal of Political Economy,* 70:215 (June 1962) reprinted in *Taxation and Welfare* (Boston: Little, Brown and Company, 1974), pp. 135–162. For a simplified exposition of the general equilibrium model used by Harberger, and its applications to a variety of taxes, see Charles E. McLure, Jr., and Wayne R. Thirsk, "A Simplified Exposition of the Harberger Model, I: Tax Incidence," *National Tax Journal,* 28:1 (Mar. 1975).

turn, that is, that the rate of saving is unresponsive to the net interest return that can be earned on savings. This is shown in Figure 13–1(b), where the total supply curve of capital is drawn vertically. When the return to capital falls from r to r' (from 8 to 6 percent), the total capital stock remains unchanged at OK (equal to $O_C O_N$). In this case, the corporation income tax does not change the total stock of capital but affects only its allocation between the two sectors. It is possible, however, that people will save less when they can realize a lower rate of return. If this occurs, the corporation income tax reduces the total capital stock below what it would otherwise have been, and also affects the allocation of the smaller total between the two sectors. This makes the determination of the incidence far more involved, and this case will be ignored on the grounds that empirical evidence suggests the supply of saving is not very responsive to modest changes in interest rates.

What does it mean to accept Harberger's conclusion that owners of capital bear the full burden of the corporation income tax? If Harberger is correct, then the incidence of the tax is equivalent to a proportional tax (of 25 percent in the preceding example) on capital income wherever capital is employed. In interpreting this, it is important to realize that the noncorporate sector actually contains about half the capital in the United States: The major uses of capital in the noncorporate sector are in agriculture and homeownership. Homes represent a way to invest in capital, and it is the major form of capital ownership for millions of families. (The capital income from homeownership is partly in the form of housing services directly consumed, a form of in-kind capital income.) Thus, people who purchase their own homes will realize a lower return because of the corporation income tax. The same is true for people with savings accounts; their interest rate will be lower. Stockholders of corporations, of course, also bear a burden. In this connection, it should be noted that the millions of workers who own stock indirectly in the form of pension funds are also affected. (In 1974, 30 percent of all corporate stock was owned by pension funds.) In short, the burden of the corporation income tax is spread widely through the population, even though most of the people who bear this burden are unaware of it.

Although people bear a burden in proportion to their income from capital, this does not mean that the burden is proportionate to total income of families. Typically, families with higher incomes receive a larger share of their incomes in the form of capital income. Thus, the burden of the corporation income tax will be a larger fraction of total family income for families in the higher income ranges. Consequently, the incidence is progressive. Pechman and Okner, for example, estimate that the corporate income tax as a percent of total family income is 1.7 percent for the poorest 10 percent of families, but 8.1 percent for the

375

wealthiest 10 percent.[2] (The overall average for all families is 3.9 percent.)

Alternatively, some scholars do not believe that the incidence of the corporate tax falls exclusively on capital income. Because many corporations have a degree of market power, it is felt that they may simply raise prices. Although this view has never been developed carefully in a general equilibrium model,[3] it is frequently suggested that consumers of corporate products do bear at least some of the burden. Unfortunately, empirical studies have been unable to resolve this issue.

A major reason for considering the incidence of any tax is to determine whether the distribution of the tax burden among families is fair. In terms of vertical equity, we have seen that the corporation income tax is progressive if the general equilibrium analysis we have stressed is correct. More can be said when horizontal equity is considered. If we accept the value judgment that families with the same total incomes *from whatever source derived* should bear the same tax burden, then the corporate tax is inequitable whichever view of incidence is correct. Under the first view (capital owners bear the burden) of two families with the same total income, the family with the larger share of capital income (as opposed to, say, labor income) will bear a larger burden. Under the second view (consumers of corporate products bear the burden) of two families with the same total income, the family that spends a larger fraction of its income on corporate products will bear a larger burden. Thus, at least in terms of horizontal equity, the corporation income tax is quite inequitable.

Welfare Cost

In addition to the direct burden of the corporation income tax, there are two major ways in which it produces a misallocation of resources.[4] First, it leads to a misallocation of a given capital stock between the corporate and noncorporate sectors of the economy. Second, it leads to too small a total capital stock. The welfare costs associated with both of these distor-

---

[2] Joseph A. Pechman and Benjamin A. Okner, *Who Bears the Tax Burden?* (Washington, D.C.: Brookings Institution, 1974), p. 61. Actually, this distribution of the burden is based on the assumption that half the burden is borne by stockholders and half by all owners of capital, but the same general pattern would hold if the entire burden were allocated in proportion to capital income.

[3] Actually, Harberger in his initial paper on the subject also examined the incidence of the corporation income tax on the assumption that all corporations had a degree of monopoly power and found that the results were largely unaffected: Capital owners still would bear virtually the entire burden.

[4] There are also a number of other misallocations because of special provisions in the tax law, such as mineral depletion allowances. We will ignore these here, but the interested reader may wish to consult Arnold C. Harberger and Martin J. Bailey, eds., *The Taxation of Income from Capital* (Washington, D.C.: Brookings Institution, 1969).

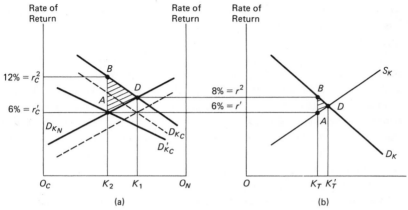

Figure 13–2. Welfare cost of the corporation income tax.

tions can be illustrated in Figure 13–2, which is similar to Figure 13–1.

Consider first Figure 13–2(a). In the last section, we saw that the equilibrium under the tax occurred where the net returns to capital in both sectors were equal. This is shown at K_2 in (a) with $O_C K_2$ in the corporate sector and $O_N K_2$ in the noncorporate sector. The gross return to capital differs between the two sectors: It is 12 percent in the corporate sector and 6 percent in the noncorporate sector. Capital is misallocated between the two sectors because it is more productive in the corporate sector than in the noncorporate sector. Although investors will be guided by the net returns, it is the gross returns, or true physical productivities, that are relevant for efficiency considerations. With the allocation at K_2, there are investment projects with yields just below 12 percent in the corporate sector that will not be undertaken because investors are interested in the after-tax yields. The after-tax yield on an investment paying a gross return of 11.9 percent will be only 5.95 percent, less than the return realized in the noncorporate sector. Thus, a reallocation of capital from the noncorporate sector to the corporate sector will increase the real return on the total capital stock, but the corporate tax inhibits that reallocation. The result is a welfare cost.

Efficiency requires that the gross yields in the two sectors be equal, and this condition occurs at K_1. The corporate tax produces underinvestment of $K_1 K_2$ in the corporate sector (and overinvestment of $K_1 K_2$ in the noncorporate sector). By reducing capital from K_1 to K_2 in the corporate sector, projects yielding from 8 to 12 percent (along D_{KC} from point D to point B) are sacrificed, and projects yielding from 8 percent to 6 percent in the noncorporate sector (along D_{KN} from point D to point A) are undertaken. The net loss from this reallocation of $K_1 K_2$ between the sectors is the difference between the returns on these projects in the two

377

sectors. This is shown by area BAD, the loss involved in investing K_1K_2 less in the corporate sector (area DBK_2K_1) minus the gain from investing this capital in the noncorporate sector instead (area DAK_2K_1).

It is difficult to estimate empirically the size of the welfare cost due to the corporation income tax, in part because it is necessary to consider simultaneously all taxes that affect capital income. Nonetheless, existing estimates strongly suggest that the welfare cost is relatively large compared to other taxes of equal yield. Michael J. Boskin has estimated that the welfare cost may have been about $24.7 billion in 1972, a large part of which is attributable to the corporation income tax.[5] This means that the welfare cost of the corporate tax per dollar of revenue is probably higher than for any other major tax.

Because of the magnitude of this welfare cost, many economists have recommended fundamental changes in the corporation income tax. One way to avoid this welfare cost, if feasible, would be to tax capital income in both sectors at the same rate. If this were done, the demand curves showing the net returns in the two sectors would be shown by the dotted lines in Figure 13–2(a). With this tax of 25 percent on capital income wherever earned, the equilibrium allocation would be at K_1, with capital efficiently allocated between the two sectors. With capital taxed equally, there is no incentive to move capital from one sector to the other. Note that owners of capital would be no worse off than under the corporate tax; they would still receive a net return of 6 percent.[6] Resources, however, would be allocated more efficiently.

There is, in addition, a second type of welfare cost due to the corporate tax if people save less when they receive a lower net return. This is shown in Figure 13–2(b). At a net return of 6 percent, the total capital stock is OK_T [this is equal to O_CO_N in (a)]. If this capital stock is allocated efficiently between the two sectors, the gross yield on capital in both sectors will be r^2, or 8 percent. If, however, savers respond to the net yield of 6 percent and save less because of this lower return, too small a total capital stock will result. The welfare cost due to this misallocation is shown by the area BAD in (b). (Note that this welfare cost would not be avoided by taxing capital income equally in both sectors because the net return would then still be below the gross return in both sectors.) Unfortunately, there is little evidence to indicate the size of this welfare cost, but most economists believe it is small compared to the welfare cost shown in (a) because it is believed that saving decisions are relatively insensitive to changes in interest rates. [In other words, S_K

[5] Michael J. Boskin, "Efficiency Aspects of the Differential Tax Treatment of Market and Household Economic Activity," *Journal of Public Economics*, 4:1 (Feb. 1975).

[6] This is true once capital has been allocated so that the net return is equal everywhere, that is, in the long run. In the short run, capital would temporarily be earning more in the corporate sector and less in the noncorporate sector.

in (b) is thought to be fairly inelastic, meaning that the reduction in the total capital stock will be small.]

In summary, it appears that the corporation income tax is an inefficient tax compared to other methods of raising revenue. It also gets low marks on equity grounds. Why then is this tax relied on so heavily? The most plausible answer stems from a public choice perspective. The corporation income tax is a hidden tax par excellence because those who bear its burden are largely unaware of it. This makes it very attractive politically. In addition, it appeals to popular prejudices because it can be depicted as a tax making "business pay its fair share," although, as we have indicated, it is misleading to consider businesses per se as bearing the burden of this or any other tax.

Social Security Payroll Tax

In our earlier discussion of the social security system, the expenditure part of the program was emphasized, and it was assumed that workers bore the burden of social security taxes. Having now discussed the principles of tax analysis, it is appropriate to consider the tax side of the social security system more carefully.

Incidence and Welfare Cost

Social security payroll taxes are levied on wage and salary incomes up to a ceiling amount and are therefore taxes on labor incomes. Our earlier analysis of the federal income tax, which also taxes labor income, indicated that such a tax will be borne fully by workers if labor is in perfectly inelastic supply. As a first approximation, this suggests that workers bear the full burden of social security taxes. There are some differences between the social security payroll tax and the federal income tax, however, that require additional discussion.

One difference is that the social security tax is composed of two parts, one levied on the employee and the other on the employer. As of 1978, the employee pays a tax rate of 6.05 percent on the first $17,700 of earnings, and the employer must also pay a 6.05 percent tax on these earnings. It is sometimes argued that splitting the tax into employee and employer portions has some relevance for the incidence of the tax.

Figure 13–3 will help us examine the impact of splitting the tax into employer-employee portions. In the absence of the tax, the wage rate would be $2.10. Now suppose that a payroll tax of 5 percent is levied on both the employer and employee. Employers are still willing to pay a total compensation of no more than $2.10 per manhour; it makes no difference to them whether part of their outlay goes to the government or

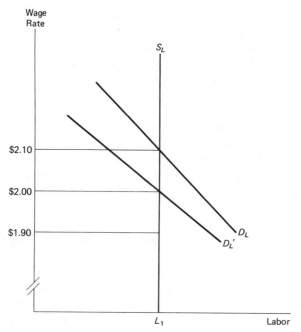

Figure 13–3. Social security tax and wage rates.

to the workers. Faced with a 5 percent tax, the maximum that they will now pay *to the employee* is $2.00 per hour because the total wage cost will still be $2.10, with $0.10 per hour going to the government. This is shown by the D_L' curve. Employees will receive $2.00 per hour and will pay a 5 percent tax on that sum, so their net wage rate will be $1.90. Thus, the $0.20 tax per manhour leads to a reduction in the net wage received by employees by an amount equal to the full amount of the tax.

It makes no difference how this $0.20 tax per manhour is split into employee and employer portions. If it were paid entirely by employers, employees would receive a wage rate of $1.90 and pay no payroll tax. If, on the other hand, the tax were levied entirely on employees, they would receive a wage rate of $2.10 from their employers and then pay a $0.20 tax, so their net wage rate would still be $1.90. The major effect of splitting the tax into employer-employee portions is not on the actual incidence of the tax, but on its visibility; workers may be unaware that they bear a tax burden as a result of the employer portion of the tax.

The conclusion that splitting the tax has no impact on the actual incidence is not equivalent to asserting that the incidence lies fully with the workers. Where the incidence lies depends on the elasticity of labor supply; if labor supply is perfectly inelastic, as drawn in Figure 13–3, then workers bear the full burden. As indicated in Chapter 12, most economists believe that labor is very inelastically supplied, so the conclusion that workers bear the full burden may be approximately correct.

There is one special feature of the social security tax that differs from the federal income tax and may have some bearing on its affect on labor supply decisions. Under the social security tax, if a worker earns more and incurs an additional tax liability, he may not view the tax as a net loss to him. Because the worker's future social security pension will be larger the more taxes he pays, there is an offsetting benefit associated with paying higher taxes. Thus, in Figure 13–3 workers may not believe their net wage has fallen from $2.10 to $1.90 because they will receive a pension when they retire. If this is so, it becomes more likely that the quantity of labor supplied remains unchanged in response to the tax. This point should not be pushed too far, however, because the link between taxes paid by a worker and his subsequent pension is not very strong. Indeed, for working wives, payment of social security taxes often produces no increase in the family's ultimate pension.

In all, it seems reasonable to conclude that workers bear the full burden of both the employee and employer portions of the social security tax. It should be mentioned, however, that this analysis has ignored the expenditure side of the social security system. If saving falls in response to the provision of pensions, then the combined (balanced-budget) impact of the tax and expenditure will produce further effects. Because a reduced capital stock means less capital per worker and lower productivity per worker, the D_L curve in Figure 13–3 will shift downward (or rise less rapidly over time), reducing wage rates still further. The impact of the entire social security system on saving is usually ignored in an analysis of the tax, and this is reasonable if the differential incidence approach is adopted. (Recall that, with the differential approach, we compare different taxes to finance the same expenditures on pensions. Then the effect on the capital stock, and hence the position of D_L, will be the same under alternative taxes.)

Assuming that workers bear the full burden of the tax, it is often argued that the social security tax is regressive because it applies only to the first $17,700 in earnings. In addition, it does not apply to capital income, which is more important in the higher income classes. This view is not fully correct; actually, the tax burden is quite progressive at the lower end of the income scale. Most low income families receive a large share of their total incomes in the form of government transfer payments (see Table 7–8) that are not subject to the tax. Consider a family with earnings of $3000 and transfers of $3000. It will pay a social security tax of about 12 percent, or $360, on its earnings, but this tax is only 6 percent of its total income. Middle income families receive most, if not all, of their incomes in the form of earnings so the social security tax will be close to 12 percent of their total incomes. Only for high income families with earnings above the ceiling does the average tax rate begin to decline.

Like the federal income tax, the social security tax can also produce a welfare cost by distorting labor supply decisions. Taxpayers will work less and be worse off than under an equal-yield lump sum tax (see Figure 11–2). Applied to the social security tax, however, there are two qualifications to this generalization. First, because the welfare cost is produced by the marginal tax rate on earnings, there will be no welfare cost for workers earning above the ceiling. People already earning $30,000 will pay no additional tax if they earn $1000 more, so the tax will not affect their labor supply decision at the relevant margin. Second, the linking of taxes paid by individuals to their future pension may reduce the distortion in labor supply decisions. Individuals are less likely to work less to avoid some of the tax if this means that they will receive a smaller pension when retired.[7]

1977 Social Security Tax Reform

In the mid-1970s the social security system began to run sizable deficits: Annual outlays were exceeding annual taxes, and the already small trust funds were being depleted. Several factors contributed to this deficit, but the most important were increases in benefit levels that were not accompanied by adequate tax increases. In 1972 Congress voted a 20 percent across-the-board increase in benefits when it was anticipated that tax revenues at previously legislated rates would increase faster than they later actually did. Congress also adopted a plan that was intended to make social security inflationproof and increase benefits automatically as the price level rose. Unfortunately, the plan had the unintended effect of increasing benefits faster than the price level rose—a mistake that was realized almost immediately but not corrected until 1977.

By 1976 retirement benefits were much higher than a decade earlier. In 1965 a 65-year-old single retiree earning the median wage would have received a pension equal to 31 percent of his earnings the year before his retirement. By 1976 this fraction—called the replacement rate—had risen to 43 percent. Moreover, this ratio did not include Medicare benefits. If Medicare benefits were counted, the replacement rate in 1976 was closer to 50 percent, or nearly 65 percent higher than a decade before.

The rapid increase in benefits was largely responsible for the deficits

[7]Note how this differs from the federal income tax. Under the income tax, if a worker earns more and thereby pays $100 more in taxes, this is completely a net loss to the worker because the additional tax payment brings with it no additional government benefits. Under the social security payroll tax, paying $100 more in taxes may result in a larger pension on retirement.

in the mid-1970s. How to put social security back on a pay-as-you-go basis, with current taxes and expenditures in balance, became a major issue. (This was called the "short-run financial issue" by many analysts, to distinguish it from the long-run problems expected in the twenty-first century due to demographic changes.) One option, that of reducing benefits, was never seriously considered. Instead, attention was focused on how to raise additional tax revenue. We will consider the three major alternatives that were discussed, and then explain the final Congressional compromise.

Using General Tax Revenues. President Carter (among others) once proposed to use general federal revenues to supplement payroll tax revenues in financing benefits. This approach would avoid an increase in the social security tax, but would alternatively necessitate higher federal income (or other) taxes. One reason for proposing this method of financing is that the federal income tax is more progressive than the social security payroll tax. Consequently, using general revenues would place most of the increased tax burden on high income families.

In evaluating this option, and the others, it is most important to consider how future benefits are affected. If benefits went up only for those who paid the additional taxes (as "individual equity" required), that is, mainly for higher income families, then this proposal would not increase taxes or benefits for low income families. This is not, however, what advocates of this approach had in mind. Instead, benefits would still be related only to taxable earnings (under the social security payroll tax), not to taxes paid. Consequently, benefits would be increased across the board regardless of whether individuals paid any additional (federal) tax. Because the benefit formula is tilted in favor of those with low earnings records, most of the benefits financed out of general revenues would go to those with low earnings, and most of the taxes would be paid by those with high incomes.

In short, the proposal to use general revenues was essentially a proposal to make the system more redistributive than before, that is, more heavily in favor of those who had low incomes before retirement.

Raising the Ceiling on Taxable Earnings. Another method of increasing revenue is to continue to rely on the payroll tax as the sole source of revenue but to increase the ceiling on taxable earnings without increasing the tax rate. For example, the ceiling might be increased from $17,700 to $25,000. Because the tax rate would remain the same, the tax on people earning below $17,700 would not increase at all. All of the additional tax burden would be placed on those earning over $17,700, with the largest increases falling on those earning $25,000 and more. (Recall that all those earning over $25,000 would pay taxes on the first $25,000 of their earnings instead of the first $17,700, so the tax increase would be larger for someone earning $30,000 than for someone earning $20,000.) Consequently, this is a progressive change in the payroll tax.

This method of increasing revenues raises two issues. First, it requires a large increase in the ceiling to raise even a moderate amount of additional revenue. For example, in 1978 it would have required a 63 percent increase in the ceiling to increase revenues by only 10 percent. The reason is that 85 percent of earners earned less than the ceiling, so the higher ceiling would apply only to the 15 percent earning above $17,700. Second, once again we must consider what happens to future benefits. Benefits for those with high earnings would have to be increased in the future. Nonetheless, low earners would also benefit, because the benefit formula favors them and benefits are based on taxable earnings and not on taxes actually paid. Thus, those with low earnings would benefit without paying any higher taxes.

Increasing the Tax Rate. A final option considered was to increase the tax rate while leaving the ceiling unchanged (or, more precisely, having the ceiling increase at the same rate already scheduled by the existing law). If the tax rate were increased, from, say, 12.1 to 15 percent, and the ceiling were maintained, an additional tax burden would be placed on all wage earners. The additional burden would be progressively distributed at low income levels and regressively distributed at high income levels. In this case, higher pensions could be provided to low income retirees without violating individual equity because they would bear some of the additional tax burden while employed. Even in this case, there would be some further redistribution in favor of low earners because of the nature of the benefit formula. It would, however, be less for an increase in the tax rate than for either of the other two options, because those with low earnings would pay a larger share of the tax increase.

The 1977 Amendments. Late in 1977 Congress voted approval of a social security tax increase that was estimated to increase social security taxes by $227 billion over the next decade, the largest peacetime tax increase in history. Congress rejected the use of general federal revenues, but increased both the tax rate and the ceiling on taxable earnings. The results are shown in Table 13–1.

The three columns to the left show how the system would have changed based on legislation enacted prior to 1977. The tax rate would have increased to 12.9 percent by 1986, and the taxable ceiling would have been raised to $29,400. (The rate of increase in the ceiling was at approximately the same rate as average earnings were expected to rise, so the same proportion of total earnings would have been taxable in 1986 as in 1977.) Under the new law, the tax rate will be about 10 percent

Table 13–1. Impact of 1977 Social Security Tax Reform

Year	Taxes Under Previous Law			Taxes Under New (1977) Law		
	Tax Rate	Earnings Ceiling	Maximum Tax	Tax Rate	Earnings Ceiling	Maximum Tax
1977	11.7%	$16,500	$1930	11.7%	$16,500	$1930
1981	12.6	21,900	2760	13.3	29,700	3950
1986	12.9	29,400	3792	14.3	40,200	5748

higher by 1986—14.3 percent instead of 12.9 percent—and the earnings ceiling will be more than a third higher—$40,200 instead of $29,400.

For all those earning less than $29,400 in 1986, the new law means that social security taxes will be about 10 percent higher. However, for those earning over $40,200, the tax will increase from $3792 to $5749, an increase of more than 50 percent. Thus, Congress decided to increase taxes most heavily for the 15 percent of workers who are expected to earn above $29,400 in 1986, and especially for the 5 percent or so who will be earning above $40,200. The major beneficiaries, of course, will be those already retired, or soon to be retired, who will receive pensions based on a much higher level of taxes than they had to pay while employed.

Perhaps the most important issue is how this will affect incentives to save. Any of the options considered would reduce incentives to save, because they all involved continuing the higher benefit levels. Congress could have reduced benefits rather than increasing taxes, and this would have given increased incentive to supplement future social security pensions by saving more. The actual tax increase adopted by Congress, however, raises especially serious questions because it most strongly affects those with high income who normally do most of the economy's saving. (One advantage of a low ceiling is that it gives incentive for those who earn above the ceiling to supplement their social security pension by saving privately.) It seems likely that the social security tax increase of 1977 will make the question of how social security affects private saving even more crucial in the future.

Property Taxation

Property taxation as it is used in the United States is primarily a tax of local governments. Property taxes are levied by almost all local governments and are their major source of revenue. In 1975 property taxes produced $50 billion in revenue for local governments, totaling more than 80 percent of all local revenue. Because the nature of the tax is determined independently by local governments, there is wide variation in rates and in the definition of taxable property.

In general, the tax is levied on the assessed value of real property, including land, homes, buildings, and equipment owned by businesses, and sometimes consumer durables such as automobiles. Although most people encounter the tax in their role as homeowners, half of the total revenue raised by property taxes accrues from the taxation of business property.

There have long been two conflicting views about who bears the burden of property taxation. One view holds that the tax is eventually reflected in higher prices of goods produced using taxed property and so would be borne by consumers. With this view of incidence, the burden of the tax is approximately proportional to income. The other view is that the tax is borne by owners of property—which would make the tax progressive. Recently, these two views have been reconciled [8] and partially incorporated into a third approach. The "new view" is best explained by first analyzing a uniform national property tax and then considering what difference it makes when there are many local property taxes levied at different rates.

National Property Tax

Property is simply another name for what economists usually refer to as capital. Property, or capital, is a durable asset that produces a flow of services (income) over a period of time. It is important to understand that taxing the value of property has the same effect as taxing the income generated by that property (such as the corporation income tax). Consider a piece of property with a market value of $10,000 that yields an income of $800 per year, a rate of return of 8 percent. A property tax of 2 percent on the market value would yield $200 in tax revenue per year. Similarly, a tax on the property (capital) income of 25 percent would also yield $200 per year. These two taxes have identical economic effects: A 2 percent tax on the market value of an asset that yields 8 percent takes one fourth of the return to the asset, just as does a tax of 25 percent on the income from the asset. Thus, the taxation of property and the taxation of capital incomes (as under the corporation income tax) can be analyzed in the same way.

Let's consider a national property tax levied at a rate of 2 percent on the market value of all capital. Before the tax, the rate of return to capital is 8 percent, so the property tax is equivalent to a 25 percent tax on the income from capital. To prepare for the analysis of different property

[8] Peter M. Mieszkowski, "The Property Tax: An Excise or a Profits Tax?" *Journal of Public Economics*, 1:73 (Apr. 1972).

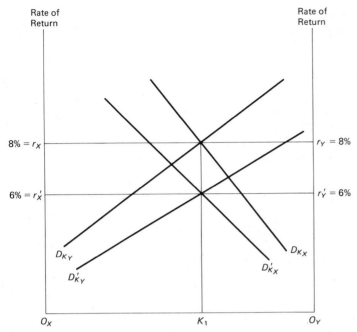

Figure 13-4. Incidence of a national property tax.

taxes in different localities, let's divide the nation into two geographic localities and call them X and Y. Because the property tax applies at the same rate in both localities, there is no incentive for capital owners to shift capital from one locality to another. If capital is in perfectly inelastic supply, its before-tax return is unchanged and capital owners bear the entire burden in the form of a lower after-tax return.

Figure 13-4, similar to the earlier diagram used for the corporation income tax, illustrates this analysis. Now, however, capital (property) employed in geographic locality X is measured to the right from O_X, and capital employed in locality Y to the left from O_Y, so $O_X O_Y$ is the total stock of capital. D_{KY} and D_{KX} show the productivities of capital in the two localities. Before the tax is imposed, $O_X K_1$ is employed in X and $O_Y K_1$ in Y, with the rate of return equal to 8 percent in both localities. A national property tax of 2 percent is equivalent to a 25 percent tax on the return to capital in both localities, making the net return to capital 25 percent below its gross return. D'_{KX} and D'_{KY} show the after-tax returns available for alternative allocations of capital. Equilibrium still occurs at K_1 because the after-tax returns are equal at 6 percent in both localities. [Just as suggested by Figures 13–1(b) and 13–2(b), the lower net return may have an effect on the size of the total capital stock, but that aspect of the problem is ignored here.]

This analysis implies that the owners of capital bear the full burden of a national property tax; property owners receive an unchanged gross return on their capital but must pay a tax of 25 percent to the government. The prices of goods and services produced using the input, capital, are not affected. Renters pay no higher rents for apartments, whereas the owners of apartments receive the same gross return, and a lower net return, on their investment. Homeowners pay the same prices for homes and receive the same gross return (partly in the form of housing services directly consumed) but a lower net return because of the tax payment. (Note also that property owners have no incentive to invest less in housing and more in stocks because the net return on stocks is also lowered to 6 percent.) Only owners of capital bear a burden. The incidence will be progressive because capital income is a larger proportion of total income in higher income classes.

System of Local Property Taxes

The United States does not have a national property tax, but instead a multitude of local property taxes. If all localities tax property at the same effective rate, the analysis above would still be correct. However, localities employ a wide variety of effective rates ranging from about 1 to 5 percent, with an average around 2 percent. The analysis must therefore be modified to incorporate the diversity of effective rates, but the earlier framework can be easily adapted to accomplish this.

Suppose that locality X levies a 1 percent tax on property holders, and locality Y utilizes a 3 percent tax, or an average for the two localities of 2 percent. These taxes correspond to levies on capital income of 12.5 percent and 37.5 percent. The effects of these two taxes on the allocation of capital between the localities is easily worked out. In the short run, before capital can move, the after-tax return to capital in Y will be reduced by more than in X. The net return available to investors is therefore higher on investments in the locality with lower taxes. In the long run, capital will move from Y to X until the net returns are equalized. In equilibrium, the net returns to capital will be the same in both localities and will be lower than the 8 percent return achieved before the taxes were levied.

Figure 13–5 illustrates this analysis. The heavier tax in Y shifts D_{K_Y} down proportionately more than the lighter tax in X affects D_{K_X}. The short run effect would be for the net return in Y to fall to aK_1, but to fall only to bK_1 in X. Thus, capital owners can achieve a higher after-tax return in X and will move capital there. Equilibrium occurs at K_2, where K_1K_2 units of capital have moved from Y to X to produce the same net return of 6 percent in both localities. Equal after-tax returns at

388

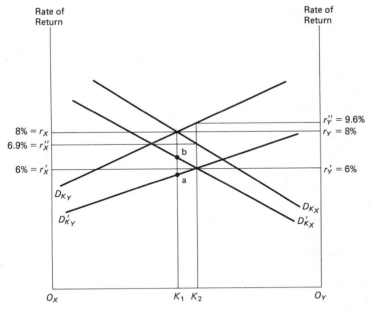

Figure 13-5. Incidence of local property taxes.

6 percent mean, of course, that the before-tax returns diverge: In Y the before-tax return is 9.6 percent, whereas in X it is 6.9 percent.

In terms of its effect on capital income realized by capital owners, these two property taxes at rates of 1 and 3 percent have the same effect as a national property tax at a rate of 2 percent. In both cases, the net return to all owners falls from 8 percent to 6 percent. In this sense, a system of hundreds of local property taxes of different rates has an effect on capital income akin to a national property tax levied at the average rate of all localities taken together. On the basis of this analysis, many economists now believe that owners of capital bear the burden of the *combined* effect of many different local property taxes.

There are, however, still other effects to consider. With a national property tax, there are no effects on prices of goods and services. When local governments use property taxes at different rates, some prices are affected. In locality Y, with the higher than average tax rate, the gross return necessary to attract capital has risen from 8 to 9.6 percent. This higher cost will be reflected in higher prices for goods and services produced with capital employed in that locality. Consumers and renters in locality Y will therefore bear some burden. The opposite occurs in locality X. The gross return has fallen from 8 to 6.9 percent, so lower net prices result.

With higher prices in localities with above average tax rates and lower prices in localities with below average tax rates, the overall price level for the entire nation is not affected. If the aggregate effect on consumers in all areas is considered, there is no net burden—some lose but others gain. Owners of capital bear the full burden of the property taxes taken all together.

This approach reconciles the apparent differences between the view that capital owners bear the burden and the view that output prices are affected. Prices are affected, but in some areas they go up and in other areas they go down. This means that our view of the effects of property taxation depends on whether we are looking at the overall effects for the nation as a whole or at the effects within a specific locality. Then, what is the incidence of the system of property taxes as a whole? The answer is that capital owners bear the burden. Because positive and negative price effects cancel out—consumers, on average, are not burdened by property taxes. If by contrast, we consider the effects within a single locality, and if I am a local government official and ask who *in this locality* will be burdened if we raise property taxes here, the answer is that local consumers (who pay higher prices) bear a large share of the burden. Although prices to consumers in other areas will go down slightly, that is not relevant where the effects within one locality are being examined rather than those nationwide.

The welfare costs of the system of property taxes are of two types. First, the capital stock is misallocated, with too little capital in high tax areas and too much in low tax areas. Second, by driving down the net return on capital, saving may fall and produce too small a total capital stock. These welfare costs are illustrated in our earlier treatment of the corporation income tax in Figure 13–2.

Our brief treatment of property taxes has stressed the broad and general consequences of this tax on investment. A fuller treatment would incorporate more carefully the fact that land is a form of capital that cannot move from one region to another and the distinction between goods produced and consumed in a locality versus those produced in one locality and sold elsewhere.[9] In addition, the way property taxes are administered by local governments is a source of concern to many people. Because property (e.g., homes or factories) is not frequently sold and therefore does not have an accurately revealed market value, administrators must rely on assessments to estimate the value of property. A frequent criticism of the tax is that some types of property are assessed at higher ratios of their true market value than other types of property. In fact, some localities apparently intentionally assess business property at

[9] For a fuller discussion of these and many other issues related to property taxation, see Henry J. Aaron, *Who Pays the Property Tax?* (Washington, D.C.: Brookings Institution, 1975).

higher rates than homes, implying that the effective tax rate varies between the different types of properties. This type of treatment, whether intentional or not, raises further questions about equity and efficiency.

Debt Finance

Governments do not finance all expenditures through explicit use of taxes. One important alternative method of finance is for the government to issue and sell bonds to the public. In effect, the government borrows money from the public to finance its expenditures. Financing expenditures through debt issue, or deficit financing, is engaged in primarily by the federal government, because there are economic (and frequently constitutional) limits to the use of this option by state and local governments.[10]

For the federal government, debt finance has been an important source of funds in recent years. From 1961 to 1970 the average annual federal deficit was $6 billion. Because federal expenditures averaged $140 billion a year over this decade, 4.3 percent of total outlays were financed by debt. From 1971 to 1976 the average annual federal deficit was $30 billion, or 11 percent of average federal outlays. By 1976 interest payments on the outstanding federal debt (the sum of past deficits and surpluses) were $35 billion, almost 10 percent of all federal spending.

Although not technically a form of taxation, debt finance raises the same question: Who actually bears the burden of government programs financed by borrowing from the public.

Incidence

Two sharply opposing views are held on the incidence of debt finance. One holds that government borrowing, just like private borrowing, shifts the burden of paying for current expenditures into the future when the debt is repaid. The other view holds that current expenditures impose a burden on the economy at the time the spending and borrowing take place. In trying to disentangle the issues involved, it will initially be assumed that when people buy government bonds their purchases will be financed by a reduction in consumption spending. This means that private saving available for investment and capital formation does not fall. Although such an assumption is probably invalid, it allows us to momentarily disregard complications that arise when future productive

[10] Wallace E. Oates, *Fiscal Federalism* (New York: Harcourt Brace Jovanovich, 1972). **391**

capacity is affected. (That aspect of debt finance will be examined in the next section.)

Suppose the government sells bonds to the public and uses the proceeds to finance the construction of a dam. The argument that this operation imposes no burden in the future runs as follows: To build the dam now, concrete, manpower, energy, and so on will be used today. These resources must be withdrawn from alternative uses in the private sector, thereby reducing the output of private goods and services. Because the output of private goods falls in the present, the sacrifice involved in constructing the dam occurs in the present and is borne by the present generation.

But what happens if the debt is repaid in some future year? If the government raises taxes at some future date to purchase the bonds back from the public (retire the debt), doesn't this impose a burden? Not so, according to this argument. In the future, the taxes are collected from the same groups (the general public) that receive the proceeds. Repayment of the debt is a transfer among those living at the time, and no net burden is imposed on future generations. In particular, debt repayment does not divert resources into the public sector, so private sector output of goods and services is unaffected.[11]

A similar argument applies to taxes used to pay interest on government bonds before the principal is repaid. Citizens pay taxes to finance interest payments, but they also own the bonds and receive the interest payments. There is no net burden, just a transfer of funds among the public.

This view of debt finance, conveniently summarized in the expression "We owe it to ourselves," was almost universally held in the economics profession from the 1930s until 1958. In 1958 James Buchanan published a book that argued that the burden of debt finance was shifted to future generations.[12] No one, according to Buchanan, bears a burden at the time the expenditure financed by debt is carried out. Although it is certainly true that the resources used in the government-built dam must come from the private sector, this does not mean that any person bears a burden in the relevant sense of sacrificed utility or well-being. Citizens who give up control over resources when they purchase bonds do so *voluntarily* in return for the government's promise of interest and principal to be paid in the future. They reduce current consumption in return for

---

[11] In the discussion that follows, it is assumed that the government sells the bonds to the general public rather than to other governmental institutions. When the government sells bonds to the Federal Reserve System, the effect is to increase the money supply. This is not really borrowing, but a form of "disguised money creation." See James M. Buchanan and Marilyn R. Flowers, *The Public Finances,* 4th ed. (Homewood, Ill.: Richard D. Irwin, 1975), pp. 333–336.

[12] James M. Buchanan, *Public Principles of Public Debt* (Homewood, Ill.: Richard D. Irwin, 1958).

bonds, which permit greater consumption later; their lifetime consumption does not fall. Accordingly, it seems correct to say that no one bears a burden at the time the government borrows the money to build the dam.

To determine who does bear a burden, it is necessary to examine what happens in the future. Suppose the debt is retired in a later year. According to the earlier view, taxpayers lose and bondholders gain, so there is no net burden. In contrast, according to Buchanan, although taxpayers lose, bondholders do not gain, so there is a net burden falling on taxpayers when the debt is retired. Bondholders do not gain because they simply exchange one asset (bonds) for another (money). This exchange represents no more of a gain for bondholders than when a person takes a $100 bill to the bank and exchanges it for five $20 bills. Taxpayers, on the other hand, lose when they pay the higher taxes to retire the debt. Consequently, there is a net burden in the future from debt finance.

A similar argument applies to taxes used to pay interest on the government debt. Bondholders do not gain, because the promised interest payment was just sufficient to induce them to purchase the bonds in the first place. (Put another way, a bondholder could have purchased a private asset and received the same interest return as on the government bond, so there is no differential advantage to receiving interest on government bonds.) Taxpayers, however, bear a burden in paying taxes to finance interest payments. So the necessity of raising taxes to pay interest also creates a burden in time periods after the government expenditure is undertaken.

Now we come to a fairly subtle point that partially reconciles the two views. It can be most simply explained with an example. Suppose the government finances the dam by borrowing in year 1 and announces that it will levy a $100 tax per person in year 2 to purchase back the bonds. All persons in year 1 will know that their taxes will be $100 higher in year 2. They will then "feel" the burden in year 1 because they know their lifetime taxes will be higher as a result of the government borrowing in year 1. The act of government borrowing carries the obligation to levy higher taxes in the future, and, if taxpayers realize this, they will know that the present value of their lifetime disposable incomes is lower. Hence they will *feel* (bear) the burden in year 1, although the actual payment is postponed until year 2.

In this example, the burden is felt by taxpayers in the present because they anticipate the higher future taxes. This suggests the element of truth in the first view described, although the arguments used to justify that view were largely irrelevant. Practically speaking, however, Buchanan's position may be more relevant. To hold that people perceive a burden when the government borrows, it is necessary to believe that citizens are well informed about current spending and tax policies—and about the future consequences of present government policy. It is plausible to suppose, however, that few people know how much government spending is financed by borrowing or what borrowing means for future tax policy, much less for their own taxes. If this is so, the general public may perceive no burden when the government deficit-finances, as Buchanan argues, and may recognize that burden only when higher taxes must actually be paid in the future. This possibility is strengthened by the fact that some people will die before the debt is retired—if it ever is—or before much interest must be paid.

There is clearly a real burden involved with the government finances expenditures by borrowing, and the real issue seems to be, at what point in time do people recognize that burden?

Impact on Capital Markets

It was assumed that government borrowing does not depress private investment, but instead that people reduce consumption spending to purchase bonds. This will generally be untrue. Government must compete with other borrowers when it sells its bonds, and it is likely to bid away funds that would otherwise have financed private investment.

Figure 13–6 shows the results of this process. The S-curve shows the amount of current income people will save at alternative rates of interest: It is drawn as very inelastic, in line with our earlier discussion. The I-curve shows the demand for funds to invest as related to the interest rate that must be paid. In the absence of government borrowing, equilibrium occurs with $100 billion of investment and saving at a 5 percent interest rate. At any given interest rate, every $1 the government borrows means that the amount of saving that can be channeled into private investment must fall. Government borrowing reduces the effective supply of funds available for private investment. If the government borrows $30 billion, this shifts the effective supply-of-saving curve to the left by $30 billion. $S - B$ becomes the effective supply schedule confronting private borrowers, and the new equilibrium occurs at an interest rate of 6 percent, with $75 billion in private investment.

In this example, government borrowing bids up the interest rate to 6 percent and induces people to save $105 billion, $5 billion more than before. Thirty billion dollars of this total is used, however, to finance government expenditures, leaving only $75 billion for private investment. Government borrowing of $30 billion here leads to a reduction of $25 billion in private investment (and a $5 billion decrease in consumption). The amount by which private investment falls depends on the elasticities of the S- and I-curves. The more inelastic the saving schedule, the greater is the reduction in investment. If the saving schedule is very

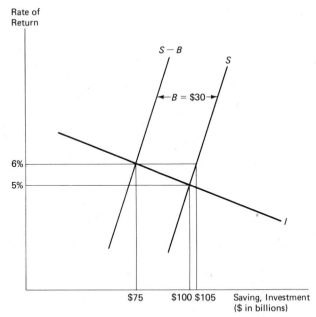

Rate of
Return

$S - B$

S

←$B = \$30$→

6%

5%

I

$75 $100 $105   Saving, Investment
($ in billions)

Figure 13–6. Effect of debt finance on capital markets.

inelastic, as drawn in the diagram, private investment will fall by almost as much as the government borrows.[13]

When debt finance leads to a reduction in investment (rather than consumption, as earlier assumed), a different type of burden is produced. The nation's capital stock grows more slowly, and future productive capacity is sacrificed. In effect, people end up owning government bonds rather than real capital that augments productivity. Aggregate output (income) is lower in subsequent years, so people bear a burden in the form of lower incomes in the future. The results are quite similar to those produced by the social security system when it reduces saving.

The sacrifice in future output occasioned by debt finance depends on the productivity of private investment. In Figure 13–6 the $25 billion in sacrificed investment projects would have produced returns between 5 and 6 percent, with the marginal investment sacrificed having a yield of 6 percent, equal to the interest rate paid by the government on its debt. In reality, however, the interest rate paid by the government on its bonds is well below the real return sacrificed in the private sector. Because of property taxes and the corporation income tax, the net return paid to owners of capital is well below its gross, or real, productivity.

[13]Empirical evidence suggests that the saving supply schedule is quite inelastic, but not perfectly so. See Michael J. Boskin, "Taxation, Saving, and the Rate of Interest," *Journal of Political Economy,* 86(2) Part 2:S 3 (Apr. 1978).

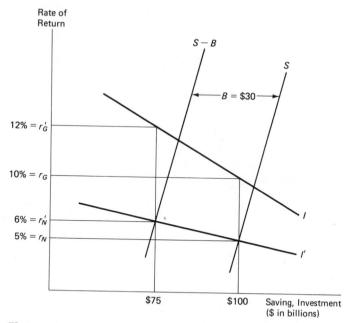

Figure 13–7. Debt financing in the presence of capital taxes.

Government must compete only with the net return people can obtain in private investments and can therefore divert resources away from projects with real returns substantially above the interest rate paid on government bonds.[14]

Figure 13–7 shows the effect of government borrowing in the presence of taxes on the return to capital. The I-curve continues to show the real return to private investment, but because some of that return accrues to government the net return is shown by I'. (It is assumed that the tax rate on the return to capital invested is 50 percent.) Equilibrium in the absence of government borrowing occurs at a rate of saving and investment of $100 billion, with net return to savers of 5 percent, equal to half the before-tax return of 10 percent realized by the investment. Now when the government borrows $30 billion, investment falls by $25 billion, and the net return rises to 6 percent as before. In this case, however, investment projects yielding between 10 and 12 percent are sacrificed. Although the government pays an interest rate of 6 percent, this is

[14]This is not precisely correct because the interest on government bonds is taxable under the federal individual income tax. It is not, however, subject to the corporation income tax and property taxes that fall on most capital income. For example, for corporations to pay stockholders a return of 5 percent (with the 5 percent subject to federal individual income tax), their investments must yield perhaps 10 percent before corporate and property taxes. Government bonds would only have to pay 5 percent to compete with corporate stock.

sufficient to bid resources away from investment projects yielding just under 12 percent.

Because investment projects with high yields are sacrificed, debt finance is likely to impose a substantial cost in the form of reduced future productive capacity. Of course, almost all ways of financing government expenditures will cause some reduction in private investment. An income tax that raises $30 billion will reduce private investment by $3 billion if people save 10 percent of their incomes. Government borrowing, however, has a more concentrated impact on private capital markets than any other form of taxation.

Most students encounter the subject of debt (or deficit) finance in courses on macroeconomics, where its impact on the overall level of output is stressed. Our microeconomic analysis may seem strange at first glance, but there is really no inconsistency if the models are correctly interpreted. Our analysis assumes full employment, but even if there is unemployment the analysis remains valid, although it must be interpreted carefully. If there is unemployment, it is conceivable that debt finance will have the effect of increasing aggregate output, and therefore have a macroeconomic effect that tends to increase private investment. The relevant analysis is to compare alternative macropolicies that achieve full employment. If monetary expansion is used to achieve full employment, the level of private investment will be greater than when debt finance is used. Thus, in comparing alternative full employment policies, debt finance leads to lower investment than when taxes are used to finance government expenditures and monetary policy is used to achieve full employment.

Other Considerations in Debt Finance

Nothing said in the preceding analysis indicates that the government *should not* finance expenditures by issuing debt. In arriving at that normative judgment, it is necessary to compare debt finance to other revenue sources. By its nature, debt finance tends to impose costs on people in years subsequent to the time the expenditure is undertaken to a greater degree than do taxes. There are situations where that pattern of costs may be desirable. For example, the government may be undertaking a project with high initial costs that will yield benefits for a number of years in the future. If we subscribe to the benefit theory of taxation, it would be desirable to finance the project in a way that imposes costs in the future on people who benefit. Debt finance may achieve that effect in a crude way.

Of course, the government does not limit the use of debt to financing long-range investment projects. Because its burden is often shifted to the future, and even then its burden may be difficult to perceive (e.g., lower productive capacity), it is an attractive revenue source for any type of expenditure from a political point of view. Recognizing the political temptation to finance greater expenditures by using debt, some economists have suggested that the government be required to balance its budget, if not each year, at least over a period of years. This might, however, interfere with the use of debt finance as a macroeconomic policy tool.

Cumulative Impact of Capital Income Taxes

When the effect of transfers and taxes on labor supply was examined, the importance of the effective, or cumulative, marginal tax rate on earnings was emphasized. Even though the tax rate in each policy separately might be low, when a person pays several taxes or receives several transfers (or both) the effective marginal tax rate is often quite high, and that is the relevant rate to consider in judging how much work incentives are affected. The same principle applies to the taxation of income from capital. Several taxes fall on capital income, with the most important being the corporation income tax, property taxes, and the federal individual income tax. Even though the individual rates might not be thought high enough to have a major effect on saving (and hence the capital stock), the combined effect could be substantial.

An example will illustrate the importance of this point. Suppose $1000 worth of capital invested in a business enterprise produces an annual income of $100. Property taxes at a rate of 2 percent of the $1000 are paid, so $20 of the capital income is property tax liability. Eighty dollars remains as net income subject to the corporation income tax (because the property tax is deductible in computing net income for corporation tax purposes). Assuming a rate of 40 percent for the corporate tax, $32 more in taxes is paid. This leaves the business with $48 in after-tax "profits." If this is paid as dividends, recipients will find the $48 taxed at their marginal rate under the income tax. Alternatively, if the $48 is reinvested in the corporation, the value of its stock will rise and owners will be taxed according to the capital gains provision in the income tax. On average, suppose the $48 is taxed at a rate of 19 percent. Then the net income received by the owner of capital, after all taxes are paid, is $39. The effective tax rate on the $100 in capital income is 61 percent.

These numbers are hypothetical but were chosen to agree with a study done by Michael Boskin in which he estimated an average tax rate of 61 percent for capital invested in businesses.[15] Although the effective rate

[15] Boskin, "Efficiency Aspects of Differential Tax Treatment . . . ," op. cit.

varies among individuals—because it depends on the taxpayer's marginal bracket in the federal income tax—the 61 percent figure provides an idea of the average burden of taxes on the income generated by capital invested in businesses. By contrast, the average tax on labor earnings is only 29 percent, although the marginal rate for most persons is well above that figure (see Table 11–5). Capital income is taxed far more heavily than labor income by the U.S. tax system.

What are the effects of these taxes on capital income? There are two important effects, both of which were discussed in the context of the corporation income tax. First, because these taxes do not strike all industries and localities at the same rate, the allocation of the capital stock among various uses is affected [see Figure 13–2(a)]. Second, because the net return realized from owning capital is reduced, people may save less, and the total capital stock may be reduced [see Figure 13–2(b)]. It is this second effect that will be considered further here because it depends on the combined impact of taxes on capital.

We wish to determine whether people save less because the net return realized is reduced by taxes on capital income. Put differently, would people save more if they could keep the full before-tax return on any additional saving? If the answer is yes, then the cumulative impact of capital taxes is to reduce saving, capital stock, and productive capacity below what they would otherwise be. This simply means that there would be a welfare cost as shown in Figure 13–2(b).

It is important to be clear on what it means to say that people save too little because of taxes on capital income. To save more, it is necessary to consume less. Consuming less (saving more) now makes it possible to consume more in later years because of the real productivity of capital. The relevant question is whether the higher future consumption that saving makes possible is worth more than the consumption sacrificed when we save. The answer depends on the rate of return realized by saving. The real before-tax return on capital invested in corporate businesses is approximately 12 percent.[16] That is a real (adjusted for inflation) return reflecting the physical productivity of investments in businesses.

Empirical evidence suggests that people would save more at a higher rate of return, but the magnitude of the effect (the elasticity of the saving supply schedule) is doubtful.[17] To provide a subjective test to see if it is reasonable to suppose that people would save substantially more, consider the following: A sum is invested at 12 percent; if the interest is reinvested each year, the amount will double every 6 years. If you are 20

[16] Martin S. Feldstein, "National Saving in the United States" in E. Shapiro and W. White (eds.), *Capital for Productivity and Jobs* (Englewood Cliffs, N.J.: Prentice-Hall, Inc., 1977), pp. 124–154.

[17] Michael J. Boskin, "Taxation, Saving, and the Rate of Interest," op. cit.

years old now, and save $1000 at 12 percent, this sum will grow to $128,000 by the time you are 62. Then you can consume the interest on $128,000, $15,000 a year, for the remainder of your life and still leave $128,000 to your heirs. Would you be willing to save more if faced with this prospect? We would, and we suspect that most other people would too.

People may save less now because the after-tax return realized is far below 12 percent. With a 61 percent tax on capital income, the net rate of return on an investment yielding 12 percent is under 5 percent. At a 5 percent return, saving an additional $1000 at age 20 will yield $8000 at age 62. It is certainly plausible that people would save significantly less because of taxes on capital income. If so, the welfare cost due to a reduced capital stock would be substantial. That welfare cost, however large it is, could be reduced by reducing taxes on capital income. To keep government revenue from falling, it would be necessary to increase taxes on labor income, which would produce an additional welfare cost by further distorting labor supply decisions. Feldstein, however, has estimated that the gain from reducing capital income taxation would be greater than the loss from increasing labor income taxation.[18] It must be stressed, however, that there is no consensus on this issue; the size of the welfare cost produced by the taxation of income from capital is unknown. We do know that capital income is very heavily taxed (in comparison to labor income), but exactly what effect this has on saving has not yet been resolved.

Appendix: The Distribution of Tax Burdens by Income Class

How are tax burdens distributed among income classes? Is the overall tax system progressive, proportional, or regressive? Now that we have examined the incidence of each major tax separately, we are in a position to consider these important questions. In this section we discuss the results of a recent study that estimated the incidence of the tax system in 1976.[19]

There are two important steps in any tax incidence study. First is the estimation of the before-tax incomes of households. A comprehensive

[18] Martin Feldstein, "The Welfare Cost of Capital Income Taxation," *Journal of Political Economy*, 86(2) Part 2: S 29 (Apr. 1978).

[19] Edgar K. Browning and William R. Johnson, "Taxes, Transfers, and Income Inequality," paper presented at a conference on Regulatory Change in an Atmosphere of Crisis: The Current Day Implications of the Roosevelt Years (forthcoming in conference volume), Washington State University, April, 1978. This paper presents preliminary estimates from the authors' study, *The Distribution of the Tax Burden* (Washington, D.C.: American Enterprise Institute, forthcoming).

measure of income is desirable for reasons discussed in earlier chapters. Thus, available estimates of money income, or adjusted gross income, must be augmented by adding types of income that are usually excluded from these statistics. The employer portion of the social security tax must be added to money income received by persons since it represents income that would have been received in the absence of the tax (i.e., before-tax income). Similarly, all indirect business taxes must be added. In addition, in-kind transfers, imputed income of owner-occupied housing, and retained corporate earnings are types of income that should be included. After adjustments of this type are made, we have a broad measure of before-tax income. Income estimated in this way is nearly 25 percent greater than the money income actually received by households.

The second step in a tax incidence study is to assign the tax burden of each tax to households. To accomplish this, it is necessary to rely on tax incidence theory to provide guidelines as to the incidence of different taxes. In this case the following incidence assumptions are used: Individual income taxes are allocated to the taxpayers themselves; payroll taxes are allocated in proportion to covered earnings; corporate income and property taxes are allocated in proportion to capital income; and sales and excise taxes are allocated in proportion to factor earnings (labor plus capital income). Note that the incidence assumptions used depend on the theoretical analysis deemed appropriate for each tax; because, however, we do not know with certainty how all taxes affect the economy, the competitive assumptions used here may not be fully correct.

Table 13–2 shows the results of calculations based on these assumptions, with households classified by before-tax income quintiles. In 1976 all taxes together were 29.3 percent of the broad measure of income; the average tax rate, taking all households together, was therefore 29.3 percent. The overall tax system, however, was quite progressive, with the tax burden on the lowest quintile equal to 10.7 percent and rising steadily up through the income distribution, reaching 36.1 percent for the top quintile. The average burden per household in the top quintile is $16,700 but only $430 for the bottom quintile.

The modest tax rate for low income households is largely the result of the fact that most of their income is in the form of government transfers. Nearly two thirds of the income in the bottom quintile is in the form of cash and in-kind transfers that are untaxed.[20] For example, even though social security and unemployment insurance (payroll) taxes are about 13

---

[20] Note that the fraction received as transfers reported here, two thirds, differs from that shown in Table 7–8. In Table 7–8 households were ranked by their before-tax, before-transfer incomes. When ranked by their before-tax, after-transfer incomes, many households with large transfers are no longer in the lowest quintile and so the share of income received as transfers is lower. For purposes of estimating tax burdens, a broad measure of income (including transfers) should be used as the basis for ranking households in the income distribution.

Table 13–2. Average Tax Rates by Quintiles of Households in 1976 (percentages)

Quintile	Sales and Excises	Payroll	Income	Corporate and Property	Total
First	2.1	4.2	1.6	2.7	10.7
Second	3.7	6.5	4.2	3.4	17.8
Third	4.8	8.5	7.5	3.3	24.0
Fourth	5.2	8.2	10.4	3.6	27.3
Fifth	5.4	5.0	13.2	12.5	36.1
All Quintiles	4.9	6.4	10.3	7.7	29.3

Source: Edgar K. Browning and William R. Johnson, "Taxes, Transfers, and Income Inequality," paper presented at a conference on Regulatory Change in an Atmosphere of Crisis: The Current Day Implications of the Roosevelt Years (forthcoming in conference volume), Washington State University, April 1978.

percent of labor income for low earners, labor income makes up less than one third of total income in the lowest quintile so the tax as a percent of total income is only 4.2 percent. Higher income households receive most of their incomes as labor and capital income that is subject to several taxes. Therefore, the progressivity of payroll (up to the fourth quintile, where the ceiling on taxable earnings begins to have effect), corporate, property, and sales and excise taxes primarily reflects the much greater importance of transfers in lower income classes. The progressivity of individual income taxes reflects the non-taxability of transfers in addition to the graduated rate structure of these taxes.

Sales and excise taxes are shown as progressive components of the tax system in Table 13–2. Earlier tax incidence studies have estimated that these taxes are regressive by allocating them in proportion to consumption outlays.[21] (Because consumption is a larger fraction of income at low income levels, any tax allocated in proportion to consumption will be regressive.) It has recently been argued that this procedure is incorrect and that these taxes should be allocated in proportion to factor income (as in Table 13–2).[22] The question of how to allocate sales and excise taxes is of more importance than might be suggested by the fact that they produce only one sixth of all tax revenue because under certain theories part of the corporate, property, and payroll taxes are assumed to effect the economy in the same way as sales and excise taxes.

To understand what is involved here, refer back to our earlier analysis of a general sales tax in Chapter 10. There we explained that such a tax left relative product prices unchanged but depressed factor prices. If

[21] Pechman and Okner, op. cit.; Richard A. Musgrave, Karl E. Case, and Herman Leonard, "The Distribution of Fiscal Burdens and Benefits," *Public Finance Quarterly,* 2:259 (July 1974).

[22] Edgar K. Browning, "The Burden of Taxation," *Journal of Political Economy* (forthcoming August 1978); Edgar K. Browning and William R. Johnson, *The Distribution of the Tax Burden,* op. cit.

absolute product prices (and hence the price level) are unaffected, a person whose only income is a government transfer bears no burden, because the purchasing power of his transfer is unchanged; only those with factor incomes are burdened. Alternatively, suppose that the sales tax led to an increase in absolute product prices (the price level rises) with no change in factor prices. This is a conceivable outcome because microeconomic theory does not permit us to predict what happens to absolute prices; it deals with relative prices. (Note that here also factor prices have fallen *relative to* product prices.) In this case, however, a person with a fixed government transfer bears a burden under the sales tax because its purchasing power is decreased, and the burden is roughly in proportion to his consumption outlays.

To argue, as previous studies of tax incidence have, that sales and excise taxes are borne in proportion to consumption outlays, it is necessary to assume that both the price level rises exactly in proportion to the size of the tax *and* that the money value of the transfers is unchanged. Both of these assumptions are open to question, especially the latter. In fact, under existing legislation the money value of most transfers will rise automatically if product prices rise. A person whose only income is a social security pension, for instance, will bear no burden if a general sales tax leads to higher prices because his pension will automatically increase because it is linked to the consumer price index. About three fourths of all cash and in-kind transfers are indexed in this fashion. Even for those transfers that are not explicitly linked to consumer prices, it appears likely that legislators make ad hoc adjustments in transfer payments in response to any changes in the price level.

For these reasons it seems plausible to assume that the real value of transfers is unaffected by sales and excise taxes. Under these conditions it is incorrect to allocate these taxes in proportion to consumption outlays; instead, they should be allocated in proportion to factor income. Because factor income is a smaller share of total income for low income households, the burden of sales and excise taxes will be progressively distributed as shown in Table 13–2.

As pointed out earlier in this chapter, some economists have been uneasy relying on competitive assumptions in tax incidence studies. It has been suggested that part (or all) of the employer portion of payroll taxes, corporate income taxes, and property taxes are "shifted to consumers" rather than borne in proportion to labor and capital incomes. How would this, if correct, affect our estimates in Table 13–2? Actually, not very much at all. If these taxes are "shifted to consumers," then they should be treated as if they were sales or excise taxes themselves—and allocated in proportion to factor incomes. Thus, if the corporate income tax is borne in proportion to factor income rather than in proportion to capital income, it would still be quite progressive, only slightly less

403

so than as shown in Table 13–2. (Compare the degree of progressivity under corporate and property taxes versus sales and excise taxes.) On the other hand, if the employer portion of payroll taxes is "shifted to consumers," this tax will be more progressive than shown in the table because sales and excise taxes are more progresive than payroll taxes. On balance the degree of progressivity of the tax system will not be much different from that shown in Table 13–2, even if noncompetitive incidence assumptions are appropriate.

Supplementary Readings

Aaron, Henry J. *Who Pays the Property Tax?* Washington, D.C.: Brookings Institution, 1975.

Boskin, Michael J. "Efficiency Aspects of the Differential Tax Treatment of Market and Household Activity," *Journal of Public Economics,* 4:1–25(Feb. 1975).

———. "Taxation, Saving, and the Rate of Interest," *Journal of Political Economy,* 86 (2) Part 2:S3–S28(Apr. 1978).

Brittain, John. *The Payroll Tax for Social Security.* Washington, D.C.: Brookings Institution, 1972.

Browning, Edgar K., and William R. Johnson. *The Distribution of the Tax Burden.* Washington D.C.: American Enterprise Institute, forthcoming.

Buchanan, James M., and Richard E. Wagner. *Democracy in Deficit.* New York: Academic Press, 1977.

Feldstein, Martin. "The Welfare Cost of Capital Income Taxation," *Journal of Political Economy,* 86 (2) Part 2:S29–S52(Apr. 1978).

Ferguson, James M. *Public Debt and Future Generations.* Chapel Hill: University of North Carolina Press, 1964.

Harberger, Arnold C. *Taxation and Welfare.* Boston: Little, Brown and Company, 1974, Chapters 6, 7, 8, and 9.

McLure, Charles E., Jr. "The 'New View' of the Property Tax: A Caveat,"*National Tax Journal,* 30(1):59–68(Mar. 1977).

———, and Wayne R. Thirsk. "A Simplified Exposition of the Harberger Model, I: Tax Incidence," *National Tax Journal,* 28(1):1–28(Mar. 1975).

Pechman, Joseph A., and Benjamin A. Okner. *Who Bears the Tax Burden?* Washington, D.C.: Brookings Institution, 1974.

FEDERALISM

The United States has a federal form of government, with one central government, fifty state governments, and thousands of local governments. The existence of a multiplicity of government units raises a number of interesting questions: What is the rationale for so many different levels of government? Are some types of economic policies better carried out by local governments rather than by the federal government? How does the free movement of people and businesses among local government units affect their performance? These are a few of the questions that will be considered in this chapter.

Overview of State and Local Expenditures and Taxes

A casual observer of contemporary affairs could easily believe that the federal government overwhelms lower levels of government in terms of its economic impact. In a sense this is probably true: The federal government spends almost 50 percent more than the combined expenditures of all state and local governments. If only domestic expenditures (thereby excluding national defense) are considered, however, state and local outlays are on a par with federal outlays. For many persons, the governmental services provided by subnational levels of government are more important in their day-to-day lives than those provided by the federal government.

Table 14–1 shows the major expenditures of state and local governments in 1975. Total expenditures were $266.2 billion, an average of about $1200 per capita. Education was the single most important expenditure category, with outlays of $87.9 billion, fully a third of all expenditures. Local governments accounted for nearly three fourths of the total spent on education. Other major categories of expenditures by state

Table 14–1. State and Local Expenditures,
Fiscal 1975 ($ in billions)

Function	1975
Total	$266.2
Education	87.9
Highways	22.5
Public Welfare	28.2
Health and Hospitals	18.8
Police and Fire	11.8
Social Insurance	18.5
Utility and Liquor Stores	17.3
Other	61.2

*Source: Facts and Figures on Government Finance,
1977* (New York: Tax Foundation Inc., 1977),
Table 113, p. 137.

and local governments included highways, public welfare, and health and hospitals, but none of these categories accounted for significantly more than 10 percent of total outlays.

Not all expenditures by state and local governments are funded by their own taxes. Some expenditure programs are partially or wholly financed by the federal government through grants (subsidies) given directly to lower levels of government. In 1975 the federal government made grants totaling $47.1 billion to state and local governments, thereby financing about a sixth of the total expenditures of subnational governments out of federal taxes. State governments also make similar grants to local governments. These "intergovernmental grants" have become increasingly important in recent years, and their rationale and consequences will be considered later in the chapter.

Sources of revenue for state and local governments are shown in Table 14–2. Although they use much the same types of taxes as the federal government, the relative importance of the taxes differs greatly. Property taxes are the single largest source of revenue and are used almost exclusively by local governments. Sales and excise taxes, relatively unimportant at the federal level, provide nearly a third of state and local tax revenue. These taxes are levied primarily by state governments. By contrast, income and payroll taxes are less important for state and local governments (primarily used by state governments) than for the federal government, although they have been growing rapidly in recent years. Note that state and local taxes, at $161.6 billion, account for only three fifths of the total revenue. Federal grants and "charges and miscellaneous" provide about a fifth each. (The "charges and miscellaneous" category includes such revenue sources as license fees, sewage fees, and receipts from the operation of state liquor stores.)

Table 14–2. State and Local Revenues, Fiscal 1975
($ in billions)

Source	1975
Individual Income Tax	$ 21.5
Corporation Income Tax	6.6
Sales and Excise Taxes	49.8
Property Taxes	51.5
Payroll Taxes	20.1
Other Taxes	12.1
Total Taxes	161.6
Charges and Miscellaneous	53.1
Grants from Federal Government	47.1
Total Revenue	261.6

Source: Facts and Figures on Government Finance, 1977 (New York: Tax Foundation, Inc., 1977), Tables 119 and 124, pp. 145 and 151.

One important characteristic of our federal system cannot be shown in tables such as Table 14–1 and 14–2, which combine the accounts of all subnational governments. This characteristic is the great diversity of tax and expenditure policies to be found among states and localities. Not all subnational governments use the same taxes or spend the same amounts on the various programs, because they are largely independent units making their own individual tax and expenditure decisions. Table 14–3 indicates the variation in total expenditures per capita among states. New York, with an expenditure of $1611 per capita, was 50 percent above the national average and more than twice the level of Arkansas. Some of this variation simply reflects the fact that per capita incomes are

Table 14–3. State and Local Expenditures, Selected States, Fiscal 1975

State	Expenditures per Capita	Expenditures as a % of Personal Income of State
Arkansas	$ 728	17.8%
California	1261	21.2
Connecticut	1059	16.4
Georgia	925	19.6
Indiana	827	15.9
Maryland	1244	20.1
New York	1611	26.2
Virginia	974	18.5
Average, All States	$1077	19.9

Source: Facts and Figures on Government Finance, 1977 (New York: Tax Foundation Inc., 1977), Tables 117 and 118, pp. 143–144.

higher in certain states, but the second column shows that some states spend a substantially larger share of their income than others. When state and local expenditures as a percentage of personal income are considered, New York still leads the way, but now Indiana falls to bottom place. Even greater differences exist among local governments. This diversity is important because if all subnational governments were to choose identical policies there would be little reason to have a multitude of different governments.

Economic Advantages of Subnational Governments

To some people, it is an article of faith that a local government will perform more efficiently than a state government, and a state government more efficiently than the federal government.[1] Other people believe the opposite. Actually, what requires emphasis is that some governmental functions are more efficiently performed by lower levels of government whereas other functions are carried out better by the federal government. For some types of policies, local government is better, but care is needed in determining exactly what policies are more suitable for local governments.

In our earlier discussion of market failure, we defined public goods and externalities and showed the potential efficiency gains from government policies. It is now time to recognize that there are frequently geographic or spatial dimensions to the provision of public goods. Consider, for example, the public provision of a police force in Richmond, Virginia. This provides benefits to virtually all Richmond residents, but very few benefits accrue to residents of Charlottesville, Virginia, and even fewer benefits, if any, to residents of San Diego, California. There are *nonrival* benefits from the police force in Richmond, but they do not extend over the entire U.S. population. Instead, the benefits are concentrated mainly on people living in or near Richmond, and diminish rapidly as one moves farther away.

Such a public good, with benefits concentrated geographically, is referred to as a local public good, as distinguished from a national public good such as national defense. Similarly, there are local externalities such as the pollution of a particular lake or stream. Note that whether a good is a "local" or "national" public good is really a matter of degree. Not all "local" public goods benefit only those who live in a specific locality (tourists and shoppers in Richmond may benefit from police protection), and not all "national" public goods benefit everyone in the na-

---

[1] This section and the following one draw heavily on Wallace E. Oates, *Fiscal Federalism* (New York: Harcourt Brace Jovanovich, 1972), Chapter 1.

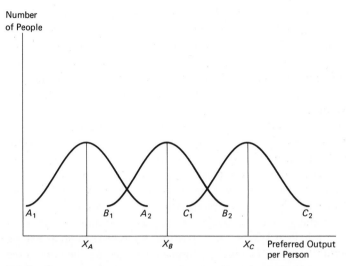

Figure 14-1.

Figure 14-1. Provision of services by subnational governments.

tion. Still, the benefits from some goods are far more limited geographically, and that is the essential point.

With respect to the provision of local public goods, it is possible for different communities to provide different levels of output. This is also true of other governmentally provided services that are not, strictly speaking, public goods at all. Because the preferences of residents are likely to vary from one community to another, a federal system of government makes it possible for consumption levels to vary with the preferences of residents. A community that wants (and is willing to pay for) a strong police force but no parks can have such a pattern of services without interfering with another community that prefers the opposite pattern of services. Thus, a federal system is capable of greater efficiency than a system that provides the same level of government services to all citizens. In principle, a federal system of many subnational governments is able to provide a range of outputs that corresponds more closely to differing preferences among communities than could a national government.

Figure 14-1 illustrates this advantage of subnational governments. Suppose there are three communities, A, B, and C, and a public good, X. The curves A_1A_2, B_1B_2, and C_1C_2 show the distribution of quantities of X preferred by residents of each community. If a national government were to provide a uniform level of X to all communities, it would probably supply a level near the overall median at X_B. This equilibrium would be very unsatisfactory for those residents of communities A and C whose preferences are at the A_1 and C_2 tails of their respective distribu-

409

tions. By contrast, if we have independent governments in the communities, three different levels of output, X_A, X_B, and X_C, could be provided. Community C, whose residents have a large demand for X, can thus get a larger output than community A, with its smaller demand. This range of outputs possible when X is provided by local governments is likely to be more efficient than a uniform level of output supplied by a national government.

In comparing the uniform level of provision, X_B, for all communities to different levels for the three communities, note that not all persons will be better off under the latter. In particular, residents of communities A and C whose preferences place them near the A_2 and C_1 tails of their respective distributions will be worse off when X_A and X_C are provided than when X_B is. This point brings us to a second major advantage of a federal system: People are free to move from one community to another. In a federal system, it is possible for people to shop around for the community whose tax and expenditure policies are the best suited to their needs. Persons in community A who prefer X_B more than X_A (whose preferences are close to A_2) can move from community A to community B. In this way, an element of individual choice among various combinations of government polcies is possible, an option that is not possible for federal policies.[2]

As a result of consumer mobility, one would ultimately expect residents of communities to have similar tastes for government policies. Some communities will emphasize good public schools and attract families with school-age children. Others will stress security and hospitals, and tend to attract retired persons, and still others may emphasize low taxes (and government services) for those who prefer private goods to government services. This process of consumers' choosing places of residence in response to differences in governmental services enhances the efficiency advantages of subnational governments. Of course, this process does not guarantee that every person will obtain exactly the type of government he would prefer. Within each community there will still be differences of opinion. Moreover, many factors in addition to government policies influence a person's choice of a location: the availability of jobs, proximity to friends and relatives, climate, and other factors play a role in a locational decision. Nonetheless, the possibility of "voting by foot" clearly enhances to some degree the attractiveness of a federal system as an institutional arrangement for providing government services.

A further advantage is that local government may be more responsive to the needs of its citizens. The political process in smaller government units may be more efficient than in larger units. Logrolling and pressure

---

[2] This advantage of a federal system was first stressed by Charles Tiebout in "A Pure Theory of Local Expenditure," *Journal of Political Economy*, 64:416 (Oct. 1956).

groups constitute less of a problem, and voters are likely to be more knowledgable about how their tax dollars are spent. In short, when government is "closer to the people," it may possess fewer inherent defects as a decision-making mechanism. It is not entirely obvious that this is always true, but it is widely believed to be so.

Finally, experimentation and innovation are likely to be greater in a federal system. With thousands of local governments, some are certain to be experimenting with new policies that are quite different from those used by the bulk of communities. Different approaches to police investigation, instruction in schools, and environmental policies will be tried. This process of experimentation can be beneficial even if some of the new policies prove to be failures. A successful policy innovation in one community can be adopted by other communities. If a new policy fails, other communities benefit from that knowledge too, and can avoid a similar error.

It is not an easy matter, however, to determine whether a new policy is a "success" or a "failure." (Indeed, since preferences of citizens differ among communities, a policy that is successful for one community might be judged a failure by another community.) Nonetheless, a federal system provides the raw material for more direct comparisons among different policy approaches than is possible in a system where one policy (of a particular type) applies to everyone. As an example, Colin D. Campbell and Rosemary G. Campbell recently compared the fiscal systems of Vermont and New Hampshire. Although taxes as a percent of personal income are 50 percent higher in Vermont, the Campbells found no evidence that public services are any better.[3] This conclusion is understandably controversial (especially among government officials in Vermont), but the important point is that a federal system makes such comparisons possible.

In summary, a system of subnational governments possesses a number of advantages. Communities can provide different levels and combinations of services more in line with the preferences of their citizens, and citizens are free to move to communities that they feel are doing a better job. The political process may be more efficient at the subnational level. Experimentation and innovation are more likely, and direct comparisons among different approaches to economic problems are facilitated.

---

[3] Colin D. Campbell and Rosemary G. Campbell, *A Comparative Study of the Fiscal Systems of New Hampshire and Vermont, 1940–1974* (The Wheelabrator Foundation, 1976).

Economic Disadvantages of Subnational Governments

Despite its advantages, a system of subnational governments is likely to be ineffective in resolving certain policy issues. For example, if local governments are relied on to provide national public goods, the result is certain to be substantial inefficiency. Each community would be responsible for its own defense against foreign aggression, but all communities taken together would probably be underdefended. The reason is that a large part of the benefits from, say, a missile system provided by one community accrue to residents of other communities. In determining how much to spend on missiles, each community would consider only the benefits its residents receive and ignore benefits to nonresidents. The free rider phenomenon is relevant here, just as it is when we consider whether an individual has incentive to contribute to the financing of a good that benefits other persons in addition to himself. Because each community has incentive to free ride, fewer resources would be devoted to defense than is justified by the interests of all persons in the nation considered together.

Efficient provision of a public good that benefits persons in all communities thus necessitates a central government. The key issue here is the geographic area over which persons necessarily benefit from provision of the good. Some goods, such as a sewer system or a police force, have benefits that extend over a limited area, and a city or county government can supply the good more efficiently because most if not all of the benefits and costs occur within one locality. Some environmental policies may have effects over larger regions and require state governments, but defense is clearly the province of the federal government. Thus, subnational governments will not be efficient in providing all types of government services.

A second area where subnational governments will be relatively ineffective is in redistributing income. If one commuity embarks on a redistributive program by taxing its higher income residents and transferring the proceeds to its poorer residents, two things will happen eventually to hinder the goal of providing assistance to the poor. First, wealthy residents can move to another community where taxes are lower. Second, poor persons in other areas can move to the community providing higher welfare benefits. As a result, average per capita income in the community will fall, and it will become impossible to finance high welfare benefits.

Thus, the very consumer mobility that is beneficial when subnational governments engage in nonredistributive programs tends to limit their use of redistributive measures. This remains true even if those with higher incomes genuinely wish to help the poor. Each wealthy individual who leaves a community has a negligible effect on the extent to which the poor are helped, and so it is in each's interest to leave. If all wealthy persons leave, of course, there can be no redistribution. This is simply the free rider problem once again.

Any significant degree of income redistribution must be carried out by a central government. Even in this case, there are limits, because wealthy persons can always leave the country, and poorer immigrants may be permitted to enter. Mobility, however, is far more restricted between countries than between regions within a country, so a national government has greater latitude in carrying out redistributive programs. Moreover, insofar as our concern is with poor persons regardless of where they reside within the nation, only a national program is capable of accommodating this goal by helping the poor in all regions.

This does not mean that local governments cannot adopt policies that benefit some residents at the expense of others, because they obviously do, but there are limits. In addition, the redistribution that occurs often takes a form that cannot be avoided by moving from the region. If a heavy property tax is placed on land owned by a wealthy person, he cannot fully avoid the burden by selling the land; the sale price will be reduced because the buyer will pay less for heavily taxed property. The immobility of property, especially land, makes it possible for local governments to engage in some redistribution, but still only to a limited degree.

A third policy area where subnational governments are relatively inefficient is in the pursuit of macroeconomic objectives. Although our primary concern here is not macroeconomics, it should be pointed out that subnational governments have little effect on employment and price levels within a specific region. These governments have no power to change the money supply, and any fiscal policies would be greatly diluted through the movement of persons and goods across jurisdictional boundaries.[4] The national government must assume the responsibility for macroeconomic stabilization policy.

Certain government functions can therefore best be performed by a central government. Although we have been referring to the "advantages" and "disadvantages" of subnational governments, it should be clear that it is not necessary to choose between total reliance on one form of government or another. Instead, the real issue should be to determine which functions are best carried out by local governments and which by the national government. The "optimal" system is obviously one that relies on both types of government, with each performing the functions it does best. Our discussion should provide some guidance in determining what level of government is best suited for the performance of dif-

[4] The proper division of responsibilities between national and subnational governments is stressed by Wallace E. Oates in "The Theory of Public Finance in a Federal System," *Canadian Journal of Economics,* 1:37 (Feb. 1968).

ferent types of policies. Still it should be recognized that there are many "in-between" cases that do not fit neatly into the categories we have considered. Some examples will be discussed later in this chapter.

Tax and Expenditure Analysis

Principles

Earlier chapters have considered general principles pertaining to the analysis of expenditure and tax programs. Many of the points made remain relevant when we turn to the consideration of fiscal activities of subnational governments. We still wish to ascertain, for example, how policies affect the distribution of income and the allocation of resources. In the context of local government policies, however, the framework of analysis is more complicated. One earlier models entirely disregarded locational aspects of government policies. For national policies, this is generally appropriate: Where a business chooses to operate or where a consumer chooses to live, work, or purchase products is generally not influenced by a national policy. Instead, emphasis is placed on the level of output, consumption, or work effort because locational decisions are not affected. On the other hand, when local government policies are considered, locational decisions must be incorporated into the analysis. Decisions by businesses about where to operate or where to sell as well as consumers' choices of where to live and work may be affected and need to be considered explicitly.

Local government jurisdictions are generally "open" economies in the sense that movement of persons and goods across jurisdictional boundaries is prevalent. In this sense, they are much like small countries engaging in international trade with neighboring countries. Goods produced in one locality are often sold ("exported") to persons in another locality, and residents often purchase ("import") goods produced elsewhere. The policies of local governments can often influence the flow of goods and services, as well as people and productive capital, across government boundaries.

If we could assume that people and productive resources were completely immobile among government jurisdictions, most of our earlier analysis would remain valid. For some specific problems, it may be reasonable to assume such immobility, not because people are unable to move, but because many policies have little *net* impact. To take an example, if a community raises taxes to finance better public schools, how will this affect locational decisions? If only the improved school system is considered, an incentive for families with children to move into the community has been created. At the same time, however, the higher taxes considered alone create incentive for people to move away. With these two opposing influences, what will the net effect be? It is entirely possible that little or no net movement of people to or from the locality will occur: the *net* attractiveness of the community as a place of residence may remain unchanged. If this is the case, an analysis that ignores locational decisions will be a reasonable approach.

This highly simplified example suggests one important general principle: It is especially important to consider both sides of the budgets of local government policies in determining whether locational decisions will be affected. A balanced-budget approach to the study of local taxes and expenditures is frequently essential. It would be a mistake to conclude that a community with better public services is a more attractive place to live; it will also have higher taxes so it will be more attractive only to those who consider the better services worth the additional tax cost.

Thus, in some situations there may be little net effect on locational decisions from local government policies. The difficulty, however, is to determine in what situations this is likely to be true. Just because the government spends and taxes more, it does not follow that no business or person will be led to relocate. For some individuals, the tax increase may impose costs in excess of the benefits derived from the expenditure, and the community will become a less attractive place. This will be true, for example, for people without children when school spending increases. The opposite may be true for other persons. In other words, it is not only the total benefits and costs for the community as a whole but also the pattern of individual benefits and costs that is relevant for locational decisions.

These remarks suggest that there may be a tendency for local governments to provide benefits to individual taxpayers in proportion to taxes paid. To see why, consider what would happen to a community that provided superb schools out of property taxes levied on all families. Clearly, families without children would be paying taxes and receiving no benefits. They would leave the community, and only those who wanted and were willing to pay the required taxes would stay. Thus, the community would end up with those who felt the schools were at least worth their tax cost. Alternatively, to avoid the departure of dissatisfied taxpayers, the community could use some of the tax revenue to provide services to those without children. In either case, the end result would be that all families received benefits roughly in line with their tax costs. This conclusion simply reflects the difficulty local governments have in redistributing income, that is, in using taxes from some people to provide benefits to other people. As suggested earlier, there is probably only a weak tendency of this sort, but it does perhaps have some effect on expenditure and tax patterns of subnational government units.

415

Why all the emphasis on locational decisions? Basically because it is the one really new element in the study of state and local government finances. Efficiency requires not only appropriate output decisions but also appropriate locational decisions—and the latter are more strongly affected by policies of subnational government than by policies of the federal government. As an example, an excise tax at the national level only reduces output, but at the local level it can have additional effects. Consider an excise tax on liquor in one state. A consumer may travel to a neighboring state or city where liquor is untaxed or less heavily taxed to stock up. The cost of time and transportation is then a welfare cost of the local excise tax—a distortion quite different from, and in addition to, that produced by a federal excise tax.

Clearly, the analysis of the expenditure and tax policies of subnational governments can be quite complicated. Although much of our analysis in earlier chapters remains valid, this analysis must sometimes be amended to explicitly incorporate influences on locational decisions. There are no simple rules to lead us to the correct conclusions in all cases. Perhaps the best advice is simply to always consider explicitly how locational decisions will be affected by any policy being examined.

Tax Competition

It is helpful to think of subnational governments as being in competition with one another. They provide public services to their residents in return for taxes. Because all communities do this, each community must offer its public services on terms sufficiently attractive to induce people and business to locate there. If any community provided deplorable services in return for exorbitant taxes, it would find its tax base eroding as people moved elsewhere. Each community is therefore subject to competition from other subnational governments. Just as with competition among private business firms, we would normally expect competition among governmental units to have a beneficial influence by inducing communities to provide a mix of services in line with the preferences of its citizens.

It is sometimes held, however, that one aspect of the competition among governmental units leads to inefficient results. Business investment in a community may be deterred by an excessive level of taxation; consequently, government officials are often reluctant to increase taxes for fear of driving away part of their tax base. Competition among neighboring communities may lead to holding down taxes to maintain a favorable climate for business. Many local government officials believe this "tax competition" results in suboptimal expenditures, arguing that "Tax competition enters into the war between communities for new industrial and commercial activities; each competing community avoids

416

making otherwise justified tax increases for fear of decreasing its attractiveness to new business."

This oversimplified view of tax competition ignores the expenditure side of the budget. If a tax increase is "justified," then the benefits from expanding public expenditures exceed the costs of higher taxes. How could providing net benefits to the community make it less attractive to business? Generally, one would expect just the opposite. It is possible, however, that the tax increase exceeds the benefits that go to business; the increased expenditures may be on public schools, for example. If this is so, however, then the community is really attempting to redistribute income from business (more specifically, its owners or consumers) to other groups. As we have already seen, subnational governments are constrained in their ability to redistribute income.

If a tax increase is really worthwhile, it should be possible for the local government to raise taxes without driving business away. There are at least two ways to accomplish this. The first is to levy the taxes on the beneficiaries of the proposed expenditure policy. Taxes on business would then be increased commensurate with any benefits received. This approach may be difficult in practice if the government is legally constrained in the form of taxes it may use. For example, it may not be possible to increase property tax rates on homeowners to finance better schools without also increasing business property tax rates. In this case, the second approach may be followed: Combine the school expenditure with another policy that directly benefits business (police services, utilities, highways, and so on). Then business, paying higher taxes and receiving commensurate benefits, will not be driven from the community by the higher tax rates.

In principle, tax competition is no barrier to efficiency in local government operations. In fact, it is a spur to efficiency because it forces government officials to keep benefits in line with taxes paid. It does inhibit localities, however, if they wish to tax some groups to finance benefits for other groups, a desirable limitation insofar as redistribution is intrinsically a function of the national government. It is understandable that local government officials do not like tax competition, but the public is probably better off because of the discipline it enforces.

"Impure" Local Public Goods

When considering public services provided by subnational governments, we saw that these services are sometimes local public goods with benefits limited to a certain geographic area. A further distinction should also be made. A good can have nonrival benefits for residents of a certain area, but the benefits per person may depend on the number of persons in the area. If so, it is called an impure local public good. A comparison between weather forecasting and police protection should clarify this distinction. A weather forecast for a particular geographic area provides nonrival benefits for residents of that area. Moreover, more people can enter the area and benefit from the forecast without reducing the benefits to the original residents. The weather forecast is a "pure" local public good.

A police force is clearly different. If more people move into the area, police services are spread more thinly over a larger population, and benefits for the original residents from a given police force will decline. (It is sometimes said that this type of good is subject to "congestion costs" from an increased population.) Benefits are still nonrival for the population, but in this case individual benefits depend on both the size of the police force and the number of people in the area. A police force is thus an "impure" local public good. It is clear that most of the services provided by local governments are more appropriately described as "impure" rather than "pure" local public goods. Fire stations, sewer services, and public schools are clearly "impure" in the sense that the larger the population the smaller the benefits per person for a given size facility.

There are important implications for the functioning of a system of subnational governments due to the prevalence of impure local public goods. Consumer mobility may be a mixed blessing in this setting. We have stressed that a person may move from community A to community B when he prefers the mix of public policies in the latter. He will benefit from the move, but the original residents of community B may suffer from the "congestion cost" his presence imposes. When the welfare of all concerned is considered, it is not obvious that the relocation leads to a better allocation of resources on balance.

This discussion, however, ignores one point: When a person moves into a community, he will also normally pay taxes there. His taxes permit, say, the police force to be expanded. If his tax payments are large enough, the expansion in the police force will be sufficient to keep benefits unchanged for the initial residents. The real question is whether the taxes newcomers contribute to the local treasury are sufficient to cover the costs their presence imposes on the original residents. If so, consumers will take account of the true costs associated with their locational decisions, and consumer mobility will function to enhance the efficiency of a federal system.

Many of the fiscal problems of local governments are due to the fact that their tax systems do not require all newcomers to pay taxes commensurate with the cost their presence imposes on the community. This is generally because taxes are not (and perhaps cannot be) levied in proportion to benefits received. For example, a family with five school-age children may purchase a modest home in a community, thereby contributing a modest sum in property tax revenues but imposing a much larger cost on the school system. To avoid the influx of newcomers who would consume more public services than they pay for through their taxes, many communities adopt restrictions on entry into the community. These restrictions take the form of zoning ordinances, limitations on the type of home that can be built, and so on. Although these restrictions are, in principle, inferior to taxing persons in proportion to the costs they impose on the other residents, they can contribute to efficiency when such a tax system cannot be implemented. Unfortunately, these restrictive practices can also be used to serve other ends.

Benefit "Spillovers"

Local government spending programs undertaken in one locality will sometimes confer benefits on residents outside their political jurisdictions. This phenomenon is called a "benefit spillover," because some of the benefits of the local expenditure policy "spill over" onto other localities. This is actually just a form of external benefit, but the literature on federalism uses the term *spillover,* presumably to emphasize its geographic aspect.

Pollution programs adopted by one subnational government often create benefit spillovers for people residing outside the community. If actions are taken to reduce pollution in a river and the river passes through a number of communities, persons residing in communities downstream will benefit from pollution abatement programs adopted by an upstream community. Similarly, a welfare program adopted in one region will benefit the nonpoor in other regions if the nonpoor care about the degree of poverty in all regions of the country. These two examples illustrate how people living outside a community can benefit from the community's policies without bearing any cost. Consumer mobility among localities gives rise to a somewhat different type of benefit spillover. A person may reside in one area but purchase goods or work in another. Thus, tourists or shoppers will benefit from the police and highway services of a town they only visit. In this case, too, nonresidents receive some benefit from the expenditure programs of a community at no cost. Benefit spillovers are significant for much the same general reason as external benefits. The political process in a community is likely to be influenced only by the benefits received by its own residents. Local voters, in determining how large an expenditure to approve, will consider only the benefits they receive and disregard the benefits accruing to outsiders. Consequently, when benefit spillovers are substantial, expenditures are likely to be too small because they will reflect only the preferences of residents and not all those who benefit from the policy.

Benefit spillovers often occur because the geographic range of benefits

419

does not precisely coincide with the political boundaries of government jurisdictions. One way to deal with them, therefore, would be to have political boundaries defined in terms of the area over which benefits accrue. Unfortunately, this would generally require a different boundary for each of many government expenditure programs. Imagine, for example, having a regional government to deal with pollution, a government encompassing a smaller area to provide police services, a still different one for schools, and so on. When the administrative and decision-making costs of operating so many overlapping governments are considered, it seems clear that this approach is far from ideal. In any event, political boundaries have been determined historically and must, for most purposes, be taken as fixed.

Thus, benefit spillovers are to a degree inevitable. Because they imply some inefficiency in local expenditure decisions, this raises the question of whether the inefficiency can or should be avoided in some way. Several approaches are possible. One is to do nothing. If only a small share of benefits accrues outside the community, the magnitude of the inefficiency will be small (for the reasons discussed in connection with the measurement of welfare costs).[5] A second approach is to rely on voluntary negotiation among governmental units. Because an inefficiency implies the possibility of mutual benefits from coordinated action, neighboring communities often have incentives to jointly undertake programs. When the number of affected communities is small, the "Coase theorem" is relevant; local governments themselves have incentives to bargain until an efficient outcome is achieved. Although relatively rare, such bargaining among neighboring governments does occasionally take place.

If the benefit spillovers affect residents in a larger number of communities, however, bargaining will be infeasible because of the free rider problem. In that event, it is possible for a higher level of government, such as the federal government, to improve matters by providing grants directly to lower levels of government. Properly designed, these intergovernmental grants can increase expenditures in cases where benefit spillovers are important. Intergovernmental grants will be considered in greater detail later.

Tax "Exporting"

A portion of the taxes levied by a subnational government is sometimes borne by persons living outside the taxing community. In this event, taxes are said to be "exported" to outsiders. There are a number of ways in which locally levied taxes can have an incidence that places part of the

[5] See Chapter 10.

tax burden on nonresidents. For example, an excise tax on a product produced in one locality but purchased by consumers in other parts of the country can achieve this result. (Care must be taken, however, not to tax the product so heavily that production will shift to another locality.) Similarly, the property tax may be applied to property owned by nonresidents that places a burden on outsiders. This is commonly the result of business property taxation.

The federal government also facilitates tax exporting through provisions in its income tax laws. For taxpayers who itemize, certain state and local taxes are deductible in computing federal income tax liability. Thus, when a locality levies a tax on its residents their federal tax payments are automatically reduced. For persons in the 40 percent federal tax bracket, for example, $1 in local taxes costs them only 60 cents because their federal tax falls by 40 cents. This loss of 40 cents in available federal revenues is a burden on taxpayers throughout the country, so part of the local tax is effectively exported to federal taxpayers in general. In the same manner, the federal income tax exempts interest on the bonds issued by subnational governments. This allows local governments to issue debt at lower interest cost; local taxpayers pay smaller taxes to finance interest payments on locally issued bonds, with the federal government losing revenue as in the previous case.

There are a number of important consequences of tax exporting. For instance, the true distribution of the burden of locally supplied government services becomes more difficult to identify. Each person will be a citizen of many local and/or state government units that export some of their taxes and will to that extent gain. At the same time each person is likely to bear some of the costs of government services supplied in other regions because a portion of these costs is exported to him. The net effect of these influences on the distribution of the tax burden is quite complex and uncertain.

Tax exporting also has important allocative effects on the tax and expenditure policies of subnational governments. Each local government, for example, has incentives to rely heavily on types of taxes that are borne largely by nonresidents. Some states are quite successful at this. Take Florida, for example. As one tax expert in Florida observed: "we have done an excellent job of shifting a large portion of the tax burden to tourists—the tax system is designed to tax the service industries quite heavily."[6] More subtle effects also occur; states are encouraged to use progressive rather than proportional income taxes, for example. A progressive state income tax places a heavier nominal burden on those in

[6]C. H. Donovan, "Recent Developments in Property Taxation in Florida: A Case Study," in Harry L. Johnson, ed., *State and Local Tax Problems* (Knoxville: University of Tennessee Press, 1969), p. 59.

higher federal tax brackets where the net burden (after the deduction) is not as great.

Expenditure decisions of local government are also affected. If 30 percent of local taxes is exported, every $1 in expenditures costs local residents only 70 cents. The unit price of supplying government services is reduced, and the tax prices of local voters are 30 percent lower. At a lower price, voters will, of course, approve larger government expenditures. Expenditures are likely to exceed the point at which marginal benefits equal true marginal costs because the residents of a community bear only part of the marginal cost.

The tendency to overspend produced by tax exporting may be mitigated by the presence of benefit spillovers. Benefit spillovers taken alone will lead to a suboptimal level of spending because residents receive only a portion of the true marginal benefits. If benefits spill over to the same degree that taxes are exported, these two distortions, which operate in opposite directions, may exactly offset each other, fortuitously leading the community to make efficient expenditure decisions.[7] Such a fortunate outcome should not be generally expected, because benefit spillovers are restricted to certain policies whereas tax exporting lowers the cost to residents of all expenditure policies.

Unlike benefit spillovers—where virtually nothing is known about the empirical significance of the phenomenon—tax exporting has been the subject of some limited empirical investigation. Charles McLure examined the extent of tax exporting among states, finding that an average of 20 to 25 percent of state tax burdens were borne by nonresidents.[8] For some states, fully 40 percent of the tax burden was exported. Unfortunately, no study has examined the extent of tax exporting for lower levels of government.

John Bowman has explored the effect of tax exporting on locally financed school expenditures.[9] He assumed that property taxes on commercial and industrial property were exported whereas taxes on residential and farm property were not.[10] In a study of independent school districts in West Virginia, he found that the degree of tax exporting was positively related to locally financed school expenditures. In fact, a 10

---

[7] This may be true in some cases with respect to tourists. Tourists often receive government services (e.g., police and highway) when they visit an area. If they bear a tax burden just sufficient to finance the services they enjoy, there is no *net* tax exporting.

[8] Charles E. McLure, Jr., "The Interstate Exporting of State and Local Taxes: Estimates for 1962," *National Tax Journal,* 20:49 (Mar. 1967).

[9] John H. Bowman, "Tax Exportability, Intergovernmental Aid, and School Finance Reform," *National Tax Journal,* 27:163 (June 1974).

[10] This is unlikely to be fully true, but it can be argued that property taxes on commercial and industrial property are "hidden taxes" that residents don't realize they bear even if they do. This would have the same political effects as exported taxes.

percent increase in the degree of tax exporting was estimated to produce a 15 percent increase in spending, suggesting a relatively high price elasticity of demand. To the extent that school districts would finance efficient levels of school expenditures if they bore all costs, this finding also implies that tax exporting leads to overly large budgets.

Despite its apparent importance, tax exporting has been given scant attention by economists. There has been little emphasis on how the inequities and inefficiencies introduced by this phenomenon could be overcome. Some partial remedies are obvious, such as eliminating the tax subsidies introduced in the federal income tax. Communities could still, however, adopt taxes that imposed some costs on nonresidents. An approach that might be worth considering is for the federal government to require subnational governments to finance all expenditures with a tax that cannot be easily shifted to nonresidents, such as a personal income tax. We leave it as an exercise for the reader to determine what disadvantages this proposal would have.

Intergovernmental Grants

Intergovernmental grants are subsidies from one governmental unit to another. Generally, these grants flow from higher to lower levels of governments. In 1977, for example, the federal government made grants of $60.7 billion to state and local governments. State governments also made grants of $52 billion in 1975 to local governments, with almost 60 percent of the total earmarked for education. These grants have become important in recent years, especially at the federal level. In 1960 federal grants were only $6 billion, or 6.5 percent of total federal expenditures. By 1977 the $60.7 billion in grants represented 15 percent of total federal expenditures.

Intergovernmental grants are of two basic types: conditional and unconditional. Conditional grants are those where the granting government specifies the way in which the funds may be spent by the recipient government. They are similar to in-kind subsidies to governmental units. In contrast, unconditional grants can be spent in any way the recipient government chooses.

As indicated in Table 14–4, conditional grants are far larger than unconditional grants. The only major program of unconditional grants at the federal level is general revenue sharing, with expenditures of $6.5 billion. Conditional grants not only are larger in total but also comprise over 400 separate programs. The major categories of conditional grant programs are shown in Table 14–4. About 70 percent of all expenditures on conditional grants is earmarked for social welfare programs.

423

Table 14-4. Federal Aid to State and Local Governments, Fiscal 1977

Type of Aid	Amount ($ billions)
Conditional-Categorical Grants	
Health	$10.2
Education, Employment,	
Training, and Social Service	12.0
Natural Resources, Energy, and Environment	4.4
Community and Regional Development	3.9
Income Security	11.4
Highways	6.6
Other	5.7
General Revenue Sharing	6.5
Total	60.7

Source: *Facts and Figures on Government Finance, 1977* (New York: Tax Foundation Inc., 1977), Table 68, p. 85.

Conditional Grants

Conditional grants must be devoted to certain specified uses. These grants are of two general types, matching and nonmatching. A nonmatching grant is a fixed sum; in contrast, the size of the matching grant depends on the recipient government's own expenditures on the specified program. For example, a matching grant formula might specify that the federal government will contribute 40 percent of the cost, and the state government must contribute the remaining 60 percent. As can be seen, a matching grant is really a form of excise subsidy that is applied to government units rather than to individuals. Similarly, a nonmatching grant is simply a form of fixed-quantity subsidy.

The analysis of matching and nonmatching conditional grants closely follows our earlier analysis of excise and fixed-quantity subsidies. There is, however, one basic difference: The recipients of conditional grants are government units and not individuals. Thus, the response of the recipient government will reflect the workings of the political processes of the local government. Before the grant, local taxpayers had to pay $100 in taxes to receive school services costing $100 (ignoring tax exporting). With a 60–40 matching grant, local taxpayers can receive the $100 in services at a tax cost of $60 because the federal government contributes the remaining $40. Thus, the tax price of each taxpayer has fallen by 40 percent, and taxpayers will prefer a larger quantity at the lower price. Because all taxpayers will be affected in this way, it seems reasonable to suppose that the local political process will approve greater expenditures under the matching grant. In effect, the matching grant lowers the price of school services to residents of the community, so they purchase more—but the decision to consume additional units is a political one.

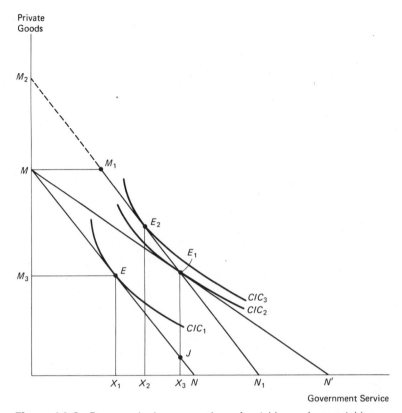

Figure 14–2. Revenue sharing: comparison of matching and nonmatching grants.

For ease of exposition, it will be assumed that the choices made by the political process of a recipient government can be represented diagrammatically by a set of community indifference curves. (Although this is a heroic assumption, the conclusions of this analysis can be demonstrated using a majority voting model.[11]) These are shown in Figure 14–2 as the CIC curves. The aggregate budget constraint of the community is MN. In the absence of any grant, X_1 of a particular government service is supplied at a tax cost of MM_3. A matching grant applied to this government service lowers its price to the community, and the budget constraint shifts to MN'. At the lower price, the community chooses X_3, and the total subsidy from the federal government is E_1J. A nonmatching grant of the same amount will shift the constraint to MM_1N_1. Under the nonmatching grant, the community will select a lower level

[11] David Bradford and Wallace E. Oates, "Towards a Predictive Theory of Intergovernmental Grants," *American Economic Review*, 61:440 (May 1971).

of the government service, X_2. A nonmatching grant has the same income effect for the community, but it does not lower the per unit price of the service as does the matching grant. Thus, the matching grant leads to greater output of the government service.[12]

The community is, however, better off with the nonmatching grant—at least in this case where the nonmatching grant is equivalent to an unconditional grant of MM_2. It should not be thought, however, that every member of the community will prefer the nonmatching grant. Taxpayers who prefer unusually large quantities of the government service will often be better off with a matching grant. In this case, the use of community indifference curves tends to obscure the distributional effects among different members of the community. Nonetheless, the matching grant results in too much output of the government service, at least if the political process functions to attain the efficient output when residents bear the entire marginal cost of supplying additional units.

Although the analysis has focused on the effects of grants on the level of government service, conditional grants often have additional effects on the structure of the economic policies of recipient governments. Medicaid, for example, is financed in part through federal matching grants to states, but the effects extend beyond simply expanding total state expenditures. To become eligible for the grants, states are required to subsidize a specific range of medical services for certain persons. In this way, the "strings" attached to conditional grants can induce states to adopt a type of program determined largely by the federal government. Sometimes these "strings" can impose great restrictions on the nature of programs, as when colleges are required to recruit a certain percentage of their faculty and student bodies from minority groups to be eligible for federal education grants. The degree of restrictions in federal grants varies greatly among programs, of course, but they often allow the federal government to exercise considerable control over some policies of subnational governments.

A major rationale for matching grants is the presence of benefit spillovers. If benefits from a local program accrue to nonresidents, the community may spend too little on its own (ignoring tax exporting). Welfare programs provide a possible example: Assistance provided to the poor by any state may benefit the altruistic nonpoor in other states. Insofar as states are relied on to provide welfare assistance, benefit spillovers provide a rationale for matching grants. In the context of welfare programs, however, the major issue is whether the national interest is sufficiently great to warrant a uniform federal assistance program rather than relying, even partially, on state governments.

[12] Note that this analysis is formally identical to our discussion of a variable quantity subsidy in Chapter 3. The same qualifications and extensions discussed there apply here, also.

General Revenue Sharing in Principle

After several years of debate, general revenue sharing was instituted by the federal government in 1972. In the latter part of that year, the Treasury Department mailed checks totaling about $2.5 billion to 37,000 state and local governments. (Because Indian tribes are considered governmental units, a check for $26 was sent to the Cortina Rancheria tribe, a tribe with one member.) By 1977 outlays on general revenue sharing had climbed to $6.5 billion.

The original conception of revenue sharing as discussed widely in the economics profession in the 1960s was a simple one. Revenue sharing was to be a system of unconditional grants to state and local governments, with the size of the grants related to population. As actually enacted, revenue sharing was far removed from this simple vision, but our discussion will be simplified if a hypothetical "pure" program is considered first.

In Figure 14–3, a community has a budget constraint relating private and local government services as shown by MN. Equilibrium occurs at point E. An unconditional revenue sharing grant of MM' is given to the community and the budget constraint becomes $M'N'$. A new equilibrium occurs at E', with X_2 in government services and M_2 in private goods being selected. Note in particular that local taxes have been

Figure 14–3. Effect of unconditional revenue sharing grant: balanced-budget approach.

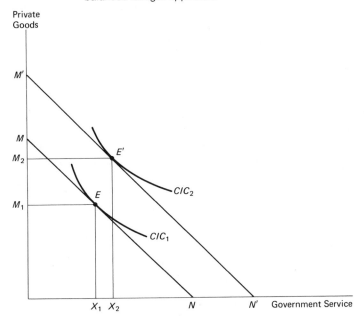

reduced from MM_1 to MM_2: The income effect of the grant encourages the community to consume more private goods by reducing local taxes.

So far, this analysis has ignored the effect of the federal taxes used to finance revenue sharing grants. Because these taxes are collected from persons in the same communities that receive the grants, they should be incorporated into the analysis. Suppose members of this community pay federal taxes equal to the revenue sharing grant the community receives. Then the before federal tax and grant constraint would be $M'N'$, and the community would be at point E' in the absence of the program. Federal taxes shift the after-tax constraint to MN, and the revenue sharing grant shifts the constraint back to $M'N'$. This balanced-budget approach implies that the local community consumes the same level of private goods and government services with revenue sharing as it would without. There is only one significant change. Before the program local taxes were $M'M_2$, but after the program, local taxes fall to MM_2, or by $M'M$, whereas federal taxes on residents rise by $M'M$. In other words, federal taxes are substituted for local taxes. Local residents pay the same total taxes, but with revenue sharing, part of the taxes that would have been paid to the local government go to the federal government and then are returned as a revenue sharing grant.

In contrast to this analysis, many people feel that a pure type of revenue sharing must have some effect on the level of government services; they believe that local governments will view the grant as "free" money and use it fully to expand local government spending. This is conceivable, especially because we are dealing with political processes that may not respond in the same way as an individual. If true, however, this argument implies that local government political processes are inefficient in a strange way: Why should local residents accept a higher level of local government spending than they are willing to pay for with local taxes just because the taxes first go to Washington and then come back to the community as a grant? It must be stressed that the real opportunities open to the communities, as summarized by the $M'N'$ constraint, are not changed in any way by the program.

Within this simple framework, revenue sharing has little effect on resource allocation. What, then, are the arguments favoring such a program? One major goal of the program was to make it easier for subnational governments to finance public services. Accepting the premise that local public services would expand (and the actual revenue sharing does contain some incentives for expansion), a possible argument favoring this outcome could be based on the existence of benefit spillovers. Benefit spillovers, however, do not exist for all local public services, so a general expansion would seem uncalled for.

A second argument holds that "all states do not have equal capacity to pay for local services" because there are gaps between "fiscal need" and "fiscal capacity." Presumably, this argument refers to the fact that average per capita income differs among communities so that the poorer communities can afford fewer public services *and* private goods. This argument seems to favor a redistribution from wealthier communities to poorer communities—a redistribution that would occur if the grants were based on population size alone. The basic question about this argument is whether we wish to redistribute income to poor *communities* or poor *persons.* A redistribution from wealthy to poor communities is a very ineffective way to help poor persons. Not only do communities with low average incomes have some nonpoor residents, but also communities with high average income have some poor residents. It would seem to make more sense to redistribute income directly to poor persons (as with the NIT) and then leave it up to the poor to vote for more local government services (more local taxes) if they want to use their transfer in that way.

A third argument is based on the extent to which federal taxes are substituted for local taxes ($M'M$ in Figure 14–3). Federal taxes might have lower collection costs than local taxes. It is not clear, however, whether this is so, at least in the relevant sense of marginal collection costs. In any case, because revenue sharing grants are less than 3 percent of total state-local expenditures, the magnitude involved is surely trivial. On the other hand, if federal taxes are substituted for local taxes, the entire tax system may become more progressive if federal taxes are more progressive in their incidence.

All in all, as Charles Goetz summed up the arguments on revenue sharing: "There is ammunition for a shaky case on either side, but a solid one for neither."[13]

General Revenue Sharing in Practice

As actually enacted, general revenue sharing was far more complex than the simple proposals originally discussed. As Wallace Oates emphasized, revenue sharing is "a highly complex fiscal program with a whole myriad of incentives, many of which the framers of the legislation most certainly did not recognize."[14]

Most of the complexity and incentives in the program stem from the procedure used to determine the size of the grant received by each subnational government. Instead of basing grants on population alone, a number of other factors are incorporated into the formulas determining what each state receives. For example, a higher relative tax effort

[13]Charles Goetz, *What Is Revenue Sharing?* (Washington, D.C.: The Urban Institute, 1972), p. 28. Goetz also considers several other inconclusive arguments.
[14]Wallace E. Oates, "Introduction," to *Financing the New Federalism,* W. E. Oates, ed. (Washington, D.C.: Resources for the Future, Inc., 1975), p. 6.

(average tax rate in the state) entitles a state to a larger grant (other things being equal), as does a lower average per capita income. To complicate matters further, two quite different formulas are used, one passed by the House and one by the Senate. Each state can select which formula will be used in determining its grant; naturally, the state will choose the formula that gives it the largest grant.

It would require an entire chapter to describe accurately how these formulas work.[15] It will suffice here to note that the net effect on the distribution of grants among states does not significantly favor states with low average incomes. Washington, D.C. (treated as a state) and New York, for example, are the wealthiest and third wealthiest states, respectively, and their per capita grants are the sixth and fifth largest in the nation. By contrast, Alabama is the second poorest state, and its per capita grant ranks 28th in the nation. Although poor states probably gain slightly on average, the net redistribution among states is slight. Perhaps no more than 10 percent of the $6.5 billion represents a net transfer among states.

The incentives in the program result from the dependence of the grant received on the level and structure of taxes levied by recipient governments. A state that increases its taxes relative to other states receives a larger grant. In this sense, revenue sharing is like a matching grant that may encourage states to expand their expenditures and taxes. The incentive to expand differs widely among states: In 1972, if Mississippi had increased its taxes by $100, it would have received $12.40 more in federal grants, whereas Ohio would have been granted only $1.30 more. Most states would have received about $5.00 more by raising their taxes $100. Some towns face even larger incentives: If Monroe, Connecticut, raised its taxes by $100, it would have received $19.60 more in grant funds. Note that the effect is the same as a matching grant that lowers the cost of financing expenditures to the locality. Although the incentives in this program alone are not large, when combined with similar incentives in tax exporting and explicit matching grants, the net subsidy rate could be substantial.

Another incentive contained in the House formula encourages states to rely more heavily on state income taxes than other forms of taxes. Because only 19 states chose the House formula, this incentive applied only to them. In some cases, the incentive is quite large. For example, Ohio could have increased its grant by 35 percent by expanding its income tax collections and reducing its sales tax collections by equal amounts.

In general, it seems that general revenue sharing does not redistribute

[15] For a more detailed discussion, see Robert D. Reischhauer, "General Revenue Sharing—The Program's Incentives," in ibid., pp. 40–87.

much between subnational governments, but it does contain significant incentives for the expansion of these governments and for greater reliance on income taxes. It is still too soon to tell how subnational governments will respond to these incentives. The basic issue is whether these governments should be encouraged to expand, and, if so, why the incentives should differ so greatly among various states and localities.

Supplementary Readings

Goetz, Charles J. *What Is Revenue Sharing?* Washington, D.C.: Urban Institute, 1972.

Oates, Wallace E. (ed.) *Financing the New Federalism.* Baltimore: Johns Hopkins University Press, 1975.

————. *Fiscal Federalism.* New York: Harcourt Brace Jovanovich, Inc., 1972.

Stigler, George J. "The Tenable Range of Functions of Local Government," in Edmund S. Phelps (ed.), *Private Wants and Public Needs,* Revised Edition. New York: W. W. Norton and Company, 1965.

Wagner, Richard E. *The Fiscal Organization of American Federalism.* Chicago: Markham, 1971.

INDIFFERENCE CURVE ANALYSIS

For students unfamiliar with indifference curve analysis, or those in need of a quick review, this appendix contains some basic fundamentals.[1] The treatment is brief, with emphasis placed on certain concepts that are relevant to the analyses developed throughout the text. Our purpose is to present a simple model of consumer behavior that permits us to determine how consumer choices among goods are affected by objective circumstances such as prices, incomes, and subsidies. The goods can be anything—beer, shoes, or public schooling. We will begin by separately explaining the way a consumer's tastes or subjective preferences can be shown by using indifference curves; then we will consider how objective conditions such as income can be represented. Next, the consumer's preferences and income will be treated jointly in a single model. Finally, several implications of the model will be examined.

The Consumer's Preferences

Consumers have different tastes or preferences, and these differences will be reflected in their consumption decisions. The consumption of goods and services provides satisfaction or utility to the consumer, and the consumer will arrange his consumption to maximize satisfaction. To understand how the consumer determines what combination of goods will maximize his well-being, we will begin by making the following assumptions about the preference patterns of the consumer:

---

[1] For a more detailed and comprehensive discussion of indifference curve analysis, see, for example, Charles F. Ferguson and S. Charles Maurice, *Economic Analysis,* rev. ed. (Homewood, Ill.: Richard D. Irwin, Inc., 1974); Edwin Mansfield, *Microeconomics— Theory and Applications* (New York: W. W. Norton, 1975); Donald S. Watson and Mary A. Holman, *Price Theory and Its Uses,* 4th ed. (Boston: Houghton Mifflin, 1977).

1. The consumer is able to rank different combinations or bundles of goods in terms of desirability. For example, suppose the consumer is confronted with three bundles of goods: one hamburger and one beer, three hamburgers and two beers, and two hamburgers and four beers. From among these groupings, the consumer is able to decide whether he prefers the third bundle to the second, or is indifferent between them, or prefers the second to the first, and so on. To say that a consumer is indifferent between two bundles of goods means that either bundle will yield the same level of utility, and the consumer has no preference for one over the other. The consumer will either prefer one bundle to another or be indifferent between them.

2. The consumer's preferences are transitive. If, for instance, there are three bundles of goods, A, B, and C, and the consumer prefers bundle A to bundle B, and bundle B to bundle C, then it follows that the consumer also prefers A to C.

3. The consumer always prefers more of a commodity to less. Going back to the hamburgers and beer in the example, the consumer would always prefer either the second or the third combination to the first because each of these involves more of both hamburger and beer than the first alternative.

Having made these assumptions, we can begin to develop our model.

Indifference Curves

Consumer tastes can be represented by indifference curves. To develop this concept, first consider the alternative bundles of goods listed in Table A-1. Assume that the groupings are deliberately arranged so the consumer is indifferent between them. In Table A-1(a), the consumer is equally satisfied with 10 units of food and 1 unit of clothing, or 7 units of food and 2 units of clothing, and so on. Similarly, each of the combinations in Table A-1(b) is as desirable as any other. Note, however, in (b) that with the same quantity of clothing more food is provided com-

Table A-1. Preferences for Food and Clothing

	(a)		(b)	
	Food	Clothing	Food	Clothing
A:	10	1	13	2
B:	7	2	10	3
C:	5	3	8	4
D:	4	4	7	5
E:	3	6	6	7
F:	2	9	5	10

pared to (a). So, given the assumption that the consumer always prefers more to less, any combination in (b) will be preferred to any in (a).

These alternative bundles of goods can be represented as points on indifference curves. An indifference curve is a locus of points indicating different combinations of goods that yield the consumer an equal level of satisfaction. In Figure A-1 an indifference curve, IC_1, has been drawn representing the alternative combinations of food and clothing detailed in Table A-1(a). Food is measured on the vertical axis and clothing on the horizontal axis. Thus, a point such as A represents 10 units of food and 1 unit of clothing. The consumer is equally well off consuming any combination of goods shown on IC_1.

Indifference curves have certain characteristics that should be noted:

1. Indifference curves are convex. Typically, an indifference curve is fairly steep at the top and relatively flat at the bottom. Its shape is a function of the relative importance of the two goods to the consumer. Starting at the top of the indifference curve and moving down it, the consumer gives up food for additional units of clothing. At A, for instance, the consumer has 10 units of food and 1 unit of clothing; at D

Figure A-1. Indifference curves.

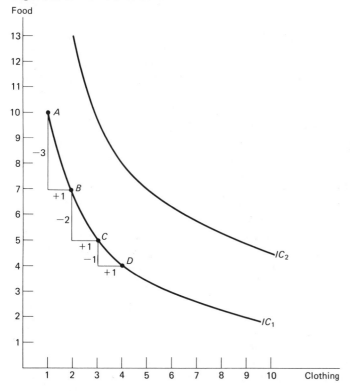

the consumer has 4 units of food and 4 units of clothing. Recall that at either point he is equally well off.

At the top of the curve, the consumer has a lot of food and little clothing; to move from point *A* to point *B* (less food and more clothing), the consumer would be willing to give up 3 units of food for another unit of clothing. As he moves down the curve to the right, however, the situation changes. The consumer has relatively more clothing and relatively less food. To move from *C* to *D,* for instance, the consumer would be willing to give up a maximum of only 1 unit of food for an extra unit of clothing. If he had more food and less clothing, as at point *A,* the consumer would have traded 3 units of food for another unit of clothing, but at point *C* he is willing only to exchange 1 unit. The rate at which the consumer is willing to trade one good for another (while maintaining the same level of utility) is called the *marginal rate of substitution.*

The marginal rate of substitution (MRS) is shown in the diagram by the slope of the indifference curve. Thus, at point *A,* the slope is $-3/1$, indicating that the MRS at that point is 3 for 1. Note that the MRS is a measure of the subjective value of one good in terms of another. At point *A,* another unit of clothing is worth 3 units of food to the consumer because that is the maximum quantity of food he will give up to acquire another unit of clothing.

Assuming that indifference curves are convex is equivalent to assuming that the MRS will decline as we move down an indifference curve, that is, the slope (MRS) will become flatter. Basically, this is an empirical proposition about the nature of people's preferences. Although it may not always be true, it makes sense as a generalization. It simply means, for example, that a person will give up *more* food to get another unit of clothing when he has a lot of food and very little clothing (as at point *A*) than when he has little food and a lot of clothing (as at point *C*). At *A,* clothing is relatively scarce, and the consumer will give up 3 units of food for another unit of clothing; at *C* he has more clothing and less food, so an additional unit of clothing is less important to him and he would give up only 1 unit of food for it.

2. Indifference curves that lie farther from the origin represent higher levels of utility than those lying closer to the origin. So far only one indifference curve has been discussed. Actually, a complete description of a consumer's tastes would involve an infinite number of indifference curves. Consider Table A-1(b) again. Recall that with all levels of clothing consumption more food is provided than in Table A-1(a). This combination of goods is represented by the indifference curve IC_2 in Figure A-1. Curve IC_2 lies farther from the origin than IC_1 and represents a higher level of utility. A utility-maximizing consumer would prefer to consume *any* combination of goods on IC_2 to *any* combination on IC_1.

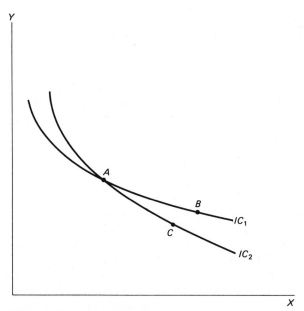

Figure A-2. Intersecting indifference curves.

Whether he is able to consume at the desired higher level is determined by his income and the prices of the two goods, factors that will be considered shortly.

3. Indifference curves cannot intersect. If indifference curves intersected, our assumption of transitivity would be violated. Figure A-2 is drawn *incorrectly* so that two indifference curves cross. Let's examine the implications. Indifference curves IC_1 and IC_2 intersect at A. On curve IC_1, points A and B yield the same level of satisfaction to the consumer because they lie on the same indifference curve. The same is true for points A and C on IC_2. Therefore, C is as desirable as A, and A is as desirable as B. This seems to imply that C and B are equally desirable. Note, however, that point B is clearly preferable to C because B contains more X and Y than point C—and we have assumed that the consumer always prefers more to less. Point B cannot be preferred to C and have the same utility as C. Thus, intersecting indifference curves are inconsistent with our assumptions.

The Consumer's Budget

In using indifference curves to explain and predict consumer behavior, we must know more than consumer's tastes. Because higher indifference curves correspond to higher levels of well-being, a rational utility-maximizing consumer will want to achieve the highest indifference curve *possible*. In maximizing utility, however, the consumer is constrained by the level of his money income. To want a villa on the Riviera is not the same as being able to afford it. Even the wealthiest individuals have budget or income constraints, because their income is not infinite. In addition to money income, the consumer must consider the prices of all relevant commodities. Price changes as well as changes in the level of the consumer's income will affect consumption patterns.

The Budget Constraint

Let's begin by assuming a consumer has an income of $1000 per year. Also assume that he is contemplating the purchase of two goods, X and Y, with the price of X $5 per unit, and the price of Y, $10 a unit. If the consumer spent his entire income on X, he could purchase 200 units ($1000/$5); if he spent his entire income on Y, he could purchase 100 units ($1000/$10). In Figure A-3, a straight line connecting 200 units of X and 100 units of Y defines the consumer's budget constraint. The budget constraint shows all combinations or quantities of X and Y that the consumer can purchase per year. The consumer can buy 200 units of X, or 100 units of Y, or various combinations of X and Y (e.g., 50 units of X and 75 units of Y, 100 units of X and 50 units of Y) that lie on the budget constraint.

The slope of the budget constraint is equal to the negative of the price ratio, P_X/P_Y (in this example $-5/10$ or $-1/2$). The slope at any point shows how much of one good must be given up to get an additional unit of the other. For the figures assumed, if the consumer wishes to consume 1 more unit of X (at a price of $5 per unit), he will have to spend $5

Figure A–3. Budget constraint.

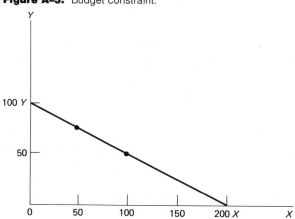

less on Y (and thereby purchase a half unit less because Y costs $10 per unit). Thus, the slope of the budget constraint is $- 1/2$ at every point because to purchase an additional unit of X always necessitates consuming a half unit less of Y.

The position of the budget constraint depends on the size of the budget. If the consumer's income increases, the budget constraint will be farther from the origin; if income falls, it will lie closer. This is illustrated in Figure A-4. Let's begin again with an income of $1000, and the prices of X and Y at $5 and $10, respectively. The budget constraint, identical to the one derived in the preceding discussion, is the line MN. If income increases to $2000, a new budget constraint will be defined by a line connecting 400 X and 200 Y, or $M'N'$; similarly, if income falls to $500, another budget line will be drawn joining 100 X and 50 Y. Note that the three budget constraints are parallel. This is because the prices of X and Y have not changed and thus the slopes (P_X/P_Y) are unaffected.

In addition to changes in income, changes in the prices of goods affect the budget constraint. To illustrate, again assume that a consumer's income is $1000 and the price of X is $5 and the price of Y is $10. The initial budget constraint is shown by the line MN in Figure A-5 connecting 200 X and 100 Y. Now assume that the price of X falls from $5 to $2.50 per unit. To reflect this change, the budget constraint pivots to MN'. Point M (100 Y) is unchanged because the price of Y is still $10; now, however, if a consumer spends his entire income on X, he can purchase 400 units. The slope of the line has been affected, becoming

Figure A–4. Changes in income.

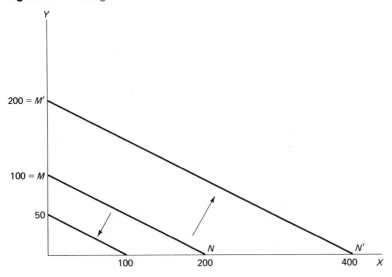

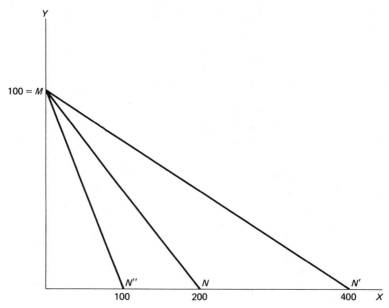

Figure A–5. Changes in price.

flatter to reflect the lower price of X. (Originally, the slope was − 1/2; after the price reduction, it becomes − 1/4.) At the lower price of X, the consumer will now have to give up only a fourth of a unit of Y (saving $2.50) to purchase 1 more unit of X. If the price of X increases, say, to $10, the budget constraint will pivot toward the origin to MN", with the steeper slope (1/1) reflecting a higher price for X (1 unit of Y must now be sacrificed to obtain an additional unit of X). In this way, the slope of any budget constraint indicates the price of one good relative to the other. At a lower price of X, the budget constraint is flatter, implying that X is now relatively lower priced than before—less Y has to be given up to purchase an additional unit of X.

The Consumer in Equilibrium

The consumer's budget constraint shows the combinations of goods he is able to choose among, and the consumer's indifference curves show how he subjectively ranks all combinations of goods. It is assumed that the consumer will choose the combination of X and Y that he prefers most from among the combinations attainable. Consider Figure A-6. The set of indifferences curves, IC_1 through IC_3, reflects the consumer's preferences. Curve IC_3 is the most preferred among these three because it rep-

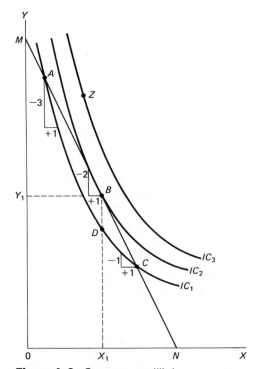

Figure A-6. Consumer equilibrium.

resents the highest level of utility. The budget constraint, *MN*, identifies the consumption options available to the consumer. Any point along *MN* (or below it[2]) such as *A* or *B* represents a real consumption possibility. Points above the constraint such as *Z* are not feasible because the consumer lacks the necessary income. Because the consumer will seek the highest level of utility possible given his budget, equilibrium will occur at *B*, where the budget constraint and *IC₂* are tangent. The consumer will purchase $0X_1$ units of *X* and $0Y_1$ units of *Y*. Note that *A* is also on the budget constraint, but *A* lies on *IC₁*; *B*, however, is on a higher indifference curve, *IC₂*, so the latter is preferred. The desire of the consumer to maximize utility also rules out the possibility of an equilibrium at a point such as *D*; although *D* is within the consumer's budget (in fact, the consumer would not be spending all his income on *X* and *Y*), it is not the highest possible level of utility attainable because

[2] Any point below the budget constraint implies that the consumer is not spending his entire income; we will assume, however, that the consumer allocates his entire income in some way between *X* and *Y*. In a more general model, saving can be considered one of the goods; thus the consumer would divide his income between consumption and saving.

it lies on a lower indifference curve. Thus, the combination of X and Y represented by the tangency at B is the equilibrium level of consumption for the consumer.

It is important to understand the meaning of the tangency between the consumer's indifference curve and his budget constraint at point B. Recall that the indifference curve reflects the consumer's subjective valuation of the benefits associated with his consumption of X and Y, and the rate at which he is willing to substitute one good for another, or the marginal rate of substitution between X and Y. The slope of the indifference curve at any point is then equal to the marginal rate of substitution. At A, for example, the consumer will be willing to exchange 3 units of Y for 1 more unit of X, at B, 2 for 1, and at C, 1 unit of Y for 1 additional unit of X. The slope of the budget constraint at all points is P_X/P_Y, the rate at which X and Y can be exchanged in the marketplace. Assume that the price of X is \$2 and the price of Y is \$1. This means that 2 units of Y can be exchanged for 1 unit of X. The slope of MN is $2/1$. At the equilibrium, B, the marginal rate of substitution between X and Y for the consumer is equal to the price ratio; that is, the rate at which the consumer is subjectively willing to substitute X for Y is just equal to the rate at which market exchange can occur. At B the consumer is willing to give up 2 units of Y for another unit of X; at a price of \$2 per unit for X and \$1 a unit for Y, this coincides with the market rate of exchange. Only at B, where the slopes of an indifference curve and the budget constraint are equal, does this condition hold.

Note that the consumer *could* consume at point A on his budget constraint, but he would then be on IC_1, a lower indifference curve than at point B. Point A is *not* an equilibrium because the MRS is greater than the price ratio. To see that this is so, note that at A the consumer is willing to give up 3 units of Y to get another unit of X but only *has* to give up 2 units of Y to consume 1 more X (because X costs twice as much as Y). This means that 1 more X costs less (a sacrifice of 2 Y) than the consumer is willing to pay (3 Y), so he will be better off consuming more X and less Y than at point A. This is shown, of course, by the fact that point B lies on a higher indifference curve than point A.

Before the analysis is continued, a modification in the model will be made. So far the consumer has been choosing between two goods, X and Y, typically dividing his budget in some manner between them. From now on the vertical axis will measure money spent on all other goods except X for a given time period, and the horizontal axis will measure the quantity of X consumed. This modification provides more flexibility. The indifference curves can now show the trade-offs between good X and money spent on other goods. The slope of an indifference curve can then show how many dollars' worth of other goods the consumer is willing to give up to acquire 1 more unit of X. With this modification, the budget constraint can be constructed as follows: Assume the consumer's income is $1000, and the price of X is $2. In Figure A-7, $0M$ ($1000) is the amount of money available to spend on other goods if the consumer purchased zero units of X (i.e., his entire money income). If he spent his entire income on X, he could purchase $0N$ units of X (500) with no money remaining to purchase other goods. By joining the two points, the budget constraint MN is derived. Given the preferences as reflected by the consumer's indifference curves, the consumer is in equilibrium at E. He is consuming $0X_1$ (200) units of X and has $0Z$ ($600) in income left to spend on goods other than X. Note that the consumer has spent (i.e., traded off), an amount of income equal to MZ ($400) to purchase $0X_1$.

As we did before, let's carefully interpret the tangency at E in Figure A-7 between the consumer's indifference curve IC_2 and budget constraint. The slope of the indifference curve now represents the rate at which the consumer is willing to trade off expenditures on other goods for additional units of X; the consumer is, in effect, placing a dollar

Figure A-7. Consumer equilibrium.

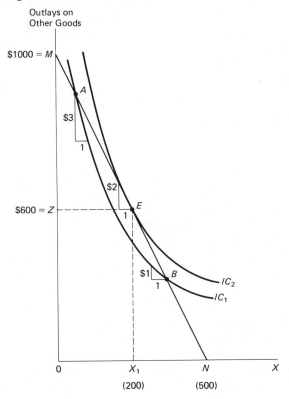

value on the benefits received from a marginal unit of X. At A, for example, the consumer is willing to pay $3 for another unit of X (willing to consume $3 less of other goods to consume 1 more unit of X); at B only $1. The budget constraint reflects the market rate of exchange between X and Y. Because Y now represents expenditures on other goods, it is measured in dollars, and the price of $1 is $1.

To the left of E on the budget constraint, the consumer places a higher dollar value on X than its market price. For instance, at A the consumer is on IC_2 and is willing to pay $3 for an additional unit of X but only has to pay the *market price* of $2. Because the benefit received from the marginal unit is greater than its cost, the consumer will purchase the extra unit. Moreover, he will continue to consume additional units as long as this condition persists, that is, until point E is reached, where the additional dollar value of benefits received from consuming 1 more unit just equals its price (in this example, at E the consumer places a value of $2 on an extra unit, which equals its market price). At point E he has attained the highest indifference curve possible. The consumer will not purchase any additional units (to the right of E) because the dollar value of benefits received from consuming additional units is less than its price—the marginal benefit is less than marginal cost. Thus, the consumer is in equilibrium at E, where the marginal benefit of an extra unit of X is equal to its price. This means that when the consumer is in equilibrium the market price of the good is a measure of the marginal value of the good to the consumer.

Having changed the vertical axis to money spent on other goods, we can now continue and consider how consumption levels of X are affected by changes in income and prices.

Changes in Income

We noted earlier how changes in income produce parallel shifts in the budget constraint. Now that indifference curves have been incorporated into the analysis, changes in the consumer's level of income and the corresponding changes in the level of consumption of X can be observed. To illustrate, consider Figure A-8(a). Given the set of preferences indicated by IC_1 through IC_3, when the budget constraint is MN, X_1 units of X are consumed. When the consumer's income increases to $0M'$, and the budget constraint is thus $M'N'$, the consumption of X rises to X_2. And, finally, when income reaches $0M''$ the consumer purchases X_3 units of X. At each income level, the consumer chooses the most preferred combination of goods from among the combinations available. A line connecting the consumer equilibria yields the *income-consumption curve*, which identifies the various quantities of X that will be consumed at different income levels. If the curve is upward sloping to the right, X is

Outlays on
Other Goods

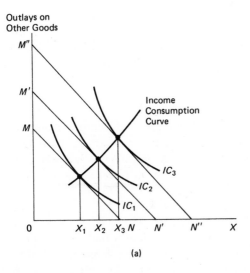

(a)

Outlays on
Other Goods

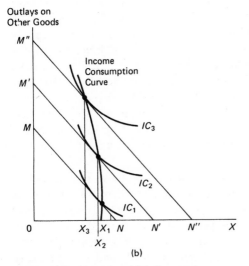

(b)

Figure A-8. Normal and inferior goods.

considered a *normal good,* that is, as income rises so does the consumption of X.

In contrast to normal goods, there are *inferior goods.* If a good is an inferior good, when income rises the quantity consumed falls. Consider Figure A-8(b). In this case, as income rises and the constraint shifts from MN to $M'N'$, and again to $M''N''$, consumption of X actually declines from X_1 to X_2 to X_3. The income-consumption curve slopes backward to the left. Typically most goods are normal goods, but it is possible to find examples of inferior goods. Perhaps, for example, as a person's income rises, his taste may turn from hamburger to filet mignon, and so hamburger, in this particular case, may be an inferior good.

Changes in Prices

So far we have considered the effects of changes in consumer income on the quantity of X consumed with prices assumed constant. Now let's hold income constant and vary the price of X and observe how the consumption of X changes. Recall that a variation in price is reflected by a change in the slope of the budget constraint; if the price of X falls, the constraint becomes flatter, pivoting to the right; if the price rises, the constraint becomes steeper, pivoting toward the origin. To begin, assume that the consumer's budget is $100 in a given time period and the price of X is $10 per unit. In Figure A-9 (a) the budget constraint is MN, and, given the consumer's preferences, equilibrium occurs with X_1 units of the good being consumed. Now let the price of X fall to $5 per unit. A new budget constraint, MN', is produced (if no X, is purchased, point M is unchanged; if all income is spent on X, 20 units can be purchased). At the lower price, X_2 is purchased, as indicated by the tangency of the highest attainable indifference curve to MN' at X_2 units of X. Finally, let price fall again—this time to $2.50 a unit. The budget constraint pivots outward to MN'', and X_3 is purchased. Each decrease in price establishes a new budget constraint and a new equilibrium. The line drawn through the tangencies depicting the equilibrium points is called the *price-consumption curve*. It shows how the consumption of X varies with changes in price.

The concept embodied in the price-consumption curve should strike a familiar note. It contains the same information as a demand curve—how the quantity consumed varies with changes in price when money income is unchanged. We are now to the point where a demand curve can be derived from the indifference curves in Figure A-9(a). On the axes of a demand curve diagram, price is measured vertically and quantity horizontally. So only a few modifications need be made to translate the information in Figure A-9(a) into a demand curve. The three prices at which X was sold, $10, $5, and $2.50, are plotted in Figure A-9(b), and the corresponding quantities of X consumed are identified. In this way, a demand curve is derived using indifference curves and budget constraints.

Because the tangency between the individual's budget constraint and indifference curve represents the point where the marginal value of the last unit of X to the consumer is just equal to its price, and these tangencies in turn define points on the consumer's demand curve, the demand curve must contain the same information. In fact, each point on

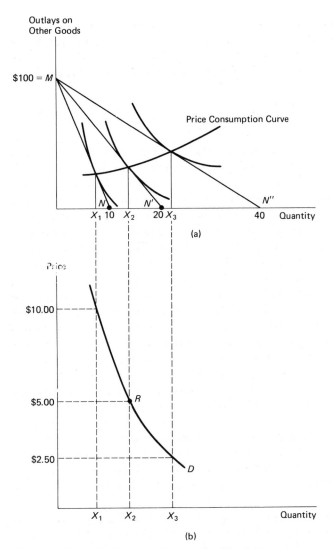

Figure A-9. Derivation of a demand curve.

the demand curve can be interpreted as a measure of the marginal benefit associated with the consumption of the corresponding unit of X. Taking this a step further, because each quantity of X is associated with a price, the price of X can be considered a dollar measure of the marginal benefit of X to the consumer: The price reflects the MRS between money spent on other goods and good X. The vertical distance between the demand curve and the horizontal axis can be taken as a measure of the marginal benefit of X; for example, the distance RX_2 is

447

a measure of the marginal value, or benefit, of the good when X_2 is the quantity consumed (that is, the consumer would be willing to pay $5 for the last unit of X). This way of measuring the marginal value of X will be useful later in the analysis of many government tax and expenditure programs.

Substitution and Income Effects of Price Changes

When the price of a good changes, the consumer is affected in two distinct ways. One effect is called the income effect and the other the substitution effect. To illustrate, suppose the price of beef falls by half. The income effect stems from the fact that the consumer is better off as a result of the price change because his budget now goes farther. The consumer can buy the same amount of beef as before and still have more income to spend on other goods and services. The price change, in effect, raises the consumer's *real* income (in the sense of the level of well-being attainable). With a higher real income, the consumer can now afford to purchase more of all the goods he consumes—including beef. So when the price of beef decreases, the consumer, as a result of the income effect, will expand purchases of beef, if it is a normal good. The substitution effect results from the consumer's decision to substitute the now cheaper good, beef, for another good such as poultry or pork. To the consumer, beef, because of its lower price, has become a relatively more attractive buy, so he will choose to consume more beef relative to other types of meat and poultry. The decrease in the price of beef has caused the consumer's consumption of beef to increase for two independent reasons. The income effect makes the consumer better off by increasing his real income, which induces him to consume larger quantities of beef. The substitution effect leads the consumer to substitute the cheaper good for more expensive ones, and in doing this his consumption of X increases.

The total effect of a price change is shown in Figure A–10 as the increase in consumption of X from A' to B'. The original budget constraint is shown by MN, with the consumer in equilibrium at A purchasing A' units of X. The lower price of X is reflected by the new budget constraint MN' with a flatter slope. The price decline involves a new equilibrium for the consumer at B, with B' units of X being purchased. The total effect of this price change, $A'B'$, as noted earlier, can be divided into an income effect and a substitution effect. When the price of a good falls, it increases the consumer's real income. However, we want to ignore the income effect for the moment and instead concentrate on how much of the increase in the consumption of X can be attributed to the consumer's substituting X for other goods. To do this

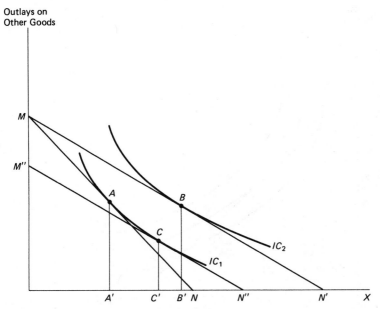

Figure A-10. Income and substitution effects.

and identify the substitution effect, the consumer's real income must be decreased by an amount sufficient to return him to his original indifference curve IC_1 in Figure A–10. (This is referred to as keeping real income unchanged.) To nullify the income effect, then, a budget constraint, $M''N''$, is constructed parallel to MN' and tangent to IC_1. The tangency occurs at C. The $M''N''$ budget constraint must be drawn parallel to MN' because we want to keep the consumer on his original indifference curve with the *new* price of X to see how the lower price of X—isolated from the income effect—causes the consumer to increase his consumption of X. The substitution effect can be identified by comparing the quantity of X consumed at the initial equilibrium, A (where the slope of MN reflects the original price), with the quantity consumed at C, where the slope of $M''N''$ indicates the new lower price of X. On the horizontal axis, the quantity $A'C'$ is the increase in consumption associated with the substitution effect.

Next comes the income effect. Assume now that the budget constraint $M''N''$ shifts to the right to coincide with MN'. The vertical distance between $M''N''$ and MN' represents the gain in real income attributable to the decline in the price of X. This rise in income alone is responsible for an increase in the purchase of X by the amount $C'B'$ because an increase in real income will induce the consumer to expand

449

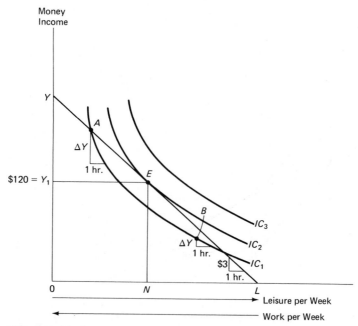

Figure A–11. Income-leisure choice.

purchases of all goods.[3] Thus, the total effect of the reduction in the price of X, $A'B'$, can be divided into a substitution effect, $A'C'$, and an income effect, $C'B'$.

An Application

To become more familiar with indifference curve theory and at the same time to lay the groundwork for some further analysis, let's examine individual labor supply decisions associated with changes in wage rates. Assume that workers can vary the amount of time they work,[4] and consider Figure A–11. On the vertical axis money income for a given time period is measured, and on the horizontal axis, reading from left to right, leisure for the same time period. The more hours worked, the less leisure time available; the more leisure consumed, the less time available to be spent at work. Because time not spent working is considered leisure time, the amount of work effort supplied can be read from right to left

---

[3] This assumes that X and the other goods purchased by the consumer are normal goods.

[4] Although many workers work an 8 hour day, they can still vary work effort with overtime, or take a second job. In addition, a worker can exercise some control over the number of hours worked by the type of job he chooses.

in Figure A–11. Indifference curves can be drawn representing the worker's preferences for income and leisure. They have a normal shape because both money income and leisure are desirable economic goods. As the worker moves down a curve to the right, money income falls as he consumes additional amounts of leisure. The slope of a curve at any point represents the rate at which the worker is subjectively willing to give up money income for leisure. At A, for example, it would require more income to induce him to work more (consume less leisure) than it would at B.

The worker's wage rate is reflected in the slope of a budget constraint showing a tradeoff between money income and leisure. The flatter the slope of the budget constraint, the lower the wage rate; the steeper the slope, the higher the wage rate. In Figure A–11, let the slope of YL reflect a wage of $3 per hour. For a worker who works a 40 hour week, weekly income will be $120. Of course, how many hours the worker will choose to work at the $3 wage rate depends on his preferences relating money income and leisure, as shown by his indifference curves. In Figure A–11, the worker's equilibrium—showing the most preferred combination of money income and leisure on his budget constraint—is point E, with weekly earnings of $120 and a labor supply of 40 hours. Note that the worker could earn more by working longer hours, at point A, but he would then be on a lower indifference curve. This simply means that the worker considers the additional earnings obtainable by working longer hours insufficient compensation for having to give up additional hours of leisure.

So far this describes a worker's equilibrium at a given wage rate. (For most consumers labor income is the major, and often sole, source of their money income—we assumed money income as given in earlier diagrams.) If the wage rate changes, the budget constraint pivots. In Figure A–12, the constraint with a $3 wage rate is shown as YL in both diagrams. If the wage rate rises to $5, the constraint pivots to Y'L. The slope (equal to the wage rate) is steeper, showing that for every hour of leisure given up (for every hour worked) more money income is received than before. At any given level of work effort, total money income will be higher at a wage rate of $5 than at a wage rate of $3.

How a worker responds to changes in wage rates is an interesting question. An increase in the wage rate has two effects on labor supply decisions: an income effect and a substitution effect. The income effect is a result of the fact that the higher wage rate raises the worker's income for any amount of work effort supplied; at higher income levels, the income effect will lead the worker to consume more of all goods, including leisure; thus, the higher income associated with higher wage rates encourages the increased consumption of leisure (and reduced work effort).

The substitution effect, on the other hand, encourages greater work

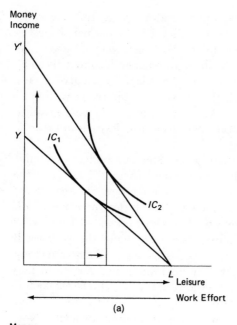

(a)

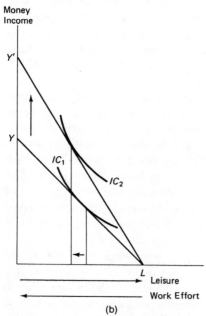

(b)

Figure A-12. Effect of wage rate on labor supply.

effort. If the wage rate rises from \$3 an hour to \$5, the price of consuming leisure increases, and the quantity consumed declines. More specifically, when the wage rate is \$3 per hour, the cost of consuming an additional hour of leisure is \$3 in foregone earnings; when the wage rate rises to \$5, the sacrifice in earnings also increases, inducing the worker to consume less leisure and to work more.

Because the income and substitution effects work in offsetting directions, it is impossible to predict whether a person will work more, or less, or the same amount, in response to changes in wage rates. If the income effect is greater than the substitution effect, then work effort will fall, as in Figure A–12(a). If, on the other hand, the substitution effect predominates, then work effort will rise in response to an increase in wages. See Figure A–12(b). If the two effects exactly offset each other, then work effort will be unchanged.

The response of labor supply to changes in wage rates is of particular interest to us in public finance because many taxes fall on labor income and consequently affect labor supply decisions with subsequent effects on the allocation of resources.

INDEX